HARK • SAMURAI
TY LITELLA • THE
SEANNE ROSEANN
E LOUNGE SINGER
OTHERS • OLYMPIA
NERDS • THEODOR
ROBINSON • BUCK
NES • GUMBY • THE
DO • ED GRIMLEY
RCH LADY • THE
HANS AND FRANZ
SPROCKETS •
WHO COULD DRIVE
• BILL SWERSKI'S
RICHMEISTER
TUART SMALLEY
JA • CAJUN MAN
LYWOOD MINUTE

SATURDAY

THE FIRST TWENTY YEARS

Edited by Michael Cader

Photographs by Edie Baskin

CADER BOOKS

HOUGHTON MIFFLIN
Boston • New York
1994

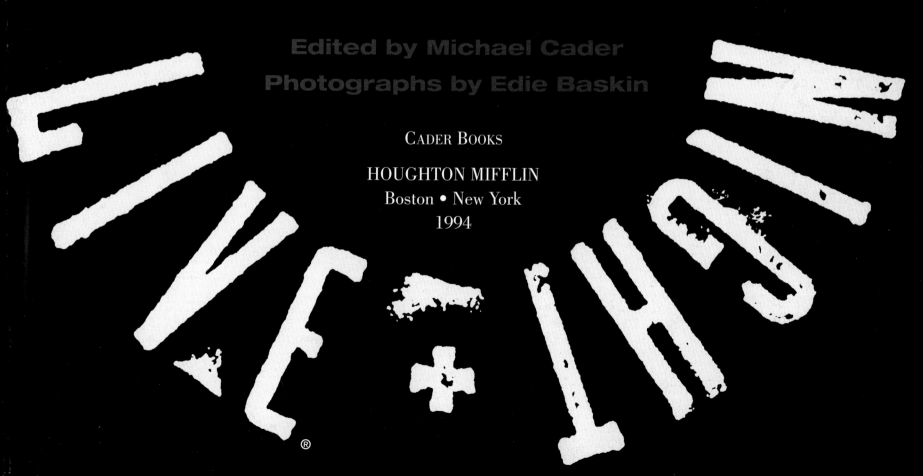

For information about permissions to reproduce selections from this book, write
to Permissions, Houghton Mifflin Company, 215 Park Avenue, New York, New
York 10003.

Library of Congress Cataloging-in-Publication Data

Saturday night live : the first twenty years / edited by Michael
Cader ; photographs by Edie Baskin.
      p.   cm.
   Includes index.
    ISBN 0-395-70895-8
    1. Saturday night live (Television program)   I. Cader, Michael.
PN1992.77.S273S23   1994
791.45'72--dc20   94-31832
                                               CIP

ISBN 0-395-70895-8

CONTENTS

Credits

Design
Charles Kreloff

Additional Photography
Norman Ng

Contributing Photography
Kate Geis
Billy Jim
Karen Kuehn
Alan Levine
Reggie Lewis
Mary Ellen Matthews
Mark Mullen
NBC Archives
Frank Ockenfels
Richard Reed
Alan Singer
Lesly Weiner
Rain Worthington
Isaiah Wyner

Associate Editor
Steve Baumgartner

Consulting Editors
Mike Bosze
John Head
Jason Korfine

Art Coordinators
Liz Gallagher
Mary Ellen Matthews

Photo Researcher
Mary Losso-Engle

Design Associate
Jessica Shatan

Interviewers
Marci Klein
Gina Marr
Fabienne Marsh

Video Researchers
Eryn Brown
Kendall LaMontagne
Cordelia Richards

Transcribers
Stephen Arenholz
Cara Sullivan

Special thanks to:
Ken Aymong
Amy Batkin
Laurie Berdan
Jim Biederman
Danny Bleier
Candace Bothwell
Leigh Anne Brodsky
Lisa Cader
Jonah Cader
Mark Caleb
Audrey Peart Dickman
Jim Downey
Eric Ellenbogen
John Engelman
Jonathan Flom
Al Franken

Jon Gartenberg
Lori Glazer
Nancy Grant
Jack Handey
Cheryl Hardwick
Ron Heyman
Tony Knight
Dan Klores
David Krell
Liz Kubik
Christopher Leonesio
Erin Maroney
Ian Maxtone-Graham
Cristina McGinniss
Neil McGuiness
Jim Medalia
Dinah Minot
Greg Mroczek
Jim Pitt
Bob Pook
Melina Root
Herb Sargent
David Saylor
Renee Schwartz
Steve Scott
Jeff Seroy
Mike Shoemaker
Howard Shore
Jim Signorelli
Amy Smith
G. E. Smith
George Stephanopoulos
Liz Welch Tirrell
Marlene Weissman
Mimi Won
John Zonars

Then and Now

A brief conversation with Lorne Michaels, the creator and producer of Saturday Night Live, about both the early days and the show in general:

Finding the show's format:

I think the very first show was over-thought. There were six months leading up to that show and six days leading up to the second show....Until you do it, you have no idea what it is you're doing. There were two musical groups, there was a Muppet segment, there was an Albert Brooks film—we were just trying to do an enormous amount. It's a clumsy metaphor, but we had the ingredients, we didn't have the recipe.

For example, we wanted to do commercial parodies—we shot a lot of them in the summer and we used five or six in the first show. We thought it would be subversive to put the commercial parodies in between, or close to, the real commercials. As we found out over time, people were annoyed because they had to watch the real commercials in a whole other way.

The network and the original show:

Most of the network pressure on the first show had been about whether George Carlin could wear jeans and a T-shirt, which was what he wanted, or a suit, which was what the network wanted. He ended up wearing a suit with a T-shirt. The network was worried about the impact on the affiliates and whether the show would be perceived as too radical—this is 1975 after all. There were a lot of worried phone calls within the network on Sunday after the show aired, but then on Monday the reviews and ratings came out and western civilization as we know it didn't end. And we had another show to do, and the network had some other problem. They moved on.

On the first season:

On the first show we did a sketch called Bee Hospital and there wasn't much audience reaction. The writers maintained that the PA system wasn't working very well and the audience couldn't hear the sketch, but maybe the piece just didn't work. In any case, I thought it was funny, and I thought it was original. But one of the most prominent notes we got from the network after that show was, "Don't do the Bees again."

Lorne Michaels, 1975

So on the second show with Paul Simon hosting we did a piece about the Bees not working. Then on the third show, the Bees appeared again, in a defiant way, with John Belushi giving a wonderful speech to Rob Reiner in the Bee Restaurant sketch. It was cocky if you're on the side of it, or you can call it arrogant if you're not. The point is that somebody was questioning our judgment about comedy. We were now a group, with its own comedic voice, and an outside voice was trying to tell us what worked and what didn't. But we already had the confidence to tell ourselves, "They're saying that it's not funny and we're saying it is."...The larger point is that by the fourth show, which Candy Bergen hosted, the show had begun to hit a rhythm. That show was probably the first one that came to look like the show that we do now.

For the fifth show, with Robert Klein, we had a late start and didn't go on until about 12:20, which we had known about in advance. So it was bumpy, but there was some good stuff in it. And then by the time we did shows six and seven, with Lily Tomlin and Richard Pryor, the cast had come forward but the audience still had come to see the hosts....It probably wasn't until show nine, hosted by Elliott Gould, that we had begun to clearly find our voice. After that, there were good shows and bad shows, but at least we knew what we were.

I don't think in terms of the show's history that the first year was necessarily the best material, or necessarily even the best cast. But it was new, and you can't ever be new again. There was this tremendous excitement of making it up as we went along. That time before order and structure was both exhilarating and frightening.

How things have changed:

Historically the week was divided in two parts—from Monday to Wednesday before the script emerged there was no show and I was worried. From Wednesday on after the read-through, there was too much show, we were too long and would have to cut and I was worried. The week has always been that way. The difference between now and then for me is that then I was worried all the time. What experience has taught me is when to worry.

When the show is at its best:

The show is working when we're doing exactly what you were hoping we would be doing, in a way that you hadn't thought we'd be doing it. In a way that is truly funny and original. That is, in the best sense, broadcasting—when a lot of people are having the same experience at the same time and talking about it the next day. That will always be the core experience of the show.

I think that there were a lot of things we tried in the beginning that worked and a lot of things that didn't work. What has remained constant, though, is the extent to which the show is about writing and performance. Whether it's Gilda Radner or Dana Carvey, when you see a performer of that caliber talking into the lens and lighting up the screen because they're doing something remarkable, and it speaks to the moment, that's the show at its best.

SATURDAY

THE FIRST TWENTY YEARS

NIGHT LIVE

THE CAST

Dan Aykroyd
Years: 1975–1979
Seasons: 4
Favorite sketch that never made it to air:
Bill Murray and I always used to do a pair of homeless men around a trash barrel. It was funny, but also kind of sad—too sad, I guess.
Favorite character:
Fred Garvin, Male Prostitute.
The *SNL* experience:
SNL was the greatest and most arduous job of my career. The immediacy of writing a piece on Monday and banking it Saturday night was incomparable to anything else and remains so.
Characters:
Bass-O-Matic salesman (and salesman for other Rovco products: Bat-O-Matic, Steroid Tulips, Mohawk Master, Chinch Range)
Beldar Conehead
Elwood Blues
Sheriff Brody, in Land Shark
Jimmy Carter
Julia Child
Bob Dole
Georg Festrunk
Fred Garvin, Male Prostitute
George, at the grill, in the Olympia Restaurant
Jimmy Joe Red Sky
Joe, one of the Ex-Police
Irwin Mainway
Dr. McCoy
Mel, in Mel's Char Palace and Mel's Hide Haven
E. Buzz Miller
Chuck Neehauser, Saint Mickey's Knights of Columbus
Eliot Ness
Richard M. Nixon
Leonard Pinth-Garnell, in Bad Playhouse
Point-Counterpoint Debater ("Counterpoint" position)
Ray, the telepsychic
Refrigerator repairman, in The Nerds
Tom Snyder
First Mate Spunk of the Raging Queen
Weekend Update anchor, 1977–1978
Bob Widette

Jim Belushi
Years: 1983–1985
Seasons: 2
Characters:
Donald Ramp, High School Chess Coach
Hank Rippy
Weekend Update critic-at-large
White Guy rapper

John Belushi
Years: 1975–1979
Seasons: 4
Characters:
Beethoven
Jake Blues
Marlon Brando
Joe Cocker
Pete Dionasopolis, owner of the Olympia Restaurant
Richard Dreyfuss
English pupil, in The Wolverines, *SNL*'s debut sketch
Harry Farber
The Incredible Hulk

Captain Kirk
Henry Kissinger
Frank Leary, Saint Mickey's Knights of Columbus
Captain Ned of the Raging Queen Samurai
Elizabeth Taylor
Weekend Update commentator ("But noooo!")
Jeff Widette
Wilderness Comedian

Dana Carvey
Years: 1986–1992
Seasons: 7
Favorite character:
Hans. That's the one that would make me laugh the most. The idea of a person, a human being, with that big of an ego with nothing going on, really makes me laugh.
Genesis of Hans and Franz:
We started playing with the voices, and then we came up with the retarded cousins [of Arnold] and then the real thing. We were at my apartment one night and we started fooling around with the idea: "You'd better work out, and if you don't work out, we could very easily come to your house and turn your muscles into the shape of a pretzel. We wouldn't even need mustard, we could just chew away." I mean, that turn is what made us, Kevin Nealon and me, one night in my apartment in New York—we literally couldn't stay in our chairs, we were laughing so hard at the idea. The idea that these fitness experts literally were into sadistic behavior and were truly violent criminals.
On doing impressions:
I get bored really fast. I get the voice and I'm real excited—"Gee, I sound like him"—and then a minute later I'm bored. But think of the word "impressionist." It's not like a "realist"—it's an *impression*. So I just take the essence and abstract it, like a lot of people do.
Characters that never made it on:
I still want to do Condescension Man, which was sort of a composite of all the things I was doing based on, basically, my father. But it was like "Well, well, well. Look at what we have here—frightened of me simply because you know that I exist….You could never be depressed. Why? Because you know me, you actually know me." It would just be pretentious celebrities coming onto the Condescension Man show.
On Church Lady:
That character was real popular in my club act but I didn't know— would I wear a dress, or what? The funny thing was Pam Downey created the look. She got two dresses, one pink chiffon and the one I wore. Some people thought I should change the pink chiffon for the air show—basically it barely got on the show, and it got in because Phil Hartman kind of lobbied for it.

It really dominated me. I mean, I was the Church Lady, and I had to stop doing it in order for anything else to get recognized, so that's why I stopped.

On Perot:

He called me at home twice. "You going to be in New York soon? My daughter would love to meet you. Would you like to come on down to Dallas? It'd be a hootenanny."

On Garth:

The day that Mike submitted Wayne's World, I had submitted this sketch: My brother Brad [was] having a show in his bedroom. He made a camera out of a coffee can, a Duracell battery, and some wire, and he was doing his little show: "Hi, today we're going to learn how to make a small radioactive device from a paper clip."...When [Mike] said, "You're Garth," he kind of gave me carte blanche to think of the character. I just said, "I guess I'll use Brad here." Mike had brown hair, so I picked blond hair, and then I had a big wig—it's so funny that now [Wayne's World spawned] these international movies. I had a big box of glasses, and I go, "I guess he's kind of a science nerd like Brad, so I'll give him these Buddy Holly glasses." And then I did the teeth and I went over to Mike and I go, "Look, I'm Garth, what do you think?" and he goes, "Okay, that's cool."

Characters:

Garth Algar, in Wayne's World
Woody Allen
Lyle Billup, The Effeminate
   Heterosexual
George Bush
Carsenio
Johnny Carson
Ching Change
Chris, Pat's special someone
Church Lady
Lyle Clarke, one of Toonces's
   owners
Grumpy Old Man
Hans, in Hans and Franz
Casey Kasem
Robin Leach
John McLaughlin, in The
   McLaughlin Group
George Michael
Dennis Miller

Mischu, apprentice of KoKo,
   the French clown
H. Ross Perot
Regis Philbin
Buddy Precisely
Dan Quayle
Keith Richards
One of A Couple of Sammies
Derek Stevens, singer of
   "Chopping Broccoli"
Jimmy Stewart
John Travolta

Chevy Chase
Years: 1975-1976
Seasons: 1
On Weekend Update:

The genesis at *Saturday Night* was when Lorne had everybody do their screen tests, which seemed kind of ridiculous because he had already been going through a month or two of choosing who would be the Not Ready for Prime Time Players. At the end of the screen test, which was in a studio right there at NBC, which was really just a kind of a news desk with lighting, [Lorne] said, "Why don't you get up and do something, Chev?" I had written this short thing about one of those things that I hated about the news back then. They'd always end with a story and

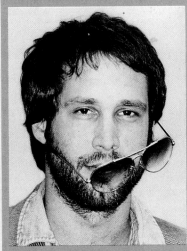

this: "[fake chuckles] Well, that's the news." So [the story] was about a baby bird born at the zoo, but it

took a twist, which was that the baby hippo that had been born a couple of days earlier unfortunately stepped on the bird and crushed it—and, of course, [the story] ended with "[fake chuckles] And now, Kate, back to you."

The thought behind it, thematically, was, "Here's an opportunity to do parody, to be funny as a newsman, and to have a phone—which they all seemed to have at that time—and use that as a vehicle for satire to say damn well what I want on the news."

I remember one of my favorites was a shot of David and Julie Eisenhower. They were walking. I guess they were marching past some army group people—maybe they were foreigners, who knows—but they were doing that, addressing the men in rank. I just said, "David and Julie Eisenhower were taken out today and shot." It just fit the picture perfectly. There was a guy named Roger Grimsby in New York. He used to say, "Good evening, I'm Roger Grimsby, and here now the news."

And I never liked that use of that conjunction or the entire phrase afterward. "Here now the news"—what the hell is that? Pretentious junk. Nothing against Roger Grimsby, but the use of it is sort of odd: "Hi, I'm Roger Elgin, and the weather's nice, isn't it?" There was a pretension I didn't like. So I at some point—I usually winged these things—I went, "I'm Chevy Chase and you're not." I mean, I had nothing else to say.

Why he made it big:

It happened for me because of some very simple things: Because of the fall, and the fact that I said my name every night. Nobody knew who Belushi was and how the hell you spell Aykroyd, so those guys were in trouble. But I had this odd name and it sticks out and there you have it.

Less funny moments:

When I came back to visit everything seemed to have changed. Nobody liked me. I came back the next year. Billy Murray was there and he got into a fight with me. We were both at fault. But it was right five minutes before the show

1975-1976 cast.

opened, and that was kind of heart-stopping, because it was hard to come out of something where I felt intimidated, like I had done something that I hadn't.

Many things didn't work; but the fact of the matter is, to me one of the great joys of that show was that you are watching a professional variety show, like *Cher* or any of the others, which are all taped, and corrections are made thereby. However, here it's live, and there's nothing better at home than to see a professional fuck up.

On hearing from someone he impersonated:
I did hear ultimately from one of Ford's sons that some of the things had hurt his feelings, and that was a shocker to me. But I figured, "Oh, well, he's the president, he can take it. I mean, he has to, he's a public figure." Of course, now my feelings have been hurt so much, I know exactly what he means.

In retrospect:
I left too early, and I felt it then, but it was a personal decision and it had to do with marrying a person who lives in California. Few people know that, besides Lorne. The assumption was I had a huge multimillion-dollar career waiting for me. Well, that just isn't true—a couple of years later I made a film.

I have always felt two terrible losses. One was not being on the show again, and the other, of course, and the most important, was my friendship with Lorne. I've always almost felt I betrayed him, but I was so totally infatuated with a girl out here, and I guess everybody but me knew that this girl was a little nutty and certainly not the one I should marry, but I didn't know. I was in love.

Even back then I knew that in my heart I should have stayed—and I should have stayed if for no other reason than that I loved Lorne and I wanted to see this show get off the ground. You

know, the first year was not a good year in terms of ratings. It was really around the second and third year, after I'd left, in John and Dan's heyday, and Billy's, that the ratings started to pick up.

Characters:
Gerald Ford
Land Shark
Mr. Spock
Weekend Update anchor

Ellen Cleghorne
Years: 1991–1994
Seasons: 3
Characters that haven't made it onto the show:
I'm dying to do Reverend High-tower, I've just got to figure out an angle that fits the show's format more. And I guess the more that I can understand about the show, the more I'll be able to fit it in; the more I'll be able to figure out an angle to get it on.
Characters:
Dr. Joycelyn Elders
Whoopi Goldberg
Queen Shenequa
Zoraida, the NBC page

Billy Crystal
Years: 1984–1985
Seasons: 1
Characters:
Muhammad Ali, in Kate and Ali
Yul Brynner
Howard Cosell

Sammy Davis, Jr.
Fernando
Joe Franklin
Lew Goldman
The Minkmans
Ricky
Willie, in Do You Know What I Hate?
Buddy Young, Jr.

Jane Curtin
Years: 1975–1980
Seasons: 5
On her Weekend Update performance:
I did the generic newswoman. A lot of people thought I was doing someone else. They knew I wasn't doing them, but they knew someone I was doing.
On Point-Counterpoint:
I don't do impressions, but you can do an attitude. I picked up on Danny's cues. He'd fire all these

things at me and I'd just fire them right back.
Memories and influences:
I learned from Gilda tremendously—just her sense of abandon when she was onstage. Laraine worked with her ears; she has this incredible ability to pick up on sounds. Billy's spontaneity; Danny's focus. John had the same abandon that Gilda had. Chevy just had this attitude.
On the SNL experience:
It made me more visible. That changes everything. It helps, it hurts, it changes your life completely.
Characters:
Anita Bryant
Joan Crawford
Joan Face
Iris de Flaminio
Betty Ford
Looks at Books host
Enid Loopner, Lisa's mother in The Nerds
Mrs. Loud
Point-Counterpoint debater ("Point" position)
Prymaat Conehead
Rula Lenska
Weekend Update anchor, 1976–1980
Betty Widette

Joan Cusack
Years: 1985–1986
Seasons: 1
Characters:
Salena, in Biff and Salena
Brooke Shields

Denny Dillon
Years: 1980–1982
Seasons: 2
Characters:
Amy Carter
Debbie
Nadine
Pinky Waxman

Character:
SNL Newsbreak anchor,
1981–1982

Robert Downey, Jr.
Years: 1985–1986
Seasons: 1
Characters:
Jimmy Chance
Rudy Randolph III
Suitcase Boy

Brian Doyle-Murray
Years: 1980–1982
Seasons: 2

Robin Duke
Years: 1981–1984
Seasons: 3
Characters:
The Pig
Wendy Whiner

Nora Dunn
Years: 1985–1991
Seasons: 6
Characters:
Cindy Adams
Ashley Ash
Babette, the international sex
  kitten
Mrs. Campbell, Wayne's mom, in
  Wayne's World

Tyne Daly
Linda Dano, Attitudes cohost
Jeane Dixon
Leona Helmsley
Dr. Norma Hoeffering
Jeane Kirkpatrick
Ann Landers
Imelda Marcos
Liza Minnelli
Martina Navritalova
Nancy Reagan
Pat Schroeder
Pat Stevens
Liz Sweeney
Dr. Denise Venetti, host of
  Learning to Feel

Christine Ebersole
Years: 1981–1982
Seasons: 1
Characters:
Princess Di
SNL Newsbreak anchor, 1982

Chris Farley
Years: 1990–1994
Seasons: 4
Characters:
Tom Arnold
B Fats, in I'm Chillin'
Bennett Brauer
Chippendales dancer
Cindy, one of the Gap Girls
Drinkin' Buddy of Middle-Aged
  Man
The Chris Farley Show host

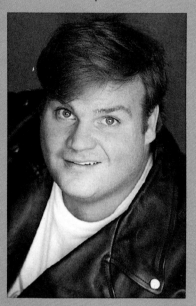

Matt Foley, motivational
  speaker
Jack Germond, in The
  McLaughlin Group
Andrew Giuliani
One of the Gyro Guys
Marco, in Il Cantore and La
  Cantoria
Todd O'Connor, in Bill Swer-
  ski's Super Fans
Mr. O'Malley, supporter of The
  Herlihy Boy
Carnie Phillips
Sandman, in The Dark Side with
  Nat X
General Schwarzkopf

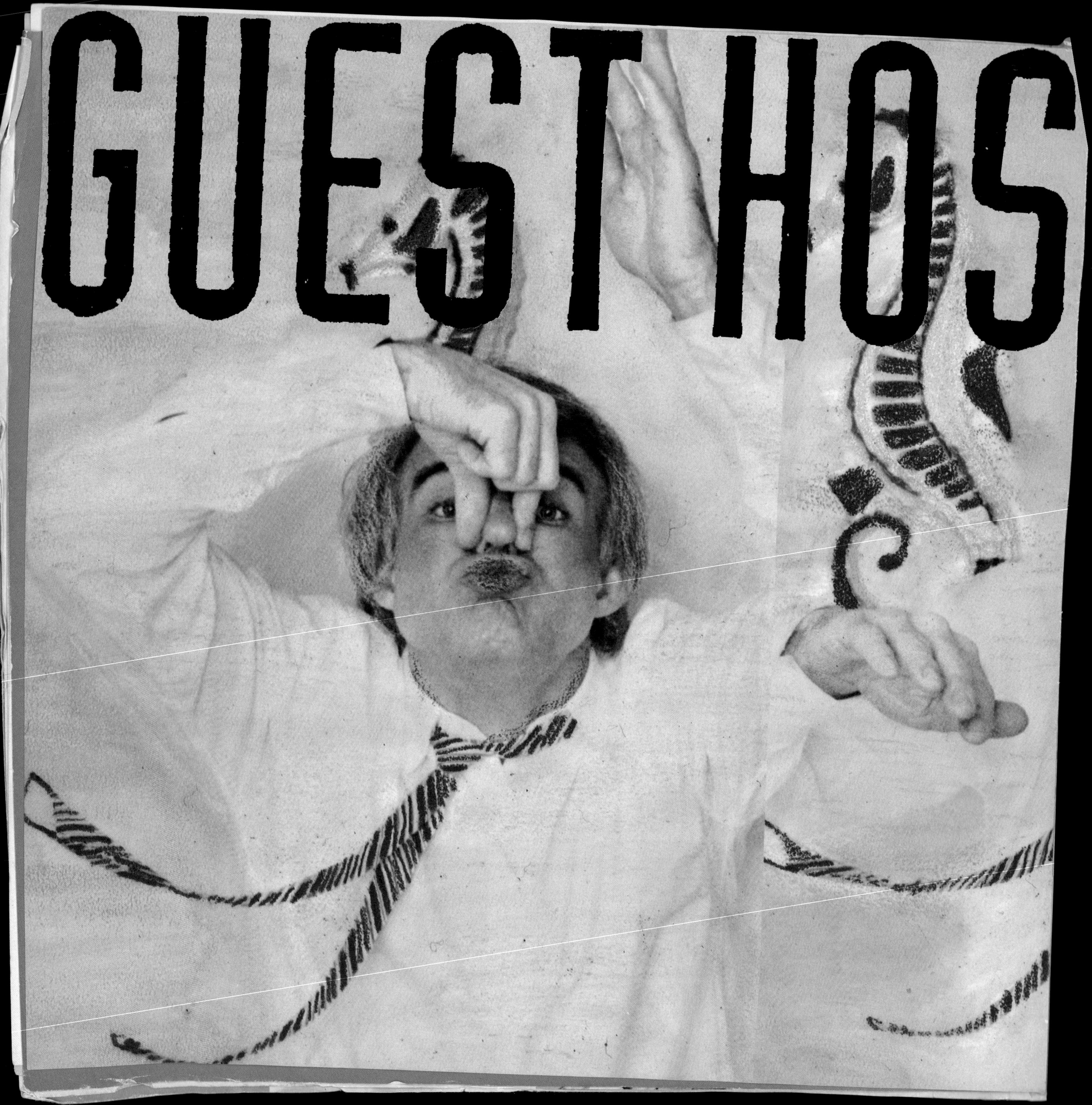
GUEST HOS

Denny Dillon
Years: 1980–1982
Seasons: 2
Characters:
Amy Carter
Debbie
Nadine
Pinky Waxman

Character:
SNL Newsbreak anchor,
1981–1982

Tyne Daly
Linda Dano, Attitudes cohost
Jeane Dixon
Leona Helmsley
Dr. Norma Hoeffering
Jeane Kirkpatrick
Ann Landers
Imelda Marcos
Liza Minnelli
Martina Navritalova
Nancy Reagan
Pat Schroeder
Pat Stevens
Liz Sweeney
Dr. Denise Venetti, host of
  Learning to Feel

Chris Farley
Years: 1990–1994
Seasons: 4
Characters:
Tom Arnold
B Fats, in I'm Chillin'
Bennett Brauer
Chippendales dancer
Cindy, one of the Gap Girls
Drinkin' Buddy of Middle-Aged
  Man
The Chris Farley Show host

Matt Foley, motivational
  speaker
Jack Germond, in The
  McLaughlin Group
Andrew Giuliani
One of the Gyro Guys
Marco, in Il Cantore and La
  Cantoria
Todd O'Connor, in Bill Swer-
  ski's Super Fans
Mr. O'Malley, supporter of The
  Herlihy Boy
Carnie Phillips
Sandman, in The Dark Side with
  Nat X
General Schwarzkopf

Robert Downey, Jr.
Years: 1985–1986
Seasons: 1
Characters:
Jimmy Chance
Rudy Randolph III
Suitcase Boy

Brian Doyle-Murray
Years: 1980–1982
Seasons: 2

Robin Duke
Years: 1981–1984
Seasons: 3
Characters:
The Pig
Wendy Whiner

Nora Dunn
Years: 1985–1991
Seasons: 6
Characters:
Cindy Adams
Ashley Ash
Babette, the international sex
  kitten
Mrs. Campbell, Wayne's mom, in
  Wayne's World

Christine Ebersole
Years: 1981–1982
Seasons: 1
Characters:
Princess Di
SNL Newsbreak anchor, 1982

Gilbert Gottfried

Years: 1980–1981
Seasons: 1
Character:
Leo Waxman

Mary Gross

Years: 1981–1985
Seasons: 4

On characters:
If I can find fault with my years at *Saturday Night Live*—I never understood repeating characters. I didn't *want* to repeat characters. I never saw the political advantage—which, of course, in retrospect, I do. I just thought it would be boring for me and boring for the audience.

Favorite impersonation:
Mary Richards.

On Alfalfa:
They picked me to play Alfalfa because Robert [Blake] said that I reminded him of Alfalfa. It wasn't exactly flattering, but it was interesting.

Uncomfortable memory:
I did Mary Richards…but there was another sketch in which I was asked to do Mary Tyler Moore, as opposed to Mary Richards. This was a monologue in which Mary was talking about her marriage to a younger man. And I was not at all comfortable with this piece. I thought it was unkind, and I didn't see any reason to satirize her marriage to a younger person. I thought, If she's found happiness, why should we make fun of it? Men do it all the time…. I was told that we really needed this piece because it was an "in-one" [a technically simple sketch involving one person playing to one camera]. On a show like *Saturday Night Live*, when you have lots of camera activity going on during the commercial, it's very helpful to have a piece that only requires one camera. So I was told that it was really needed for technical purposes.

The day before we were about to do this piece, I was about to go to the studio for a rehearsal. I stopped at Bergdorf Goodman to have lunch in one of their little lunch counters. And I was sitting there with the script in front of me and at the top of the script it said, "Mary as Mary Tyler Moore." And I was sitting there thinking, God, what can I do to get out of this. I really don't want to do this piece. And of course Mary Tyler Moore walked in the restaurant. She was with a male companion and they sat next to me. I was trembling. I had showed the waitress the script and we were laughing. And I was thinking, What should I do, should I ask her for her permission? Then I said, That's ridiculous. This is obviously insulting and it will hurt her feelings. And if I showed it to

her, it would just make her feel bad that anyone would be doing such a thing. I felt really trapped. I didn't quite know what to do. Then I thought, Well, if I have to do her, I'll just observe her body movements—but she was smoking, which no one has ever seen her do in public (at least not at that point), and nobody ever pictured her smoking. I had to disregard that completely; nobody would have understood it. So I went back to the studio and I said, "Guys, something has happened. It's a sign from God." I said, "I was just sitting next to Mary Tyler Moore. We *can't* do the sketch." They said, "No, no. You *completely* misinterpreted it." So we did do it that Saturday and then we went on Christmas break. I went back to Chicago. Three weeks later I come back to New York and the first thing that's said to me after I get off the elevator is "Gee, Mary, did you see the latest issue of *New York* magazine?" I go into Dick Ebersol's office and, apparently, the little article in *New York* magazine said that Mary had seen the scene and that she had spoken to Grant Tinker about it and she was upset…and Dick told me that he took full responsibility for it. I was devastated.

On the SNL experience:
To this day, if something bad happens to me, I feel, That's *nothing* compared to a typical week at *Saturday Night Live*.

Characters:
Alfalfa
Chi Chi
Geraldine Ferraro
Mary Richards
Brooke Shields
SNL Newsbreak anchor/reporter, 1981–1982
Dr. Ruth Westheimer

Christopher Guest

Years: 1984–1985
Seasons: 1
Characters:
Frankie, in Do You Know What I Hate?
Paul
Saturday Night News anchor, 1984–1985
Trainer, in Synchronized Swimming
Rajeev Vindaloo
Señor Cosa

Anthony Michael Hall

Years: 1985–1986
Seasons: 1
Characters:
Anthony Michael Hall, boxer (weighing in for bout with cohost)
One of the Two Joneses
Craig Sundberg: Idiot Savant

Brad Hall
Years: 1982–1984
Seasons: 2
Characters:
Larry Rolands
Saturday Night News anchor, 1982–1983

Rich Hall
Years: 1984–1985
Seasons: 1
Characters:
David Byrne
Paul Harvey
Robert Latta

Phil Hartman
Years: 1986–1994
Seasons: 8
On impersonations:
Dana's approach you could characterize as a caricature, an exaggeration. What I try to do is not an impression but an impersonation. When I do somebody, I really try to be as much like them as I possibly can and I don't like to go too far with the caricature. I like to see how close I can get because I think, in a way, that's what my talent is—that I can really get so close that it allows the audience to suspend disbelief.
Characters:
Sergei Akmudov, oversteroided weightlifter
Beev Algar, in Wayne's World
The Anal Retentive…(Chef, Sportsman, Carpenter, and more)
Wilford Brimley
Barbara Bush

Russell Clark, senior editor of *Sassy* magazine
Bill Clinton
Phil Donahue
Michael Eisner
Frankenstein
Helmut, model girly-man in Hans and Franz
Charlton Heston
Saddam Hussein
Jesus
Liberace
Mace
Ed McMahon
Ronald Reagan
Frank Sinatra
Susan, the She-Male, in Sprockets
Donald Trump
Unfrozen Caveman Lawyer

Jan Hooks
Years: 1986–1991
Seasons: 5
Characters:
Tammy Faye Bakker
Eleanor Clift, in The McLaughlin Group
Hillary Clinton
Nadia Comaneci
Bette Davis

Mia Farrow
Betty Ford
Kathie Lee Gifford
Nancy Glass, in Attitudes
Jessica Hahn
Sally Kellerman
Dee Kelly, in Attitudes
Marla Maples
Sinéad O'Connor
Sally Jessy Raphael
Nancy Reagan
Diane Sawyer
Nancy Simmons, in Wayne's World
Candy Sweeney
Ivana Trump

Melanie Hutsell
Years: 1991–1994
Seasons: 3
Characters:
Blossom
Jan Brady

Di, in The Sorority Girls
Tonya Harding
Tori Spelling

Victoria Jackson
Years: 1986–1992
Seasons: 6
On her audition:
Someone asked me, "Do you want to audition for *Saturday Night Live*?" It was really odd, because it usually goes through my agent. And I said, "Sure." They said, "Get on a plane tomorrow. We have your ticket and your hotel. Come to New York and audition." I said, "Okay," and they said, "And bring your characters." And I didn't have any. And I said, "Okay." I had a three-month-old baby and I said to my husband, "*Saturday Night Live* just called me."…So we packed up my

1981-1982 cast—formally.

1981-1982 cast—informally.

suitcase and I brought my ukulele and French maid costume because I think that they'd seen me on *The Tonight Show.*

Favorite characters:
Roseanne Barr and Zsa Zsa Gabor. All the articles in the newspapers used to say "She is the character."...I was very frustrated that they never let me do impressions, so one day one of the writers said, "Well, you're nasal, so you can only do nasal people. I know who you can do—Roseanne Barr. She's nasal."

Favorite moment:
When I say "I'm not a bimbo," and I did a hand-stand on the desk. This writer came up to me—Christine Zander—and dropped a magazine on my desk. I think it was *People.* And it had these huge letters: "I AM NOT A BIMBO." Jessica Hahn was quoting that and then taking her clothes off in *Playboy.* And it was like, "What an *idiot.*" I mean, "I'm not a bimbo. Look at my boobs." So Christine said, "This would be good for you, Vicki." And I said, "Yes, it would. That's *perfect* for me." So I made up a song in ten minutes:
Just because of the way I look,
Just because of what I wear,
Just because of how I act and fix my hair,
You think you can label me,
But don't you dare...because I am not a bimbo!
One time Al Franken said to me, "It really offends me that you act like a bimbo, because I know you're really smart." I was really hurt. Also, my voice has a congen-

ital palatal insufficiency. I'm really not trying to act like that; I *hate* women who act like that.

Fond memories:
The first time I did Roseanne, Dana Carvey was backstage. He was so sweet to me. He was standing next to me, and I said, "Dana, it's the first time I'm doing an impression." He's the master of it, and he said, "Vick, just cop an attitude. Cop an attitude." And I said, "Okay. Okay." He would hand me a cup of water and I was shaking. And he would say, "Cop an attitude." I'll never forget that. It was so sweet—the camaraderie.

Characters:
Acrobat
Roseanne Arnold
Jenny Barton, Church Lady's nemesis
Brenda Clarke, one of Toonces's owners
Zsa Zsa Gabor
Eydie Gorme, in The Sinatra Group
I Am Not a Bimbo
I Love a Cop
LaToya Jackson
Twelve-year-old Missy
Victoria's Secrets
Tina Yothers

Tim Kazurinsky
Years: 1981–1984
Seasons: 3

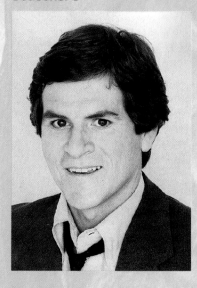

Characters:
Dr. Jack Badofsky
I Married a Monkey
Mr. Robinson's landlord
New York Post reader
David Stockman
Havnagootiim Vishnuuerheer, The
  Guru

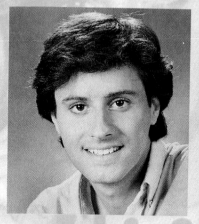

Gary Kroeger
Years: 1982–1985
Seasons: 3
Characters:
Champion of Run, Throw, and
  Catch like a Girl Olympics
Dwight MacNamara, educational-
  film narrator
Walter Mondale
Needleman the Dentist
Donny Osmond

Julia Louis-Dreyfus
Years: 1982–1985
Seasons: 3

Characters:
Nina Blackwood, MTV News
Consuela
Patti Lynn Hunnsacker
Marie Osmond
Linda Ronstadt
Spittake Talk Show host

Jon Lovitz
Years: 1985–1991
Seasons: 6
The Liar genesis:
The Liar started out as an inside
joke with a friend of mine. And I
like old movies a lot, so it was
based on a character from old
movies. That's where "Yeah, that's
the ticket" came from. I did it on
The Tonight Show, and Lorne
said, "Hey, why don't you get
together with A. Whitney Brown
and write it with him." He really
helped tremendously with
expanding the character.

It's an inside joke between a
friend of mine and I, and the next
thing you know, the whole country's doing it.
Master Thespian genesis:
This professor of mine in college
taught Shakespeare. The first
thing he did was the opening
speech from the chorus of *Henry
V:* "O! for a Muse of fire, that
would ascend / The brightest
heaven of invention." He would do
it really big, and to me it was
funny. I thought it was great and

hysterical, and I would imitate
him. Then I would say to my
friends, "I am the Master
Thespian…anytime, anyplace,
anywhere." Then I started doing it
at the Groundlings. I made him a
combination of my favorite actors:
John Barrymore, Basil
Rathbone—because they all have
great voices—and John Carradine,
because his voice was so loud, like
a cannon. So it was a combination
of all of them, filtered through me.
On his characters:
I guess all my characters are kind
of likable jerks.
True-life stories:
I did Harvey Fierstein. He didn't
like it. He came in to the show to
complain about it. His point was
that he was getting more famous as
me than as him….He came in to
talk about it and, watching him, I
realized that I was doing him quite
well. He thought I was doing a gay
stereotype. I said, "What if I
change the name?" He said, "No."
And he had his brother there who
was a lawyer. And he came out
that he basically wanted to host the
show. He wanted to do something
about outing—"Jew / Not-a-Jew,
Homosexual / Not homosexual"—
with all these pictures of people
coming up….But he's a nice guy
and I've run into him since. One
time I was walking in the street
behind him and I said [*imitating
Fierstein*], "Oh, whatta you talkin'
about?" And he said, "Oh, Jon
Lovitz, you stop that!"
Characters:
Annoying Man
Biff, in Biff and Salena
The Critic
David Crosby
David, Woody Allen's biggest fan
The Devil
Michael Dukakis
Queen Elizabeth
Harvey Fierstein
Tommy Flanagan, the pathological
  liar
Frenchie
Girl Watcher (with Tom Hanks)

Hanukkah Harry
Evelyn Quince, host of Tales of
  Ribaldry
Gene Shalit
One of the Stand-Ups
Master Thespian
Tonto

Gail Matthius
1980–1981
Seasons: 1
Characters:
Frances Lively
Rowena
Vickie
Weekend Update anchor, 1981

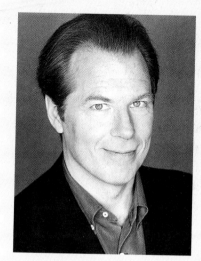

Michael McKean
Years: 1994
Seasons: 1

Tim Meadows

Years: 1991–1994

Seasons: 4

Characters:

Cyrano de Bergerac
Sammy Davis, Jr.
David Dinkins
Grandpa, in Tales from the
 Barbecue
Michael Jackson
Captain Jim, in Captain Jim and
 Pedro
Lenny Kravitz
Bernard Shaw
Clarence Thomas
Ike Turner

Dennis Miller

Years: 1986–1991

Seasons: 5

Characters:

KoKo, the French clown
Weekend Update anchor,
 1985–1991

Dennis: You know, over the years

there has been one consistent, recurrent segment of *Saturday Night Live*. That, of course, would be the really bad sketch at ten till one that makes everyone want to go to bed early. In addition to that, there has always been political content, either in the form of sketches or Weekend Update jokes. I hold a particularly fond place, near and dear to my heart, for Weekend Update. Because without it, I would probably be watching the show at home tonight, embittered and undoubtedly plotting the deaths of many of the fabulous entertainers you see here tonight.

[From the fifteenth anniversary show.]

Garrett Morris

Years: 1975–1980

Seasons: 5

Characters:

Pearl Bailey
Black Perspective host
Idi Amin Dada
Chico Escuela
Ella Fitzgerald
Inmate Johnson, Singer of "Kill All
 the Whiteys I See," in Lifer
 Follies
Uncle Remus
Grant Robinson, Jr., in The Nerds
Anwar Sadat
Tina Turner
News for the Hard of Hearing
 reporter, in Weekend Update

Garrett: I was hired by this show under terms of the Token Minority Window Dressing Act of 1968. [I get to play] all parts darker than Tony Orlando.

Cicely Tyson: Garrett, what is happening to you? Look at what you're doing! When we worked together at the Black Resentment Drama Workshop in the 1960s, I expected something really very big from you. The range you showed, your talent, your voice....Where's your integrity? What happened to it? You have talent and you're just throwing it away....Don't you know you have a responsibility as a black actor to perfect your craft? And you are here on this stage, in front of all these people on television, acting like a clown. What are you doing it for? Money?

Garrett: Well, it doesn't look bad on my résumé, you know. And I get to keep the dresses.

Eddie Murphy

Years: 1980–1984

Seasons: 4

Characters:

Black History Minute host
James Brown
Buckwheat
Bill Cosby
Dion Dion, in Dion and Blaire
Irving Flang
Tyrone Green, poet ("Cill My
 Landlord")
Gumby
Velvet Jones

Larry the Lobster pollster
Raheem Abdul Muhammed
Mr. Robinson
Little Richard Simmons
Solomon
Stevie Wonder

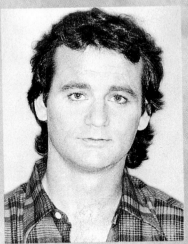

Bill Murray

Years: 1977–1980

Seasons: 4

Characters:

Richard Dawson
Todd DiLaMuca, in The Nerds
Jerry Eldini, A&R Man handling
 Candy Slice
One of the Ex-Police
Ronnie Getsetter, Connie Conehead's boyfriend
Richard Herkiman, in Shower
 Mike
The Honker
Ted Kennedy
Ted Koppel
Dick Lanky
Mr. Loud
Captain Steve McCloud, Microdentist
The Mighty Hercules
Nick the Lounge Singer
Nico, serving chips and drinks in
 the Olympia Restaurant
Stargazer Bill Murray, Celebrity
 Corner host
Director, in Stunt Baby and Stunt
 Puppy
Superman
Paco Valenzuela, host of ¡¿Quien
 Es Mas Macho?!

Weekend Update anchor,
1978–1980

Bill: Hello. I'm Bill Murray. You can call me Billy, but around here everybody just calls me "the new guy." I want to thank the producer, Lorne Michaels, for urging me to speak with you directly. You see, I'm a little bit concerned. I don't think I'm making it on the show.

I'm a funny guy, but I haven't been so funny on the show. My friends say, "How come they're giving you all those parts that aren't funny?" Well, it's not the material, it's me. It's not that I'm not funny, it's that I'm not being funny at the right time. Honest. Before, I could be funny whenever I wanted. But now, as a professional, I have to learn to pick my spots, you know. This morning I picked up my laundry, and the guy said to me, "Bill, you know, every time you come in here, you say something funny. But I saw you on the show Saturday night, and you stunk."

Mike Myers
Years: 1989–1994
Seasons: 6
Favorite character:
Linda Richman. Because it's fun to do. I know that sounds really corny, but it truly is fun. It brings me out of my sort of shy Canadian persona.
Origins of Linda Richman:
I was sort of doing Linda to her face for years [The character is based on Myers's mother-in-law, whose maiden name is Linda Richman], and then in the makeup trailer on *Wayne's World* I was doing it to make everybody laugh, and I thought, Why don't I just change it [i.e., replace "Coffee Talk" host Paul Baldwin with his Linda Richman]? I also talked to Linda and asked her if it was okay, and she said, "Sure." It's not so much an impression as it is a love letter.
Strange encounters:
Gilda Radner played my mother on

a commercial for British Columbia Hydro Electric two years before *Saturday Night Live* came out.
The moment he knew:
I've always wanted to be on the show, since I was eleven years old. I was so proud that Aykroyd was from Canada and that Lorne was from Canada. I did a project on Lorne in grade eight, as a famous Canadian that I was proud of. I watched the first show, and even after the first sketch, with Michael O'Donoghue and Belushi, I said, "I want to do this."
Odd moments:
Dennis Hopper got out of sync in the line, and so he said the line to me that was supposed to come after my line. And it worked great, because the line that he said was "I'm psychic." So it was a complete and wonderful accident. So I said to him, "How's it going," and he said, "Sixty-eight degrees." And then I went, "What's the weather like outside?" Then when he got back in sync, the first line was "I'm a bit of a psychic, you know."
Characters:
Angus, in All Things Scottish
Pat Arnold, in Bill Swerski's Super Fans
Paul Baldwin, original host of Coffee Talk
Wayne Campbell, excellent host of Wayne's World
Dieter, host of Sprockets
Queen Elizabeth
Mick Jagger

Joey Lawrence
Steve Lawrence, in The Sinatra Group
Lothar of the Hill People
Marcello, in Il Cantore and La Cantoria
Middle-Aged Man
Phillip, the Hyper-Hypo
Kenneth Reese-Evans, host of Theatre Stories
Linda Richman, host of Coffee Talk
Simon
George Stephanopoulos
Lank Thompson, Handsome Man

Kevin Nealon
Years: 1986–1994
Seasons: 8
Characters:
Michael Bolton
Sam Donaldson
Franz, in Hans and Franz
Gannon, P.I.P.I.
Rudolph Giuliani
Michael Gross
Jimmy the Doorman
Larry King
Morton Kondracke, in The McLaughlin Group
Lebee
Jay Leno
Mr. No Depth Perception
One of A Couple of Sammies
Mr. Subliminal
Tarzan
One of the Valincourt Boys
Bob Waltman
Weekend Update anchor, 1991–1994

Laraine Newman
Years: 1975–1980
Seasons: 5
Favorite character:
Lina Wertmuller is one that I really loved. It was very "inside," and I don't think anybody got it, but it tickled me more than anything in the world. The people who wrote the character—I think it was Rosie Shuster and Tom Schiller—they understood that character very well, and it was just so in accord with my sensibility. It just made me laugh.
Favorite sketches we never saw:
For the Lina Wertmuller, there was a lot of stuff I wanted in the sketch that wasn't in that involved "The Little Rascals." I just thought that the idea of "The Little Rascals" being directed by Lina Wertmuller…!

Also, we had Bill Russell, the basketball player, as a host once—and there's a great song by the Marvelettes called "Don't Mess with Bill." I wanted to do a dance number around him, with basketball cheerleaders trying to compete for Bill's affection.
Most embarrassing moment:
Well, this was the very last show that we did, and we knew it. We knew that after that it was over for all of us. We were doing a parody of *Coal Miner's Daughter* called "Cow Minder's Daughter," and I was doing this woman from India.

I was playing the guitar, I was onstage by myself in home base, and the monitor went blank. There was supposed to be a crawl over me; I could see the monitor and I knew what was supposed to happen, and it went blank, so I thought we had gone off the air. I just kind of stood there and Lorne was standing in front of me pantomiming "Sing! *Sing!*" I finally got it: He wanted me to cover for the audience's sake. Bill Murray came out and rescued my ass. He made some Polish joke, but instead replaced it with an Indian one.

On Christy Christina:
I did my feeblest of Marilyn Monroe imitations. We wanted some hook for her, which turned out to be her little laugh. It was fun for me to play a bimbo. God, it's so liberating.

Characters:
Amy Carter
Rosalynn Carter
Child Psychiatrist/Baby Mogul
Christy Christina, E. Buzz Miller's cohost
Connie Conehead
Indira Gandhi
Penny, the little girl visited by Mr. Death
Regan, in The Exorcist
Sandy, waitress at the Olympia Restaurant
Sherry
Barbra Streisand
Sunshine
Terri, in Uncle Roy
Maxine Universe
Gloria Vanderbilt
Lina Wertmuller
Nicole Westman, Microdental Hygienist

Joe Piscopo
Years: 1980–1984
Seasons: 4
Characters:
Blaire, in Dion and Blaire
Jimmy Carter
Paulie Herman, in The Jersey Guy
David Letterman

Jerry Lewis
Alfred E. Neuman
Pokey
Pudge
Dan Rather
Andy Rooney
Saturday Night Sports anchor
Frank Sinatra
"Uncle" Tom Snyder
Doug Whiner

Randy Quaid
Years: 1985–1986
Seasons: 1
Characters:
Ed McMahon
Ronald Reagan
Rudy Randolph, Jr.

Gilda Radner
Years: 1975–1980
Seasons: 5

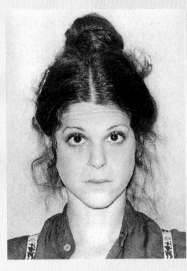

Characters:
Lucille Ball
Connie Carson
Lillian Carter
Christina Crawford
Debbie Doody
Lady Douchebag
Voice of Mrs. Ed
Bobbi Farber
Annette Funicello
Olga Korbut
Emily Litella
Lisa Loopner, in The Nerds
Judy Miller
Jackie O.
Roseanne Roseannadanna
Candy Slice
Tracy, in Uncle Roy
Baba Wawa
Rhonda Weiss
What Gilda Ate
Tammy Widette

Ann Risley
Years: 1980–1981
Seasons: 1

Chris Rock
Years: 1991–1993
Seasons: 3
Favorite character:
Nat X. I do good racial jokes. Nat X lent itself to me.
Least favorite moment:
"Superman's Funeral." I had to play Robin from *Batman*, and I'm this skinny guy, and I had on these tights. And I love Sade—I've always had posters up of Sade in my house. She's there all week and I can't even talk to her. I'm like a groupie little girl. I'm literally hyperventilating. So I finally get face-to-face with her and I am wearing this Robin suit. She's singing and she's *giggling* at me. Sade, the woman of my dreams, she can't stop laughing. I wait my whole life to meet Sade and I'm dressed up like Robin.
Favorite sketches we never saw:
"Nasty Man" was a morning show—*Regis and Kathy Lee*, but a dirty old man. It was so foul, so Snoop Doggish. There was a guy

like a pimp in the helicopter doing the traffic report: "Boy, there's a *lotta* bitches on the FDR today! I see a girl down there with no bra on—back to *you!*"
Biggest influence:
There would be no Chris Rock without Eddie Murphy.
Characters:
Luther Campbell
Arsenio Hall

Michael Jackson
Onski, host of I'm Chillin'
Hero of Tales from the Barbecue
Nat X

1985–1986 cast.

Charles Rocket
Years: 1980–1981
Seasons: 1
Characters:
Phil Lively
The Rocket Report
Weekend Update anchor,
1980–1981

Tony Rosato
Years: 1981–1982
Seasons: 1
Character:
Ed Asner

Adam Sandler
Years: 1991–1994
Seasons: 4
On the genesis of Operaman:
The guy from Fifty-seventh Street.
Some guy sings opera and gets
money in a cup. I just used to do
impressions of him, and the
Turners made it into an Update.
At first I would just do it around
the office. I originally did it like
"Operaman Sings about Grape
Juice": He doesn't like grape juice,
but he never really tried it. So they
make him drink it, and he likes it,
and so he would sing, and he was
sad, and then all of a sudden he
would get happy because he
realized he liked grape juice. So
that was the original idea. It was
really stupid, but it didn't work, so
the Turners turned it into an
Update.

On Canteen Boy:
Canteen Boy is just the boys I
knew, kids when I was growing up
in the neighborhood. He's not
retarded; he's just a silly kid who
stayed in the Scouts too long.
On the role of the audience:
When I get nothing from a crowd, I
get so upset that it bruises me for a
week. When I do something wrong,
it ruins me until the next show.
Characters:
Audience McGee
Bono
Brian, host of The Denise Show
Cajunman
Canteen Boy
Bill Cosby
Fabio, in Il Cantore and La
  Cantoria
One of the Gyro Guys
Halloween costume expert
The Herlihy Boy
Lucy, one of the Gap Girls

Operaman
Pedro, in Captain Jim and Pedro
Iraqi Pete
Axl Rose
Bruce Springsteen
One of the Valincourt Boys
Eddie Vedder

Rob Schneider
Years: 1990–1994
Seasons: 4
Characters:
Carlo, in Il Cantore and La
  Cantoria
Tiny Elvis
Frank the Doorman
One of the Gyro Guys
k. d. lang
Orgasm Guy
Soon-Yi Previn
The Richmeister
Rob Schneider's Girlfriend
  Theatre host
The Sensitive Naked Man
Tammy, the Gap Girls' rival from
  Donut Hut
Weed Guy

Harry Shearer
Years: 1979–1980;
1984–1985

Seasons: 2
Characters:
Mr. Blackwell
Ronald Reagan
Frank Reynolds
Gerald, in Synchronized
  Swimming
The Vicker
Mike Wallace

Martin Short
Years: 1984–1985
Seasons: 1
Characters:
Irving Cohen
Ed Grimley
Doug Henning
Katharine Hepburn, in Kate and
  Ali
Jackie Rogers, Jr.
Lawrence, in Synchronized
  Swimming
Nathan Thurm

David Spade
Years: 1990–1994
Seasons: 4

On the Receptionist:
I think it was Patrick Swayze who
was here and he had either an
agent or it could have been an
assistant. He was sitting reading
People magazine in the writers'
room. I walked in on him, like, at
one A.M. to tell him an idea that I
was writing, and she stepped in
between us and said, "Can I help
you?" I said, "Yeah, I just wanted

to run something by Patrick."
She said, "And you are?" And I
go, "David Spade." She goes,
"What do you do here?" or something, and I go, "I'm a writer,"
and she goes, "He's a little
stressed-out right now. He's a
little under the gun. If you could
just give him a while." I'm like,
Isn't that him right there reading
People? So I go, "Oh, okay, I'll
come back."

Then later I was getting it on
the phone when I called Lorne in
Los Angeles. No one knew who I
was at Broadway Video because
I've never been there or met them,
and I'd get "He would know you
through…?" "I'm on *Saturday
Night Live*. I'm on his show."

**On his progression as a
writer:**
The first year I didn't want to get
fired. The second year I just
wanted my sketches not to stand
out [so] you wouldn't know which
ones were mine because they were
all evenly funny, and then I
wanted to get ahead. It takes a
long time to be a good enough
sketch writer.

On Hollywood Minute:
I like Hollywood Minute for
different reasons. I like it because
creatively each joke means a lot to
me, even if it doesn't get a laugh,
because structurally it's an
important joke which surprises or
hasn't been done before or in a

way which I think is funny or
really stupid for the sake of being
stupid. And being kind of nobody
on the show and small physically
and being the biggest asshole was
funny to me.
Characters:
Christy, one of the Gap Girls
Michael J. Fox
Hollywood Minute host
Karl, the video-store owner
Don LaPre
Tom Petty
The Receptionist

Pamela Stephenson
Years: 1984–1985
Seasons: 1
Characters:
Angela Bradleigh
Cyndi Lauper

Julia Sweeney
Years: 1990–1994
Seasons: 4

Characters:
Chelsea Clinton
Mrs. Hibbert
Pat
Jane Pauley
Prylon, in Alien Spacewoman

Terry Sweeney
Years: 1985–1986
Seasons: 1
Characters:
Joan Collins
Nancy Reagan

Danitra Vance
1985–1986
Seasons: 1
Characters:
That Black Girl
Cabrini Green, the pregnant teen
Flotilla Williams, in Shakespeare
   in the Slums

1993–1994 cast.

Featured Players

Peter Aykroyd
Year: 1980
Seasons: 1

A. Whitney Brown
Years: 1986–1990
Seasons: 5
Character:
The Big Picture

Beth Cahill
Years: 1992–1993
Seasons: 1
Characters:
Pam, in the Sorority Girls
Denise Swerski

George Coe
Year: 1975
Seasons: 1

Tom Davis
Years: 1977–1980
Seasons: 3
Character:
Franken & Davis

Jim Downey
Year: 1980
Seasons: 1
Characters:
George Bush (as vice president)
Craig, in Craig's Travelers Checks
Spokesman for Citiwide Change
  Bank

Siobhan Fallon
Years: 1991–1992
Seasons: 1
Character:
Meg, in The Sorority Girls

Al Franken
Years: 1977–1980; 1986;
1989–1994
Seasons: 9
Characters:
The Al Franken Decade
Franken & Davis
Henry Kissinger
One-Man Mobile Uplink Unit
  reporter

Pat Robertson
Senator Paul Simon
Stuart Smalley
Paul Tsongas

People are going to stop thinking about themselves and start thinking about me, Al Franken. That's right. I believe we're entering the Al Franken Decade. Oh, for me, Al Franken, the eighties will be pretty much the same as the seventies. But for you, when you see a news report you'll be thinking, "I wonder what Al Franken thinks about this?" "I wonder how this inflation thing is hurting Al Franken?" And you women will be thinking, "What can I wear that will please Al Franken?" or "What can I not wear?" A lot of you are probably thinking, "Why Al Franken?" Well, because I thought of it, and I'm on TV.

Yvonne Hudson
Years: 1980–1981
Seasons: 1

Mitchell Kriegman
Years: 1980
Seasons: 1

Matthew Laurance
Years: 1980–1981
Seasons: 1

Norm MacDonald
Years: 1993–1994
Seasons: 1
Character:
Charles Kuralt

Jay Mohr
Years: 1993–1994
Seasons: 1
Characters:
Andrew McCarthy
Dick Vitale
Christopher Walken

Don Novello
Years: 1978–1980;
1985–1986
Seasons: 4

Character:
Father Guido Sarducci

Michael O'Donoghue
Years: 1975–1979
Seasons: 4
Characters:
English tutor, in The Wolverines,
  SNL's debut sketch
Mr. Mike

Paul Shaffer
Years: 1979–1980
Seasons: 1
How he became an actor:
The first time I got to read lines, I was participating with Brian Doyle-Murray and putting together an idea he had for a musical number, "Mr. Mike and Tina Turner." The idea was that Garrett would be in drag doing an impersonation of Tina Turner, and he turned out to have pretty good legs. In order to set this up, Brian Doyle-Murray said, "We need somebody to introduce this, like a rock impresario," and I'd just come from doing a sitcom called *A Year at the Top*, produced by Norman Lear and Don Kirshner. I took from that this impersonation of Kirshner. I said, "Let me introduce this number as Don Kirshner," so I wrote myself into it. And that's how I got to perform on the show. When David Letterman was starting his show, he asked to see me based on his familiarity with me on the *Saturday Night Live* show. He had seen some of the things I had done on *Saturday Night Live*, most notably the stuff with Bill Murray in the lounges. I think that's what drew his attention to me.
Embarrassing memories:
It was during that fifth season when I was getting to play some roles. Franken and Davis had

written a sketch in which they transcribed the famous Troggs tape—the Troggs were a band in the sixties who had had a song called "Wild Thing." And they use obscenities. They say the four-letter words over and over again. So Franken and Davis had the idea to use the actual lines that these guys were saying to each other but to make our scene into a medieval band rehearsing for a performance before the king and saying the words that the Troggs say on this tape. But of course we couldn't say "fuck," so we made up our own word, "flog." Laraine was in it, James Taylor was in it, I was in it, Billy was in it, and we were all saying, "You've played the flogging song before, why can't you play the flogging song again?" It went very well in the dress rehearsal, so well that I remember Al Franken coming to me, just before we went on air, saying, "The *flogging*s are getting big laughs. If you want to expand, put a few more in." So I was loose. I was saying "flogging this" and "flogging that" and actually did slip and said "fuck" on live television. And when I said it, I shocked myself. It wasn't like Madonna. Laraine's face went "Whoops," and afterwards she said, "And thank *you* for making broadcasting history." This was in '78 or '79 and I was worried about what would happen to me, and Lorne came up to me and said, "Well, you've broken down the last barrier."
On the show hosted by the Rolling Stones:
It almost became competitive: Who is the heavier here? Is it the cast of *Saturday Night Live*—who were referred to as "the Beatles of comedy"—or was it the Stones? There was a sketch which was to immediately precede the first Stones number. And this sketch

Candice Bergen and Muppets

would be the scene backstage at the Stones trailer—a security guard with a list and various people trying to get in. I was to walk up to the security guard with Billy Murray as Jerry Eldini, the rock and roll A & R man. And it was a very hip idea to see a fictional backstage with the Stones. They would, from that sketch, walk right out onto the stage and do their first number. It wasn't used. It was supposed to be in, but it had to be cut at the very last minute. I was very excited about it. I was in the makeup room having my Don Kirshner wig applied and Mick Jagger floats into the makeup room—he knows; I don't yet know. He sees me getting the wig put on. He focuses in on me slowly,

extends his finger, and says, "You're cut." So I'll always remember what Mick Jagger said to me backstage at *Saturday Night*.

Characters:
Accompanist, in Nick the Lounge
  Singer
Don Kirshner

Sarah Silverman
Years: 1993-1994
Seasons: 1

Robert Smigel
Years: 1991-1993
Seasons: 2
Characters:
One of the Gyro Guys
Carl Wollarski, in Bill Swerski's
  Super Fans

Ben Stiller
Year: 1989
Seasons: 1
Character:
Butch "Eddie Munster"
Patrick

Dan Vitale
Years: 1985-1986
Seasons: 1

Damon Wayans
Years: 1985-1986
Seasons: 1
Characters:
One of the Stand-Ups
One of the Two Joneses

Patrick Weathers
Years: 1980-1981
Seasons: 1

The Writers

We spoke to James Downey, a longtime writer for SNL and currently the show's producer, about the role of the writers.

The number one misconception it seems we just can't root out is that the show is largely improvised. A lot of otherwise fairly intelligent people will ask, "How much of what they're doing is scripted and how much are they just making it up?" as though we would put people out on television and invite them to use their imaginations. The whole show is written.

Ideally, it's a mix of performer-generated material—popular characters or impressions—and pieces that are topical; not necessarily about news events so much as things that people have been thinking about lately.

I think performers like to develop characters and then bring them back in different situations, which writers don't necessarily find all that interesting. Performers tend to like repeating things because they're the people who get approached on the street and asked, "How come you haven't been doing that character lately?" For them I think it's more about being out there on stage; the idea isn't necessarily as important as the performance. For the writers it's more about the idea, and we tend not to want to repeat things because we often feel the best jokes for that idea were done the first time out.

These days—and I notice this because I was there in the early days too—the whole show is harder to write, because TV and commercials and culture in general are a lot more sophisticated. It's not the big, fat, easy target it once was. It's also not virgin territory anymore. Back in the '70s, anything we did was, by definition, being done for the first time, and that's not the case today. It's hard to find fresh, sincere, non-ironic stuff that hasn't already been worked over.

We're not about perfection, we're about getting it on the air. It's a very raw show, and done in sort of a primitive way. We're really about that week—there's no lag time. We don't do our shows and then broadcast them months later. So we like to think that we can do things in a show at the same time that everyone in the country is thinking about them. That's probably what made the show such a phenomenon, especially in the early years.

But it's also the idea of seeing things that you'd never see anywhere else on television, like getting George Steinbrenner and putting him in a sketch where he's a boss who just can't find it in his heart to fire people. Or a piece where Wayne Gretzky is in an Elvis movie about a kid working as a busboy who is really a great hockey player. Obviously, what made that piece funny wasn't that he did this great Elvis; it was his really appealing, naive performance, and the fact that it really was Wayne Gretzky. In the same way, Ron Reagan, Jr. dancing, doing the *Risky Business* thing, was about that he really was the son of the president of the United States and it was cool to see him doing that.

I always say, "I'm not doing the show for myself and I'm not doing it for the audience. I'm doing it for my friends," who I tend to think of as having good taste and intelligence. If they tell me the show's really bad it troubles me in a way that negative mail doesn't.

We have a live audience and a live energy that comes from the show really taking ninety minutes to do. We don't stop tape in the middle and then set something up and do it again. To get from one thing to another we really have to design the show in such a way that it's perfectly compact and efficient—like those English suitcases where everything folds in on itself—and yet flows for ninety minutes.

I think that finally the show is about the performance. When the show is good, and when it's really working, it's probably because you have a very funny cast who can do a lot of different funny things that writers can take and shape and put in a context and come up with jokes for. Writers need those performers.

Larry Arnstein	Robin Duke	Mitchell Kriegman	Eddie Murphy	Marc Shaiman
Dave Attell	Bruce Feirstein	Andrew Kurtzman	Bill Murray	Harry Shearer
Dan Aykroyd	Paul Flaherty	Lanier Laney	Michael Myers	David Sheffield
Peter Aykroyd	Ellen L. Fogle	Carol Leifer	Kevin Nealon	Martin Short
Paul Barrosse	Al Franken	Neil Levy	Matt Neuman	Rosie Shuster
Anne Beatts	Leslie Fuller	Steve Lookner	Pamela Norris	Sarah Silverman
Jim Belushi	Tom Gammill	Nelson Lyon	Don Novello	Robert Smigel
John Belushi	Shannon Gaughan	Norm MacDonald	Margaret Oberman	Andrew Smith
Barry Blaustein	Eddie Gorodetsky	David Mandel	Conan O'Brien	Terry Southern
Dick Blausucci	Adam Green	Patricia Marx	Bob Odenkirk	David Spade
Joe Bodolai	Mel Green	Ian Maxtone-Graham	Mark O'Donnell	Jeremy Stevens
Jeremiah Bosgang	Mary Gross	Bruce McCall	Michael O'Donoghue	John Swartzwelder
John Bowman	Christopher Guest	Brian McConnachie	Sarah Paley	Terry Sweeney
Andy Breckman	Rich Hall	Bruce McCulloch	Joe Piscopo	Bob Tischler
A. Whitney Brown	Jack Handey	Dan McGrath	Max Pross	Tracy Tormé
Billy Brown	Bruce Handy	Douglas McGrath	Paul Raley	Bonnie Turner
Jean Carroll	Phil Hartman	Mark McKinney	Mark Reisman	Terry Turner
Chevy Chase	Tim Herlihy	Tim Meadows	Ron Richards	Jon Vitti
Billy Crystal	Nate Herman	George Meyer	Rob Riley	Eliot Wald
Greg Daniels	David Hurwitz	Lorne Michaels	Tony Rosato	Mason Williams
Larry David	Warren Hutcherson	Vanessa Middleton	Richard Rosen	Walter Williams
Tom Davis	Judy Jacklin	Marilyn Suzanne Miller	Adam Sandler	Dirk Wittenborn
John DeBellis	Dawna Kaufman	Jay Mohr	Herb Sargent	Fred Wolf
Tony De Sena	Tim Kazurinsky	Paul Mooney	Tom Schiller	Christine Zander
James Downey	Kevin Kelton	Tom Moore	Rob Schneider	Alan Zweibel
Brian Doyle-Murray	Steve Koren	Lewis Morton	Susan Schneider	

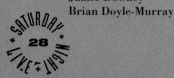

Anne Beatts

Favorite character:
Irwin Mainway, who originally appeared in a sketch Danny [Aykroyd] and I co-wrote about unsafe Halloween costumes—one of them was called Invisible Pedestrian. Irwin was so sleazy he would do anything, even—in a sketch that Rosie [Shuster], [James] Downey, and I wrote together—sell dog milk to a school lunch program. I'll always remember Jane's expression of utter disgust—she was Joan Face again—as she said, "I don't want to know where they get the dogs, Mr. Mainway, or who milks them."

Worst character:
Perhaps the best worst character Rosie and I wrote was Buck Henry as Uncle Roy. Ah, those carefree days, when we felt free to explore the lighter side of child molesting. At least Uncle Roy never hurt anyone—he was the one who got tied up. So it was all good clean fun, really.

The SNL experience:
I've often described it as a cross between summer camp and concentration camp. In those first years it was like a family— an extremely dysfunctional family where people were always slamming doors and going, "You pig! I'm going to my room and never speaking to you again!" It was also the kind of showbiz job that spoiled you for all other showbiz jobs, because you were in this kind of kindergarten for geniuses where you could play in the TV sandbox to your heart's content.

James Downey

The best show ever:
We did a show with Steve Martin (April 22, 1978) that probably came off as well as any single show that we've ever done. There was a thrill of feeling that everything went right, that we got all the breaks—it's the only time I remember having that feeling. I think if you ask most of the people from the early show, they would say that was probably the best single show we did.

A memorable near-mishap:
There was one time when Joe Montana hosted the show and the show was almost over. It was like a quarter after twelve, and I just stopped by his dressing room to talk to him. He was relaxing because most of his work was over at that point, but there was one piece remaining. There's a call box in the host's dressing room where Joe Dicso gives them warnings—like, "five minutes," "three minutes," and so on—and Montana's lawyer had turned it off because it does get distracting.

I should have known better, but I just got to sitting and talking to him, and apparently they were frantically trying to call him until with about thirty seconds to go he wasn't out there. Joe Dicso comes bursting into the door, screaming, "They're about to go on camera, where are you?" So the pages have cleared a path for him and here was Joe Montana, sprinting from his dressing room into the studio and hitting his mark at a dead run just as the red light went on. He was a little thrown just for the first twenty seconds but he got there in time, and it was just a great thing to see Joe Montana do.

Marilyn Suzanne Miller

On SNL's twentieth anniversary:
I always expected a twentieth anniversary for *SNL*. I just never expected anybody would be dead for it [John Belushi and Gilda Radner], including myself—that is, I never thought I would get breast cancer before it came along, or any of that.

Favorite characters:
I liked the sketches I wrote more than the characters I invented, although Judy Miller and the Festrunk Brothers (done with Danny [Aykroyd] and Steve Martin) are among my favorites in terms of characters. Judy Miller was based on a number of my sisters and was Gilda at her physical-comedian finest. She was without peer as a physical comedian, and there are very few places you can see this more than in this sketch.

Favorite sketch:
Probably my very favorite sketch was the one I wrote with Sissy Spacek and John Belushi, a kind of dramatic sketch where she plays this kind of southern white trash cheerleader girl, and he plays her husband who can't get it up, and they are trying, after a luckless love encounter, to figure out what's wrong.

Rosie Shuster

Favorite characters:
Lisa Loopner, whom [Anne] Beatts and I wrote. Todd's notion of what was sexy, his pelvic gyrations, used to kill me. I was happy when William Safire noticed the "not" phenomenon was born in a Nerd sketch. It once passed for wit back in junior high.

And the politically-so-incorrect Uncle Roy, the genial pervert, played by Buck Henry, based on my old babysitter, Mr. Clark. I loved seeing Buck on all fours as Uncle Roy playing Ruffy, the bad dog, leaping up on the couch and getting his butt spanked by Gilda and Laraine with a rolled up newspaper. I used to play Ruffy at home with my brother Steve.

Alan Zweibel

On watching SNL reruns:
What happens is, you're transported back, and just like if you heard an old song from seventh grade and you go, "Oh, I had a crush on that guy when that song was popular"—it's the same thing with watching the old shows.

On Gilda:
I just took one look at her and I thought that this was not only the funniest person I'd ever seen but it just struck a nerve with me. I just somehow fell in love with her.

Roseanne Roseannadanna:
I was having dinner with Gilda and I said, "Remember that character you did a couple of weeks ago in that Hire the Incompetent sketch? Why don't we take her and put her in Weekend Update and make her a consumer reporter, not unlike Rose Ann Scamardella on *ABC Eyewitness News*." And Gilda said, "Great, I'd love to do that, but can we name her Roseanne Roseannadanna?" And I said, "Well, what does that mean? How did you come up with that?" And she started singing that song "The Name Game," you know? *"Johnny, Johnny, Bobohnny, Banana...."* If you put Roseanne in there, somewhere like in the fourth verse you'll have "Roseanne Roseannadanna."

Richard Feder from Fort Lee, New Jersey, who used to write her every week, is my brother-in-law. He's a guy I grew up with, and he married my sister. I wrote the letters but I said they were from him.

1975-1976

October 11, 1975
George Carlin

October 18, 1975
Paul Simon

October 25, 1975
Rob Reiner

November 8, 1975
Candice Bergen

November 15, 1975
Robert Klein

November 22, 1975
Lily Tomlin

December 13, 1975
Richard Pryor

December 20, 1975
Candice Bergen

January 10, 1976
Elliott Gould

January 17, 1976
Buck Henry

January 24, 1976
Peter Cook and Dudley Moore

January 31, 1976
Dick Cavett

February 14, 1976
Peter Boyle

February 21, 1976
Desi Arnaz

February 28, 1976
Jill Clayburgh

March 13, 1976
Anthony Perkins

April 17, 1976
Ron Nessen

April 24, 1976
Raquel Welch

May 8, 1976
Madeline Kahn

May 15, 1976
Dyan Cannon

May 22, 1976
Buck Henry

May 29, 1976
Elliott Gould

July 24, 1976
Louise Lasser

July 31, 1976
Kris Kristofferson

1976-1977

September 18, 1976
Lily Tomlin

September 25, 1976
Norman Lear

October 2, 1976
Eric Idle

October 16, 1976
Karen Black

October 23, 1976
Steve Martin

October 30, 1976
Buck Henry

November 13, 1976
Dick Cavett

November 20, 1976
Paul Simon

November 27, 1976
Jodie Foster

December 11, 1976
Candice Bergen

January 15, 1977
Ralph Nader

January 22, 1977
Ruth Gordon

P*aul Simon walks out to home base dressed as a giant turkey. He pauses for a few moments, then takes the microphone from the stool next to him and starts singing "Still Crazy After All These Years." Afters a few bars, he stops and addresses the bandleader.*

Paul: Cut it, forget it, forget it, Richard. You know, I said, when the turkey concept was first brought up, I said there's a very good chance I'm gonna end up looking stupid if I come out wearing it. I mean, everyone said, "Oh, it's Thanksgiving, go ahead."

You know, I felt it was not in any way in keeping with my image, the lyrics, "The Boxer," any of these songs. They said, "Hey, y'know, you take yourself sooo seriously. Why don't you stop taking yourself sooo seriously for a while and loosen up a little bit and maybe people will laugh. You wanna be Mr. Alienation, you can be Mr. Alienation." Well, I didn't want to be Mr. Alienation. I wanna be a regular guy, but I feel this has just been a disaster. I'm sorry. I'm just gonna go and change....

[*He leaves the stage and walks out of the studio, toward his dressing room. He meets Lorne Michaels in the corridor.*]

Lorne: Wonderful!

Paul: You call that wonderful?

Lorne: What? You had a problem?

Paul: That was one of the most humiliating experiences of my life.

Lorne: What? The band came in late?

Paul: The band was fine… it's not the band!

Lorne: I don't understand what the problem is.

Paul: The problem is, I'm singing "Still Crazy" in a turkey outfit. Well, would you like to sing in a turkey outfit?

A*IRED:* O*CTOBER* 18, 1975

1977-1978

September 24, 1977
Steve Martin

October 8, 1977
Madeline Kahn

October 15, 1977
Hugh Hefner

October 29, 1977
Charles Grodin

November 12, 1977
Ray Charles

November 19, 1977
Buck Henry

December 10, 1977
Mary Kay Place

December 17, 1977
Miskel Spillman

January 21, 1978
Steve Martin

January 28, 1978
Robert Klein

February 18, 1978
Chevy Chase

February 25, 1978
O.J. Simpson

March 11, 1978
Art Garfunkel

March 18, 1978
Jill Clayburgh

March 25, 1978
Christopher Lee

April 8, 1978
Michael Palin

April 15, 1978
Michael Sarrazin

April 22, 1978
Steve Martin

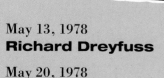

May 13, 1978
Richard Dreyfuss

May 20, 1978
Buck Henry

1978-1979

October 7, 1978
The Rolling Stones

October 14, 1978
Fred Willard

October 21, 1978
Frank Zappa

November 4, 1978
Steve Martin

November 11, 1978
Buck Henry

November 18, 1978
Carrie Fisher

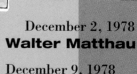

December 2, 1978
Walter Matthau

December 9, 1978
Eric Idle

December 16, 1978
Elliott Gould

January 27, 1979
Michael Palin

February 10, 1979
Cicely Tyson

February 17, 1979
Rick Nelson

February 24, 1979
Kate Jackson

March 10, 1979
Gary Busey

March 17, 1979
Margot Kidder

April 7, 1979
Richard Benjamin

April 14, 1979
Milton Berle

May 12, 1979
Michael Palin

May 19, 1979
Maureen Stapleton

May 26, 1979
Buck Henry

Steve Martin: Later, baby; got a big show to do.

Gilda Radner: Hello, Steve.

Steve: Gilda! [*He tries to kiss her but she backs off.*] Hey, if something's wrong, you might as well tell me. I don't like playing games.

Gilda: It's just that you've changed since you've been on *The Tonight Show.*

Steve: Guest-hosted *The Tonight Show.*

Gilda: Guest-hosted. I know you're doing a lot, you're on the road…

Steve: Hey, show business is my life.

Gilda: What about my life?

Steve: I don't know. I guess your life is ruined. I mean I'm a ramblin' guy; you knew that before you got involved.

Gilda: Yeah. But you could have called.

Steve: I did call. I left the name of the lotion on your tape machine. You got the message, didn't you?

Gilda: Yeah.

Steve: So everything turned out all right. Say [*He looks into his dressing room, this girl crashes early. Whatta ya say I meet you at your place about three.

Gilda: Okay. Three. [*They kiss.*] Have a good show.

Steve: Will do. Three. [*He starts walking to the locker room.*] Hey, guys, how's it going? [*Long pause.*]

John Belushi: Well, if it isn't

Mr. Big-time Show Business!

Garrett Morris: Mr. Host of *The Tonight Show.*

Steve: Guest host. I was just a guest host once.

Bill Murray: Steve, I wasn't here the last time you did the show, but from what I hear, I don't think I like you.

Steve: Why don't you just come out with what's buggin' you. I don't like playing games. I'm a ramblin' guy.

John: Okay, I'll tell ya. We all know what happened to Gilda.

Bill: We just think you got off a little easy.

Steve: Is that all? C'mon, you guys are just jealous.

Garrett: That has nothing to do with it. You've ruined the reputation of a Not Ready for Prime Time player.

Steve: Well, excuuuse me.

John: I've had just about enough!!

Bill: Don't rough him up, John. He's got a show to do.

John: Okay. We'll take care of this later.

Steve: Let me tell you guys something. I care as much for Gilda as you do. I just had a long talk with her, and there are no hard feelings. And you guys come down on me like I'm Jack the Ripper. Well, I don't need this. I'm a ramblin' guy and I'm a-ramblin'. Belushi, good luck with the opening to the show.

John: You're not going anywhere. You're opening this show.

Steve: Don't tell me what to do. [*John grabs Steve by the fingers.*]

John: C'mon, say it.

Steve: No, I won't.

John: Say it. Say it.

Steve [*In great pain*]: All right. Live from New York, it's *Saturday Night.*

AIRED: FEBRUARY 26, 1977

Bill Murray, John Belushi, Steve Martin, and Garrett Morris.

1979-1980

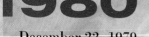

October 13, 1979
Steve Martin

October 20, 1979
Eric Idle

November 3, 1979
Bill Russell

November 10, 1979
Buck Henry

November 17, 1979
Bea Arthur

December 8, 1979
Howard Hesseman

December 15, 1979
Martin Sheen

December 22, 1979
Ted Knight

January 26, 1980
Teri Garr

February 9, 1980
Chevy Chase

February 16, 1980
Elliott Gould

February 23, 1980
Kirk Douglas

March 8, 1980
Rodney Dangerfield

April 5, 1980
Paula Prentiss and Richard Benjamin

April 12, 1980
Burt Reynolds

April 19, 1980
Strother Martin

May 10, 1980
Bob Newhart

May 17, 1980
Steve Martin

May 24, 1980
Buck Henry

1980-1981

November 15, 1980
Elliott Gould

November 22, 1980
Malcolm McDowell

December 6, 1980
Ellen Burstyn

December 13, 1980
Jamie Lee Curtis

December 20, 1980
David Carradine

January 10, 1981
Ray Sharkey

January 17, 1981
Karen Black

January 24, 1981
Robert Hays

February 7, 1981
Sally Kellerman

February 14, 1981
Deborah Harry

February 21, 1981
Charlene Tilton

March 7, 1981
Bill Murray

1981-1982

October 10, 1981
Susan Saint James

October 17, 1981
George Kennedy

October 31, 1981
Donald Pleasence

November 7, 1981
Lauren Hutton

November 14, 1981
Bernadette Peters

December 5, 1981
Tim Curry

December 12, 1981
Bill Murray

January 23, 1982
Robert Conrad

January 30, 1982
John Madden

February 6, 1982
James Coburn

February 20, 1982
Bruce Dern

February 27, 1982
Elizabeth Ashley

March 20, 1982
Robert Urich

March 27, 1982
Blythe Danner

April 10, 1982
Daniel J. Travanti

April 17, 1982
Johnny Cash

April 24, 1982
Robert Culp

May 15, 1982
Danny DeVito

May 22, 1982
Olivia Newton-John

1982-1983

September 25, 1982
Chevy Chase

October 2, 1982
Lou Gossett Jr.

October 9, 1982
Ron Howard

October 23, 1982
Howard Hesseman

October 30, 1982
Michael Keaton

November 13, 1982
Robert Blake

November 20, 1982
Drew Barrymore

December 4, 1982
Smothers Brothers

December 11, 1982
Eddie Murphy

January 22, 1983
Lily Tomlin

January 29, 1983
Rick Moranis and Dave Thomas

February 5, 1983
Sid Caesar

February 19, 1983
Howard Hesseman

February 26, 1983
Beau Bridges and Jeff Bridges

March 12, 1983
Bruce Dern

March 19, 1983
Robert Guillaume

April 9, 1983
Joan Rivers

April 16, 1983
Susan Saint James

May 7, 1983
Stevie Wonder

May 14, 1983
Ed Koch

Buck Henry, John Belushi, and Laraine Newman.

Laraine Newman: Well, I think it's pretty exciting having an eighty-year-old grandmother host the show.

John Belushi: Yeah, but what if she forgets her lines?

Laraine: Don't worry, she won't. Let me tell you something. You should be as together as Mrs. Spillman when you're eighty.

John: Don't worry; I'll be dead by thirty.

Laraine: Hi, Buck.

Buck Henry: Hey, have either of you seen Mrs. Spillman recently?

John: Yeah, I just left her dressing room about twenty minutes ago. Why?

Buck: Well, I checked in on her and she's lying on her back looking at a bowl of fruit with her radio turned up full blast.

Laraine: Well, she's eighty years old, maybe she's got a hearing problem.

Buck: No, she's acting very strange.

John: Well, she was a little nervous when I saw her. So, I just told her a few things to loosen her up. You know, that being nervous is natural, and how we're all a little nervous, too, and I found out she knows some people I met in New Orleans during Mardi Gras, and then we smoked a joint and she seemed to calm down.

Buck: You smoked a joint with Mrs. Spillman?

Laraine: One of your joints?

John: Yeah, it works for me; I figured she needed it.

Buck: Did she know what it was?

John: I told her it was a French cigarette.

Laraine: John, how could you?

Buck: John, your joints overwhelm even an experienced drug user like myself.

Laraine: What did you give her? Not the stuff with the rhino tranquilizer?

John: No! Are you kidding? To an eighty-year-old grandmother? No, we smoked a joint of Wauhauken, and Maui Wowie, blended with a little hash oil. Calmed her right down.

Buck: Well, she's in Hawaii right now with her friend, Mr. Fruit Bowl, and I've got to go out there in a minute and introduce the winner of the Anyone Can Host Contest, America's oldest living doper.

AIRED: DECEMBER 17, 1977

1984-1985

1983-1984

October 8, 1983
Brandon Tartikoff

October 15, 1983
Danny DeVito and Rhea Perlman

October 22, 1983
John Candy

November 5, 1983
Betty Thomas

November 12, 1983
Teri Garr

November 19, 1983
Jerry Lewis

December 3, 1983
Smothers Brothers

December 10, 1983
Flip Wilson

January 14, 1984
Father Guido Sarducci

January 21, 1984
Michael Palin and his mother

January 28, 1984
Don Rickles

February 11, 1984
Robin Williams

February 18, 1984
Jamie Lee Curtis

February 25, 1984
Edwin Newman

March 17, 1984
Billy Crystal

April 7, 1984
Michael Douglas

April 14, 1984
Sen. George McGovern

May 5, 1984
Barry Bostwick

May 12, 1984
Ed Koch, Billy Crystal, Edwin Newman, Betty Thomas, Father Guido Sarducci

October 13, 1984
Bob Uecker

October 20, 1984
Rev. Jesse Jackson

November 3, 1984
Michael McKean

November 10, 1984
George Carlin

November 17, 1984
Ed Asner

December 1, 1984
Ed Begley Jr.

December 8, 1984
Ringo Starr

January 12, 1985
Kathleen Turner

January 19, 1985
Roy Scheider

February 2, 1985
Alex Karras

February 9, 1985
Harry Anderson

February 16, 1985
Pamela Sue Martin

March 30, 1985
Mr. T and Hulk Hogan

April 6, 1985
Christopher Reeve

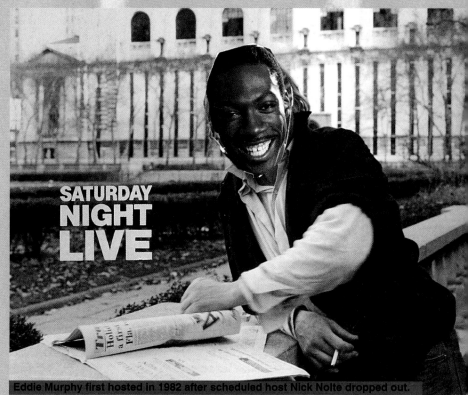

Eddie Murphy first hosted in 1982 after scheduled host Nick Nolte dropped out.

December 15, 1984
Eddie Murphy

April 13, 1985
Howard Cosell

1985-1986

1986-1987

November 9, 1985
Madonna

November 16, 1985
Chevy Chase

November 23, 1985
Pee-wee Herman

December 7, 1985
John Lithgow

December 14, 1985
Tom Hanks

December 21, 1985
Teri Garr

January 18, 1986
Harry Dean Stanton

January 25, 1986
Dudley Moore

February 8, 1986
Ron Reagan

February 15, 1986
Jerry Hall

February 22, 1986
Jay Leno

March 15, 1986
Griffin Dunne

March 22, 1986
George Wendt and Francis Ford Coppola

April 12, 1986
Oprah Winfrey

April 19, 1986
Tony Danza

May 10, 1986
Catherine Oxenberg and Paul Simon

May 17, 1986
Jimmy Breslin

May 24, 1986
Anjelica Huston and Billy Martin

October 11, 1986
Sigourney Weaver

October 18, 1986
Malcolm-Jamal Warner

November 8, 1986
Rosanna Arquette

November 15, 1986
Sam Kinison

November 22, 1986
Robin Williams

December 6, 1986
Chevy Chase, Steve Martin, and Martin Short

December 13, 1986
Steve Guttenberg

December 20, 1986
William Shatner

January 24, 1987
Joe Montana and Walter Payton

January 31, 1987
Paul Shaffer

February 14, 1987
Bronson Pinchot

February 21, 1987
Willie Nelson

February 28, 1987
Valerie Bertinelli

March 21, 1987
Bill Murray

March 28, 1987
Charlton Heston

April 11, 1987
John Lithgow

April 18, 1987
John Larroquette

May 9, 1987
Mark Harmon

May 16, 1987
Garry Shandling

May 23, 1987
Dennis Hopper

SATURDAY NIGHT LIVE 40

Featuring an auctioneer (Martin Short), a first bidder (Julia Louis-Dreyfus), Ringo Starr, Ann (Mary Gross), a second bidder (Gary Kroeger), and a third bidder (Pamela Stephenson).

Auctioneer: Do I hear forty-five thousand dollars? I have forty-five thousand dollars. Do I hear fifty? Fifty-thousand for this guitar pick used by John Lennon while recording "Eight Days a Week." No? Forty-five thousand once, forty-five twice, sold to the gentleman in the second row for forty-five thousand dollars.

Now, if you will turn to page twenty-one in your catalogues, we have Lot thirty-five, a particularly fine piece: a toothbrush used by Paul McCartney during the _Rubber Soul_ recording sessions. It's a blue, medium-bristle Oral-B 40 with one of those little pointy rubber things at the other end. Yes, madam?

First Bidder: Did Paul actually _use_ the little pointy rubber thing?

Auctioneer: It is our understanding that he did. I will open the bidding at sixty-thousand dollars. Do I hear sixty? [_A hand is raised._] Do I hear seventy-thousand dollars? [_Another hand is raised._] Do I hear eighty-thousand dollars? [_Another hand is raised._] Do I hear ninety-thousand dollars?

First Bidder: A hundred and ten thousand dollars.

Auctioneer: A hundred and ten thousand dollars once, a hundred and ten thousand dollars twice, _sold_ to the woman in the third row. Now, ladies and gentlemen, if you will turn to page twenty-two in your catalogues, we have Lot thirty-six, Ringo Starr.

Martin Short and Ringo Starr.

[_Ringo Starr enters, and Ann leads him around the room to display him._]

Auctioneer: He was for nine years the drummer with the Beatles and performed with them on all their albums and tours. As you can see, he's in very good condition. I will open the bidding at seventy-five thousand dollars. Do I hear seventy-five? Do I hear seventy-five thousand dollars for this drummer with the Beatles?

Do I hear sixty-five thousand dollars for Ringo Starr? A member of the Beatles...talented musician...owner of a large ring collection.

[_Calls on the second bidder, who has raised his hand._] Yes, sir, sixty-five thousand dollars?

Second Bidder: No, no, I was wondering about the jacket he's wearing.

Auctioneer: Yes.

Second Bidder: Was it by any chance ever worn by Paul?

Auctioneer: I'm sorry, no, sir. Do I hear fifteen thousand dollars for Ringo Starr? Fifteen thousand dollars? Good Lord, this man is a human being. Yes, madam?

Third Bidder: Hmmmm... Well, does he _do_ anything?

Auctioneer: Ah, Ann knows more about that than I would. Ann, what does he do?

Ann: Well, he, uh, plays the drums. And he has a very interesting ring collection.

Third Bidder: Can he talk?

Ann: Yes, I think so. [_She hands him a file card._] Here, Ringo, would you read this?

Ringo Starr: Live from New York, it's Saturday Night!

AIRED: DECEMBER 8, 1984

William Shatner addresses a Star Trek Convention.

Before I answer any more questions, there is something I wanted to say. Having received many of your letters over the years—and I've spoken to many of you, and some of you have traveled hundreds of miles to be here—I'd just like to say: Get a life, will you, people! I mean, for crying out loud, it was just a TV show. I mean look at you, look at the way you're dressed. You've turned an enjoyable little job that I did as a lark for a few years into a colossal waste of time. I mean, how old are you people? What have you done with yourselves? You—you must be almost 30—have you ever kissed a girl? I didn't think so! Geez. There's a whole world out there! When I was your age, I didn't even watch television. I lived! So move out of your parents' basements, get your own apartments, and grow the hell up! It's just a TV show, dammit! It's just a TV show!

AIRED: DECEMBER 20, 1986

Phil Hartman and William Shatner.

1987-1988

October 17, 1987
Steve Martin

January 30, 1988
Carl Weathers

October 24, 1987
Sean Penn

February 13, 1988
Justine Bateman

October 31, 1987
Dabney Coleman

November 14, 1987
Robert Mitchum

November 21, 1987
Candice Bergen

December 5, 1987
Danny DeVito

December 12, 1987
Angie Dickinson

December 19, 1987
Paul Simon

January 23, 1988
Robin Williams

February 20, 1988
Tom Hanks

February 27, 1988
Judge Reinhold

1988-1989

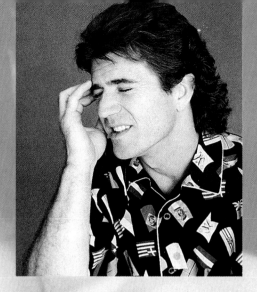

October 8, 1988
Tom Hanks

October 15, 1988
Matthew Broderick

October 22, 1988
John Larroquette

November 5, 1988
Matthew Modine

January 28, 1989
Tony Danza

February 11, 1989
Ted Danson

February 18, 1989
Leslie Nielsen

February 25, 1989
Glenn Close

April 1, 1989
Mel Gibson

April 15, 1989
Dolly Parton

April 22, 1989
Geena Davis

May 13, 1989
Wayne Gretzky

May 20, 1989
Steve Martin

1989-1990

November 12, 1988
Demi Moore

November 19, 1988
John Lithgow

December 3, 1988
Danny DeVito

December 10, 1988
Kevin Kline

December 17, 1988
Melanie Griffith

January 21, 1989
John Malkovich

March 25, 1989
Mary Tyler Moore

September 30, 1989
Bruce Willis

October 7, 1989
Rick Moranis

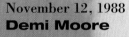

1990-1991

October 21, 1989
Kathleen Turner

October 28, 1989
James Woods

November 11, 1989
Chris Evert

November 18, 1989
Woody Harrelson

December 2, 1989
John Goodman

December 9, 1989
Robert Wagner

February 10, 1990
Quincy Jones

February 17, 1990
Tom Hanks

February 24, 1990
Fred Savage

March 17, 1990
Rob Lowe

March 24, 1990
Debra Winger

April 14, 1990
Corbin Bernsen

September 29, 1990
Kyle MacLachlan

October 6, 1990
Susan Lucci

October 20, 1990
George Steinbrenner

October 27, 1990
Patrick Swayze

November 10, 1990
Jimmy Smits

February 16, 1991
Roseanne Barr

February 23, 1991
Alec Baldwin

November 17, 1990
Dennis Hopper

December 1, 1990
John Goodman

December 8, 1990
Tom Hanks

December 15, 1990
Dennis Quaid

January 12, 1991
Joe Mantegna

January 19, 1991
Sting

February 9, 1991
Kevin Bacon

March 16, 1991
Michael J. Fox

March 23, 1991
Jeremy Irons

April 13, 1991
Catherine O'Hara

April 20, 1991
Steven Seagal

May 11, 1991
Delta Burke

May 18, 1991
George Wendt

December 16, 1989
Andie MacDowell

January 13, 1990
Ed O'Neill

January 20, 1990
Christopher Walken

April 21, 1990
Alec Baldwin

May 12, 1990
Andrew Dice Clay

May 19, 1990
Candice Bergen

SATURDAY NIGHT LIVE
44

1991-1992

September 28, 1991
Michael Jordan

October 5, 1991
Jeff Daniels

October 12, 1991
Kirstie Alley

October 26, 1991
Christian Slater

November 2, 1991
Kiefer Sutherland

November 16, 1991
Linda Hamilton

November 23, 1991
Macaulay Culkin

December 7, 1991
Hammer

December 14, 1991
Steve Martin

January 11, 1992
Rob Morrow

January 18, 1992
Chevy Chase

February 8, 1992
Susan Dey

February 15, 1992
Jason Priestley

February 22, 1992
Roseanne & Tom Arnold

March 14, 1992
John Goodman

March 21, 1992
Mary Stuart Masterson

April 11, 1992
Sharon Stone

April 18, 1992
Jerry Seinfeld

May 9, 1992
Tom Hanks

May 16, 1992
Woody Harrelson

Jan Hooks, Dolly Parton, Victoria Jackson, and Nora Dunn.

Announcer: On the outer reaches of our galaxy spins the planet Estrogena, where there evolved an advanced race of women: Planet of the Enormous Hooters

Queen: Bring the deformed one to me.
Courtier: Look! Her breasts are so small, they look like melons.
Prisoner: Oh, please stop belittling me!
Queen: You are a disgrace to our planet. I hereby banish you to the planet Earth where your undersized breasts will go unnoticed and you may live your life in anonymity.

QUEEN PLAYED BY NORA DUNN
COURTIER PLAYED BY VICTORIA JACKSON
PRISONER PLAYED BY DOLLY PARTON
AIRED: APRIL 15, 1989

Tom Hanks: Believe it or not, this is the fifth *Saturday Night Live* I have been lucky enough to host. Now, the first time you do the show, you can't believe you're here. You can't believe it. Your head buzzes with excitement. The second time you do the show, it means you were *funny* enough to be asked back—and you're pushing a movie.

The third time you do the show, the second time didn't go so well, and you have something to prove to yourself. The fourth time you do the show, you're just blatantly pushing a movie.

But the fifth time you do the show is the most special time of all, because you get this—a membership card in the Five-Timer Club. Come with me. I'm gonna give you a chance to look in on one of the most exclusive clubs in the world.

Sean the doorman [*Conan O'Brien*]: Welcome, Mr. Hanks. Once again, congratulations on your fifth appearance.

Tom: Thank you, it's a real thrill.

Sean: Mr. Hanks, would you like your club robe now?

Tom: Boy, would I! Thank you…

Sean: Sean.

Tom: Sean.

Paul Simon: Tom! Congratulations! Welcome aboard!

Tom: Thanks, Mr. Simon.

Paul: Please, call me Paul.

Tom: Okay [*Excited*]… "Paul."

Paul: You know, we've had our eye on you ever since your third show. We knew you'd make five.

Tom: Wow, that's flattering.

Paul: Yes. There was some concern after *Joe Versus the Volcano*, but you made it, and good for you.

Tom: Thanks.

Paul: Step into the reading room. I think you'll like it. Steve, look who's joined us.

Steve Martin: Tom, Tom, old bean! Let's have a look at you. That robe fits you smashingly.

Tom: Thanks, Mr. Martin.

Steve: Please, call me Mr. *Steve* Martin.

Tom: Thanks, Mr. Steve Martin.

Steve: Whoa! I think someone needs to learn the club handshake.

[*Steve and Paul demonstrate an intricate handshake.*]

Steve: Tom, sit down. Y'know, I hope you appreciate the responsibility that comes with being a fiver. Let's be frank—it takes a certain caliber of performer to earn that fifth show.

Elliott Gould: Hey, Steven! You really oughta take a dip. The pool's a perfect eighty degrees.

Steve Martin, Paul Simon, Tom Hanks, and Elliott Gould.

Steve [*To Tom*]: He practically lives here.

Elliott: Tom Hanks! Welcome aboard!

Tom: Hi, Mr. Gould.

Elliott: *Mazel tov*, old man. Y'know, it *is* much easier to get five nowadays. Nothing against you, Tom. Let's get you fixed up. Care for some supper?

Tom: Sure.

Elliott: Waiter!

[*Jon Lovitz enters as a waiter, with menus.*]

Jon: Here you are, Mr. Gould. Welcome, Mr. Hanks.

Tom: Jon, you work here?

Jon: Work is work.

Steve: I'll have the Chevy Chase, and easy on the ham this time.

Jon: Good choice, Mr. Steve Martin.

Tom: Wow. So many choices. What do I do?

Steve: Try the Anthony Michael Hall. It's surprisingly good.

Paul: I'll have the Joe Piscopo.

Steve [*Disapprovingly*]: Really.

Jon: And to drink?

Tom: I'll have a beer.

Jon: Anyone else?

Elliott: I'll have a Jenny Craig protein shake.

Sean: Jon, we're having that problem again at the door.

Jon: I'll handle it. Mr. Nader, I've told you before, this club is for members only.

Ralph Nader [*Holding a tattered script*]: But I've hosted the show! I swear!

Jon: Sorry, sir, five-timers only!

Ralph [*With friends*]: See—there's Steve Martin, there's Paul Simon… Tom Hanks just joined!

Jon: Out! All of you! Out! I got rid of him, gentlemen.

Paul: Very good, Jon.

Elliott: I smell something burning.

Jon: My muffins!

Tom: Well, everyone, this has been a thrill, but I have to go finish the rest of the monologue.

Elliott: What are you talking about, Tom? You can do it from here.

Tom: What?

Steve: Of course! You're a five-timer! You don't need to be there! You can phone it in!

Tom: Really?

Paul: Sure! Elliott, hand him the club phone.

Elliott: This is a direct line to the studio.

Tom: Hey, great!

Steve [*Handing him a pipe*]: Make yourself comfortable, boy! Say whatever you want!

Tom: Well, okay. [*Into phone*] Uh… We've got a great show! Edie Brickell is here!

All: Well done, good job, son.

Tom: We'll be right back!

AIRED: DECEMBER 8, 1990

1992-1993

September 26, 1992
Nicolas Cage

October 3, 1992
Tim Robbins

October 10, 1992
Joe Pesci

October 24, 1992
Christopher Walken

October 31, 1992
Catherine O'Hara

November 14, 1992
Michael Keaton

November 21, 1992
Sinbad

December 5, 1992
Tom Arnold

December 12, 1992
Glenn Close

January 9, 1993
Danny DeVito

January 16, 1993
Harvey Keitel

February 6, 1993
Luke Perry

February 13, 1993
Alec Baldwin

February 20, 1993
Bill Murray

March 13, 1993
John Goodman

March 20, 1993
Miranda Richardson

April 10, 1993
Jason Alexander

April 17, 1993
Kirstie Alley

May 8, 1993
Christina Applegate

May 15, 1993
Kevin Kline

1993-1994

September 25, 1993
Charles Barkley

October 2, 1993
Shannen Doherty

October 9, 1993
Jeff Goldblum

October 23, 1993
John Malkovich

October 30, 1993
Christian Slater

November 13, 1993
Rosie O'Donnell

November 20, 1993
Nicole Kidman

December 4, 1993
Charlton Heston

December 11, 1993
Sally Field

January 8, 1994
Jason Patric

January 15, 1994
Sara Gilbert

February 5, 1994
Patrick Stewart

February 12, 1994
**Alec Baldwin and
Kim Basinger**

February 19, 1994
Martin Lawrence

March 12, 1994
Nancy Kerrigan

March 19, 1994
Helen Hunt

April 9, 1994
Kelsey Grammer

April 16, 1994
Emilio Estevez

May 7, 1994
John Goodman

May 14, 1994
Heather Locklear

Most Frequent Hosts

Steve Martin
Hosted: 12 times
Surprise Shots: 4
Recurring Characters:
Theodoric of York
Charles Knerlman, in The Nerds
Georg Festrunk
First Hosted: October 23, 1976
Most Recently Hosted:
December 14, 1991

On Festrunks:
I had this character that I was doing in my act—sort of an obnoxious guy—and Danny had this idea to do the Czechoslovakian brothers. I said I could just put this character—it would fit right in. And so he came up with that. I was doing wild-and-crazy-guy stuff in my act, so I put that in....

When we rehearsed it the first week, we could hardly make it through rehearsal, we thought it was so funny. We were laughing our heads off. That's a good sign. Actually, it doesn't mean anything—it could be good or bad; I have had the opposite reaction too....

So we were pretty thrilled with ourselves. The first time we did it, it was received kind of okay. But what happened between that time and the second time we did it is the audience kind of got it. The second time we did it there was this big surprise of applause. And it just kind of exploded very, very quickly.

Enjoyable characters/roles:
I like to play game-show hosts. When I was a kid I was always parodying them anyway. We did a *Jeopardy!*-type game, only it was a combination of *Jeopardy!* and *Family Feud*. And the answers were all "What seventeen-year-old said...?" I think Nora Dunn played Jeane Kirkpatrick; she was playing a very smart person who couldn't believe that the answers to all the literature questions were Ernest Hemingway.

Least favorite moments:
The monologue was always really difficult for me. I had to really work on that. And I really worried it to death trying to get it right.

Other thoughts:
There's the contribution of Lorne Michaels. Lorne was extremely gracious in putting me on the show. He was reluctant at first, then he became one of my best friends.

Buck Henry
Hosted: 10 times
Surprise Shots: 3
Recurring Characters:
Uncle Roy
The foil, in Samurai
Mr. DiLaMuca
Co-star with stunt babies and stunt puppies
First Hosted: January 17, 1976
Most Recently Hosted:
May 24, 1980

Paul Simon
Hosted: 4 times
Musical Guest: 9 times
Surprise Shots: 2
First Hosted: October 18, 1975
Most Recently Hosted:
December 19, 1987
Most Recently Appeared as Musical Guest: May 15, 1993

Tom Hanks
Hosted: 6 times
Recurring Characters:
Girl Watcher
Mr. Short Term Memory
One of the Stand-Ups
Uri, in the Sabras shopping network
First Hosted: December 14, 1985
Most Recently Hosted:
May 9, 1992

Elliott Gould
Hosted: 6 times
Surprise Shot: 1
First Hosted: January 10, 1976
Most Recently Hosted:
November 15, 1980

Danny DeVito
Hosted: 5 times
First Hosted: May 15, 1982
Most Recently Hosted:
January 9, 1993
Also appeared as a "Special Guest" on February 21, 1987

Candice Bergen
Hosted: 5 times
First Hosted: November 8, 1975
Most Recently Hosted: May 19, 1990

I had no idea why Lorne asked me to do the show. I didn't know Lorne and I didn't know the show. I just watched the tapes that he brought to the office and said yes on the spot.

It was terrifying. I had no background in that kind of thing. I was totally unqualified for it. I don't know why I did it except that I really loved doing it and it was my idea of heaven to be doing the show.

Amusing memories:
I remember the first show I had a skit with Gilda. I was having such a good time, I boggled my line and called Gilda by my character's first name. And I started laughing and Gilda was great about it and I continued laughing throughout the sketch. It never occurred to me that there should be some professionalism at play. We were having so much fun. I remember that Lorne had never seen anyone break character so completely without any qualms. I had no shame. I was howling during the sketch. When I look back at it now, I can't believe it.

Repercussions from the world at large:
Once I was a spokesperson for Polaroid and I had done a Polaroid commercial at the Grand Canyon shooting Polaroids. We did a takeoff on that, with the Grand Canyon in the background and me sitting on the same log with a camera; but instead of a Polaroid, a piece of Velveeta cheese came out of the camera. And I certainly heard from Polaroid on that one. They weren't thrilled. I was their spokesperson. I wasn't supposed to be shooting Velveeta out of their camera.

On SNL, twenty years later:
When I do watch [the '70s shows] now, I can see how I've grown older because I don't respond to the comedy the way I used to. I find myself watching it and squinting. And everyone else is just howling. When I first watched the show and when Lorne first showed me those tapes, I was so stunned. It was so thrilling. It was such wonderful comedy and it was groundbreaking. It was really like a

comedy lab…and now, when I look at it, I feel like a geezer because I don't get a lot of it.

Favorite Moments:
One of my favorite moments was doing the Bee Capades on the Christmas show. I was wearing this Sonja Henie skating outfit in red velvet with an ermine muff—and with my skates on, with skate guards. Everybody else was wearing their bee suits and their antennae were bouncing. I remember that the elevator men never looked at us. They just stared straight ahead. Finally, it was nothing more than spelling out "N-O-E-L" with the bees lying on the ice. At the time it seemed like the inmates had gotten into the system.

John Goodman
Hosted: 5 times
Recurring Character:
Police Chief Wilson, in Wayne's World
First Hosted: December 2, 1989
Most Recently Hosted:
May 7, 1994

Eligible for membership soon:

Alec Baldwin
Hosted: 4 times
First Hosted: April 21, 1990
Most Recently Hosted:
February 12, 1994

Effect on his private life:
My wife has repeatedly threatened divorce since I cajoled her into cohosting with me in 1994.

People who have hosted and been the musical guest, on separate occasions:

Art Garfunkel
Deborah Harry
Madonna
Paul Simon
Sting
Frank Zappa

People who have hosted and been the musical guest on the same show:

Desi Arnaz
Johnny Cash
Ray Charles
Hammer
Deborah Harry
Quincy Jones
Kris Kristofferson
Olivia Newton-John
Dolly Parton
Paul Simon
Ringo Starr
Sting
Lily Tomlin
Stevie Wonder
Frank Zappa

Shows with no host:

February 20, 1977
March 15, 1980
April 11, 1981
October 3, 1981
April 3, 1982
March 24, 1984
October 6, 1984
March 2, 1985
May 4, 1985
November 7, 1987

L PARODIES

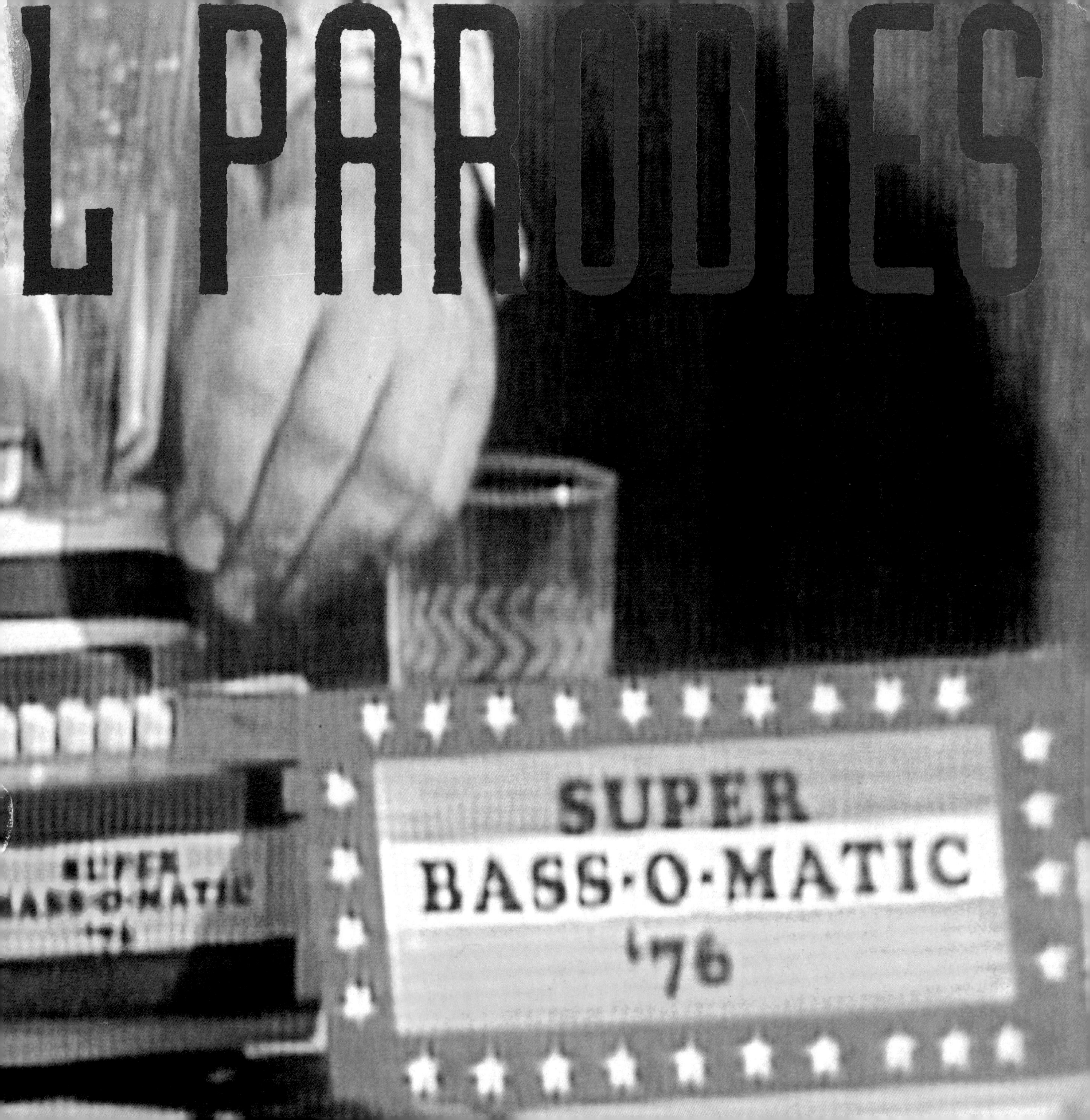

Mel's Char Palace

Hi, I'm Mel, from Mel's Char Palace. Where you find your own cow, you cut your own steaks. You select your cow from over two hundred head. You stun it, you cut it, you charbroil it. You cut your own steaks. We give you the saw. You cut your own sirloin tips, blades, and roasts.

"OVER 3000 STUNNED"

You find it, you stun it, you cut it. As big and as thick as you want it. Only at Mel's Char Palace. Our saws are light. Here's Mrs. Mel—show them how to start the saw. Yeah, she does it—so can you. Route 17, Paramus.

Quarry Cereal

Quarry contains no preservatives, no additives, no artificial flavoring—because Quarry isn't grown, it's mined.

Here's a cereal that is pure, one hundred percent rocks and pebbles.

A hearty, old-fashioned flavor the whole family will enjoy.

"Donuts of Champions"

Little Chocolate Donuts

A Decathlon Champ says he owes his success to his main source of nutrition: Little Chocolate Donuts. "They taste good, and they've got the sugar I need to get started in the morning. That's why Little Chocolate Donuts have been on my training table since I was a kid."

Super Bass-O-Matic

Announcer: How many times has this happened to you? You have a bass and you're trying to find an exciting new way to prepare it for the dinner table. You could scale the bass, remove the bass's tail, head, and bones, and serve the fish as you would any other fish dinner. But why bother, now that you can use Rovco's amazing new kitchen tool, the Super Bass-O-Matic 76. Yes, fish-eaters, the days of troublesome scaling, cutting, and gutting are over, because Super Bass-O-Matic 76 is the tool that lets you use the whole bass, with no fish waste and without scaling, cutting, or gutting.

Here's how it works: Catch a bass, remove the hook, and drop the bass—that's the whole bass—into the Super Bass-O-Matic 76. [*Drops bass into blender and covers top.*] Now, adjust the control dial so that the bass is blended just the way you like it. [*Turns blender on and reduces fish to a pulp.*] Yes, it's that simple.

Woman [*Drinks the final product*]: Wow, that's terrific bass.

Announcer: We've got fish here, fast and easy and ready to pour, mmm-mmm. Super Bass-O-Matic 76 comes with ten interchangeable rotors, a nine month guarantee, and a booklet, *1001 Ways to Harness Bass.*

Super Bass-O-Matic 76 works great on sunfish, perch, sole, and other small aquatic creatures. [*Throws a sample of each in and blends them.*]

Super Bass-O-Matic 76, it's clean, simple, and after five or ten fish it gets to be quite a rush. Super Bass-O-Matic 76—you'll never have to scale, cut, or gut again.

Hey You

Not all women are looking for Mr. Right. Sometimes they might just want a little company. That's why Oldbat created Hey You. Just one whiff does the trick. For those occasions where you can't afford to be subtle.

Hey You, for the special someone you never expect to see again. Hey You, the perfume for one-night stands.

Droolers

In America today, certain oppressed minorities are still treated like second-class citizens—some simply because of a harmless little affliction. I refer to those with saliva disbursement difficulties, or as we are sometimes called, droolers. We at the Droolers' Anti-Defamation League are working to correct the negative image of droolers propagated by the media. For example, how many people know that many famous individuals throughout history—the great philosopher Spinoza, authoress Charlotte Brontë, and world leader Mahatma Gandhi—were actually droolers?

There is no reason why a drooler cannot function as a useful, active member of society—sealing envelopes for small businesses, for instance. Like anything else, drooling is a handicap, but it is a handicap that can be licked.

New Dad

Yes, it's New Dad. A radically new concept in family insurance coverage. Within seconds after old Dad is out, we'll have New Dad there to take his place.

Princess Grace for Tarn-Off

Rovco's new tarnish remover: It cleans crown, jewels, and scepters before you can say, "Let them eat cake."

Evelyn Woodski

Hel-lo. My name is Ev-e-lyn Wood-ski and I am the flounder–founder of the Evelyn Woodski School of Speed-Re-a-ding. Re-ah-ding. Redding? [*Asks off camera*] Which is it? Re-ah-ding?

Dick Cavett School

You know America has over a hundred and four billion square feet of swamplands and everglades. Much of it is uncivilized; all of it is wet. That's why the trained hydroplane operator has a solid employment future. Today the best courses in hydroplane and hovercraft operation are being offered by the Dick Cavett School of Hydroplane Operation. In three short weeks you'll learn all the skills of this exciting field at our fifty-eight-acre training swamp near Beaumont, Texas; or you can keep your present job and learn at home. Call this toll-free number now and we'll send you my informative booklet, *The American Presidency and Hovercraft Speed-tuning.*

Vampire

I was an ugly child . . . a hideous teenager, with fur on my ears and webbed fingers. But now I am young and beautiful. How do I do it? The answer is in this, my beauty regimen book. My book tells how I drink the blood of Girl Scouts and Brownies. It tells how I eat the face of young virgins. It even tells how I have all my bones replaced with those of cheerleaders and pom-pom girls.

Car Yummies

I'm sure your whole family loves cheese, but one member never gets enough—your car. That's why we created Car Yummies. Shaped like little traffic signs, Car Yummies provides all the essential additives your car needs plus a hearty cheddar flavor that automobiles really go for. Car Yummies—gives your car pep and lets it know you care.

Colon Blow

Announcer: Hold it! Is that what you're having for breakfast?
Customer: Sure. Haven't you heard? Fiber is really good for you.
Announcer: Well, there's fiber. And then there's high fiber. Try this.
Customer: Hmmm! Colon Blow. Sounds delicious—but is it really higher in fiber than my oat bran cereal?
Announcer: Take a guess. How many bowls of your oat bran cereal would it take to equal the fiber content of one bowl of Colon Blow?
Customer: Two?
Announcer: Guess again.
Customer: Three?
Announcer: A little higher.
Customer: Four?
Announcer: Keep tryin'.
Customer: Five?
Announcer: Nooo. You'll have to do better than that.
Customer: Seven?
Announcer: Guess again.
Customer: Eight?
Announcer: We'll give you one more guess.
Customer: Nine.
Announcer: Not even close. It would take over thirty thousand bowls of your oat bran cereal to equal the fiber content of Colon Blow. To eat that much oat bran, you'd have to eat ten bowls a day, every day, for eight and a half years.
Customer: Wow! I think I get the picture. Colon Blow must be the highest-fiber cereal on the market.
Announcer: Not anymore. Now there's new Super Colon Blow.
Customer: Super Colon Blow?
Announcer: It would take two and a half million bowls of your oat bran to equal the fiber content of one bowl of Super Colon Blow.

Colon Blow and you in the morning!

Warning: May cause abdominal distension. Consult a physician.

Action Cats

Uh-oh! It's the big cat with the big guns!

But he's no match for Missile Missy!

And they all give way for Stego-Puss! Collect all twenty-two Action Cats, including Skele-Kitty, Laser Gal, Cat-Atomic, Spider Cat, and all the rest.

Then you'll say, "Action Cats are awesome!"

Jiffy Express

At Jiffy Express we know how important it is to be on time.
And we also know sometimes you just can't make it. That's when you call Jiffy. We'll take the package—and the blame.

When your package has to be there overnight, call the other guys. When it has to be there three weeks ago, call us!

We'll backdate the receipt, "age" the package according to your specifications, and even simulate international misrouting!

Jiffy Express. When you've got no one else to blame, call us.

Swill

When I want mineral water, I keep it simple, and I keep it domestic.

I drink Swill, the water that's dredged from Lake Erie.

Nothing's added to Swill—it comes straight from the lake to you.

Happy Fun Ball

It's Happy. It's Fun. It's Happy Fun Ball!
Yes, it's Happy Fun Ball. The toy sensation that's sweeping the nation. Only fourteen ninety-five at participating stores.
Warning: Pregnant women, the elderly, and children under ten should avoid prolonged exposure to Happy Fun Ball.
Caution: Happy Fun Ball may suddenly accelerate to dangerous speeds.

Happy Fun Ball contains a liquid core, which, if exposed due to rupture, should not be touched, inhaled, or looked at.

Do not use Happy Fun Ball on concrete.

Discontinue use of Happy Fun Ball if any of the following occurs: itching, vertigo, dizziness, tingling in extremities, loss of balance or coordination, slurred speech, temporary blindness.

If Happy Fun Ball begins to smoke, immediately seek shelter and cover head.

Happy Fun Ball may stick to certain types of skin.

When not in use, Happy Fun Ball should be returned to its special container and kept under refrigeration.

Failure to do so relieves the makers of Happy Fun Ball, Wacky Products, Incorporated, and its parent company, Global Chemical Unlimited, of any and all liability.

Ingredients of Happy Fun Ball include an unknown glowing substance which fell to Earth, presumably from outer space.

Happy Fun Ball has been shipped to our troops in Saudi Arabia and is also being dropped by our warplanes on Iraq.

Do not taunt Happy Fun Ball.

Happy Fun Ball comes with a lifetime guarantee.

Accept no substitutes!

Chia Head

You look good now . . . but you could look better. You've tried all the hair replacement products, but nothing seems to work. Well, now there's a

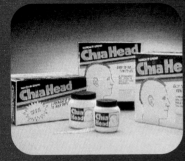

solution—Chia Head. Scientists and gardeners at the Chia Institute in Chia, Wisconsin, have finally found the answer to male baldness.

Just apply the Chia Mud to your scalp. Then add the Chia Seed. Sprinkle with water, and get a good night's sleep. You'll see results immediately.

And with your new Chia Hair you'll attack the day with new confidence. So if you have male pattern baldness, get the edge—the Chia edge.

Buzz Pen

No matter what you have to remember, the Buzz Pen's gliding ball tip and tungsten blade guarantee clarity for you and a smooth, stylish cut your friends will appreciate.

Shimmer

New Shimmer is a floor wax *and* a dessert topping. Here, I'll spray some on your mop and some on your butterscotch pudding.

H & L Brock

Hi, I'm Lowell Brock for H & L Brock with more of my seventeen reasons why you should bring your taxes to us instead of H & R Block. Reason number one: We are willing to cheat for you. Take, for example, this little item: Reason number two, our bogus receipt service. We can fabricate entire business trips using our collection of all the standard receipt forms used by legitimate restaurants, airlines, car rentals, or any expense remotely related to your business.

White Guilt Relief Fund

[*With Garrett Morris:*] If you would like to relieve your guilt, I'm willing to accept money as a representative victim of four hundred years of repression. Send your check or money order to White Guilt Relief Fund.

Fluckers

And so, with a name like Fluckers, it's got to be good. Hey, hold on a second. I have a jam here called Nose Hair. Now, with a name like Nose Hair you can imagine how good it must be. Mmm-mmm!

Excuse me, gentlemen, but are you familiar with a jam called Death Camp? That's Death Camp—just look for the barbed wire on the label. With a name like Death Camp, it must be so good, it's incredible—just amazingly good jam.

Dog Vomit, Monkey Pus. We offer a choice—two of the most repulsive brands of jam you ever heard of. And with names like these, this stuff has got to be terrific. We're talking fabulous jam here.

Save your breath, fella. Here's a new jam we just put out called Painful Rectal Itch. So if it's great jam you're after, try this one—the brand so disgusting you can't say it on television. Ask for it by name.

Norman Bates School for Motel Management

[*With Tony Perkins:*] You can be your own boss while earning big money in this rapidly expanding field. Best of all, you learn at home, in the privacy of your own shower.

Are you motel material? Let's find out with a simple quiz.
Question one: A guest loses the key to her room. Would you:
(a) Give her a duplicate key
(b) Let her in with your passkey
(c) Hack her to death with a kitchen knife

Autumn Fizz
The carbonated douche. Don't leave him holding the bag.

Bathwater of the Stars
Come to me, Roy Waddmaker's Bathwater of the Stars, in the heart of Beverly Hills. Serving your needs since 1974. And just look at the selection. Thousands to choose from—enough bathwater to sink a battleship in and every drop of it personally approved by a notary public. For pennies a day you could be making herb tea with this bonded quart of Doug McClure, filling your steam iron from this jar of Cicely Tyson, raising tropical fish in this gallon of Dan Duryea, and much more.

Soft Drink Test
New sugar-free Zing, tastes better than Phlegm.

Toads
When you're at home or you're on the road and you got to stop and crave the toad—Del Slater's, Del Slater's, Del Slater's fab toad ranch. Where the best ninety-nine cent toad steak is served.

Vibramatic
Soothes hard-to-reach places, and slices and dices salad.

Jesse Owens
A special offer for a medallion saluting a dying breed, the Great White Athlete.

The Navy
Port of call: Bayonne, New Jersey. The Navy adventure. It's not just a job, it's $96.78 a week.

Green Cross Cupcakes
Why take chances? When it comes to cupcakes, feed them Green Cross Cupcakes—cancer-free never tasted so good.

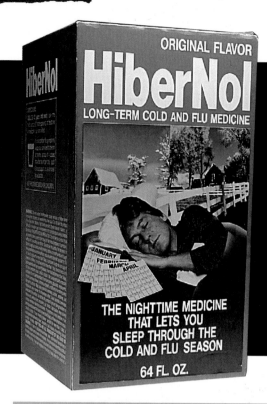

ORIGINAL FLAVOR

HiberNol
LONG-TERM COLD AND FLU MEDICINE

THE NIGHTTIME MEDICINE THAT LETS YOU SLEEP THROUGH THE COLD AND FLU SEASON

64 FL. OZ.

Hibernol

You don't have to suffer through the cold and flu season this year, thanks to Hibernol.

Modern medicine is years away from finding cures for colds and the flu. But that doesn't mean you have to suffer. Other flu medicines help you sleep for eight or ten hours—Hibernol lets you sleep through the entire flu season, usually between two and three months. You can't buy stronger medication—in this country!

Unlike other medicines, which only contain mild sedatives, Hibernol contains a powerful narcotic that lets you sleep, and sleep, and sleep!

As you sleep, living off stored body fat, the cold runs it course…and in fact, other colds and flus may come and go…but you won't know it—because you're out cold and nothing's going to wake you.

Hibernol: It knocks your cold out while you're out cold. From the makers of Comadose.

Chameleon XLE

Finally, a luxury sedan engineered for the inner-city driving experience. The Chameleon XLE has everything you would expect in a luxury car of its class. A spacious cockpit. Soft leather seating, fine wood, and Berber carpeting.

Every inch of the Chameleon XLE is a pinnacle in urban design. Authentically distressed fenders give way to a partially padded roof of blistered vinyl. This is craftsmanship no one will steal.

There's attention to detail. Like three mismatched wheel covers and one exposed rim in school-bus yellow. Standard.

A broken taillight repaired with gaffer's tape. Standard.

A Buick body with a driver's-side door from an Oldsmobile Delta 88. All standard. While under the hood, a simulated transmission-fluid drip whispers, "There is nothing of value here. I'd move on if I were you." A car thief takes one look at this and keeps right on walking.

The Chameleon XLE. They might tow it away, but they'll never steal it.

Available in primer red, primer black, and primer gray.

Green & Fazio

Barry Green, senior partner: Have you been in an accident? Have you witnessed an accident? Have you suffered psychological damage from hearing someone describe an accident he saw?

Hello, I'm Barry Green of the law firm Green & Fazio, here with another Litigation Myth.

Myth number four: You cannot file a suit for an accident in which you were not involved. False.

We at Green & Fazio realize that when an accident occurs, it's not just those involved who suffer. That's why we've been pioneers in whole new areas of accident litigation, including bystander trauma . . . phantom whiplash, and . . . near-collision stress disorder.

Why not come in for a free consultation and let us help you collect the money you didn't even realize you were entitled to.

Myth number eight: In order to be successful, a law suit must have merit. False.

At the law firm of Green & Fazio we know that some of the best lawsuits are nuisance suits. At Green & Fazio we don't have to win your case to make you money. We can win by simply agreeing to drop the suit, accept a settlement, and leave the defendant in peace. Today's large corporations and wealthy individuals don't need the headaches, the harassment that long, protracted litigation involves. And no one harasses defendants like Green & Fazio. Why? Because at Green & Fazio, you don't pay a cent unless you win a settlement. That's right. We don't see a dime until you see three dimes. That's why we never give up.

Another lawyer [*speaking on the phone*]: I'm afraid I have some bad news. The people suing you are represented by Green & Fazio. As your lawyer, I urge you to settle. I know those bastards. Believe me, you don't want the headache.

Green & Fazio. Experts in nuisance suits since 1978. 1-800-HARASSS.
The extra "S" is for extra harassment.

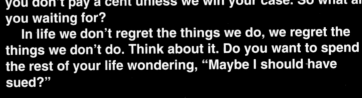

GREEN & FAZIO
LAW OFFICES

DIAL **1-500-HARASSS**

The extra **S** is for extra harassment

Green & Fazio 2

Barry Green, senior partner: Hello. Have you attained your financial goals? Is your economic future secure? Do you have the money you need to buy the things you want? If your answer is no, ask yourself these questions:
- •Have you been injured or shot while committing a burglary?
- •Have you survived a suicide attempt made on public property?
- •Has a bartender sold you a drink which led to your involvement in a fatal hit-and-run accident?

If so, then we at the law firm of Green & Fazio can help you achieve financial independence through litigation. If this sounds too good to be true, listen to some of our clients.

Woman dressed in furs and jewels: I didn't realize it at the time, but throwing myself in front of that subway car was my first step on the road to financial independence. Thank you, Green & Fazio

Man lounging poolside: Sure, I'm grateful the medics pulled me from the wreck. But they didn't have to dislocate my shoulder. No one can give me back my shoulder the way it was before it was dislocated, but thanks to Green & Fazio, at least I have financial independence.

Man playing tennis: The construction site was posted No Trespassing. But, let's be frank. What does a No Trespassing sign mean when you're as drunk as I was? They can have their four million back. Who will give me back my tooth?

Barry Green: So why haven't you sued? Maybe like many people, you think it's too expensive. But at Green & Fazio you don't pay a cent unless we win your case. So what are you waiting for?

In life we don't regret the things we do, we regret the things we don't do. Think about it. Do you want to spend the rest of your life wondering, "Maybe I should have sued?"

Green & Fazio. Everyone hates us but our clients.

Phone Company

[*With Lily Tomlin:*] Here at the Phone Company we handle eighty-four billion calls a year. Serving everyone from presidents and kings to the scum of the earth. We realize that every so often you can't get an operator, for no apparent reason your phone goes out of order, or perhaps you get charged for a call you didn't make.

We don't care.

Watch this—just lost Peoria.

You see, this phone system consists of a multibillion-dollar matrix of space-age technology that is so sophisticated, even we can't handle it. But that's your problem, isn't it? Next time you complain about your phone service, why don't you try using two Dixie cups with a string. We don't care. We don't have to. We're the Phone Company.

Fidoflex

Are you like most people? Do you long for a German shepherd that tells time? Well, help is here. Introducing Fidoflex, the digital watchdog. The only watch that nurses its young, and the only dog you can wear underwater.

FX 70

The new FX 70 cheese slicer and processed cheese cartridges. Only $69.75 for all your cheese needs. Hey, what do you say—cheese!

Santi Wrap

Disposable lap-shaped paper covers for sanitary protection when sitting on Santa's lap.

Long Distance

A grandfather is waiting for his beloved grandson to call with a chess move. The call is late, and Grandpa rants about the rotten kid.

Puppy Uppers

Puppy Uppers pep up your pooch, plus they help control his weight. When my Skippy gets too frisky, I give him these: Doggie Downers. Doggie Downers mellow out your mutt.

Compulsion

Somewhere between cleanliness and godliness lies Compulsion. The world's most indulgent disinfectant. From Calvin Kleen.

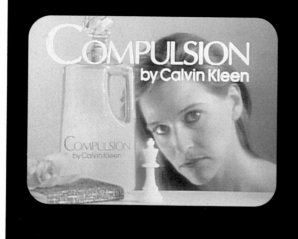

Nikey Turkey

Holiday Time everyone gets together,
Shows up for dinner with my father and mother.
Family at the table getting crazy and loud, sayin',
"Ain't enough food to feed this crowd."
"The bird's too small to feed us all!"
But yo' mama says pump it! Pump it up now.
Pump it!
Get a Nikey Turkey and pump it.
Make it big, now!
Pump it, pump it up.
The first turkey dinner was 1620,
The Pilgrims had it in the land of plenty.
Nothin' was chill with the harvest down,
But the red brother knew he had enough to go 'round.
He knew to pump it!
Pump it up now! Pump it! Pump the bird!
If the holiday table ain't looking too full,
Get a Nikey Turkey.
It's adjustable.
And pump it!

If it doesn't say Nikey, it's not a turkey.

Dysfunctional Family Christmas

This record album offers songs for families who have a tough time with the holidays. You get hit after dysfunctional hit:
"Let's Pretend We Like Each Other (This Christmas)"
"I've Got My Drinking Under Control for the Holidays"
"Peace on Earth? Where?"
"Ballad of the Codependent"
"Can't You Let It Drop, It's Christmas"
"What I Want, You Can't Buy Me"
"Fruitcake and Shame"
To order, call 1–800–GET–HELP.

Balz-Off

When I started back to work, there weren't enough hours in the day. It seemed that life was divided between my job and family. I was exhausted and run-down. So I asked my doctor what to do, and he recommended this: Balz-Off.

Balz-Off's time-release formula lasts a full twenty-four hours. Two Balz-Off tablets with breakfast and he's home all evening and glad to be there.

And unlike the leading hormonal suppressant, there's no mess and no embarrassing alteration of secondary sexual characteristics.

Here's how Balz-Off works: Hormonal signals build up here, in the freedom center. These signals are sent to the brain, where they cause pressure and confusion. But Balz-Off effectively blocks these signals, eliminating aggression, restlessness . . . and the desire to buy stereo equipment.

Balz-Off. In regular and new Italian strength.

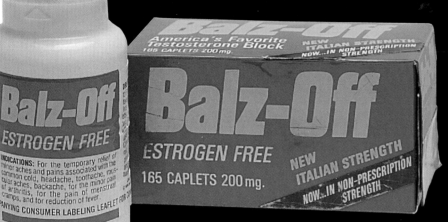

Ass Don't Smell

Scrubbing doesn't work. Perfumes only cover it up. And who has the time to soak? Forget all that junk.

And step up to Ass Don't Smell. The name says it all.

Steroid Cereal

Hi, I'm Fran Tarkenton. You know, it takes strength and stamina to play pro football. You need to replace lots of lost muscle tissue fast, and sometimes your metabolic system just can't pull it off alone. That's why I start each day with a big bowl of Sugar-Frosted Anabolic Steroids. This cereal is a delicious synthetic derivative of male hormones, and in one eight-ounce bowl I get more than my body would produce in three years.

Angora Bouquet

A woman and her husband are raking leaves in their suburban backyard.
Woman: Hi, I'm beautiful but stupid, and I've found the soap that helps me stay that way.

My husband says I look natural and unspoiled, and he loves the way I never bother him with my opinions.

Let's face it . . . good looks and complex human emotions just don't mix. I guess that why I use Angora Bouquet with pH Formula 23.

Angora Bouquet's thousands of tiny tranquillizers penetrate your skin to wash reality away and make your mind and skin as clear as a baby's.

You see, Angora Bouquet actually contains methaqualone, the same tranquillizing agent that is found in those large white pills I often come across in Bill junior's jeans pockets when I do the laundry. [*She's obviously raking the leaves the wrong way.*]
Husband: Honey, why don't you try the other side of the rake. Here, you can get a little more leaves that way.
Woman: I guess that's why my soap is Angora Bouquet with pH Formula 23.
Announcer: Angora Bouquet. Washes your brain as well as your face.

Afro Lustre Hair Spray

[*With Julian Bond:*] *You've come a long way, Negro,/To get where you've got to today./You've got your own hair spray now, Negro./You've come a long, long way.*

Pilson's Feed Bag Dinner

The feed bag dinner is ideal for people on the run: all you do is strap it onto your face and eat.

Royal Deluxe
A car with a ride so smooth that a circumcision can be performed inside of it. We went to Temple Beth Shalom in Little Neck, New York, and asked Rabbi Meyer Teppletz to circumcise eight-day-old Benjamin Kantor while riding in the backseat of the elegant Royale Deluxe Two.

Performing circumcision is a demanding, time-honored art.

It requires a sure hand . . . and a steady cutting surface.

Kromega
A watch so complex, it takes two to work it. It's like asking a stranger for the time.

Epoxy-Dent
Denture adhesive so strong that a denture wearer can hang from a helicopter.

Elvis's Coat
The King may be gone but his coat lives on, as we see in this concert starring Elvis's music and Elvis's coat.

Roaches
Even the best houses get roaches. So why not protect your house with this house. The Roach Brothel. By Red Light. Roaches make out, but they don't get out. Price negotiable.

Grandparents
How to Talk to Your Grandparents, the record album that makes everyone's life a little richer.

Saveco
America's number-one chain of recalled-products discount centers. Hey, nobody likes to pay retail or even wholesale prices. That's why there's Saveco. Let me tell you what we do. Every time the U.S. government orders a product recalled, we buy them.

Craig's Traveler's Checks
Buy your traveler's checks from Craig. He's always there when you need him. He never leaves his apartment.

Jewess Jeans
She's the Jewess in Jewess Jeans. You don't have to be Jewish, but it helps.

Nerf Crotchbat

Don't worry, Mom—because these crotchbats are Nerf!

In six different hot neon crotch colors and styles. Choose the crotchbat that fits you.

Nerf, Nerf, Nerf, Nerf, crotch-bats,
Swing away at home or at school.
If your crotchbat's not Nerf, you're a fool.
Nerf, Nerf, Nerf, Nerf, crotch-bats,
Not aluminum bat, pole, or stick,
It's a crotch surprise that'll give you a kick.
Nerf, Nerf, Nerf, Nerf, crotch-bats,
A hard steel core, covered with Nerf.
You'll know the difference as you hit the turf,
Nerf, Nerf, Nerf, Nerf, crotch-bats,

The Love Toilet

You've found that one special someone, and you never want to be apart. You dine together. You play together. You sleep together. You even bathe together. So why not share the most intimate moment of them all . . . with the Love Toilet.

Because when you're in love, only five minutes apart can seem like an eternity.

Handi-Off

You've tried sanding them off. You've tried slamming them off. And mitts just hide the problem. There's no way around it: you've got extra fingers.

It's time for Handi-Off.

Subtract your extra digits with Handi-Off.

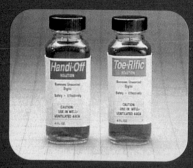

And now there's new Toe-Rific for toes.

Coldcock

There's only one malt liquor that'll get your head hummin'. Coldcock's the one you never see comin'.

I have yet to see the man that could drink a whole can.

First Citywide Change Bank 1

When you do only one thing, you do it better.
At First Citywide Change Bank we just make change.
First Customer: I needed to take the bus, but all I had was a five-dollar bill. I stopped by First Citywide, and they were able to give me four singles and four quarters.
Bank Representative: We will work with the customer to give that customer the change that he or she needs. If you come to us with a twenty-dollar bill, we can give you two tens, we can give you four fives—we can give you a ten and two fives. We will work with you.
Second Customer: I stopped by my First Citywide branch to change a fifty. I guess I was in kind of a hurry, and I asked for a twenty, a ten, and two fives. Their computers picked up my mistake right away, and I got the correct change.
Bank Representative: We have been in this business a long time. With our experience, we're gonna have ideas for change combinations that probably haven't occurred to you. If you have a fifty-dollar bill, we can give you fifty singles. We can give you forty-nine singles and ten dimes. We can give you twenty-five twos.
Come talk to us.
We listen to you.
Bank Representative: We are not going to give you change that you don't want. If you come to us with a hundred-dollar bill, we're not going to give you two thousand nickels—
We want your business.
Bank Representative:—unless that meets your particular change needs.
We will give you . . . the change . . . equal to . . . the amount of money . . . that you want change for.
First Citywide Change Bank. Our business is making change.
Bank Representative: That's what we do.

First Citywide Change Bank 2

Bank Representative: A lot of people don't realize that change is a two-way street. You can come in with sixteen quarters, eight dimes, and four nickels, we can give you a five dollar bill. Or we can give you five singles.
　Or two singles, eight quarters, and ten dimes. You'd be amazed at the variety of the options you have.
First Customer: I was driving through Pennsylvania on the tollway, and to save time, I was using the exact-change lanes. I had just run out of quarters and I was getting a bit nervous when I spotted a sign for a Citywide branch at the next exit. Let me tell you, it was a pretty good feeling.
Bank Representative: I have had people come in with wrinkled ten-dollar bills to exchange for new crisp bills to put in birthday cards. We can handle special requests like that, usually in the same day.
Second Customer: I'd just returned from a business trip to London, and all the cash I had was a five-pound note. Citywide wasn't able to convert it to dollars, but they did give me four guineas, two crowns, four shillings, and ten pence.
Bank Representative: All the time our customers ask us, "How do you make money doing this?" The answer is simple: Volume. That's what we do.

At FIRST CITIWIDE CHANGE BANK
We just make change.

At FIRST CITIWIDE CHANGE BANK
Our business is making change.

Jesus in Blue Jeans

How many times have we seen a youngster listen to a rock and roll recording and then talk back to his parents and fornicate? Never forget that it's only a short skip from the phonograph needle to the hypodermic needle. Rock and roll is the Devil's music—until now, because for just nine ninety-eight, you can now use this same music to deliver your children from evil. It's all here in my new born-again rock and roll collection, *Jesus in Blue Jeans*. You get twenty-four great rock hits, but no sex and no drugs—just good rockin' love songs to God. So send for my record today—or burn in hellfire eternal.

Macho Wipes

Hi, I'm Lauren Hutton. I like my martinis dry, my steaks rare, and my men hard. My men like to work hard, play hard, and when they come home they want to wipe hard. They want Macho Wipes—it's one tough toilet paper that's not afraid to roll up its sleeves and get the job done.

Lungs

Clearly, it's not the poor cigarette that causes cancer—it's the lung.

Aussie Free

Aussie Free. The quick and easy way to get rid of those troublesome Australians.

Brush with Death

If your kids won't take dental hygiene seriously give them a Brush with Death. This time, you're not dealing with the tooth fairy.

Day-Off

That's right, Day-Off's exclusive anti-antihistamine formula provides you with all the outside symptoms of a cold. Day-Off lasts all day long—plenty of time to get the sympathy you need.

Diet Pills

How does Helen Sherman do it all? She's smart, she takes Speed. Speed, the tiny blue diet pills you don't have to be overweight to need.

Happy's Mayonnaise

I bet I know what you're hankering for—a heaping helping of real mayonnaise! Hi, I'm Happy. And I'd like to invite you all out to Happy's Mayonnaise Palace—the biggest and most fun mayonnaise parlor anywhere.

Mr. & Mrs. T's Bloody Mary Mix

Now, if any man tries to tell me he doesn't like Mr. and Mrs. T's Bloody Mary Mix, I say to him, Shut up, old man, shut up. And then I kill him to death. I kill the man who doesn't drink it. I kill him—but I pity him first. It's a bloody shame. It's Mr. and Mrs. T's Bloody Mary Mix. Buy it or I'll kill you.

Rubik's Grenade

A toy inspired by the popular game.

65

Kannon Camera
A camera that's so simple anyone can use it, even Stevie Wonder. Stevie and Jon Newcombe team up to show how it works.

Foldgers
Set in a hospital where, unbeknownst to them, patients' blood is replaced with Foldgers crystals.

Bush Series
In the first paid political announcement we learn how tall various presidents were and how tall President Bush is. And how much shorter Dukakis is.

In the second installment we learn that the parents of past presidents, including George Bush, were all born in America. The Dukakises come from Greece.

And in the third installment we see pictures of past presidents and learn about their heritage. "Vote for Bush—he's whiter."

Sports Illustrated
Hello, I'm Paulina Porizkova. Today we live in a climate of increasing censorship: There's the Meese Commission, the Moral Majority, and the banning of *Playboy* and *Penthouse* from 7-Elevens.

That's why, more than ever, the young man in your household needs *Sports Illustrated's* annual swimsuit issue. It's filled with dozens of photos of today's Top models wearing practically no clothes at all, and it's mixed in with enough sports scores and essays on thoroughbred racing to make it acceptable in any American home.

Tomb
The Tomb of the Unknown Soldier is opened up for the first time in sixty-five years. Geraldo Rivera is on hand to do the honors.

Pork
I spent eight years preparing for the next fifteen seconds tuning myself to run like a fine machine. Striving for excellence. I could've had anything for lunch, but I chose pork because my body can handle it. Pork—eat it, while you're still healthy.

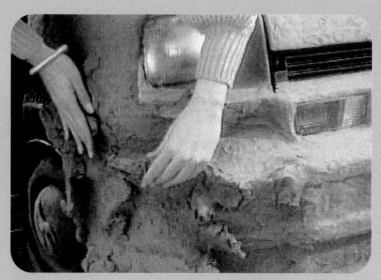

Adobe

The sassy new Mexican import. German engineering and Mexican know-how help to create the first car to break the two-hundred-dollar barrier. That's because it's made out of clay.

Canis

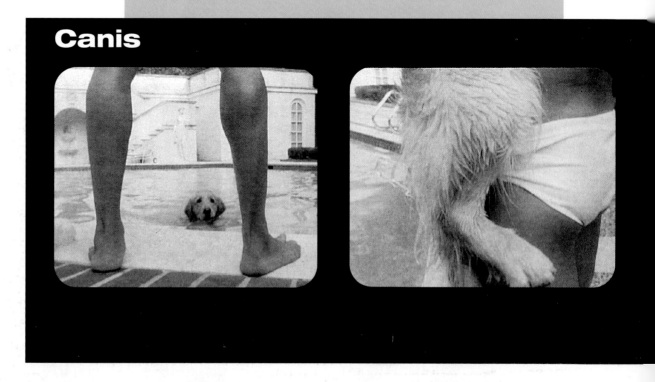

Hedley and Wyche

Hedley and Wyche, the British toothpaste that makes brushing a pleasure. That's because its mild cleaning agent is enhanced by two teaspoons of pure cane sugar. And it tastes great on a cracker! You don't have to brush your teeth every week—but you just might want to.

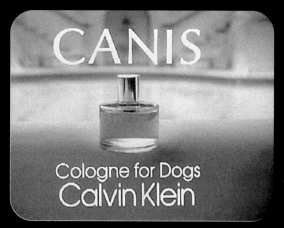

Cologne for dogs. From Calvin Klein.

Time-Life Books
Time-Life Books presents *The Grenada Experience*, a series designed to help you celebrate the greatest military triumph of our generation. Forty-eight comprehensive volumes—one for every hour of this explosive period in American history.

Metrocard 1
A bank representative calls a female customer to tell her she is spending too much money, and there is too much activity on her card. When the woman tells him that it's really none of his business, he points out that with one button he can obliterate her credit and ruin her Christmas.

Metrocard 2
A distressed traveler who discovers he has lost his credit card calls for a replacement. The customer service representative, annoyed by the request, bluntly tells him that she's not "the credit-card fairy."

Fur Commercial
Hello, I'm Alexander Johnson of Alexander's Fur World and we're having our year-end, better-off-dead sale. Furs, furs, furs— choose from hundreds of full-length minks. Every one of these animals was raised in the lap of luxury and, I'm sorry to say, committed suicide due to personal problems. [*Flash: depressed minks.*] And that's not all, we have a fabulous collection of evil, murdering, vicious coyotes—every one a confirmed bunny killer convicted by a jury of environmentalists and executed under humane conditions. Believe me, they're better off dead. So come with a clear conscience, and remember they're animals, for crying out loud, that's what they're there for.

Crystal Gravy

Clearly just like Mom used to make.
Gravy has a whole new taste.
"I can't see any lumps."
Seasoned and simmered.
Stirred and cleared.
Absolutely.
You can see through it.
Someone just got a taste of the future.
Lighter.
Crisper.
Old-fashioned.
You can see your meat.
Crystal Gravy.
Turkey-style and clear brown gravy.
You've never seen a gravy like this.

Cluckin' Chicken

Hey, Clucky—why's the Cluckin' Chicken so chick-a-licious?

Everybody knows why. It's 'cause I'm flame broiled! Yow-zee-yow-dow! But that's not all. I'm cooked *fresh!*

First my head's cut off. Heads up! Then I'm plucked and gutted—my intestines are pulled out. Trust me, you don't want 'em!

Then the pieces of me get flame-broiled. Finally, I'm served to you—where you chew me, swallow me, and convert me into waste matter. Bein' dead never tasted so go-nobbity-good!

Earthies

You don't just throw them away, you plant them.

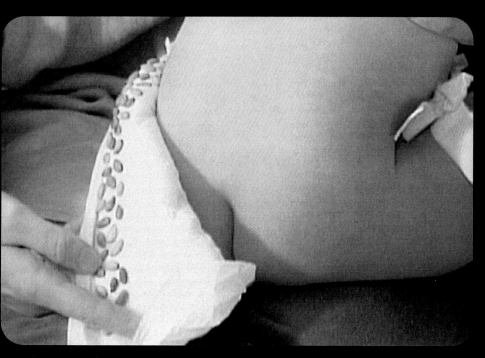

Earthies are the only diapers lined with seeds.
Once planted, Earthies' unique absorbent liner protects
the young seedling as it begins to grow. In a short time, an
ear of corn emerges from the diaper-enriched soil.

Beatle Classics
*Ten Beatle Classics You Kind of
Know the Words To*, sung by the
Kind of Know the Words To
Singers.

Einstein Express
Einstein Express—when it absolutely, positively has to be there
the day before yesterday.

Thirtysomething
Introducing, in talkative and self-
doubting fashion,
Thirtysomething cereal, shaped
like all the characters in *thirtysomething*.

Yard-a-Pult
A new product that helps get rid of
unnecessary waste. You put
unwanted items in a dishlike
container and catapult them into
your next-door neighbor's yard.

McDonald's
A cashier at the Russian McDonald's offers a new Happy Meal.
When you purchase certain food
items, you'll receive a gift soap,
spool of thread, needle, or toilet
paper.

Funeral Home
Winston-McCauley Funeral Home
provides care, compassion, dedica-
tion and absolutely no sex. In fact,
if an employee does not live up to
the standards and has sex with any
dead body, the mortician will be
suspended and they will discount
the customer's bill.

Savalas
[*With Phil Hartman:*] I'm Telly
Savalas. And if you're like me, you
like to be near the action. And
when there isn't any action, then
you gotta make your own. And,
baby, that's when you need to join
the Player-With-Yourselves Club.
That's right, baby. The Player-
With-Yourselves Club Card entitles
you to masturbation privileges at
hotels all over the world. Who loves
yourself, baby?

Schmitts Gay
An empty and dingy pool is magi-
cally filled with water and gorgeous
men clad in bikinis. "If you've got
a big thirst and you're gay, reach
for a cold tall can of Schmitts
Gay."

THE EARLY

YEARS
Great Sketches (1975-80)

Candice Bergen and the Bees.

The Bees

Featured in *SNL*'s inaugural show and in eight of the first ten episodes, the Bees are the first of the show's recurring characters. In the course of their nineteen appearances they get swatted with rolled-up newspapers, are featured in their own "Bee Centennial Minute," and sing be-bop and "The Battle Hymn of the Republic" (what did you expect—"*The Sting*"?). Mentally deranged Bees appear in "One Flew Over the Hornet's Nest," and Killer Bees swarm into the homes of innocent Californians ("Your pollen or your life, *señor*!") and liberate the imprisoned swine flu ("When times were hard, my family was poor. The swine flu took us in. The swine flu taught us to read").

Most touching of all, though, is the continuing saga of the Bees' struggle to make it, both on *SNL* and in America, the land of milk and honey. In the second show host Paul Simon is forced to tell a disconsolate band of cast members dressed as Bees that the sketch has been cut. In the third show host Rob Reiner stops a sketch to complain about their presence: "I was told when I came on this show that I would not have to work with the Bees!" The Bees, he rants, "don't work" and "are horrendous." John Belushi cuts him off: "I'm sorry if you think we're ruining your show, Mr. Reiner. But you don't understand. We didn't ask to be Bees. See, you've got Norman Lear and a first-rate writing staff, but this is all they came up with for us. Do you think we *like this*? No. No, Mr. Reiner, but we don't have any *choice*."

Jane Curtin and Gilda Radner

Dan Aykroyd and John Belushi

In truth, Belushi did not like performing the Bees at first. But the Blues Brothers, in their very first appearance, were in the guise of the Bees, singing "King Bee." Over a three-year period the Bees were among the most frequently broadcast characters. Through hard work and determination they rise to success in a country once run by wasps, who call them names—flower suckers, antennaheads, flying barber poles, queen stuffers—and make racist jokes ("What's black and white and yellow all over? A dead Bee covered with a newspaper").

As one Bee explains to a rambunctious Wendy (Jodie Foster) in a *Peter Pan*–esque adventure: "Bees are a state of mind. Bees are like Muppets with a longer contract, don't you understand?"

FIRST AIRED: OCTOBER 11, 1975

The Bee-All That Ends All

A brief look at the final episode of the Bees:

As "Bad News Bees" opens, adolescent Bee campers are speculating on the big baseball game that is to be played the next day—all except for Alan (John Belushi), who is caught reading a *Playbee* magazine: "Boy, I'd sure like to get into her honey sac!" Alan confesses he never "did it," but Artie (Dan Aykroyd) claims that he was involved in a swarm's "gangstang."

The Bees' adult coach (Walter Matthau) quiets the conversation: "When you're my age, you should stick it to the queen as often as I do." The coach leaves and turns out the lights; after a brief pause someone's bedsprings start to squeak: "Hey, Alan, would you pull your stinger somewhere else?" The coach returns, yelling that they were told to go to sleep; the young Bees blame Alan for keeping them awake—he has been "buzzing off." Alan denies it, but there's honey all over his sheets.

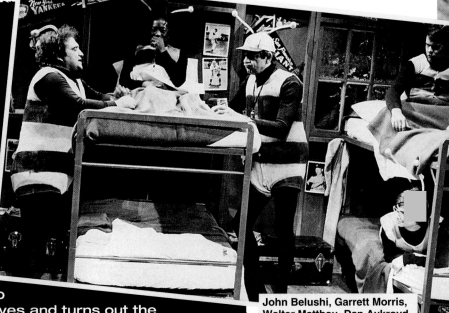

John Belushi, Garrett Morris, Walter Matthau, Dan Aykroyd (top), and Charlie Matthau

Land Shark

The script for the original Land Shark episode, with Gilda Radner, Laraine Newman, Jane Curtin, and Candice Bergen playing victims, features Matt Cooper (John Belushi), Sheriff Brady (Dan Aykroyd), and the Shark (Chevy Chase):

Gilda: Who is it?

Voice [Mumbling]: Mrs. Ramilarghhh?

Gilda: Who is it?

Voice: Plumber.

Gilda: Plumber? I didn't ask for a plumber. Who *is* it?

Voice: Telegram.

Gilda: Oh. Telegram. Just a moment.

[*She opens the door. The head of the Shark appears, and she is pulled away, shrieking. Dissolve to the sheriff's office. Wearing a snorkel mask, he is examining a body.*]

Matt Cooper: Oh my God. You can't tell me this woman was killed by falling out of a tree.

Sheriff Brady: What was it?

Matt Cooper: Land Shark. The cleverest species of them all.

[*Dissolve to another apartment.*]

Laraine: Yes?

Voice: Mrs. Arlsburgerhhh?

Laraine: Who?

Voice [Pause]: Mrs. Johanes-burrrr?

Laraine: Who is it?

Chevy Chase

Voice: Flowers.

Laraine: Flowers? From whom?

Voice: Plumber, ma'am.

Laraine: I don't need a plumber. You're that clever Shark, aren't you?

Voice: Candygram...

Laraine [*convinced she knows*]: Candygram my foot. Get out of here before I call the police. You're the Shark and you know it.

Voice: I'm only a dolphin, ma'am.

Laraine: A dolphin?...Well...Okay.

[*The Shark's jaws engulf her. Dissolve back to the sheriff's office. Cooper peeks anxiously into container on his desk, then turns away in revulsion.*]

Matt Cooper: Oh my God!

Sheriff Brady: What is it?

Matt Cooper: Egg salad again.

[*Dissolve to another apartment.*]

Jane: Who is it?

Voice: Land Shark.

Jane [*laughing*]: Oh, Walter.

[*She opens the door. The Shark attacks her to piercing screams. Dissolve to sheriff's office.*]

Matt Cooper [*On the phone*]: Hello, Walter. I have some good news and I have some bad news. First the good news. Betty and I are having a party tonight. Come on over, you'll have a great time. Now, the bad news: You'll be coming stag. Good-bye, Walter.

[*Dissolve to another apartment. Candice is reading a paper with the headline, "More Shark Killings," and listening to the radio.*]

Radio Newsman:...considered the cleverest of all sharks. Unlike the great white, which tends to inhabit the waters of harbors and recreational beach areas, the Land Shark may strike at any place, anytime. It is capable of disguising its voice and generally attacks young single women. Experts at the University of Miami's Oceanographic Institute suggest that the best way to scare off the Shark in the event of an attack is to hit or punch the predator in the nose. Now for the weather...

[*Doorbell rings.*]

Candice: Who is it?

Voice: Sorry to disturb you, ma'am. I am from the Jehovah's Witnesses and thought you might be interested in a copy of our journal, *The Watchtower.*

[*She has tiptoed over to the door with a large wooden mallet.*]

Candice: Why, certainly, I'd be very interested.

Voice: Would you mind opening the door, ma'am?

Candice: Sure, just a second.

[*She opens the door a crack and smacks the unseen visitor on the head with the mallet. The door opens, and to her horror, Garrett Morris, in a suit, drops journals on the floor and reels into the apartment, his face bloodied.*]

Candice: Oh...sorry!

2 Laraine opens the door to accept a candygram and is eaten. Matt Cooper and Sheriff Brady go to Patricia's (Jane Curtin's) house and warn her. She opens the door when the Shark pretends to be Matt: "I left my goggles . . ." The Shark announces on the radio advice about how best to deal with him: "Graciously invite the fish into your living room, offer him a soda pop, and maybe some Oreos, some cookies—just make him feel at home."

3 Louise Lasser is nervous about hosting a live television show, and she runs into her dressing room. Cast members try to coax her out. The Shark's voice offers a telegram, a candygram, hairstyling ("I'm here to do your braids"), and finally, the "cover of *Time* magazine," which draws her out. And it's not the Shark at all, just Chevy Chase.

4 Gilda opens her door at two in the morning on Halloween ("Candygram." "Look, I'm all out of candy") once she thinks it's UNICEF. She gets eaten. The Shark enters, and Chevy sticks his head through the mouth and announces the show.

5 Charles Lindbergh (Buck Henry) has trouble staying awake during his transatlantic flight. Land Shark offers "maps, Paris maps," a "compass," and finally "amphetamines." When Lindy realizes it's a Land Shark, who is running, not swimming, he knows he has made it to France.

6 John Zacherle presents a scary episode of "Mystery Theatre," in which the Shark once again comes delivering a candygram to Julia Louis-Dreyfus—only this time, the Shark appears on a television monitor outside Julia's door.

Candygram.

FIRST AIRED: NOVEMBER 8, 1975

Dan Aykroyd and Laraine Newman

E. Buzz Miller

E. Buzz: How about that one? Thirty-three inches long! Ever see a worm thirty-three inches long?
Christy: I don't know!
E. Buzz: I bet you don't!

E. BUZZ MILLER PLAYED BY DAN AYKROYD
CHRISTY CHRISTINA PLAYED BY LARAINE NEWMAN
AIRED: FEBRUARY 25, 1978

Dan Aykroyd

Tom Snyder

Speaking of heat, you're quite the dancer. Well, heck, I can—haha! haha!—well, let's get a wide shot of this. I can boogie as well as the next guy!

PLAYED BY DAN AYKROYD
AIRED: OCTOBER 7, 1978

Gilda Radner

Judy Miller

Oh, it's the show of the day, it's the show of the way, I am in it, oh, yes, I am, oh, it's the show of your life, it's the JU-DY MIL-LER SHOW! Presenting the big famous and you know who it is… star of the show…and here it is—the person who is also a bride named Judy Arlene Miller!

Hello. You know, I am the most beautiful person in the whole wide world.

PLAYED BY GILDA RADNER
AIRED: OCTOBER 29, 1977

SAMURAI

John Belushi

Samurai

John Belushi and Richard Pryor

John Belushi and Buck Henry

🔪 "Samurai Hotel," the first sketch, features the Samurai (John Belushi) and another bellhop (Richard Pryor) dueling over who is going to carry a guest's bags. "Your *mama-san*!" cries the bellhop in between grunts. He smashes the desk with his sword, and the Samurai takes the luggage, saying, "I can dig where you're coming from." These are the only words the Samurai has ever spoken in English.

🔪 Buck Henry begins to order in the "Samurai Delicatessen," but the Samurai interrupts, his sword pointing to the "Take a Number Please" machine. Henry complies and waits until the Samurai grunts up to his number.

The ropes on hanging salami are severed, a tomato is sliced in midair, and bread is split against the Samurai's skull. "Nice work, but can you please trim away some of the fat on the corned beef?" The request nearly prompts the Samurai to commit hara-kiri, and is retracted. "Oh, listen, can you break a twenty?" With his saber, the Samurai does.

SAMURAI DIVORCE

🔪 It's "Samurai Divorce Court," featuring Futaba versus Futaba. Pounding her forehead, Mrs. Futaba (Jane Curtin) charges mental anguish; Mr. Futaba explains his side of the story, sliding his sword in and out of its case. "Adultery," the judge (Peter Boyle) concludes. Some possessions are to be divided, literally: A concertina is halved by blade, and a rare gong is busted against Mr. Futaba's pate. Finally, the couple fight over custody of their daughter, Bingo; she's about to be split between them at the freeze-frame.

Jane Curtin, John Belushi, and Peter Boyle

John Belushi and Buck Henry

In "Samurai Stockbroker" John Belushi's sword accidentally strikes Buck Henry, playing the unhappy client Mr. Dantley, in the forehead. On tape you can clearly see Henry staggering back from the blow.

Buck Henry brings his set to Samurai TV Repairman. "Inspected by number eighty-nine" complains Henry—and the Samurai turns wistful: "*Mama-san!*" he cries. The Famous TV Repairman's School only trained him on black-and-white sets, but he tosses the set around, hits it with his sword, plunges two knives into the top grill—and the picture comes out perfect.

Buck Henry is relating a disturbing dream to Samurai Psychiatrist. The doctor slices two oranges off a tree and prompts the patient to identify his diagnosis: "Castration complex."

SAMURAI OPTOMETRIST

The "Samurai Optometrist" teases his customer (Buck Henry) about his eyesight, using his sword as a cane. "If I wanted to be entertained, I'd go see a comedian, not an optician," huffs Henry, prompting the Samurai to threaten hara-kiri. "Wait! I meant optometrist."

Samurai mumbles the Rolling Stones' "Shattered" as he chops his counter without breaking the lenses. "Shatterproof—but what about the frames? Do you have any tortoiseshell?" The Samurai creates them from a convenient turtle. "You know, I could save myself all this trouble if I had bifocals …" The sketch is frozen as the sword swings toward the glasses Henry wears.

Other Samurai adventures:
"Samurai Baker"
"Samurai Night Fever"
"Samurai B.M.O.C."
"Samurai Dry Cleaner"
"Samurai Tailor"
"Samurai General Practitioner"

FIRST AIRED: DECEMBER 13, 1975

John Belushi and Dan Aykroyd

Don Marsala (Dan Aykroyd) hires Samurai Hit Man to kill, as soon as possible, both Don Cornelius and Don Kirschner. He is to prepare lunch for them at their favorite restaurant—Benihana's. A simulated dining area is wheeled in, with Cornelius and Kirschner represented by heads of cabbage. The Samurai demonstrates that he can fry beef professionally, but refuses to issue the kiss of death. His price rises to seventeen thousand dollars and carfare back to Detroit, after which he kisses and chops down the cabbages.

THE END

The Mr. Bill Show

I's so good to see all you bright faces out in front of the TV set. We're going to have a great time today!" Mr. Bill. joined by his dog, Spot, always greets the day with high hopes. But Mr. Hands, who molds our Play-Doh hero and serves as our announcer ("Mr. Hands is really short and has ten fingers"), always seems to have other things in store for Mr. Bill. The trouble usually focuses around his "good friend" Sluggo: "I don't even like him," Mr. Bill squeaks. "He hurts me all the time!" And so goes the life of Bill.

"Oh nooooo"—Mr. Spot has been flattened by a fist, just after he arrived. Good friend Sluggo comes to shake hands. "What's that in his hands? No! No! Nooooooo!" Mr. Bill has been knifed in the gut. And Dr. Sluggo—Sluggo with a little stethoscope—says Mr. Bill's leg must be amputated. "Try standing up," Mr. Hands encourages, and Mr. Bill falls flat.

Mr. Hands suggests a deep-sea mission; he drops Mr. Bill into a deep pot of water. After our hero's rescue, Mr. Hands brushes Mr. Bill's teeth—and in the process his nose, mouth, and right eye are brushed off. No time to rest—it's on to a skydiving adventure! But Mr. Bill's parachute doesn't open and he plummets to the ground.

2 "You need exercise," Mr. Hands decides, and aids Bill with a pull-up that rips out a tiny left arm. Doctor Sluggo recommends, and inflicts, acupuncture. No time to recover—Mr. Bill has a party to go to! "Let's wash up!" Mr. Hands douses his friend with a mysterious liquid marked "XXX"; next thing you know, Mr. Bill is on fire. "Why, why, why?" Mr. Hands deposits Mr. Bill at a doorway and rings the bell. Out comes a partygoer, who sees no one—but unknowingly winds up with Mr. Bill pâté on the sole of his shoe.

3 Mr. Sluggo is very hungry, so Mr. Hands offers him Spot. Ohhhhh! Spot's gone, save for his tail, which is sticking out of Sluggo's mouth. Mr. Hands suggests some grooming; he begins with a vigorous hair brushing that tears off the top of Mr. Bill's skull. "I don't want to be bald," Mr. Bill squeals; fortunately, Mr. Hands has a "mod-look toupee," giving Mr. Bill a Beatlesque appearance.

Mr. Hands introduces the world-famous magician the Amazing Sluggo. Sluggo, in silver hat and cape, is going to levitate Mr. Bill. Mr. Bill is held aloft over poison-tipped spikes and told, "Okay, Mr. Bill, levitate yourself!" The traditional sawing-in-half trick results in three pieces of Mr. Bill.

4 Spot looks mighty dirty to Mr. Hands. But don't worry, he's got some warm water—boiling, in fact—to make Spot feel fresh and clean. Mr. Bill made so much money last year, he should get professional tax advice. H&R Sluggo figures that Mr. Bill owes an arm and a leg, which are promptly detached and mailed to the IRS. Mr. Bill's face gets stamped "Paid."

Here comes Mr. Bill's girlfriend, Miss Sluggo; no matter what Mr. Bill says, they look so in love that Father Sluggo names them man and wife. A flying bag of rice knocks off Mr. Bill's skull. Head and body are reunited in a van heading for Niagara Falls; Mr. Hands gives the honeymooners an enthusiastic send-off over the road's edge.

5 Today promises to be a lot of fun: Mr. Bill and Mr. Hands are having their own circus! Spot looks mighty hungry, so Sluggo brings dog food (with a skull-and-cross-bones label). Mr. Hands ties some helium balloons around Bill's fingers and wrist. "Too tight! Too tight!" The fingers are lopped off, and the helium pulls the arm out of the socket. "Oh, Mr. Bill, you lost your balloon." Ringmaster Sluggo runs the circus. Mr. Bill performs a daring high-wire act, but he slips and lands on a specially made net—which is flat against the floor. No circus would be complete without the shoot-the-man-out-of-the-cannon stunt, which ends the episode with a bang.

6 Mr. Bill is moving to New York. He and Mr. Hands meet Mr. Sluggo and Spot downtown. Sluggo curbs Spot, and the dog is flattened by a passing car. "Cleaning up after your dog" takes on new meaning. The two visit the top of the Empire State Building. "Let's get a little closer for a more spectacular view!" "No, no, no, nooooooo…"

7 The decorator arrives at Mr. Bill's new apartment: he's a limp-wristed Sluggo, who says Mr. Bill just *must* have a nice dogskin rug. Mr. Hands, rolling pin in hand, happily obliges. Sluggo recommends some new furniture, and brings in the perfect table. "But it only has three legs," cries Mr. Bill. Mr. Bill's left leg becomes the table's fourth. Sluggo thinks the room should be recolored, and Mr. Bill is inadvertently caught between the wall and the roller. "Oh, Mr. Bill, we got some paint on you. We'll have to wash your clothes." Mr. Bill and his clothes get the best washing quarters can buy.

8 Mr. Bill's going fishing, and Mr. Hands outfits him with a fisherman's hat; the hooks in the fabric dig into Mr. Bill's head. What is Mr. Hands going to do for bait? "Here comes Mr. Bill's dog…" Spot is hooked. Say, what a catch: they reel in deep-sea diver Jacques Sluggo, who's happy to show Mr. Bill his new harpoon. Finally, a fish bites, and Mr. Hands lets Mr. Bill reel him in; Mr. Bill gets yanked into the air, then falls into a dolphin's mouth.

9 Animal Trainer Sluggo has Spot roll over into glass shards, with Mr. Hands's help. Even Mr. Hands's help can't get Spot all the way through the ring of fire! Mr. Bill arrives and sees Spot's charred remains: "Mr. Hands, I'm beginning to think you're not such a good friend. You always let that bully Sluggo pick on me! I think I'm going to punch him in the face, huh?" But they're out of time, and Mr. Bill gets a last-minute conk on the head.

10 A messenger has brought a summons. It reads, "Mr. Bill's gonna get it," although Mr. Hands tells Mr. Bill, "It says here you're being sued by Mr. Sluggo because your dog Spot bit him on the leg and has rabies." The Honorable Judge Sluggo presides. To prove Spot doesn't have rabies, Mr. Hands gives a blood test—oops! Spot is sucked into the hypodermic. Uh-oh! The jury (all frowning Sluggos) thinks Spot *does* have rabies. Only one thing to do: Here comes Mr. Bill's mom…and she testifies that "Mr. Bill is the nicest son a mother could ever have." DA Sluggo interrogates Mother Bill in private; she returns with black eyes and a sudden change in testimony: "Mr. Bill is a spoiled brat and has committed many felonies recently." The jury decides to throw the books at Mr. Bill, literally. As Mr. Hands sees it, Mr. Bill's only option is to plead insanity. Judge Sluggo accepts the plea ("Yayyyyy!") and authorizes shock treatment ("Noooo!").

11 Mr. Bill weighs in at 190 (with Mr. Hands's help) and resolves to lose weight—with help from Sluggo LaLanne. The barbell is too much for Mr. Bill's arms and crushes his chin. "And now for those shoulders, stretch this spring"; Mr. Bill goes flying. A brick wall stops him flat: "You're slimmin' up already," Mr. Hands encourages. Mr. Bill is forced into the steam box and comes out pencil-thin. Time to cool off with a refreshing shower; what's left of Mr. Bill seeps down the drain.

12 Mr. Bill has left a note: "Went shopping. Be back later." Once Mr. Hands leaves, Mr. Bill calls from the closet. "Oh, I'm sorry I had to tell a fib, but I didn't want Mr. Hands to know where me and Spot are! You know, I'm beginning to wonder if we're very safe around him anymore. I'm even beginning to think that he likes Mr. Sluggo more than he likes me, because he always lets him pick on me. And the mean things he does to poor little Spot." But Mr. Hands reappears. He teaches that "it's good to return borrowed things promptly" and returns Mr. Bill's bowling ball.

13 Mr. Bill and Spot hitchhike, in disguise. A driver stops and revs his engine until Mr. Bill and Spot choke on the exhaust. It's Mr. Hands! He's been "worried sick." "Let's shake hands, and then it'll be like old times again." Mr. Hands helps Mr. Bill buckle up for safety: "Not too tight, that's too tight, ohhhhh."

14 Today we see a movie, *Sluggo's Follies*, featuring the hilarious antics of Vaudeville Bill, Mr. Bill's grandfather. A pair of hands wins the first laughs by pulling a banana peel from under Vaudeville Bill's feet. The hands douse the burning comic with a bucket of water. The Amazing Sluggo, the knife thrower, hurls five knives into Vaudeville Bill's gut. Angry that no knives hit the balloons, the all-Sluggo audience throws food at the stage. The kitchen sink drops onstage to end the act. "Oh, no! I didn't like that movie! Poor Granddaddy."

15 Today we're all going to see *Saturday Night Live*! Mr. Hands graciously allows Mr. Bill to pass through the revolving door first—but the spinning door thrusts Mr. Bill through the air and into a wall. Badge-wearing NBC Page Sluggo tears Mr. Bill's ticket, and in the process rips Mr. Bill's right hand from its wrist. Mr. Bill takes his seat, the last in the house. He's eager for the traditional opening line, and delivers it himself: "Live from New York, It's *Saturday Ni*— ohhhhhh!" A latecomer heedlessly sits on the tiny Mr. Bill.

16 It's "The *All-New* Mr. Bill Show" with a mirrored disco ball and "an all-new cast, yay!" No more Sluggo and Mr. Hands, Mr. Bill says, " 'cause I think they were holding us back." He introduces the really versatile and witty and cute guest Miss Sally. They show home movies of how they met at the beach—but first Mr. Hands stops in to return the projector. Whoops! It drops onto the doughy Miss Sally.

On-screen, Mr. Bill is at a Coney Island beach. A Frisbee decapitates Spot. Mr. Hands shares his tips for a great tan: Sluggo Quick Start Lighter Fluid for protective lotion, and a magnifying glass to speed tanning. Miss Sally returns the Frisbee and accepts an invitation to stay for lunch. Sally's jealous (and human-size) boyfriend kicks sand into Mr. Bill's face.

Once the movie's over, Spot barks that Mr. Bill has gone home. "Spot, between you and me, I like the set the way it used to be." *Snip!* The mirrored ball plunges onto Spot.

17 The doorbell rings: "It's probably Mr. Hands. Let's pretend we're not here and he'll go away!" But Mr. Hands knocks harder and harder until the door crashes in on Sally. Mr. Bill says he has a cold and won't be coming into the studio. Mr. Hands offers home remedies. First, "plenty of aspirin," and he dumps a thousand tablets on Mr. Bill. Next, "keep warm," and he scalds Mr. Bill with a hot-water bottle. The bottle leaks, but Mr. Hands covers Mr. Bill with an electric blanket. Eventually Mr. Bill's house burns down.

18 The good news: Mr. Bill, Miss Sally, and Spot are living in Pleasant Stay Trailer Park while a new home is built by their insurers. The bad news: Mr. Hands is the contractor. Miss Sally is crushed by bricks, and Mr. Bill stands cemented into the foundation. Insurance Agent Sluggo stops by to say his company won't pay a cent; Mr. Bill did not check his Sluggo of Omaha policy's fine print, which has an expiration date of "yesterday."

19 "I hope you're ready to have fun today, because we're all going to see a psychiatrist! Yay!" Mr. Bill finds himself on I. M. Häns's couch, recalling his birth: When the stork dropped him in Sluggoville (town credo: "We Hate the Bills"), Dad's head got knocked off by the earthbound bundle of joy.

The doctor uncovers Mr. Bill's chronic nightmare. In it, Mr. Bill is rafting in a sink when hands open the drain. Mr. Bill falls all the way to a fiery hell, ruled by a horned, tailed Sluggo, whose pitchfork impales the plummeting Mr. Bill. "Obviously, you feel manipulated by these so-called hands." Häns's diagnosis? Paranoia. "Oh, no—those hands are real. And you know what? You look mighty familiar. I want a second opinion." Häns's associate Dr. Sluggo agrees that Mr. Bill is crazy, and a lobotomy is performed via scissors.

20 Mr. Bill traces a lot of the problems he's been having lately to the people he hangs around with—and he doesn't mean Spot. Mr. Bill reports a threat on his life to Sergeant O'Hanahan. He blames Sluggo and Mr. Hands: "I want them locked up, okay?" When Mr. Bill describes his tormentors, the renderings look like Mr. Bill and Spot. It's Mr. Bill who gets arrested, and in the most painful way, he learns why it's called the slammer.

21 Extra, extra, read all about it: "Mr. Bill Gets 20 Years in Sing Sing." Warden Sluggo has said Mr. Bill will be out real soon if Sally's nice to him. Mr. Hands tries to help Bill escape by yanking the bars out with a rope tied to his car. The other end of the rope is tied to Mr. Bill's neck, so the plan fails, and Mr. Bill is stuck in the bars. A little dynamite should loosen them right up. Mr. Bill is blasted into the prison yard, where the warden orders him to stand. Trapped under debris, Mr. Bill can't obey, and the guards open fire.

22 Mr. Bill recounts his first Christmas, when Santa Sluggo buried Spot under stocking stuffers and gave baby Bill an up-close look at his model train. Then there was the Christmas when the Sluggo-in-a-box sprung open to splatter Spot, reshaping him as a tree-top star. Little Billy got a pierced palm from stringing popcorn and "made such a great living ornament" before Mr. Hands "lit the tree" with a lighter. And so on.

23 As Mr. Bill lounges poolside in Los Angeles, he is invited to a big party at Ken and Barbie's. Mr. Hands suggests some coke; Mr. Bill says he's trying to stick with diet sodas. However, Agent Sluggo says he only has coke, and a burlap bag drops onto Mr. Bill and his car. That coke buy turns out to be real expensive—even the house must be sold, and the Sluggo Realty sign is planted into Mr. Bill's foot. Mr. Hands talks Mr. Bill into lunch at the San Ansluggo's Fault picnic area. The ground splits between Mr. Bill's feet and closes once he has fallen into its chasm.

24 Mr. Bill makes a rare appearance outside "The Mr. Bill Show." Chevy Chase returns to rummage through a roomful of old *SNL* costumes and props—and finds Mr. Bill stranded amidst the memorabilia. This time, there is no Mr. Hands or Mr. Sluggo to hurt Mr. Bill. A stumbling Chevy, however, proves just as dangerous to his Play-Doh pal.

Mr. Bill, Sluggo, and Spot

Oh nooooo.

FIRST AIRED: FEBRUARY 28, 1976

Star Trek

Featuring Mr. Spock (Chevy Chase), Captain James T. Kirk (John Belushi), Mr. Sulu (Akira Yoshimura), Lt. Uhura (Doris Powell), Mr. Scott (Dan Aykroyd), Dr. McCoy (Dan Aykroyd), Herb Goodman (Elliott Gould), and Curtis (Garrett Morris).

John Belushi

Announcer: The following program is brought to you in living color by NBC.

Spock: Captain Kirk to the bridge! Captain Kirk to the bridge!

Kirk: Yes, Mr. Spock.

Spock: Sensors are picking up an unidentified vessel, Captain, headed straight toward us.

Kirk: Range, Mr. Sulu?

Sulu: Point four zero light years, sir, and closing fast.

Kirk: Lieutenant Uhura, open a hailing frequency.

Uhura: I've been trying to reach them but there's no response, sir.

Kirk [*Into microphone*]: This is Captain James T. Kirk of the starship *Enterprise*. Identify yourself. [*To Uhura*] Put them on the viewscreen, full magnification.

Uhura: Aye aye, sir.

Kirk [*Into microphone*]: Repeat— identify yourself.

[*Bridge screen shows a maroon 1968 Chrysler limo "driving" through space*]

Kirk: What kind of ship is that, Mr. Spock?

Spock: Fascinating, Captain. It would appear to be an early gas combustion vehicle, at least two or three hundred years old.

Kirk: Run it through the computer. Find out what those little numbers mean. I want answers.

Spock: Process visual feed. Analyze and reply.

Kirk: I have a hunch, Mr. Spock, that we are about to face a menace more terri-fying than the flying para-sites of Ingraham B; more insid-ious than the sand-bats of Manark 4; more bloodthirsty than the vampire clouds of Argus 10. I have a hunch that "thing" out there is deadlier than the Romulans, the Klingons, and the Gorns all rolled into one.

Spock: Here is the readout, Captain. The computer has identified the alien vessel as a 1968 Chrysler Imperial with a tinted windshield and retractable headlights.

Kirk: And the little blue and orange numbers?

Spock: That's called a "California license plate," and it's registered, or was in 1968, to a corporation known as "NBC." Wait, there's something more. The computer isn't sure, but it thinks this NBC used to manufacture cookies.

Kirk: Could that be some sort of illusion, Mr. Spock?

Spock: It's no illusion, Captain. Scanner readings indicate two life forms inside that craft.

Kirk: Mr. Sulu, increase speed to warp factor eight.

Sulu: But, sir, that's only for the most extreme emergencies. The ship can't take it.

Kirk: You heard my order, Mr. Sulu.

Sulu: Aye aye, sir.

Kirk [*Voiceover*]: Captain's Log, Stardate 3615.6. On a routine delivery of medical supplies to Earth Colony 9, we are being chased through space by an automobile three centuries old, owned by a company that manufactured cookies. It would all seem silly if it weren't for this feeling of dread that haunts me, a sense of impending doom.

Sulu: They're right behind us, Captain.

Kirk: Let's lose them, Mr. Sulu. Prepare for evasive action. Helm hard to port!...Hard to starboard!...Hard to port!

Spock: Frankly, Captain, I'm exhausted.

Kirk: Me, too. Stabilize, Mr. Sulu.

Sulu: Look, Captain! It's no use. We can't shake them.

Kirk: Then we'll give them a fight they won't forget. [*Into intercom*] All hands! Man your battle stations! This is not a drill! Red alert! Man your battle stations! Red alert!

Spock: But, Captain—

Kirk: Lock phasers on target, Mr. Sulu.

Sulu: Phasers locked on target, sir.

Spock: But, Captain, you can't—

Kirk: Stand by to fire.

Sulu: Phasers standing by, sir.

Spock: But captain, we don't know who the aliens are or what they want. To kill them without warning would be highly illogical.

Kirk: Fact—their intentions are unknown. Fact—I am responsible for the lives of 430 crewmen. And fact—I can't afford to take any chances. Fire main phasers! [*Nothing happens.*] I said, "Fire main phasers!"

Sulu: I'm trying, sir. Nothing is happening.

Kirk: Arm and lock photon torpedoes, Mr. Sulu.

Sulu: They're not working either, Captain.

Kirk: Deflectors up.

Sulu: Captain, the helm does not respond. The controls are dead.

Spock: We're slowing down, Captain. We're stopping.

Kirk: Bridge to engine room, acknowledge.

Scotty: Scotty here, Captain.

Kirk: What in blazes is going on, Scotty?

Scotty: I dinna know, Captain. We're losing power and I don't know why.

Kirk: Well, do something, man. Go to manual override. Cut in auxiliary systems.

Scotty: Saints preserve us, Captain, but even the emergency systems are out.

Kirk: Well, fix it, Scotty. I don't care how, but fix it. The lives of 430 crewmen hang in the balance. Kirk out.

Spock: Life support systems are still operative, Captain.

Kirk: But for how long, Mr. Spock, for how long? Lieutenant Uhura, inform Starfleet Command of our situation.

Uhura: All communications are dead, Captain.

McCoy: Jim, Jim, I—I…Jim—

Kirk: Great God, man, spit it out.

McCoy: The aliens have boarded us, Jim. And they're headed this way.

Kirk: But how, Bones? How did they get on board? Did they beam on? Did they suddenly materialize?

McCoy: No, they just sort of stepped out from behind the curtains.

Spock: Describe them, Doctor.

McCoy: There's two of them. Bipeds, humanoid in appearance. Their clothing is drab except for a bright piece of cloth worn around the neck of the leader.

Spock: Was there anything else odd about their clothing?

McCoy: I'm a doctor, not a tailor, dammit! Wait, there was one other thing about them that seemed a bit strange. They spoke English! Quick, Jim, I hear them coming up the turbo-lift! They'll be here in seconds!

Kirk: We'll be ready for them, Doctor.

[*Kirk, Spock, and McCoy quickly whip out their phasers and train them on the turbo-lift doors.*]

Kirk: Welcome aboard the starship *Enterprise.* I'm Captain James T. Kirk, representing the United Federation of Planets.

Goodman: Hi, I'm Herb Goodman, head of programming for the network.

Kirk: Stand back. I won't hesitate to shoot.

Goodman: Can I have your attention? Curtis, you want to turn off those sound effects?

Curtis: Sure thing.

Goodman: Everyone, please, can I have your attention? I have an announcement to make. Due to low Nielsens, we at NBC have decided to cancel "Star Trek."

Kirk: Fire at my command.

Goodman: On your way out, stop by the cashier's office and pick up your checks.

Kirk: Set phasers on "stun." Fire.

McCoy: They're not firing, Jim.

Kirk: Try "kill."

McCoy: Nope, still nothing.

Goodman: You'll make sure the property department gets those things back, won't you, fellows?

Spock: Most peculiar, Captain. I can only conclude that they possess some sort of weapons deactivator, in which case I shall merely render him unconscious with my famous Vulcan nerve pinch.

Goodman: Of course, if it was up to me, you could keep them—as souvenirs, give 'em to your kids, whatever. But, you see, they're planning to market a complete line of Trekkie merchandise, and I have to send these to Taiwan to be copied.

[*Spock tries to knock him out with the Vulcan nerve pinch. Goodman thinks he's admiring his suit…*]

Goodman: Isn't that fabric something? You just can't buy material like this in the States. No way! But I was lucky enough to find this great little tailor who flies in from London four times a year— Oh, Nimoy, we'll need those ears back too, I'm afraid.

[*He pulls off the tips of Spock's ears and pockets them.*]

McCoy: For God's sake, man, we're on a five-year mission to explore space, the final frontier, and dammit, we've only been out three years!

Goodman: Sorry, but it's those Nielsens. If it was up to me, of course…

Kirk: What are these "Nielsens" that the alien keeps mentioning, Mr. Spock?

Spock: If I remember my history correctly, Captain, Nielsens were a primi-

Dan Aykroyd, John Belushi, Chevy Chase, and Elliott Gould

tive system of estimating television viewers once used in the mid-twentieth century.

McCoy: If Man were meant to fly, he'd have better ratings, is that what you're saying, Mr. Goodbody, whatever your name is? Come on, George, Nichelle, let's go tie one on.

Uhura: I'm with you, Kelley.
Sulu: Maybe I'll just go home.
Kirk: Belay that kind of talk, Doctor McCoy.

McCoy: Forget it, Bill. We lost. It's over. Are you coming, Leonard?
[Spock tries nerve pinch on McCoy]
McCoy: Knock it off, you joker!
Kirk: Wait, Mr. Spock. We have yet to try Vulcan mind meld, where you actually enter the alien's brain, merge with his intelligence, and read his thoughts.
Spock: I entered Mr. Goodman's mind while you were talking to Dr. McCoy, Captain.
[Curtis enters, not really noticed, and starts to pry apart the set with a crowbar.]
Spock: It was all…all dark and empty in there. And…and there were little mice in the corners and spiders had spun this web—
Kirk: Spock!
Spock: I kept bumping my head on the ceiling, and once—
Kirk: Snap out of it, Spock!
Spock [With a shudder]: It's okay, Captain. I'm all right now.
Goodman: What do you think, Curtis? Any chance we can sell this junk to "Lost in Space"?
Curtis: Well, it all comes apart.
Kirk: Hey, get away from there!
Curtis: Right on, Buck Rogers! Is that an order?
Kirk: No, it can't end like this. I won't let it! This is my ship! I give the orders here! I give the commands! I am responsible for the lives of 430 crewmen, and I'm not going to let them down! There's got to be a way out!
Curtis: Let's go, boys!
[Enter five or six NBC stage-hands who start taking set apart.]
Spock: You are becoming quite emotional, Captain. Needless to say, my trained Vulcan mind finds such open displays of emotion distasteful. Emotion, you see, interferes with logic, and it is only by dealing with problems in a logical, scientific fashion that we can arrive at valid solutions. Now, with regard to the alien takeover of the Enterprise, I would suggest that we seek some new alternative, based upon exact computer analysis, of course, and taking into consideration elements of—
[Suddenly breaks down into sobbing wacko] Oh, God! I don't believe it! We're cancelled! How could they do this? Everybody I know loves the show! I have a contract! What about my contract! I want my ears back!
Goodman: Curtis, can you give me a hand here?
Curtis: I have a couple Valium in my tool box. Maybe that'll help.
Kirk: So it's just me, is it? Well, I've been in tougher spots. Surrender? No way. I'd rather go down with the ship.
Goodman: Oh, Shatner, your agent called you. Something about a margarine commercial. He said he'd call back.
Kirk: Captain's log, final entry. We have tried to explore strange new worlds, to seek out new civilizations, to boldly go where no man has gone before. And except for one television network, we have found intelligent life every where in the galaxy. Live long and prosper. Captain James T. Kirk, SC 937-0176 CEC.
[Pull back to show him alone in what is now obviously a set in a TV studio, with some of set broken up and one piece turned around so one can read "Star Trek Bridge #4" crudely painted on the back. Continue pulling back to show cameras, booms, technicians.]

AIRED: MAY 29, 1976

Baba Wawa

1 Baba Wawa tells why she left NBC for her new five-million-dollar deal at ABC: "Tom Snyduh. I simpwy cannot see his eahs. Have you eveh noticed that? It's the way the man weahs his haih. Wight ovuh his eahs. It looks like he cuts his haih in Howwand owa something." And when will her new job start? "As soon as I learn to pwonounce Hawwy Weasoneh."

2 Tonight's guest is "an actuah wiving wegend—the incwedibuh Mahweena Doitchwand" (Madeline Kahn). What is it wike to be a wiving wegend? "It has been a weawwy wich experience."

Baba is impwessed and wants to know how Mahweena stays so swim. "Swimming keeps me swim. My daiwy wegimen incwudes me swimming twewve waps in my poow, and it's wonduhfuh foh my wegs." Apparently, she's also "had evwything wifted"—even her "wegs" and "weah."

3 "I wiv to diwect, I diwect to wiv." Tonight's guest is the bwiyant and pwowific filmmaker Weena Wutmyuwwah (Laraine Newman). Weena concludes: "I want you in my next film, saying the word 'pwowetawianism' over and over again. Of course you must gain two hundred pounds. You *will* gain two hundred pounds. You will be an obese, grotesque pig with stretch marks—obscene, repulsive, disgusting cow. You will be so fat, it will be *hilarious*!" Baba reminds her that she's "awweady unduh contwact."

4 "Hewwo. This is Baba Wawa. This is my wast moment on NBC. I want to wemind you to wook fow me awong with Hawwy Weasoneh weeknights at seven o'cwock. I want to take this oppuhtunity to apowogize to NBC. I don't wike weaving; pwease twust me, it's not sowah gwapes. But watheh, that anothuh netwohk wecognizes in me a gweat tawent fowah dewivvuhwing wehwevent news stowies with cwysah cwawity to miwwions of Amewicans. It's the onwy weason I'm weaving. Weawwy."

5 Guest Indiwa Gandhi, pwime ministuh of powiticawwy twoubuhd India (Laraine Newman), faces a grilling: "Indiwa, wet's be fwank. Is India today democwatic?" The PM replies: "In the past eighteen months I have heard not a single whimper of complaint. Oh, maybe one or two feeble little peeps, but no complaints." Baba asks if she knows she has a pimento on her forehead; Indira demands that the "untouchable one" keep her fingers away.

BABA WAWA AT LARGE

6 Baba interviews the candidates for First Lady "in a fwee-fowm fowum, fwank and fwiendly, whewe we weawwy welate." Does either one still sleep with her husband? Betty Ford (Jane Curtin) answers: "After lunch, before dinner, in elevators, behind big statues—I'm sleeping with my husband whenever I can." Rosalynn Carter (Laraine Newman) is equally forthright: "As you know, my husband and I lust after each other in our minds." Eventually Baba concludes: "I mean weawwy, who does deserve to be Fiwst Wady? Me. Baba Wawa. Fiwst Wady of Tewevision."

7 Tonight "we have the gweatwy wespected and wuhld-wenowned cweatoh of shuttuwe dipwomacy. Sometimes contwavewsial, but to my mind, a weawwy weguwah guy. Secwetawy of State Henwy Kissinjuh (John Belushi)." Baba asks about a statement attributed to him: "Powuh is the gweatest aphwodisiac." Well, yes, he explains: "Have you ever sat in a nuclear warhead?" The year 1973 was his high point—"when I won the Nobel Peace Prize for ending the Vietnam War." His low point? "1975, when the Vietnam War ended."

8 Baba is at home, "which you aww saw on my wast speciaw, and you weawwy wiked a wot, wemembew?" For her next special, instead of wasting time with extraneous personalities like the president, she interviews someone she respects: "me." There will be a rare opportunity to see some of her favorite trinkets: "My wings, my wugs, my dwapes, my wecods, my pwants, my wipstick, also my wange. Also my wadiator, my wadio, my wecowd pwayew, my waincoat, my nasal aspiwatoh, and my best fwiend, Wita Taywor."

9 Baba interviews the Asian film star Godziwwa (John Belushi). "You know, a lot of people think I'm from Japan or a Muppet, but I'm Hawaiian. I was born in a crater off the coast of Oahu." Apparently his egg was hatched by wawmth of a wava fwow duwing a vowcanic ewuption.

10 Baba interviews "the man mawwied wongest to Wiz Taywuh, Mr. Wichawd Buwton (Bill Murray).

But wet's get down to bwass tacks. A wot of peopuh awe cuwious to know, awe you still a wush who dwinks wike a jewwyfish?" Moving on: "You wed and woved Ewizabeth Taywuh. You showuhed huhw with emewawds and wubies, the wawgest wock in the wuhwld. What was Ewizabeth Taywuh weawwy wike, Wichawd?" "Intelligent, talented, and a very hot tomato."

11 Baba recently accompanied Egyptian president Anwar Sadat on his visit to Israel, and now she is quizzed by Weekend Update anchors Dan Aykroyd and Jane Curtin. Jane wants to know the situation there: "The'we tweating me tewifficawwy! They fwew me fiwst-cwass, and they put me up in the Jewusawem Howiday Inn—only hewe we caww it the High Howiday Inn. That's a wittle Iswaewi joke." For her sign-off, as they say in Isweal: *Shawom!*

12 "There's a woman to see you," Henry Higgins (Christopher Lee) is told, "and I can't understand

Gilda Radner and Burt Reynolds

a word she's saying." It's Baba Wawa! "You must be Henwy Higgins, wuhwd wenowned winguist!" She goes on to explain: "Baba Wawa could become as big as Waltew Cwonkite—if I could only leawn to talk cowwectwy!" She repeats after him: "The wain in Spain stays mainwy in the pwain." But she's hopeless, and after a couple of weeks Higgins takes on her impediment: "I've wuined youwah caweeah!"

13 In "The Pepsi Syndrome" a spilled cola results in nuclear catastrophe. Baba Wawa appears wive from Two Mile Island's nucweaw weactow site, where wumows are wunning wampant that the pwesident has been exposed to weethaw wevvehs of wadiation and has gwown to incwedibwy widicuwous pwopowtions. He's weawwy, weawwy wawge.

14 From Panama it's "A Christmas Gift from the Shah (Bill Murray) and His Friends." "Hello! My name is Mohammad Reza Pahlevi, but you know me by just my short name, Shah." Panamanian strongman Omar Torrijos (Tom Davis) gives the Shah a piñata in the shape of the Ayatollah, filled with Chiclets and Demerol. Meanwhile, Anwar Sadat (Garrett Morris) and Baba Wawa "twim the twee with fifty wittle Amewican fwags." Baba sings "Wudowf the Wed-Nosed Weindeewh."

15 Baba is with a man who has been wabeled a wecwuse, a wenegade, and a webewh: Mahwon Bwando (Burt Reynolds). Baba asks about his Indian name, which translates literally to "Flesh Balloon of the Deep." Then she joins him under the covuhs ("I wove the way winen feews on the wegs"). Baba wraps it up: "Is Bwando stiww gwowing? Is he stwetching himsewf as an actuh or mewhewee, wittewawwy, as a bag of fwesh? Owa someday, wiww we see Mahwon Bwando fwoating wayziwee ovuh the Supuh Boww with the wowds 'Good Yeaw' pwinted on his wump?"

FIRST AIRED: APRIL 24, 1976

John Belushi and Gilda Radner

The Widettes

Betty: We're having macaroni and cheese in about five minutes.

Jeff: OK. But I'm going to have a couple of Ho-Ho's to tide me over. [*Jeff exits.*]

Betty: Honestly, I don't know where he puts it.

BETTY WIDETTE PLAYED BY JANE CURTIN

JEFF WIDETTE PLAYED BY JOHN BELUSHI

BOB WIDETTE PLAYED BY DAN AYKROYD

AIRED: DECEMBER 16, 1978

Dan Aykroyd. John Belushi. and Jane Curtin

Dan Aykroyd

Julia Child

Oh, now I've done it—I've cut the dickens out of my finger. Well, I'm glad in a way this has happened. We have never really discussed what to do. First we must stop the bleeding. The best way is to put pressure on the apron like so, then raise your hand above your head so the blood doesn't pump all the way up...

PLAYED BY DAN AYKROYD

AIRED: DECEMBER 9, 1978

Franken and Davis

Mr. California: Hi, I'm Brad Gutner, a business undergraduate at Death Valley State College. In the summer I work for the Boraxo company, where I teach handicapped children to drive the 20-mule team. My watchwords can be found in the last four letters of American: I can.

Mr. Arkansas: Hi. My name's Lyle Kadonia. I'm a speech therapy major, I plan to be a speech therapist and teach handicapped children speech therapy, because I believe that speech therapy can better help people to better understand each other.

MR. CALIFORNIA PLAYED BY TOM DAVIS

MR. ARKANSAS PLAYED BY AL FRANKEN

AIRED: SEPTEMBER 24, 1977

Tom Davis and Al Franken

Laraine Newman, Dan Aykroyd, and Jane Curtin

Beldar: I am Beldar. This is Prymaat. We are emissaries from the planet Remulak, which is located many light-years outside of this solar system. Twenty Earth years ago the five High Masters of Remulak dispatched a fleet of starcruisers to this solar system—

Connie: Starcruisers?

Beldar: Metallic disks powered by an anti-gravity-field reactor.

Prymaat: Flying saucers, dear.

Connie: Oh, come on, you guys, there's no such thing as flying saucers.

Beldar: Your mother and I were instructed to pilot our machine to Earth, seize all major centers of radio and television communications and inform the people of Earth that we of the planet Remulak were taking over their world.

Prymaat: Your father was to make it clear to the Earth people that the two of us were to be called "the Timekeepers," that we would remain here for seven centuries, that we were to end all wars, that the Earth weapons were useless against us, and that they would destroy them if they did not follow our instructions.

Connie: I ask you, then...what happened?

Beldar: I lost the speech I was supposed to make. I had a

speech: "People of Earth. I am the Timekeeper from the planet Remulak. Your weapons are useless against us…" I lost the rest of it. The instructions, times, dates, place, orders for the UN. I don't know where. I lost it.

Connie: But—but what became of your flying saucer?

Prymaat: It's at the bottom of Lake Michigan.

Beldar: Your mother was at the control panel.

Prymaat: No, it was you who was guiding us.

Beldar: No, my dear, you were responsible for the control—

Connie: But did your planet not send a rescue ship for you?

Beldar: Well, our planet cut back on their space program, and I had to get a job here on Earth as a driving instructor.

Prymaat: In order to be less obvious on Earth we took the names Fred and Joyce Conehead.

Beldar: And then, my dear, you were born. And when your little cone was shown to us, we knew we had to stay here on Earth. We named you Connie.

Prymaat: And besides, the schools are better here.

Beldar: I took out a mortgage on this house. Your mother joined a few clubs. Perhaps one day the High Masters of our planet will dispatch a fleet of starcruisers to rescue us.

Prymaat: But until then just do all your homework and tell everyone you come from France.

The Coneheads

Now the Coneheads live in a comfortable, colonial-style suburban home in Parkwood Hills, New Jersey. They're just like any other family—except for their large heads. Beldar (Dan Aykroyd) and his wife, Prymaat (Jane Curtin), may sound detached but they live with zest: "Consume mass quantities!" is their robotic cry. Their diet ranges from human favorites like "starched disks with vegetable matter and molten lactate extract of hooved mammals sprinkled with fish flesh" (i.e., anchovy pizzas) to items best appreciated by Remulakian taste buds, such as

insect repellent strips and fiberglass insulation. A six-pack or two washes everything down.

Carnal appetites are indulged with furry senso-rings—providing daughter Connie (Laraine Newman) is not around, which is often, since, like any teen, she has "absorbed all the knowledge there is to know," and enjoys "interacting" with her human friends. Prymaat is resourceful when it comes to the failure of earthling methods: "If you want to do something right, use your own cone."

The Life and Times of the Coneheads:

1 Connie reports that telling friends she is from France "is an insufficient answer." She has a date with Ronnie Getsetter (Bill Murray), and when he arrives the Coneheads display the normal hospitality: "Would you like to satiate yourself with some beer and potato chips?" Instructed to "return at the time coordinates we have agreed upon," the kids are off—leaving the parents to "play some ringtoss."

2 The door signal rings, and IRS agent Eli Turnbull (Steve Martin) appears: "Is this the Con Ed residence?" He has questions about some of their deductions: "You claimed two thousand dollars for stocking caps, seven thousand dollars for beer, and two thousand dollars for titanium." Their strangeness scares him off, and once again they play ringtoss: "You have stimulated me! You have stimulated me! You have stimulated me!"

3 The Coneheads' neighbors, Bobbi (Gilda Radner) and Larry "the Farb" Farber (John Belushi), have invited them over. They look at family pictures from Disney World, which, Connie explains, is "a vast man-made construction which duplicates human psychosexual experiences through tension-releasing fantasy mechanisms." They play a game of Scrabble, but the Coneheads insist on using French words like *sebfarg* and *alatu*: "Larry doesn't know French words because he's a salesman." And when Larry displays his wares—an old-fashioned, cone-shaped hair dryer—the Coneheads jump out the window in terror.

4 A telephone repairman (Elliott Gould) arrives to install thirty-five extensions. "We need them. We are from France," Prymaat says. But in reality, the devices are useless to them—except that "the bonding polymers and the paint are a nutritional delicacy."

Merkon, the High Master's messenger (Garrett Morris), makes a surprise visit and the Coneheads are eager for news: "Did the Blackfarbs win the Protoid Bowl?" "No, the Barkolians kicked their cones! Ha-ha!" Beldar is told they can go home in one hundred and twenty-five Earth years: "We'll have to start packing soon." The telephone man finds senso-rings under Connie's bed, and she is sent directly to her sleeping chamber and denied the privilege of consuming mass quantities.

5 Dr. Ray Blondish (Buck Henry) of the Air Force Aerospace Defense Command appears with a metallic pyramid that "fell from the sky into the parking lot of a Taco Bell in downtown Tucson." The space object is addressed to Beldar. It's an emergency message, directing the Coneheads to return to Remulak.

They fly home in the Chrysler Building and bear gifts for their leader: "This substance is known as beer. Suck back a couple of these." High Master Kuldroth (John Belushi) has chosen Connie as his genetic mate. "Why get married?" she says. "Let's just get it on." Indeed, her cone has already been honed, and Kuldroth denounces her as "nothing more than a common *flathrag.*"

6 It's Halloween, a "miserable Earth festival" for "human young ones who move through the night demanding small consumables." The Coneheads dispense handfuls of fried eggs and six-packs of beer to the little

humans. Neighbors Carl (Bill Murray) and Sharleen Van Arsdale (Gilda Radner) are "extremely upset to find six-packs of brewski in the children's trick-or-treat bags." But they dismiss it as a quirky French custom, and are invited to stay by the Coneheads: "We will honor your Halloween ritual by paying homage to the symbolic vegetable orb."

7 The Coneheads face the Mels (Joe, played by Steve Martin; Mrs. Mel, played by Gilda Radner; and Joe junior, played by John Belushi) on *Family Feud.* Host Richard Dawson (Bill Murray) asks, "Name something people like to bite." Beldar's answer, "protoid capsules," falls short, but Prymaat scores well with "organically inactive meat or vegetable matter between two starched planes" (sandwich), and Connie hits with "the big one." Joe is bitter: "Well, we knew they'd win when we saw the size of their heads." But the bonus round doesn't go quite as well:

Dawson: All right, name a famous explorer.
Beldar: Zythron the Insistent.
Dawson: The biggest holiday of the year?
Beldar: The Moons of Meepzor.
Dawson: A place you keep your valuables?
Beldar: In a muldroth ion field.
Dawson: A mode of transportation?
Beldar: The foam shoe.
Dawson: Something you eat with eggs?
Beldar: Fiberglass.

Jane Curtin, Steve Martin, and Dan Aykroyd

10 It's colder than a *larckors mip* and the Coneheads are in a bad mood. "There is no human custom which says the female spousal unit may not collect the tree particles." Frank Zappa appears to take Connie to one of his concerts ("a voluntary gathering of humans to absorb sound patterns"). Connie is embarrassed: "Excuse my parental units if they have presented square doctrines." Zappa can't help laughing his way through the sketch; and when he and Connie leave, Beldar and Prymaat eat his records: "What fine compressed petroleum binding polymers."

11 The Coneheads take in a triple sci-fi feature. Fellow patron John Belushi shares his joint with Beldar, who takes a huge drag, consuming a gram of hash in one toke. "Enjoyable plant fibers." Beldar gets the munchies, and then he starts laughing uncontrollably. "Oh, no, Daddy's freaking" ("Inappropriate social behavior induced by the mass consumption of psychoactive substances"). The usher kicks them out.

12 Lorne Michaels previews "The New Coneheads," returning next season, once again with Beldar (Phil Hartman), Prymaat (Nora Dunn), and Connie (Victoria Jackson). They still come from France: "Yeah, that's the ticket. We're from France." Lorne boasts, "Their cones, I might add, are bigger than ever....Of course, a lot has changed since we did the original Coneheads. Times are more complex, and today we have the duty to inform as well as entertain. So we won't shy away from serious issues we feel the Coneheads should speak out on." These issues include Beldar's alcoholism. Lorne reads a testimonial letter from Dan Aykroyd ("I just wanted to offer my seal of approval to 'The New Coneheads' ").

We are from France.

FIRST AIRED: JANUARY 15, 1977

8 Beldar is having an affair with human Jill Clayburgh: "I've never been with anyone from France before." When Prymaat asks Beldar why he comes home late, he says, "A large meteorite fell from the sky. I stopped to examine it." Apparently, that's the third meteorite this month. She catches him red-coned—literally—and with senso-rings behind his back. But then she gets a phone call from Jerry; apparently, she has been with a human as well. They make up, and hone "right here on the floor."

9 Kuldroth is coming for an inspection, and Beldar and Prymaat's cones are on the block: "You said the High Master would not visit us for at least three hundred years!" Kuldroth notes that Connie is "growing into a beautiful *krotmar*." Of course, he and Merkon want to see the *meevgun* marshes for stocking the starcruisers and the fuel ports for the protoid pumps. Meanwhile, Richard Dreyfuss arrives at the house, in the midst of a *Close Encounters* quest. The Coneheads pass Dreyfuss off as the Supreme Refueling Attendant for the protoid station on Earth, and he is sent to Remulak for training.

Theodoric of York

Featuring William (Dan Aykroyd), Theodoric (Steve Martin), Brungilda (Gilda Radner), Joan (Jane Curtin), Isabelle (Laraine Newman), Hunchback (John Belushi), and Drunkard (Bill Murray).

Voiceover: In the Middle Ages medicine was still in its infancy. The art of healing was conducted not by physicians but by barbers. The medieval barbers were the forerunners of today's men of medicine, and many of the techniques they developed are still practiced today. This is the story of one such barber.

William: Hello, Theodoric of York. Well, it's springtime, and I've come for my haircut and bloodletting.

Theodoric: Hello, William, Son of Malcolm the Tanner. Have a seat. Brungilda, you start on William's hair, and I'll open a vein here.

Brungilda: Yes, Theodoric.

Theodoric: How's that baby I delivered last Christmas when your wife died?

William: Oh, the little fellow is deformed.

Theodoric: Oh, that's right, I remember now.

[*Theodoric takes a medieval scalpel and "cuts" William's vein. William bleeds into bowl.*]

William: Ahhh . . .

Voiceover: And now it's time for another episode of…"Theodoric of York, Medieval Barber."

Theodoric: There you go. Looks like I have another patient. I'll be back in a minute to see how you're doing.

William: Right. Thank you.

Joan: Hello, Theodoric, Barber of York.

Theodoric: Hello, Joan, Wife of Simkin the Miller. Well, how's my little patient doing?

Joan: Not so well, I fear. We followed all your instructions: I mixed powder of staghorn, gum of arabic with sheep's urine, and applied it in a poultice to her face.

Theodoric: And did you bury her up to her neck in the marsh and leave her overnight?

Joan: Oh, yes. But she still feels as listless as ever, if not more.

Theodoric: Well, let's give her another bloodletting. Brungilda—

Brungilda: Yes, Theodoric.

Theodoric: —take two pints.

Brungilda: Yes, Theodoric.

Joan: Will she be all right, Barber?

Theodoric: Well, I'll do everything humanly possible. Unfortunately, we barbers aren't gods. You know, medicine is not an exact science, but we are learning all the time. Why, just fifty years ago, they thought a disease like your daughter's was caused by demonic possession or witchcraft. But nowadays we know that Isabelle is suffering from an imbalance of bodily humors, perhaps caused by a toad or a small dwarf living in her stomach.

Joan: Well, I'm glad she's in such good hands.

Hunchback: Is this Theodoric, Barber of York?

Steve Martin, Bill Murray, John Belushi, and Laraine Newman

Theodoric: Say, don't I know you?

Hunchback: Sure, you worked on my back.

Theodoric: What's wrong with your friend here?

Hunchback: He broke his legs.

Drunkard: I was at the festival of the vernal equinox and I guess I had a little bit too much mead and I darted out in front of an oxcart. It all happened so fast, they couldn't stop in time.

Theodoric: Well, you'll feel a lot better after a good bleeding.

Drunkard: But I'm bleeding already.

Theodoric: Say, who's the barber here?

Drunkard: Okay, okay. Just do something for my legs.

Theodoric: Well, the three of us'll get you

up on the gibbet here….Okay. Now this is gonna hurt a little. What we're doing is separating your broken bones…and if you don't feel better tomorrow, we'll just cut his legs off about here.

Drunkard: Okay. I'm pretty sure I'm gonna feel better tomorrow.

Theodoric: I guess this will teach you to go easy on the mead. Brungilda, put a few leeches on his forehead.

Drunkard: Thank you.

Theodoric [to William]: When was the last time you came in for a worming?

William: I guess I'm due, but I don't have the time today. Please accept my payment—this fine, fat goose.

Theodoric: Thank you. Brungilda will give you your change….So how's the little patient doing?

Joan: She's worse. She's looking pale.

Theodoric: Well, if she's not responding to treatment, I'm afraid we'll have to run some more tests. Brungilda, bring me the Caladrius bird.

Joan: Caladrius bird?

Theodoric: Yes. The Caladrius bird is placed beside a patient. If the bird looks at the patient's face, she will live; but if it looks at her feet, she will die. Okay now, Freddy, c'mon out. [*Bird flies out of cage.*] I don't know how to interpret that. Did you see, Brungilda?

Brungilda: No.

Theodoric: Well, I guess, take another pint from Isabelle, and while you're at it, take two pints from the bird.

Brungilda: She's dead.

Joan: Dead! Dead! I can't believe it! My little daughter dead!

Theodoric: Now, Mrs. Miller. You're distraught, tired; you may be suffering from nervous exhaustion. I think you'd feel better if I let some of your blood.

Joan: You charlatan! You killed my daughter, just like you killed most of my other children. Why don't you admit it? You don't know what you're doing.

Theodoric: Wait a minute. Perhaps she's right. Perhaps I've been wrong to blindly follow the medical traditions and superstitions of past centuries. Maybe we barbers should test those assumptions analytically, through experimentation and a "scientific method." Maybe this scientific method could be extended to other fields of learning: the natural sciences, art, architecture, navigation. Perhaps I could lead the way to a new age, an age of rebirth, a Renaissance. [*He thinks for a minute.*] Nah!

Voiceover: Tune in next week for another episode of "Theodoric of York, Medieval Barber," when you'll hear Theodoric say…

Theodoric: A little bloodletting and some boar's vomit and he'll be fine.

AIRED: APRIL 22, 1978

> ## "*I write the songs that make the whole world sing...I write the notes and the words and eeeeverythiiiiing.*"

A self-described "kinda fun guy," Nick (Bill Murray) is the Mr. Versatile of show business. He'll sing anywhere, and he can sing any song with his own unique stylings. His last name changes with every appearance, depending upon the location: He's Nick Winters at the ski lodge; Nick Rails on the Auto Train. His regulars include accompanist Paul (Paul Shaffer) and Jimmy Joe Red Sky (Dan Aykroyd)—"He's an Indian, and they *don't* lie, I love that"—who always seems to be working wherever Nick appears.

Bill Murray, Laraine Newman, and Buck Henry

Nick's Career:

1 It's Happy Hour in the Zephyr Room at beautiful Lake Minnehonka's Breezy Point Lodge, and Nick Summers salutes couples who are celebrating their anniversaries: "Mrs. Alquist (Gilda Radner), do you still love him as much as you ever did?" She answers, "Yes, I do." "If you had it all to do over again, would you do it?" "No." "Is there a song I can sing for you?" "No!"

Waterskiing instructor Skeeter Miller (Elliott Gould) is sitting with a "pretty young miss," Mrs. Campbell (Laraine Newman), who brusquely confirms that her husband is laid up with a broken ankle.

Paul plays the "Catch of the Day" fanfare as fishing and snowmobile instructor Jimmy Joe Red Sky presents a big fish. "I *am* a fun guy," Nick reminds his audience, "and I hope that you had fun tonight. And there's one thing I'd like you to remember: '*Sing...*'—that's right!—'*Sing a sooooong*'—this is my seventh summer up here! '*Make it simple....*'"

2 Nick Winters is at the Powder Room up here at Meatloaf Mountain. He spots "a cute little girl" (Gilda Radner) with a cast on her leg and signs it with his standard inscription: "Don't eat yellow snow." Nick identifies hostile "celebrity" Heinz Kleimer (Elliott Gould), head of the ski school, here with a "pretty snow muffin" hiding her face (Laraine Newman): "My husband is exhausted and *I don't ski.*" She has no requests, but Nick knows "there's only one way anybody likes it, and that's with plenty of snow! '*That's the way, uh-huh, uh-huh, I like it, uh-huh, uh-huh!*'"

Jimmy Joe Red Sky brings both a weather report and a porcupine hit by his Sno-Cat. Nick leaves the "powder animals" with a theme from a hit movie: "*Star Wars/Nothing but Star Wars/Gimme those Star Wars/Don't let them end.*"

Nick the

Bill Murray

Lounge Singer

3 Nick Springs is at the Honeymoon Room of the Pocomount. A newly married couple, the Shoemers (John Belushi and Gilda Radner), sit in; they are covered in calamine lotion—victims of nude sunbathing gone awry.

Nick finds "*Mrs.* Liebowitz" (Laraine Newman): "Oh, are you the wife of the man who injured himself when he slipped in the heart-shaped tub?" She's with "this crazy nut," Jeff Greenspoon (Richard Dreyfuss), the guy who booked Nick. "You know, Jeff is a Jew, but he's always been more than fair with me." He sings them a special "Hava Nagila."

Groundskeeper Jimmy Joe Red Sky appears with a stiff squirrel: "I was cleanin' out the pool and I found dis guy in the filter. I put in lots of chlorine so don't open your eyes under water for a few days."

4 "*I've been through the desert on a horse with no name*": Nick Sands entertains at Sands Strip North Oasis, "located here on Nevada 287, which of course feeds into 15A, which winds down into Las Vegas and is therefore technically the Strip through the Strip North—hence the Strip North." Nick is a twenty-percent owner of the Strip

Gilda Radner, Kirk Douglas, and Bill Murray

North: "Right now I'm doing my twenty percent for you people." Jimmy Joe "Ten Percent" Red Sky appears with a snake he backed over.

5 "My name's Nick Rails and I'll be your entertainment, like it or lump it, all the way to Orlando." Nick mingles on the Auto Train with army urologist Dr. Rye Slate (Dan Aykroyd), to whom Nick dedicates the theme from *M*A*S*H*. Nick asks the Saulfreys (John Belushi and Laraine Newman), "What car do you drive?" He then observes: "You know, I'm fascinated by how many Jews drive German cars. When they showed *Holocaust*, I had a Volkswagen, but the next morning I went out and threw up all over it. Had to get rid of it. And I'm not even Jewish."

6 " *Hey! You! Get ooooff of my cloud'*—and stay off!" The setting is TransEastern's VIP lounge, "where the special people get the other people off of their cloud." Celebrities include Pearl Bailey (Garrett Morris), traveling with Mrs. Bob Hope (Maureen Stapleton). "Gosh, what a pleasure," Nick Wings burbles, " *'Thaaaaanks for the memories'*—Go ahead, finish it!" Mrs. Hope doesn't know the words.

"I adore *Heart Like a Wheel*!" he screams at Linda Ronstadt. "And I adore you! Look at that cute little schnozzola!" Her bodyguard (John Belushi) knocks Nick down. The flight boards as Nick's "Scarborough Fair" clears the room.

7 Nick Borealis winds up his tour of distant early-warning bases: "I must say the view here at Cape Farval will always be frozen in my memory. Ha!" His selections include "Papa Was a Rolling Stone": "Mine was, anybody else?" A career soldier causes Nick to wonder in song, *"War! Hooh! What is it good for? Absolutely nothing*." He comments on the long days and nights in Greenland—"Does anybody really know what time it is? Do any of you dudes care?"—before his special guests arrive: It's the Swankmates (Laraine Newman, Jane Curtin, and Gilda Radner)—"here by the good graces of the folks at *Swank* magazine."

8 A drunken Nick Collins works Greg Lieberman's Bar Mitzvah. Nick feared the crowd would be "a bunch of religious stiffs," but, he says, "nope—you guys are as nuts and screwed up as any of my buddies." He moves straight to his version of "There's No Business Like Show Business": *"There's no people, like the chosen people/There's no people I know.*"

9 Nick Lava plays Trader Nick's, "a little bit of Hawaii right here in the Buffalo and Niagara Falls area." The audience includes the Posniaks (Buck Henry and Laraine Newman), who are relocating from the Love Canal: "Ouch!" Nick quiets some rowdy high schoolers and meets the prom queen (Gilda Radner): "And how did you get to be senior prom queen?" he asks. "How did you get into show business?" she responds. "Well, I wasn't elected unanimously!" Nick says *aloha* with "Stairway to Heaven."

10 In the Paddlewheel Lounge of the *Riverboat Queen*, Nick Rivers apologizes about the engine trouble that will keep the passengers away from New Orleans: "But hey! *I* think the Mardi Gras we had in Cincinnati at the dock was just as good, and I mean that."

Nick sends complimentary weenies to the women before bursting into an energetic rendition of "Celebration." Why? The American hostages in Iran were released this year.

11 *"Everybody have fun tonight./Everybody Wang Chung tonight!"* Nick Slammer plays the Crestwood Minimum Security Prison Detention Center and Warehouse: "I never had a warmer reception, and if you're talking about a debt to society, as far as Nick Slammer is concerned, you guys have paid it in full." Nick meets Gerry Clark (Kevin Nealon) and his "bitch," Ivan Boesky (Jon Lovitz). Gerry and Ivan are kind of shy in public, but *"when they get behiiiind cloooosed dooooooors…."*

Nick introduces the "Head Screw," Warden Haney (Phil Hartman), and sings of him: *"Every breath you taaaaaake,/Every mooove you maaaaake,/ He'll be watching youuuuuu."*

FIRST AIRED: APRIL 16, 1977

Laraine Newman, Buck Henry, and Gilda Radner

Uncle Roy

Father Dan Aykroyd expresses misgivings: "Any forty-five-year-old who has nothing to do but babysit...I just think it's kind of weird, that's all."

UNCLE ROY PLAYED BY BUCK HENRY
AIRED: NOVEMBER 11, 1978

Garrett Morris, Dan Aykroyd, and Margot Kidder

Fred Garvin, Male Prostitute

No ifs, ands, or buts about it, you're spending the night—with Fred Garvin, Male Prostitute....I have a work order here that specifies that I am to roger you roundly 'til 6:15 in the morning.
PLAYED BY DAN AYKROYD
AIRED: MARCH 17, 1979

Gilda Radner, Bill Murray, Dan Aykroyd (center), Rick Nelson (right), and others

¡¿Quien Es Mas Macho?!

Paco: Question Numero Uno, Jorge, Graciela. ¿Quien es mas macho— Fernando Lamas...o Ricardo Montalban? ¿Fernando Lamas...o Montalban?
Jorge: ¿Ricardo Montalban?
Paco: ¿Ricardo Montalban es muy macho...porque?
Jorge: ¡Porque Cordoba es automobil muy macho!
Paco: No. Fernando Lamas es un paquito mas macho. Graciela? [*They kiss*] ¡Muy caliente! Questione bonus. La questione es en tres partes. Escucha bien. ¿Quien es mas macho? David Janssen, Lloyd Bridges, o Jack Lord. Repeto, David Janssen, Lloyd Bridges, o Jack Lord.
Eliot Ness: Okay, Paco—get your hands up and keep them there!
Paco: ¡Dios mio, es Eliot Ness!

PACO VALENZUELA PLAYED BY BILL MURRAY
JORGE LOPES PLAYED BY RICK NELSON
GRACIELA CORTES PLAYED BY GILDA RADNER
ELIOT NESS PLAYED BY DAN AYKROYD
AIRED: FEBRUARY 17, 1979

Mr. Mike

You know, in the past twenty, thirty years, we've seen a lot of rock and roll stars come and go. But there was one man, one man who stayed on top right from the very beginning, and I guess that's why they called him The King. Of course, I'm speaking about Mr. Elvis Presley. Yes! Yes! There was a man. You know, when Elvis died, I think a small piece of all of us died with him. I know that's how it was with me. I was home watching television the other afternoon, and I happened to catch *Spinout*, a great Presley movie with an incredible cast—Nancy Sinatra, Bill Bixby. I was watching this movie, and a funny thought occured to me. I thought, what if someone took steel needles— say, fifteen, eighteen inches long— and plunged them, plunged them into Elvis Presley's eyes. What would his reaction be? We can only guess—but I think it might go something like this.

MR. MIKE PLAYED BY MICHAEL O'DONOGHUE
AIRED: MAY 26, 1979

Michael O'Donoghue

John Belushi, Dan Aykroyd, and Garrett Morris

Miles Cowperthwaite

Miles: Captain Ned, I learned from my shipmates, was a very manly, virile, manful person, and a firm believer in strict discipline, corporal punishment, and nude apartment wrestling. If there were any doubts as to Captain Ned's severity, they were quickly dispelled that very afternoon, when a scuffle broke out on deck.
Spunk: That's my tanning spot! You, you're in my spot! That's my spot! Where's my towel?
Sailor #1: You are daft. I've been here all morning. Now run along, you are blocking my sun.
Spunk: Don't you give me any back-sass, you tan tease!
[*Ned breaks up the fight.*]
Ned: Is this how men act on a man's ship? Where is your manliness?
Spunk: Captain! I threw the first blow. If anyone is to be punished, let it be me. I ask only that whatever you do, please don't put me in a tight-fitting Lassie costume and make me eat from a monogrammed dog dish.
Sailor #2: Captain, I encouraged this fight, punish me. Make me wear nipple-pinching clothespins, sir.

MILES COWPERTHWAITE PLAYED BY MICHAEL PALIN
FIRST MATE SPUNK PLAYED BY DAN AYKROYD
CAPTAIN NED PLAYED BY JOHN BELUSHI
SAILOR #1 PLAYED BY GARRETT MORRIS
SAILOR #2 PLAYED BY TOM DAVIS
AIRED: MAY 12, 1979

Festrunk Bro

Two wild and crazy guys, Georg (Dan Aykroyd) and Yortuk Festrunk (Steve Martin) are political refugees who escaped the 1975 riots in Bratislava by "throwing many rocks at a Russian tank." In Czechoslovakia they had medical degrees ("There, we were brain surgeons"), but now they have to work as salesmen. Their product: decorative bathroom fixtures.

They have many swinging hobbies and "enjoy a great deal many interests, like meeting girls and being next to their big American breasts." With their trademark look—loud unbuttoned polyester shirts and tight trousers—"it is certainly not difficult now for any women to notice our bul-ges." After all, they boast, "there is no other pair of Czechoslovakian brothers who cruise and swing so successfully in tight slacks."

Cliff (Garrett Morris) is their neighbor and swinging American buddy. He reminds the brothers of the Ethiopian engineering students they knew back in Bratislava, so they take to him fondly.

The Festrunks' Adventures:

1 The brothers try to pick up two women, Lynn (Jane Curtin) and Barb (Gilda Radner), who are playing Ping-Pong: "Not to be polite, but what are your names?"

Dan Aykroyd and Steve Martin

They start putting the moves on the foxes—"You young girls seem to know that we are talking to you in a very swinging way"—and make their version of small talk: "How much do you weigh?" The boys show off their disco dancing and go in for the kill: "You know, you American girls have such big breasts all the time!" "Well, I guess you must like us by now, so please give us the number of your apartment so we can go up and have sex with you right now."

Lynn suggests they meet somewhere first, at a place called the Holland Tunnel. Georg says confidently, "Of course, we swing there often." The brothers are told to go to the middle and wait by the guy in the glass booth. The girls promise to be there—"as soon as we slip into our big American breasts."

2 Two foxes, specially selected by a computer dating service, are coming to the bachelor pad tonight. As Yortuk says, "In America the most swinging people use computers to find others who will have sex with them."

Yortuk greets the women enthusiastically: "Take off your coats so we can see your big American breasts." And Georg says reassuringly, "Don't worry about birth control devices for sex, we have many." But these foxes are Croatian—the sisters, Bobka (Laraine Newman) and Bobsina (Jane Curtin), chaperoned by their uncle Kravosh (John Belushi). "Sorry to be placing a bum trip on *my*

ners

mind, but before having sex, you will be buying us an expensive meal and many Pepsis."

Female versions of Georg and Yortuk, the women immediately set their sights on Cliff. "I have just seen this black person who would be much better to swing with us in America," says Bobka. And Bobsina adds, "So now, we will be taking off your pants." As the girls ravage Cliff, the Festrunks and Uncle Kravosh hit the town, three wild and crazy guys.

3 Georg and Yortuk are expecting two hot models from the fox bar who are coming "to give themselves to the Festrunk brothers." Apparently they had to go to the Statue of Liberty first, where "the American park rangers distribute birth control devices." Georg laments, "Poor foxes, every time they are having sex they must go to the closest national monument."

Cliff tells them that they have been hosed. "Hosed, count me in!" cries the unwary Yortuk. Once Cliff explains, Yortuk understands: "We sure have a drag." "The Festrunk brothers do not cruise correctly for foxes," the saddened boys conclude, and vow never to swing again.

But the girls arrive after all, and it's the brothers' turn to console Cliff: "Many American girls enjoy you too. They enjoy your protruding buttocks all of the time."

4 The Festrunks complain to the bartender (Bill Murray) that all the chicks are frightened by their "bul-ges." They spot a group of women (Gilda Radner, Jane Curtin, Laraine Newman) and introduce themselves: "two swinging guys who enjoy doing many things and can come on to you now."

A swinging rap session ensues, with the brothers' famous mix of conversation starters: "Tell me, Debbie, when you have sex, are you loud?" Georg has brought along electrical devices to use for sex, namely, a Czechoslovakian "vibrating machine"—basically a drill with a pink feather duster attached to the end. The contraption scares the women, but he doesn't seem to notice: "So, aren't you getting hot yet?" After more chitchat Georg gets to the point: "We have talked long enough, let us choose partners for sex." And Yortuk says: "Here is something—look at our slacks. It is because of you that our pouches are stretching."

The women make a getaway, but the brothers take it in stride, since apparently they never had much success in Czechoslovakia either.

Fox-es!

First aired: September 24, 1977

Steve Martin, Dan Aykroyd, Jane Curtin, and Gilda Radner.

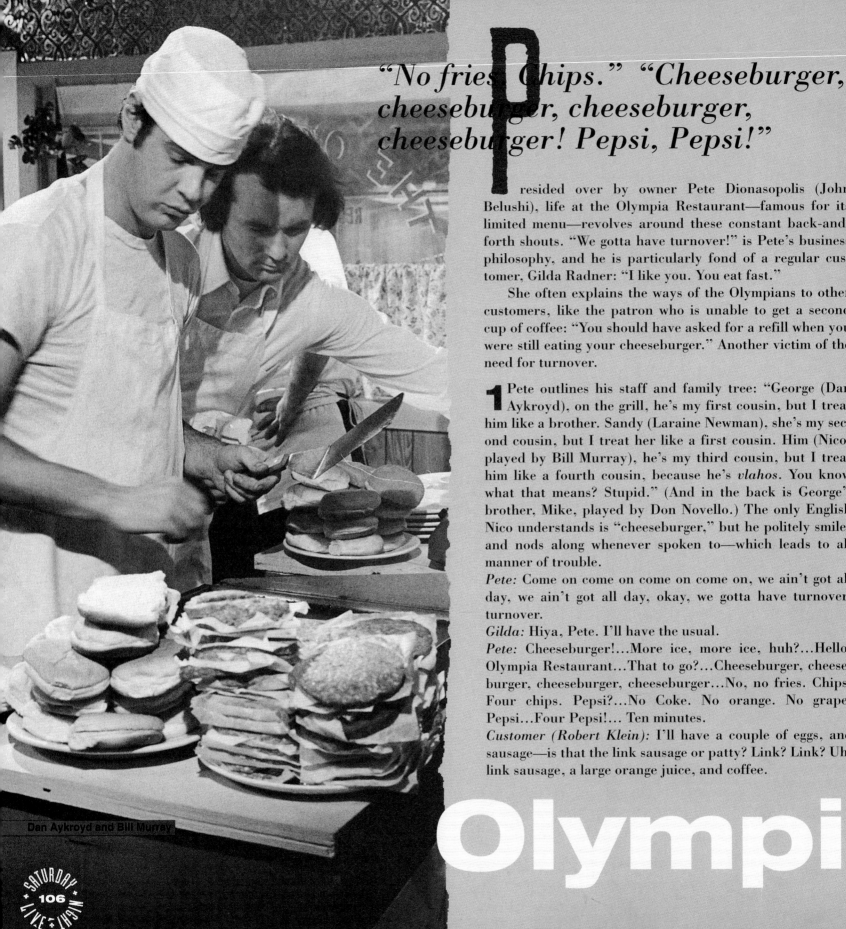

"No fries. Chips." "Cheeseburger, cheeseburger, cheeseburger! Pepsi, Pepsi!"

Presided over by owner Pete Dionasopolis (John Belushi), life at the Olympia Restaurant—famous for its limited menu—revolves around these constant back-and-forth shouts. "We gotta have turnover!" is Pete's business philosophy, and he is particularly fond of a regular customer, Gilda Radner: "I like you. You eat fast."

She often explains the ways of the Olympians to other customers, like the patron who is unable to get a second cup of coffee: "You should have asked for a refill when you were still eating your cheeseburger." Another victim of the need for turnover.

1 Pete outlines his staff and family tree: "George (Dan Aykroyd), on the grill, he's my first cousin, but I treat him like a brother. Sandy (Laraine Newman), she's my second cousin, but I treat her like a first cousin. Him (Nico, played by Bill Murray), he's my third cousin, but I treat him like a fourth cousin, because he's *vlahos*. You know what that means? Stupid." (And in the back is George's brother, Mike, played by Don Novello.) The only English Nico understands is "cheeseburger," but he politely smiles and nods along whenever spoken to—which leads to all manner of trouble.

Pete: Come on come on come on come on, we ain't got all day, we ain't got all day, okay, we gotta have turnover, turnover.

Gilda: Hiya, Pete. I'll have the usual.

Pete: Cheeseburger!...More ice, more ice, huh?...Hello, Olympia Restaurant...That to go?...Cheeseburger, cheeseburger, cheeseburger, cheeseburger...No, no fries. Chips. Four chips. Pepsi?...No Coke. No orange. No grape. Pepsi...Four Pepsi!... Ten minutes.

Customer (Robert Klein): I'll have a couple of eggs, and sausage—is that the link sausage or patty? Link? Link? Uh, link sausage, a large orange juice, and coffee.

Dan Aykroyd and Bill Murray

Olympia

Nico: Cheeseburger?

Customer: No, I don't want a cheeseburger. Eggs, couple of eggs, eggs—do you speak English? Eggs, couple of eggs, over lightly, with sausage, *café, café.*

Pete: No no no no—no eggs. Cheeseburger.

Customer: When do you stop serving breakfast?

Pete: Now. No breakfast.

Customer: No breakfast?

Pete: Nope.

Customer: I just want a couple of eggs.

Pete: No breakfast! Cheeseburger, huh?

Customer: Shut up. I don't want a cheeseburger.

Pete: Come on come on come on, don't give me that. Come on, let's go, let's go, we gotta have turnover. You want a cheeseburger, everybody got a cheeseburger, you want a cheeseburger? Come on, cheeseburger?

Customer: I don't want a cheeseburger. It's too early for a cheeseburger.

Pete: Too early for cheeseburger? Look—cheeseburger, cheeseburger, cheeseburger, cheeseburger, cheeseburger, cheeseburger, cheeseburger, cheeseburger, cheeseburger, cheeseburger, cheeseburger, cheeseburger, cheeseburger.

[*George throws thirteen cheeseburgers on the grill.*]

Pete: What do you want, what are you going to have?

Customer: I'll have a cheeseburger.

Pete: One cheeseburger.

George: No more cheeseburger.

Pete: No more cheeseburger.

Customer: I'll have a hamburger, then.

Pete: Hamburger.

George: No more hamburger.

Pete: No hamburger. No cheeseburger, no hamburger, no burger.

George: No cheeseburger, no hamburger, no burger.

Customer: How 'bout a couple of eggs, then?

Pete: Eggs.

Jane Curtin, Laraine Newman, Gilda Radner, and John Belushi

Customer: Over lightly?

Pete: Scrambled.

Customer: All right, scrambled.

Pete: And what to drink?

Customer: Coke.

Pete: No Coke, Pepsi.

Customer: All right, Pepsi.

Pete: One Pepsi!

Nico: One Pepsi!

2 Sandy trains a new waitress (Jill Clayburgh), whom Pete berates for ordering cheeseburgers incorrectly: "You don't say it right!" He tries to teach her, repeating the

Restaurant

5 We learn where the plunger is kept (under the counter) and how the Olympians keep bugs away. A customer (Garrett Morris) reports seeing "a roach about the size of a cat walk behind this napkin holder." Fresh bug spray soon coats food, air, and customers, while George crushes the stunned insect with his burger spatula. The regular customer, Gilda, announces her upcoming wedding, so Pete presents her with a free bag of chips: "I'll open them when I open the other gifts."

Coca-Cola salesman John Pittman (Walter Matthau) and the new area distributor Lambros "Lamb Roast" Petropopolous (Brian Doyle-Murray) speak to Nico about switching to Coke. Pittman "talks drachmas" to Nico, who lowers the price and seals a better deal with uncomprehending nods. The familiar refrain is now "No Pepsi, Coke. We switch!"

What you can't get at the Olympia Restaurant

No tuna. Cheeseburger?

No grilled cheese.

No orange today. Pepsi?

No club, no tea. Cheeseburger.

No grape.

No root beer.

No hamburger, cheeseburger.

word over and over again—and George keeps throwing more burgers on the grill. The trainee breaks down in hysterics, and a customer (Jane Curtin) asks, "Can somebody get her a glass of water?" "No water, Pepsi."

3 A customer (Jane Curtin) asks Pete how he cooks his burgers. "Good," he replies. "No, I mean, in what manner are they cooked?" "They are cooked *good*, what do you mean?" He's distracted when a lamb gets loose in the basement again. Al from Rent-a-Doberman (Buck Henry) tries to rent Pete some security, but the dogs are too expensive.

4 Everyone is sad: Pete is on his way back from Greece. In his absence, the restaurant has been redecorated—there is even a new mural by Nico. Furious, Pete throws out all the customers (among them, Ron Wood and Charlie Watts at the counter): "But we're not finished eating." Pete's car is then stolen with his wife in the backseat, not to mention his luggage. He wakes from his daze only to whack Nico with a menu.

6 After a fire the Olympia is limited to take-out service. Two policemen (Garrett Morris and Buck Henry) comment that the scent of burnt rubber might make the cafe "smell a little better than usual."

The insurance adjuster, Mrs. Laramore (Jane Curtin), arrives to a muted welcome: "I'm sorry, I thought maybe you were from the Health Board." Pete blames sparks for the fire, as he did five years ago with another fire. His losses include two hundred dollars for a picture of Spiro Agnew (autographed) and five hundred dollars in napkins. The adjuster asks about personal property—"umbrellas, golf clubs, anything like that?"—and Pete recalls his four-hundred dollar golf clubs. In fact, everybody lost golf clubs: "We all golf together after work. That's why we keep them here." Mrs. Laramore balks, however, upon learning that Nico lived in the back room. "Okay, forget about his golf clubs." The adjuster leaves and Pete is empty-handed, so he does the traditional thing: "We are Greeks. We dance."

FIRST AIRED: JANUARY 28, 1978

Lord and Lady Douchebag

Featuring a Noblewoman (Laraine Newman), a Nobleman (Peter Aykroyd), a Butler (Garrett Morris), Lord Worcestershire (James Downey), Lord Salisbury (Harry Shearer), Lord Wilkinson (Tom Davis), Lady Wilkinson (Jane Curtin), the Earl of Sandwich (Bill Murray), a Servant (Brian Doyle-Murray), Lord Douchebag (Buck Henry), and Lady Douchebag (Gilda Radner).

Noblewoman: What a splendid party. I do believe everyone of any importance in England is here tonight.

Nobleman: Who would miss a party given by Lord Salisbury?

Butler[Announcing]: Lord and Lady Wilkinson.

Lord Worcestershire: A marvelous entertainment, Salisbury. These chopped steaks are terrific, especially with this delicious mushroom sauce.

Salisbury: Thank you. Coming from you, Worcestershire, that certainly is a compliment. Lord and Lady Wilkinson, welcome.

Worcestershire: Tell me, Wilkinson, what the deuce is the purpose of two swords?

Wilkinson: It's simple, really. Let's say you're an attacker. My first blade straightens you upright, while the second clips you neatly at the ankles.

Lady Wilkinson: And there's

Lady Wilkinson, for attacking your opponent's underarms and legs.

Butler [Announcing]: The Earl of Sandwich.

Nobleman: Tell me, have you seen Lord Cardigan?

Noblewoman: I understand he was turned away at the door.

Nobleman: Lord Cardigan? Why, in heaven's name?

Noblewoman: He wasn't prop-

erly attired. Evidently he came in a sweater.

Nobleman: Odd. I saw Lord Ascot, and he got in.

Butler[Announcing]: The Duke and Duchess of Argyll.

Worcestershire: You know Sandwich, were the Sandwich Islands named after your family?

Sandwich: Oh no. Everyone asks me that, but I'm afraid nothing ever has been named after a member of my family.

Servant: Excuse me, your lordship, but would you care for one of Lord Salisbury's steaks?

Sandwich: Yes I would. Would you bring it to me with a couple slices of pumpernickel please?

Servant: Yes.

Butler [Announcing]: Lord and Lady Douchebag.

Salisbury: Well, well, well, I was just asking Lord Sandwich, "Where the devil are those Douchebags?"

Lady Douchebag: Well, it has been impossible to get him out

of his workshop. He has been working night and day.

Salisbury: You, Douchebag? Well, I wasn't aware you dabbled in that sort of thing. What in heaven's name are you working on?

Douchebag: Well, I would be happy to tell you, but perhaps after you have finished eating.

Salisbury: Well, here is Chambers right now. Would you like something to eat?

Douchebag: We're not too hungry right now—just a plate of raw vegetables.

Salisbury: Would you like some dressing with that?

Lady Douchebag: Just some vinegar and water, thank you.

Sandwich: Douchebag, how are you? I haven't seen you in the House of Lords in ages. Don't tell me for the first time in memory we are going to have a House of Parliament without a Douchebag?

Douchebag: My dear Sandwich, Parliament has always had its share of Douchebags and it always will.

Salisbury: Spoken like a true Douchebag. I have often heard the King speak of your family, and of yours as well: "Give me a Sandwich and a Douchebag, and there is nothing I cannot do."

Sandwich: Hear, hear.

Salisbury: So tell me, Douchebag, when are you going to show us that invention of yours?

Sandwich: Yes, Douchebag, just what kind of invention are you sitting on?

Douchebag: Well, it's a long story. Why don't we go out to the garden and I'll explain it to you.

Sandwich: Tell me, did Lady Douchebag help you in the project?

Douchebag: Help? Why, she was the inspiration.

AIRED: MAY 24, 1980

James Downey, Bill Murray, Brian Doyle-Murray, Harry Shearer, Buck Henry, and Gilda Radner

Lisa Loopner (Gilda Radner) and Todd DiLaMuca (Bill Murray) are nerds. She's known as Four Eyes, he's called Pizza Face, and the two are nearly inseparable. Lisa's a bit of a late developer; or as Todd puts it: "You really ought to put some Band-Aids on those mosquito bites you got there."

As for Todd, he knows his manners—"If I said *h-e-dou-ble-hockey-sticks* at home, my mom would beat the *c-r-a-*you-know-what outta me"—but he is often found applying various forms of special noogies onto Lisa's head. What's going on between the two of them? Todd, Lisa claims, is not her boyfriend: "He's a boy and he's a friend, but he's certainly not my boyfriend." Todd, though, is definitely "a Scorpio with hormones rising."

Mrs. Loopner (Jane Curtin) enjoys making egg salad: "It gives me pleasure. That and ironing contour sheets." Todd thinks she's repressed—"Her shoulders are up

The Nerds

around her ears"—but Lisa claims, "That's because her bra straps are too tight." Mr. Loopner, God rest his soul, died because "he was born without a spine—it was always just a matter of time." He invented the Slinky, but unfortunately he didn't call it Slinky and he didn't patent it. He did sue the Slinky people for five million dollars and lost. His oft-remembered motto was "Happiness is a Norge full of Tang and egg salad!"

Todd's father, Marshall (Buck Henry), has a small crush on Mrs. Loopner, and particularly admires her stunning housecoat. As for Todd's mother: "We lost Mrs. DiLaMuca some twelve years ago, at Expo '67."

1 Dan Aykroyd, a disc jockey, introduces the latest thing in music—Nerd Rock. Why did this new band call themselves the Nerds? "We didn't. Other people did." They're giving away copies of their new album, *Trying Desperately to Be Liked*. Songs include "I'll Give You My Lunch Money," "I Can't Help It If I Have Egg Salad on My Retainer," and "Let My Head Up Out of the John and I'll Give You Tomorrow's Lunch Money." As Lisa puts it: "We're young, we're gifted, and we're Nerds. It's our turn to be popular." But no one calls in for free copies of the album.

2 Lisa and Todd are Jane Curtin's guests on "Looks at Books." They discuss their book, *Whatever Happened to the Class of '77?* It's about thirty of their classmates and what has happened to them since last June. They follow such exciting characters as Scott Kendall, who mowed lawns all summer and is now going to junior college

in South Dakota, and Ricki Gale, who made a picnic and got salt in the cupcakes and sugar in the potato salad. "And one chapter is about a girl who got cooties," Lisa tell us. "That's so funny, it's not even funny. A noogie for that!"

3 Todd is invited to stay for dinner, over Lisa's protests, since she's afraid he'll embarrass her in front of her piano teacher. "Todd's a boy. Mr. Brighton's a man." Todd notes, "If my skin cleared up, I'd be shaving now." Lisa's comeback: "When your skin clears up, they'll be making snowballs in Hell."

Mr. Brighton (Michael Palin) presses Lisa against the keyboard to kiss her, and Todd walks in on them: "I have no need to go on living—I'll just commit noogie suicide."

The piano teacher is shown out, and Lisa and Todd play "Heart and Soul." "Lisa, did you ever have a lollipop kiss?" Todd asks. "No, what's that?" "Close your eyes and pucker up"—and she does. "Sucker."

4 Lisa and Todd have entered Dialing for Toast in the Science Fair. Charles Knerlman (Steve Martin), "the real dreamy president of the Science Club," known to Todd as Chaz the Spaz, has built a mystery project: Top Secret. "Nothing special—I just put together a plutonium bomb." How did he get the plutonium? "None of your beeswax."

Grant Robinson, Jr. (Garrett Morris) from Harriet Tubman High has entered Fun with Friction. Todd notes, "Why, Ms. Loopner, I seem to recall a little fun-with-friction experiment last Thursday in your rec room." Todd says he noticed Grant immediately, since he's "the only Negro here." Mrs. Loopner brings egg salad, and Todd and Charles make a sandwich—with Lisa.

5 As Lisa is dressing for the prom, and Mrs. Loopner warns that when a perfectly nice young man like Todd "feasts his eyes on you in that get up, his hormones are going to go berserk." Lisa says she doesn't like Todd in that way, and her mother retorts: "Your father and I never liked each other. But our love triumphed over our mutual dislike. I did my wifely duty and you're the living proof of that." Fortunately, Lisa is saving herself for her one true love, Marvin Hamlisch.

Gilda Radner, Bill Murray, and Jane Curtin

Mrs. Loopner lays out the facts of life: "Making a baby, it's like making egg salad. You, the woman, produce the eggs, and the man furnishes the mayonnaise. Of course, you don't need chopped celery. Oh, I've just given you my egg salad recipe, and I was saving that for your twenty-first birthday."

Todd's right on time—half an hour early—with his father (Buck Henry) as chauffeur. He gives Lisa a graduation gift "Here's those special prom noogies that you ordered."

6 Todd and Lisa are vying for the same honor. Lisa says, "I'm going to be president of the Chess Club and you're going to be president of the Pepperoni Pizza Face Club!" Todd needs help with his homework. He's studying underdeveloped nations, he tells her as he stares down her blouse. Mrs. Loopner's poor old Norge refrigerator is on the fritz. The repairman (Dan Aykroyd) has them in hysterics because his pants are riding way too low. He ends up taking the fridge down to the shop to be fixed. It's an especially sad moment for Mrs. Loopner: "You were too young to remember, but they took your father away like that." Lisa sniffs, "First Daddy, and now the Norge."

7 Lisa is in the hospital for an operation to correct a deviated septum. She has visits from her "nice young Negro friend," Grant Robinson, and Todd: "Oh my gosh, you've had your busts removed!…I call this your hope chest: Keep hoping, Lisa." The ambulance comes with special get-well-soon noogies: "Don't worry, these have all

Bill Murray, Gilda Radner, and Dan Aykroyd

been sterilized." Charles Knerlman pays a visit too. He would have come sooner, but he was out buying expensive gifts, including a record, *Marvin Hamlisch Does It to Marvin Hamlisch*. Todd gives her a dollar. "I forgot to wrap it." The rivals start fighting, and Mrs. Loopner has to administer forty lashes with a wet noodle to both of them.

8 Todd and Lisa have had too many franks and beans. "Pee-yew! Someone cut the cheese!" "Shut up, Todd. He who smelt it, dealt it." Mr. Brighton comes to give Lisa another piano lesson. He starts to attack her—"Lisa, you stir my manhood"—but Mrs. Loopner interrupts. Todd stumbles in. "I can't see anything. These goggles are defective." Lisa says, "It's your brain that's defective, Todd. That's my mom's bra!" Mrs. Loopner comments: "Those kids and their hormones. They run me ragged."

Mr. Brighton tries to shake Mrs. Loopner's hormones loose—"but don't worry, they're still stuck." Todd is em-

pathetic: "These Loopners are dynamite-looking dames. It's hard to keep your hands off them."

9 Lisa is crushed: "I've lost Todd. He's in love with another woman." It's Mrs. Loopner's nurse, Michelle (Kate Jackson), who has been helping out since she broke her arm. He "hasn't given me noogies for two weeks," Lisa complains. "I keep waiting for the noogie patrol and it never comes...and what's worse, his skin cleared up."

How can Lisa compete with the nurse, who has "those cool firm mountains of vanilla ice cream"? "All I got," she laments, "are these miserable maraschino cherries."

The real problem is that Lisa has her period ("I've been stricken"), and Mrs. Loopner explains, "Someday you may want to use the lower half of your body"—and this is nature's own Drano, keeping the plumbing clear.

10 Mr. Dunwoodie (Ted Knight) struggles to direct the Nativity play at school, and pretty much everything goes wrong. Lisa is playing Mary, and Todd is Joseph ("My wife is great with pillow").

Lisa sniffles audibly while they adore Him in silence. Todd cracks, "If you guys were really wise, you would have brought gold, frankincense, and Dristan." He praises her performance as Mary: "I happen to know you're one of the few girls at Gus Grissom High who's physically correct for the part." Then he decks her head with Christmas noogies.

11 Milt DiLaMuca (Richard Benjamin), Todd's groovy older brother, is lending Todd his pad for a hot date with Lisa. Todd checks the details: "How do you dim the lights? Is the Mateus chilled? Is the new Chuck Mangione album here? How do you unfold the bed?"—and most important of all, "Where's your Brut?" When Lisa arrives, Todd suggests that Milt make like an amoeba and split.

Todd starts putting on the moves, bewitched by her scent—Vicks VapoRub. "Haunting. I'll never forget it." Mrs. Loopner arrives early, just as Todd is pulling out the sofabed. She administers a stern lecture: "A young woman's virginity is like a hard-boiled egg. It's safe as long as you keep it cold, in the Norge, in its shell. The second it cracks open and the mayonnaise gets in, it could go rotten...especially at room temperature." But Todd is clear: "Let me reassure you, Mrs. Loopner, it never even got close to the mayonnaise stage."

12 "We've been through this a zillion times, Todd, and the answer to your pathetic animal needs is still *n-o* spells no!" Todd says she's giving him a painful

Bill Murray and Gilda Radner

case of lover's noogies—that's when your head turns all blue and swells up. Mr. DiLaMuca arrives with two tickets to a chess tournament and, at Todd's urging, asks Mrs. Loopner to go with him: "But Enid Loopner—she's a whole lot of woman."

As it turns out, Lisa and her mom go to the tournament, and Todd and his father stay at the Loopners' house to keep an eye on the boiling eggs. They amuse themselves by looking at Mr. DiLaMuca's Belgian postcard collection—except for the two that are stuck together ("They were the best ones").

13 Todd is running for student body president, but he has no real platform, just a bunch of stupid slogans like "Vote for Todd, he's like a God." Grant is Todd's bodyguard, since during a rally someone tried to pull his pants down. "Oh, no! The mooning incident! Don't tell me they're trying to bring that up again," Lisa moans.

But Belinda (Laraine Newman) is clear: "The day Todd threw a moon in study hall, he blew his chances of becoming president. No ifs, ands, or butts." Apparently Shelley Fabish (Harry Shearer) has documented photos of the May 1978 mooning. Arnie (Paul Shaffer) notes, "I have examined the photos closely and I must say they made me extremely nauseous." Shelley threatens to print the photos unless Todd pulls out. "The school paper will never print those photos," Lisa comments. "They're too gross."

Noogie patrol.

FIRST AIRED: JANUARY 28, 1978

The House Band

Musical guests come and go every week on *SNL*, but the house band has been a vital and versatile element of the show since its inception. Every time a sketch opens with a theme song or features an original composition, the house band is the force behind the music. Of course they also play the show's opening and closing themes and they play into and out of commercial and station breaks. And although home viewers don't get the opportunity to enjoy it, the band warms up the audience before the show with a rousing set.

When *SNL* debuted, most comedy/variety shows patterned their music after the big band sound of the forties and fifties; think of "Johnny's Theme" from *The Tonight Show*. But original music director Howard Shore had roots in rock and roll and jazz and he wanted to begin a new chapter in television music. Influenced by Junior Walker, Shore led ten or more musicians through sax-driven rhythm and blues.

Current musical directors Cheryl Hardwick and G.E. Smith have maintained the band's R&B and jazz repetoire of original compositions and cover songs. In the late seventies, band member Paul Shaffer wrote some disco-flavored pieces for the mix. When sketches require a particular recording the encyclopedic Hal Willner has provided needle drop music—for the past fifteen years.

In the early years band members would often appear in sketches, most notably in King Tut and as the All-Nurse Band. As the show has evolved, the amount of music played has increased and the band has focused more on musical business.

Over the years the show's sound has grown richer, with finer technology capturing an accomplished house band and a wide roster of musical guests. The end result is one of the most unusual and diverse collections of music anywhere.

G.E. Smith and the Saturday Night Live Band, 1993.

Paul Shaffer and Howard Shore.

Howard Shore and his All-Nurse Band.

Beatles Offer

Lorne Michaels: Hi. I'm Lorne Michaels, the producer of *Saturday Night*. Right now we're being seen by approximately twenty-two million viewers, but please allow me, if I may, to address myself to just four very special people—John, Paul, George, and Ringo—the Beatles. Lately there have been a lot of rumors to the effect that the four of you might be getting back together. That would be great. In my book the Beatles are the best thing that ever happened to music. It goes even deeper than that. You're not just a musical group. You're a part of us. We grew up with you.

It's for this reason that I am inviting you to come on our show. Now, we've heard and read a lot about personality and legal conflicts that might prevent you guys from reuniting. That's something which is none of my business. That's a personal problem. You guys will have to handle that. But it's also been said that no one has yet to come up with enough money to satisfy you. Well, if it's money you want, there's no problem here.

The National Broadcasting Company has authorized me to offer you this check to be on our show. [*Displays check*] A certified check for three thousand dollars. Here it is right here. Dave—can we get a close-up on this? Which camera? Oh, this one. Here it is. A check made out to you, the Beatles, for three thousand dollars. All you have to do is sing three Beatles songs. "She loves you yeah, yeah, yeah." That's one thousand dollars right there. You know the words. It'll be easy.

Like I said, this is made out to the Beatles—you divide it up any way you want. If you want to give Ringo less, it's up to you. I'd rather not get involved. I'm sincere about this. If this helps you to reach a decision to reunite, it's well worth the investment. You have agents. You know where I can be reached. Just think about it, okay? [*Shows check again*] Thank you.

AIRED: APRIL 24, 1976

Beatles Offer 2

Lorne Michaels: Hi, I'm Lorne Michaels, producer of *Saturday Night*. A short while ago I went on the air and addressed myself to John, Paul, George, and Ringo—the Beatles. At that time I invited them to come on our show, and told them that I was authorized by NBC to pay them in the sum of three *thousand* dollars. That was three *thousand* dollars for just three songs. Well, about a month has gone by. We've heard from the Monkees, Freddy and the Dream-

Lorne Michaels.

ers, Peter and Gordon, Herman's Hermits, the Cowsills, and Lulu; but still no word from the Beatles. I'm not discouraged and neither is NBC. Because of the recent acclaim we've received, I have the weight to go to the network and convince them that it is worth it for them to sweeten the pot. John, Paul, George, and Ringo—NBC is now prepared to up the original offer from three thousand to three thousand, two hundred dollars. Can we get a close-up of the check. Which camera is it? As you can see, it's a check for three thousand, two hundred dollars, made out to you, the Beatles. Off the record, this increase comes to an extra *fifty* dollars for each of you. That's if you split it equally—I'm still not sure what your situation with Ringo is. Also, NBC has decided that they will also take care of your hotel accommodations. Don Pardo, tell the Beatles what they can expect when they come to get that check for three thousand, two hundred dollars.

Don Pardo: It'll be my pleasure, Lorne. First of all, the lads from Liverpool will be picked up by a radio-dispatched Checker cab that will whisk them to the Cross Town Motor Inn, located in the heart of New York's fashionable Garment District. Once there, they will check in in the recently renovated lobby; and then it's off to their rooms via round-the-clock elevator service. They'll be treated like royalty as pitchers of ice water are hand-delivered to their rooms, and they can drink that water from glasses sanitized for their convenience. Oops—Ringo spilled a little something on his jacket? No problem—not with prompt forty-eight-hour dry cleaning service! "In by Tuesday, out by Thursday." And let's just put a shine on those shoes, too, with a free shoe shine cloth. And, Lorne, since the Beatles will be staying in separate rooms, the four Mop Tops can still speak to each other as much as they want because there is no charge for room-to-room calls. And, after a hard day's night, the Beatles can sleep as late as they like with a leisurely checkout time of 10 A.M. That's the Cross Town Motor Inn, a hotel tradition, hosting New York's visitors since 1971. Yeah, yeah, yeah! Back to you, Lorne!

Lorne Michaels: Thank you, Don Pardo. John, Paul, George, and Ringo, that's where we stand right now. Thirty-two hundred dollars, and free hotel accommodations. Now it's your move. I've always respected you, you were always my favorite group, and I always liked Yoko, even at the beginning when everyone was having problems with her. I would like to see you do our show, and so would the American people. You know where I can be reached. I'm waiting to hear from you.

AIRED: MAY 22, 1976

King Tut

Steve Martin: I'd like to talk seriously just for a moment. One of the great art exhibitions ever to tour the United States is the Treasures of Tutankhamen, or King Tut. But I think it's a national disgrace the way we have commercialized it with trinkets and toys, T-shirts and posters. And three months ago I was up in the woods and I wrote a song. I tried to use the ancient modalities and melodies. I'd like to do it for you right now. Maybe we can all learn something.

(King Tut.
King Tut.)
Now when he was a young
man
He never thought he'd see
People stand in line
To see the boy king.
(King Tut.)
How'd you get so funky?
(Funky Tut.)
Did you do the monkey?
(Born in Arizona,
Moved to Babylonia,
King Tut.)

(King Tut.)
Now if I'd known
They'd line up just to see
him, I'd have taken all
my money

And bought me a museum.
(King Tut.)
Buried with a donkey.
(Funky Tut.)
He's my favorite honky.
(Born in Arizona,
Moved to Babylonia,
King Tut.)

(Tut! Tut!) Dancing by
the Nile!
(Disco Tut! Tut!) The
ladies love his style!
(Boss Tut! Tut!) Walkin'
for a mile.
(Rockin' Tut! Tut!) He
ate a crocodile.
(Ooooooo, wah-oooo . . .)
He gave his life for
tourism.

[Sarcophagus opens for
sax solo; Steve breaks in
with "Golden Idols! He's
an Egyptian!" and offers
saxophonist an electric
blender.]

(King Tut.)
Now when I die,
Now don't think I'm a
nut.
Don't want no fancy
funeral,
Just one like old King
Tut!
(King Tut.)
He could have won a
Grammy.
(King Tut.)
Buried in his jammies.
(Born in Arizona,
Moved to Babylonia.
Born in Arizona,)
Got a condo made o'
stone-a.
(King Tut.)

Performed by Steve
Martin
Aired: April 22, 1978

Steve Martin

Gilda Radner.

Candy Slice

"IF YOU LOOK CLOSE"
I am sexless
I sing loud
Know that always gets the crowd
I talk dirty
And I'm proud
No dry cleaning is allowed

I am funky
I don't bathe
I am rock'n'roll's new slave
I am punky to the grave
I can't sing but I can rave

Watch my blouse
It's got da rhythm
High-heel feet
Pants to go with 'em

I am hot
Don't need no bra
Got what it takes
To make a staaaaaaar

If you look close
You can see my tips
'Cause I want ya to
But don't want ya
To know that I do

CANDY SLICE PLAYED BY GILDA RADNER
AIRED: DECEMBER 9, 1978

Little Richard Simmons

Eddie Murphy enters as Little Richard. He has processed hair, a pencil-thin mustache, and lipstick, and wears a Richard Simmons jogging suit opened almost to the navel. He leads his background exercisers and the audience in simple calisthenics. The first set is to the tune of "Ready Teddy."

Ready, set, go, fat, go.
I know a gal whose butt hangs low.
She's flabby,
Yeah, she's flabby,
Oooh, she's flabby,
Fatty, fatty, fatty,
If she stepped on your foot,
She'd mash your toe.

[Tune segues to "Good Golly, Miss Molly"; Richard leads crowd to jog in place.]

Good golly, Miss Molly
Looks like a hog.
Ooooh!
Good golly, Miss Molly
Looks like a hog.
Well, you better start a-runnin'
Because it's much too late to jog.
From the early, early mornin'
To the early, early night,
You're just a fat disgusting blob of
cellulite.
Good golly, Miss Molly,
Good golly, Miss Molly,
Good golly, Miss Molly
Looks like a hog.

[After sax player in tights does a solo, Richard switches the exercise to torso bends to the tune of "Tutti Frutti."]

Tutti-frutti, all roody,
Tutti-frutti, all roody,
Tutti-frutti, all roody,
Tutti-frutti, all roody,
Tutti-frutti, all roody,
Wop bom a loo mop, a mop bam boom.
Know a girl named Daisy.
The girl is fat and lazy.
Know a girl named Daisy.
The girl is fat and lazy.
Blubber to the east,
Blubber to the west,
The bitch got long and flabby breasts.
Tutti-frutti, all
roody,
Tutti-frutti, all
roody,
Tutti-frutti, all
roody,
Wop bom a loo
mop, a mop
bam boom!

AIRED: OCTOBER 3, 1981

LIFER FOLLIES

I'm gonna get me a shotgun and kill all the whiteys I see.

I'm gonna get me a shotgun and kill all the whiteys I see.

When I kill all the whiteys I see,

Then Whitey won't bother me.

I'm gonna get me a shotgun and kill all the whiteys I see.

Then I'll get a white woman who's wearing a navy blue sweater.

INMATE JOHNSON PLAYED BY GARRETT MORRIS
AIRED: JANUARY 24, 1976

David Byrne

You may ask yourself,
Why such a big suit?
You may ask yourself,
Can this suit be taken
in a little?
You may ask yourself,
Does this store have
any mirrors?

DAVID BYRNE PLAYED
BY RICH HALL
AIRED: NOVEMBER 3,
1984

Rich Hall.

Season's Greetings from Tarzan, Tonto, and Frankenstein

Away in manger
No crib for bed
Little Lord Jesus
Lay down sweet
head
Stars in sky
Look down where
lay
Little Lord Jesus
Asleep in hay

TARZAN PLAYED BY
KEVIN NEALON
TONTO PLAYED BY
JON LOVITZ
FRANKENSTEIN
PLAYED BY PHIL HARTMAN
AIRED: DECEMBER 19, 1987

Kevin Nealon, Phil Hartman, and Jon Lovitz.

Chopping Broccoli

And my lady,
She went downtown.
She bought some broccoli.
She brought it home.

She's chopping broccoli.
She's chopping broccoli.
She's chopping broccoli.
She's chopping broccoli.

DEREK STEPHENS PLAYED BY DANA CARVEY
AIRED: OCTOBER 11, 1986

Dana Carvey, Sigourney Weaver, and Phil Hartman.

Hanukkah Harry

On Moische! On Herschel! On Schlomo!
Says Hanukkah Harry eight nights a year.
On Moische! On Herschel! On Schlomo!
Means that Hanukkah Harry is here.
Delivering toys
For Jewish girls
and Jewish
boys—
We dance the hora
Around the
menorah
When Hanukkah
Harry is here!

HANUKKAH HARRY
PLAYED BY JON
LOVITZ
AIRED: DECEMBER
16, 1989

Jon Lovitz.

Tonight Song

Victoria Jackson: Steve, wanna run lines for our scene?
Steve Martin: We have a sketch together? Is it on cue cards?
Victoria: I guess so.
Steve: Then what's the problem? [*Chris Farley presents Martin with an artifact.*] My old King Tut costume! I remember this. This was back when the show *meant* something. Back… when I used to care.

Something's out there…
Something's in the air…
Don't know how,
Don't know why,
Got a feeling tonight's the night
I'm actually gonna try…
Not gonna phone it in tonight.
Not gonna go through the
   motions tonight.
This time I'm really gonna do
   the best I can…
Mr. Cue Card Man, put those
   down over there.
For some reason tonight, I
   care!

Victoria: You care?
Steve: That's right!

That's why I'm not gonna
   phone it in tonight.
Not gonna read my screenplay
   during the songs tonight.
I could walk through my parts
And still be hilarious, I've done
   it so often before.
But look at these faces! Look
   at this fat guy!
He wants more! He wants
   mooooore!

Audience Member: Hey, I'm
not that fat!

Steve: Please!

So many times I faked it
Just because I could.
I'm that good!
But twenty percent won't do
   tonight.
Mike Myers:
Mr. Martin, I'll do it for you
   tonight.
Julia Sweeney:
Gonna do something different
   tonight.
Something says not to just do
   Pat tonight…
Tim Meadows:
I don't have any lines.
I'm not in the show.
But something tells me that if I
   were
I'd be rarin' to go…
Chris Farley:
Not gonna get liquored up
   tonight.
I'm not gonna have a drink
   tonight.
I'm not gonna drink
Till Update is through—
That's a promise to you, the
   viewer.
Yes! After the show, I'll drink
   till I spew,
But for now I'm clearheaded
   for you.
Phil Hartman:
I hide behind these wigs and
   this makeup
But tonight I'm going to let
   myself shine through.
Yes, they're gonna see the real
   Phil Hartman tonight!

Steve: I wouldn't do that, Phil!
Phil: Okay!
Steve: Follow me everyone.
Let's go make an effort!

All: Not gonna have dead air
   tonight.

Gonna seem as if we care
   tonight.

Kevin Nealon: But Steve, why
do you care? Aren't you rich?

Steve:
I'm worth seventeen million
I could buy and sell you and
   you and you a thousand
   times over,
But tonight, there's a show to
   do!

Joe Dicso: Five minutes to
Monologue, Mr. Martin!
Steve: Thanks, Joe!

Joe:
I can't ever get fired.
I've got a union job.
But somehow tonight it doesn't
   matter
That I'm in with the mob…

Stagehands: Gonna move our
   lardasses tonight,
We're gonna move our fat
   Teamster asses tonight…

Lorne Michaels: Steve, what's
going on?
Steve: We're going to do our
best tonight, Lorne!
Lorne: But Steve, the show's
on automatic pilot. I don't even
come in until Saturday.
Steve: Lorne, don't you see?
That's not the way it was in the
seventies. Back in the seventies, people cared, they

believed in something. Now it's
the eighties, and everything's
yuppie, yuppie, yuppie, spend,
spend, spend!
Lorne: Steve, it's the nineties.
Steve: Whatever! You see,

I've always wanted to see
How good I could be.
I just want to know.
Lorne:
Then go, Steve, go,
And have a great show!
All: We're gonna learn our
   lines,
Do our parts well,
Then we'll go back to coasting,
But not while Steve's host,
'Cause…
We're…
Not gonna phone it in tonight.
Not gonna sleepwalk through
   tonight!
Steve:
I made it happen!
All:
Steve made it happen!
Steve:
Now it's in sight!
All:
Now it's in sight!
Steve:
Live from New York… !
Line?
It's Saturday …
All:
Night!!!!

Aired: December 14, 1991

Adam Sandler's "Christmas Song"

So many presents,
So little time,
Santa won't be coming to my house
    this year
'Cause I tried to drown my sister and
    I pierced my ear.
Oh, Mama made it perfectly clear:
Santa don't like bad boys.
Especially Jewish ones!

Gnip Gnop and Lego blocks
Are what I desire,
So why'd I have to set the pizza guy's
    hair on fire?
I told him I was sorry—I'm a liar,

So no toys for me.
I don't deserve 'em!

I couldn't wait for a Big Wheel
As the holiday neared,
But then I told my grandma that she
    had a beard.

[Spoken interlude.]
Dear Santa . . . you know what my
    problem is,
Why I can't be good.
It's a fear of intimacy.
You see, my whole life, whenever I
    met someone really great like you,
And I keep feeling I'm getting too
    close to them,
Something inside of me makes me
    want to screw it up.
So in a weird way, the reason I'm so
    bad
Is because I love you so much, Santa.

Rock 'Em Sock 'Em Robots
Is what I was hoping for,
But then I made a death
    threat
To Vice President Gore.
Oh, Santa won't be knocking
    at my door
'Cause he's a big fat whore.
What made me say that?

Chutes and Ladders would be
    so good indeed,
So why'd I have to sell that
    cop a bag of weed?
So, Santa, please give me my
Easy Bake Oven.
I swear I thought billy goats
Were made for lovin'.

So, Santa, won't you accept
    my apologies,
Santa, can't you see, I'm beggin'
    you, please,
Oh, Santa, next year I'll do you
    right,
Live from New York, it's Saturday
Night.

Aired: December 11, 1993

Frank Gifford: Good evening. I'm Frank Gifford. The sports world was rocked this week by the surprise retirement of Michael Jordan. In a last ditch effort to get him to change his mind, some of the biggest names in music have come together to record a hastily put together benefit song. Ladies and gentlemen, "Rock for Michael."

James Taylor [To the tune of "Fire and Rain"]:
I've seen Magic and I've seen Bird,
I saw Kareem retire but I never said a
    word,
But I always thought I'd see you play one
    more time again.

David Pirner [To the tune of "Runaway Train"]:
Runaway Mike, better come back.
Got season tickets, can't get my money
    back.
Don't you know you're so crowd pleasin'.
Won't you stick around one more season?

Steven Tyler [To the tune of "Dream On"]:
Play on, play one more year.
Play for the fans and play for the cheers.
Play the Sonics, play the Knicks too.
Even the Celtics—
We'll still root for you.

The Proclaimers [To the tune of "500 Miles (I'm Gonna Be)"]:
I've seen you score
Five hundred points.
I want to see you score
Five hundred more.
Just to be the man
Who could say he saw a man
Score a thousand points
On the basketball floor.
    Michael Jordan!
    Michael Jordan!
    Michael Jordan!
    Michael Jordan!
    Michael, hey!
    Michael, ho!
    Michael Jordan!

Rock for Michael

Snoop Doggy Dogg [*To the tune of "Who Am I? (What's My Name?)"*]:
Bow-wow-wow,
Yippie-yo, Yippie-yay
Keep Jordan in the mother [bleeped] house!

Dr. Dre:
Michael Jordan,
Where you think you're goin'?
With your tongue hangin' out
And your bald head showin'!

Snoop:
Don't you know
You're in a higher class?
So come on back
Before I pimp-slap your [bleeped].

Eddie Vedder [*To the tune of "Even Flow"*]:
Even . . . please don't quit yet.
Even . . . you're the best dribbler.
Even . . . who's Pippen gonna pass to?
Even . . . golf is so boring, oh, yeah!

Tyler [*To the tune of "Dream On"*]:
Play on, play one more year.
Play against Isiah, play against Laimbeer.
Take the basketball, throw it through the hoop.
Do a three-sixty—
And slam an alley-oop.

The B-52's [*To the tune of "Love Shack"*]:
If you stop playing, you'll get as big as a whale!
Everybody's playing.
Everybody's staying, baby.
Michael! Don't forget your endorsement money!
Everybody's playing.
Everybody's staying, baby.

Meat Loaf [*To the tune of "Paradise by the Dashboard Light"*]:

Michael, sleep on it.
Michael, baby, won't you sleep on it.
Won't you sleep on it?
Give us an answer in the morning.

Vedder:
I gotta know right now!

Loaf:
Let him sleep on it.
Michael, baby, won't you sleep on it.
Won't you sleep on it?
Give us an answer in the morning.

All [*To the tune of "Dream On"*]:
Play on, play one more year.
Bulls can't win without you.
Its very very clear.
Play on!
Play on! . . .

Tyler:
. . .Play on, Michael!

Michael, we want you to keep playin', and . . .

Tyler and Joe Perry: Live from New York, It's Saturday Night!

FRANK GIFFORD PLAYED BY PHIL HARTMAN
JAMES TAYLOR PLAYED BY KEVIN NEALON
DAVID PIRNER PLAYED BY DAVID SPADE
THE PROCLAIMERS PLAYED BY MIKE MYERS AND NORM MACDONALD
SNOOP DOGGY DOGG PLAYED BY TIM MEADOWS
DR. DRE PLAYED BY ELLEN CLEGHORNE
EDDIE VEDDER PLAYED BY ADAM SANDLER
THE B-52'S PLAYED BY ADAM SANDLER, MELANIE HUTSELL, AND JULIA SWEENEY
MEAT LOAF PLAYED BY CHRIS FARLEY

AIRED: OCTOBER 9, 1993

The following is a complete list of every musical guest ever to appear on the show and the songs they played.

1975–1976

OCTOBER 11, 1975
Janis Ian
"At Seventeen"
Billy Preston
"Nothin' From Nothin'"
OCTOBER 18, 1975
Paul Simon and Art Garfunkel
"The Boxer"
"Scarborough Fair"
Paul Simon
"Marie"
"My Little Town"
"American Tune"
Art Garfunkel
"I Only Have Eyes for You"
Randy Newman
"Sail Away"
Phoebe Snow
"No Regrets"
Paul Simon, Phoebe Snow, and the Jesse Dixon Singers
"Gone at Last"
OCTOBER 25, 1975
Joe Cocker
"With a Little Help from My Friends"
NOVEMBER 8, 1975
Esther Phillips
"What a Difference a Day Makes"
"I Can't Stand a Little Rain"
NOVEMBER 15, 1975
ABBA
"Waterloo"
"S.O.S."
Loudon Wainwright III
"Bicentennial Certainty"
"Unrequited to the Nth Degree"
NOVEMBER 22, 1975
Lily Tomlin with Scred
"I Got You Babe"
Lily Tomlin with Howard Shore and His All-Nurse Band
"St. James Infirmary"
DECEMBER 13, 1975
Gil Scott-Heron
"Johannesburg"
"A Lovely Day"
DECEMBER 20, 1975
Martha Reeves
"Higher and Higher"
The Stylistics
"You Make Me Feel Brand New"
JANUARY 10, 1976
Anne Murray
"Long-Distance Call"
"Boogie with You"
JANUARY 17, 1976
Bill Withers
"Ain't No Sunshine"
Toni Basil
"Wham"
JANUARY 24, 1976
Neil Sedaka
"Breaking Up Is Hard to Do"
"Lonely Night"
JANUARY 31, 1976
Jimmy Cliff
"Many Rivers to Cross"
"The Harder They Come"
"Wahjaka Man"
FEBRUARY 14, 1976
Al Jarreau
"We Got By"
"Pretty as a Picture"
FEBRUARY 21, 1976
Desi Arnaz

"Cuban Pete"
"Babalu"
FEBRUARY 28, 1976
Leon Redbone
"Ain't Misbehavin'"
"Big-Time Woman"
MARCH 13, 1976
Betty Carter
"Music Maestro, Please" / *"Swing Brother Swing"*
"I Can't Help It"
APRIL 17, 1976
Patti Smith
"Gloria"
"Generation"
APRIL 24, 1976
Phoebe Snow
"All Over"
"Two-Fisted Love"
John Sebastian
"Welcome Back"
MAY 8, 1976
Carly Simon
"Half a Chance"
"You're So Vain"
MAY 15, 1976
Leon and Mary Russell
"I Want to Satisfy You"
"Daylight"
MAY 22, 1976
Gordon Lightfoot
"Summertime Dream"
"Spanish Moss"
MAY 29, 1976
Leon Redbone
"Shine On Harvest Moon"
"Walking Stick"
JULY 24, 1976
Preservation Hall Jazz Band
"Panama"
JULY 31, 1976
Kris Kristofferson
"I've Got a Life of My Own"
Kris Kristofferson with Rita Coolidge
"Eddie the Eunuch"
Rita Coolidge
"Hula Hoop"

1976–1977

SEPTEMBER 18, 1976
James Taylor
"Shower the People"
"Road Runner"
"Sweet Baby James"
SEPTEMBER 25, 1976
Boz Scaggs
"What Can I Say"
"Lowdown"
OCTOBER 2, 1976
Joe Cocker
"You Are So Beautiful"
"Feelin' Alright"
OCTOBER 16, 1976
John Prine
"Hello In There"
"The Bottomless Lake"
OCTOBER 23, 1976
Kinky Friedman
"Dear Abbie"
OCTOBER 30, 1976
The Band
"The Night They Drove Old Dixie Down" / *"Stage Fright"* / *"Life Is a Carnival"*
"Georgia"
NOVEMBER 13, 1976
Ry Cooder
"Tattler"
"He'll Have to Go"
NOVEMBER 20, 1976
Paul Simon and George Harrison

"Here Comes the Sun" / *"Homeward Bound"*
Paul Simon
"50 Ways to Leave Your Lover"
"Bridge Over Troubled Water"
"Something So Right"
NOVEMBER 27, 1976
Brian Wilson
"Back Home"
"Love Is a Woman"
"Good Vibrations"
DECEMBER 11, 1976
Frank Zappa
"I'm Slime"
"Lagoon"
"Peaches and Regalia"
JANUARY 15, 1977
George Benson
"Masquerade"
"Gonna Love You More"
JANUARY 22, 1977
Chuck Berry
"Johnny B. Goode"
"Marie" / *"Carol"*
JANUARY 29, 1977
Leo Sayer
"When I Need You"
"You Make Me Feel Like Dancing"
Donny Harper Singers
"Sing a Song"
FEBRUARY 20, 1977
Randy Newman
"Louisiana 1927"
"Marie"
"Kingfish"
"Sail Away"
FEBRUARY 26, 1977
The Kinks
"You Really Got Me"
"Sleepwalker"
MARCH 12, 1977
Richard Baskin
"One I Love You"
"City of One-Night Stands"
MARCH 19, 1977
Levon Helm
"Ain't That a Lot of Love"
Dr. John
"Sing Sing Sing"
The Meters
"I Got to Get My Name Up in Lights"
MARCH 26, 1977
Santana
"Black Magic Woman"
"Gypsy Woman"
APRIL 9, 1977
Tom Waits
"Eggs and Sausages"
Tom Waits with Susan Nickerson
"In a Cadillac"
Brick
"Dazz"
APRIL 16, 1977
Roslyn Kind
"I'm Not Anyone"
Kate and Anna McGarrigle
"Kiss and Say Goodbye"
"Heart Like a Wheel"
APRIL 23, 1977
Alan Price
"In Times Like These"
"Poor People"
Neil Innes
"Shangri-La"
MAY 14, 1977
Joan Armatrading
"I'm Not In Love"
"Down to Zero"
MAY 21, 1977
Jennifer Warnes
"Right Time of the Night"
Kenny Vance
"The Performer"

1977–1978

SEPTEMBER 24, 1977
Jackson Browne
"The Pretender"
"Runnin' On Empty"
OCTOBER 8, 1977
Taj Mahal
"Queen Bee"
OCTOBER 15, 1977
Libby Titus
"Fool"
OCTOBER 29, 1977
Paul Simon
"So Kind"
"Slip Sliding Away"
NOVEMBER 12, 1977
Ray Charles
"I Believe in My Soul"
"Oh! What a Beautiful Morning"
"What'd I Say"
NOVEMBER 19, 1977
Leon Redbone
"Champagne Charlie"
"Please Don't Talk About Me When I'm Gone"
DECEMBER 10, 1977
Willie Nelson
"Blue Eyes Crying in the Rain"
"Whiskey River"
"Something to Brag About"
DECEMBER 17, 1977
Elvis Costello
"Radio, Radio"
"Watching the Detectives"
JANUARY 21, 1978
Randy Newman
"Short People"
Dirt Band
"On the Loose with the Blues"
"White Russia"
JANUARY 28, 1978
Bonnie Raitt
"Give It All Up or Let Me Go"
"Runaway"
FEBRUARY 18, 1978
Billy Joel
"Only the Good Die Young"
"Just the Way You Are"
FEBRUARY 25, 1978
Ashford and Simpson
"Don't Cost You Nothing"
"So, So Satisfied"
MARCH 11, 1978
Stephen Bishop
"On and On"
Art Garfunkel
"Crying in My Sleep"
"All I Know" / *"Scarborough Fair"*
MARCH 18, 1978
Eddie Money
"Two Tickets to Paradise"
"Baby Hold On"
MARCH 25, 1978
Meat Loaf
"No Place to Go"
"Two Out of Three Ain't Bad"
APRIL 8, 1978
Eugene Record
"Have You Seen Her?"
"Trying to Get to You"
APRIL 15, 1978
Keith Jarrett
Instrumental
Instrumental
Gravity
Instrumental
APRIL 22, 1978
Blues Brothers
"I Don't Know"
MAY 13, 1978
Jimmy Buffett
"Son of a Sailor"
Gary Tigerman

"White Oaxacan Moon"
MAY 20, 1978
Sun Ra
"Space is the Place"
"Space-Loneliness"

1978–1979

OCTOBER 7, 1978
The Rolling Stones
"Beast of Burden" / *"Respectable"* / *"Shattered"*
OCTOBER 14, 1978
Devo
"Satisfaction"
OCTOBER 21, 1978
Frank Zappa
"Dancing Fool"
"Meek"
"Rollo"
NOVEMBER 4, 1978
Van Morrison
"Wavelength"
"Kingdom Hall"
NOVEMBER 11, 1978
The Grateful Dead
"Casey Jones"
"I Need a Miracle" / *"Good Lovin'"*
NOVEMBER 18, 1978
Blues Brothers
"Soul Man"
"Got Everything I Need, Almost" / *"Get Back to You"*
DECEMBER 9, 1978
Kate Bush
"Them Heavy People"
"The Man with the Child in His Eyes"
DECEMBER 16, 1978
Peter Tosh with Mick Jagger
"Don't Look Back"
Peter Tosh
"Bush Doctor"
JANUARY 27, 1979
The Doobie Brothers
"What a Fool Believes"
"Taking It to the Streets"
FEBRUARY 10, 1979
Talking Heads
"Take Me to The River"
"Artists Only"
FEBRUARY 17, 1979
Rick Nelson
"Hello, Mary Lou" / *"Travellin' Man"* /
"Fools Rush In"
"Dream Lover"
Judy Collins
"Hard Times for Lovers"
FEBRUARY 24, 1979
Delbert McClinton
"B Movie"
MARCH 10, 1979
Gary Busey
"Stay All Night"
Eubie Blake and Gregory Hines
"Low-down Blues" / *"I'm Just Simply Full of Jazz"* / *"I'm Just Wild About Harry"*
MARCH 17, 1979
The Chieftains
"If I Had Maggie in the Woods"
"Morning Dew"
APRIL 7, 1979
Rickie Lee Jones
"Chuck E.'s in Love"
"Coolsville"
APRIL 14, 1979
Ornette Coleman
"Times Square"
MAY 12, 1979
James Taylor
"Johnny Comes Back"
"Up on the Roof"
"Millworker"

MAY 19, 1979
Linda Ronstadt and Phoebe Snow
"The Married Men"
"It's in His Kiss"
MAY 26, 1979
Bette Midler
"Married Men"
"Martha"

1979–1980
OCTOBER 13, 1979
Blondie
"Dreaming"
"The Hardest Part"
OCTOBER 20, 1979
Bob Dylan
"Gotta Serve Somebody"
"I Believe in You"
"When You Gonna Wake Up"
NOVEMBER 3, 1979
Chicago
"I'm a Man"
"Street Player"
NOVEMBER 10, 1979
Tom Petty
"Refugee"
"Don't Do Me Like That"
NOVEMBER 17, 1979
The Roches
"Bobby's Song"
"Hallelujah"
DECEMBER 8, 1979
Randy Newman
"It's Money That I Love"
"The Story of a Rock and Roll Band"
DECEMBER 15, 1979
David Bowie
"The Man Who Sold the World"
"TVC-15"
"Boys Keep Swinging"
DECEMBER 22, 1979
Desmond Child and Rouge
"Goodbye Baby"
JANUARY 26, 1980
The B-52's
"Rock Lobster"
"Dance This Mess Around"
FEBRUARY 9, 1980
Marianne Faithfull
"Broken English"
"Guilt"
FEBRUARY 16, 1980
Gary Numan
"Cars"
"Praying to the Aliens"
FEBRUARY 23, 1980
Sam and Dave
"You Don't Know Like I Know"
"Soul Man"
MARCH 8, 1980
The J. Geils Band
"Love Stinks"
"Sanctuary"
MARCH 15, 1980
James Taylor and Paul Simon
"Cathy's Clown" / "Sunny Skies" /
"Take Me to the Mardi Gras"
David Sanborn
"Anything You Want"
APRIL 5, 1980
Grateful Dead
"Alabama Getaway"
"Saint of Circumstances"
APRIL 12, 1980
Anne Murray
"Lucky Me"
"Why Don't You Stick Around"
APRIL 19, 1980
The Specials
"Gangsters"
"Too Much, Too Young"
MAY 10, 1980
Amazing Rhythm Aces
"Who Will the Next Fool Be" /
"Third-Rate Romance"

Bruce Cockburn
"Wondering Where the Lions Are"
MAY 17, 1980
3-D
"All-Night Television"
MAY 24, 1980
Andrew Gold
"Kiss This One Goodbye"
Andraé Crouch and The Voices of
Unity
"Can't Nobody Do Me Like Jesus"

1980–1981
NOVEMBER 15, 1980
Kid Creole and the Coconuts
"Mister Softee"
"Grace of God"
NOVEMBER 22, 1980
Captain Beefheart and His Magic
Band
"Hot Head"
"Ashtray Heart"
DECEMBER 6, 1980
Aretha Franklin
"United Together"
"Can't Turn Me Loose"
Keith Sykes
"B.I.G.T.I.M.E."
DECEMBER 13, 1980
James Brown
"Rap Payback"
"I Got You (I Feel Good)" / "Small
Man" / "Please Please Please"
Ellen Shipley
"Fotogenic"
DECEMBER 20, 1980
The Pirates of Penzance
"I am the very model of a modern
Major-General" / "Oh, is there
not one maiden breast" / "Poor
wandering one" / "Go ye, heroes"
"O Come Emmanuel" / "Joy to the
World" / "The First Noel"
JANUARY 10, 1981
Jack Bruce and Friends
"Dancin' On Air"
"Livin' Without Jah"
JANUARY 17, 1981
Cheap Trick
"Baby Loves to Rock"
"Can't Stop"
Stanley Clarke Trio
"Deep in the Night"
JANUARY 24, 1981
Joe "King" Carrasco
"Baby, Don't Bug Me"
14 Karat Soul
"I Wish That We Were Married" /
"This Time It's for Real"
FEBRUARY 7, 1981
Jimmy Cliff
"Gone Clear"
"I Am the Living"
FEBRUARY 14, 1981
Deborah Harry
"Love TKO"
"Johnny"
Funky 4 + 1 More
"That's the Joint"
FEBRUARY 21, 1981
Todd Rundgren
"Time Heals"
"Healer"
Prince
"Party Up"
MARCH 7, 1981
Delbert McClinton
"Giving It Up For Your Love"
"Shotgun Rider"
APRIL 11, 1981
Junior Walker and the All Stars
"(I'm a) Road Runner" / "Shotgun"
"How Sweet It Is" / "What Does It
Take"

1981–1982
OCTOBER 3, 1981
Rod Stewart with Tina Turner
"Hot Legs"
Rod Stewart
"Young Turks"
OCTOBER 10, 1981
The Kinks
"Destroyer"
"Art Lover"
OCTOBER 17, 1981
Miles Davis
Instrumental
OCTOBER 31, 1981
Fear
"I Don't Care About You"
"Beef Bologna" / "New York's
Alright If You Like Saxophones" /
"Let's Have a War"
NOVEMBER 7, 1981
Rick James
"Super Freak"
"Give It to Me Baby"
NOVEMBER 14, 1981
The Go-Go's
"Our Lips Are Sealed"
"We Got the Beat"
Billy Joel
"Miami 2017"
"She's Got a Way"
DECEMBER 5, 1981
Meat Loaf
"Promised Land"
"Bat Out of Hell"
DECEMBER 12, 1981
The Spinners
"Then Came You" / "I'll Be
Around" / "Working My Way
Back to You"
JANUARY 23, 1982
The Allman Brothers Band
"Midnight Rider"
"Southbound"
"One Way Out"
JANUARY 30, 1982
Jennifer Holliday
"And I Am Telling You I'm Not
Going"
"One Night Only"
FEBRUARY 6, 1982
Lindsey Buckingham
"Bwana"
"Trouble"
FEBRUARY 20, 1982
Luther Vandross
"Never Too Much"
"A House Is Not a Home"
FEBRUARY 27, 1982
Daryl Hall and John Oates
"You Make My Dreams"
"I Can't Go for That"
"You've Lost That Lovin' Feeling"
MARCH 20, 1982
Mink DeVille
"Love and Emotion"
"Maybe Tomorrow"
MARCH 27, 1982
Rickie Lee Jones
"Pirates"
"Lush Life" / "Woody" / "Dutch"
APRIL 10, 1982
John Cougar
"Hurts So Good"
"Ain't Even Done With the Night"
APRIL 17, 1982
Johnny Cash
"I Walk the Line" / "Folsom Prison
Blues" / "Ring of Fire"
Elton John
"Empty Garden"
"Ball and Chain"
APRIL 24, 1982
Charlie Daniels Band
"Still in Saigon"
"The Devil Went Down to Georgia"

MAY 15, 1982
Sparks
"Mickey Mouse"
"I Predict"
MAY 22, 1982
Olivia Newton-John
"Physical"
"Make a Move on Me"
"Landslide"

1982–1983
SEPTEMBER 25, 1982
Queen
"Crazy Little Thing Called Love"
"Under Pressure"
OCTOBER 2, 1982
George Thorogood and The
Destroyers
"Bad to the Bone"
"Back in Wentzville"
OCTOBER 9, 1982
The Clash
"Straight to Hell"
"Should I Stay or Should I Go"
OCTOBER 23, 1982
Men at Work
"Who Can It Be Now"
"Down Under"
OCTOBER 30, 1982
Joe Jackson
"Steppin' Out"
"Another World"
NOVEMBER 13, 1982
Kenny Loggins
"Heart to Heart"
"I Gotta Try"
NOVEMBER 20, 1982
Squeeze
"Annie Get Your Gun"
"Pulling Mussels from a Shell"
DECEMBER 4, 1982
Laura Branigan
"Gloria"
"Living a Lie"
DECEMBER 11, 1982
Lionel Richie
"You Are"
"Truly"
JANUARY 29, 1983
The Bus Boys
"The Boys Are Back In Town"
"New Shoes"
FEBRUARY 5, 1983
Joe Cocker and Jennifer Warnes
"Up Where We Belong"
Joe Cocker
"Seven Days"
FEBRUARY 19, 1983
Tom Petty and the Heartbreakers
"Change of Heart"
"The Waiting"
FEBRUARY 26, 1983
Randy Newman
"I Love L.A."
"Real Emotional Girl"
MARCH 12, 1983
Leon Redbone
"Sweet Sue"
"When You Wish Upon a Star" /
"I Ain't Got Nobody"
MARCH 19, 1983
Duran Duran
"Hungry Like the Wolf"
"Girls on Film"
APRIL 9, 1983
Musical Youth
"Pass the Dutchie"
"Never Gonna Give You Up"
APRIL 16, 1983
Michael McDonald
"If That's What It Takes"
"I Can't Let Go Now"
MAY 7, 1983
Stevie Wonder
"Overjoyed"
"Go Home"

MAY 14, 1983
Kevin Rowland and Dexy's Midnight
Runners
"Come On, Eileen"
"The Celtic Soul Brothers"

1983–1984
OCTOBER 8, 1983
John Cougar
"Pink Houses"
"Crumblin' Down"
OCTOBER 15, 1983
Eddy Grant
"I Don't Wanna Dance" / "Electric
Avenue"
"Living on the Front Line"
OCTOBER 22, 1983
Men at Work
"Doctor Heckyll and Mr. Jive"
"It's a Mistake"
NOVEMBER 5, 1983
Stray Cats
"She's Sexy + 17"
"I Won't Stand in Your Way"
NOVEMBER 12, 1983
Mick Fleetwood's Zoo
"Tonight"
"Gary Thinks He's a Rabbit"
NOVEMBER 19, 1983
Loverboy
"Working for the Weekend"
DECEMBER 3, 1983
Big Country
"In a Big Country"
"Fields of Fire"
DECEMBER 10, 1983
Stevie Nicks
"Stand Back"
"Nightbird"
JANUARY 14, 1984
Huey Lewis and the News
"Heart and Soul"
"I Want a New Drug"
JANUARY 21, 1984
The Motels
"Suddenly Last Summer"
"Remember the Nights"
JANUARY 28, 1984
Billy Idol
"White Wedding"
"Rebel Yell"
FEBRUARY 11, 1984
Adam Ant
"Strip"
"Goody Two Shoes"
FEBRUARY 18, 1984
The Fixx
"One Thing Leads to Another"
"Red Skies at Night"
FEBRUARY 25, 1984
Kool & the Gang
"Celebration"
"Joanna"
MARCH 17, 1984
Al Jarreau
"Mornin'"
"Trouble in Paradise"
APRIL 7, 1984
Deniece Williams
"Let's Hear It for the Boy"
"Wrapped Up"
APRIL 14, 1984
Madness
"Our House"
"Keep Moving"
MAY 5, 1984
Spinal Tap
"Christmas with the Devil"
"Big Bottom"
MAY 12, 1984
The Cars
"Magic"
"Drive"

1984–1985

OCTOBER 6, 1984
Thompson Twins
"Hold Me Now"
"The Gap"
OCTOBER 13, 1984
Peter Wolf
"Lights Out"
"I Need You Tonight"
OCTOBER 20, 1984
Andraé Crouch
"Right Now"
Wintley Phipps
"Tell Me Again"
NOVEMBER 3, 1984
Chaka Khan
"I Feel for You"
"This Is My Night"
NOVEMBER 10, 1984
Frankie Goes to Hollywood
"Two Tribes"
"Born to Run"
NOVEMBER 17, 1984
The Kinks
"Do It Again"
"Word of Mouth"
DECEMBER 1, 1984
Billy Squier
"Rock Me Tonight"
"All Night Long"
DECEMBER 8, 1984
Herbie Hancock
"Rockit"
"Junku"
DECEMBER 15, 1984
The Honeydrippers
"Santa Claus is Back in Town"
"Rockin' at Midnight"
JANUARY 12, 1985
John Waite
"Saturday Night"
JANUARY 19, 1985
Billy Ocean
"Caribbean Queen"
"Loverboy"
FEBRUARY 2, 1985
Tina Turner
"What's Love Got to Do With It"
"Better Be Good to Me"
"Private Dancer"
FEBRUARY 9, 1985
Bryan Adams
"Somebody"
"Run to You"
FEBRUARY 16, 1985
Power Station
"Some Like It Hot"
"Get It On (Bang a Gong)"
MARCH 30, 1985
The Commodores
"Night Shift"
"Animal Instinct"
APRIL 6, 1985
Santana
"Say It Again"
"Right Now"
APRIL 13, 1985
Greg Kihn
"Boys Won't"
"Lucky"

1985–1986

NOVEMBER 9, 1985
Simple Minds
"Alive and Kicking"
NOVEMBER 16, 1985
Sheila E.
"Hollyrock"
"A Love Bizarre"
NOVEMBER 23, 1985
Queen Ida
"La Louisiane" / *"Frisco Zydeco"*

DECEMBER 7, 1985
Mr. Mister
"Kyrie"
"Broken Wings"
DECEMBER 14, 1985
Sade
"The Sweetest Taboo"
"Is It a Crime"
DECEMBER 21, 1985
Dream Academy
"Life in a Northern Town"
The Cult
"She Sells Sanctuary"
JANUARY 18, 1986
The Replacements
"Bastards of the Young"
"Kiss Me on the Bus"
JANUARY 25, 1986
Al Green
"Going Away"
"True Love"
FEBRUARY 8, 1986
The Nelsons
"Walk Away"
"Do You Know What I Know"
FEBRUARY 15, 1986
Stevie Ray Vaughan
"Say What"
"Change It"
FEBRUARY 22, 1986
The Neville Brothers
"The Big Chief"
"The Midnight Key"
MARCH 15, 1986
Rosanne Cash
"Hold On"
"I Don't Know Why"
MARCH 22, 1986
Philip Glass
"Lightning"
"Rubric"
APRIL 12, 1986
Joe Jackson
"Right and Wrong"
"Soul Kiss"
APRIL 19, 1986
Laurie Anderson
"My Brian"
"Baby Doll"
"Day the Devil"
MAY 10, 1986
Paul Simon
"You Can Call Me Al"
"Homeless"
"Graceland"
MAY 17, 1986
Level 42
"Something About You"
E. G. Daily
"Say It, Say It"
MAY 24, 1986
George Clinton
"Take It to the Stage"
"Do Fries Go With That Shake"

1986–1987

OCTOBER 11, 1986
Buster Poindexter
"Oh Me, Oh My"
"Baby It's Cold Outside"
"Smack Dab in the Middle"
OCTOBER 18, 1986
Run-D.M.C.
"Walk This Way"
"Hit It, Run"
NOVEMBER 8, 1986
Ric Ocasek
"Emotion in Motion"
"Keep On Laughin'"
NOVEMBER 15, 1986
Lou Reed
"I Love You, Suzanne"
"Original Wrapper"

NOVEMBER 22, 1986
Paul Simon
"Diamonds on the Soles of Her Shoes"
"The Boy in the Bubble"
"The Late Great Johnny Ace"
DECEMBER 6, 1986
Randy Newman
"Roll With the Punches"
"Longest Night"
DECEMBER 13, 1986
The Pretenders
"Don't Get Me Wrong"
"How Much Did You Get for Your Soul"
Chrissie Hynde and Buster Poindexter
"Rockin' Good Way"
DECEMBER 20, 1986
Lone Justice
"I Found Love"
"Shelter"
Buster Poindexter
"Zat You, Santa?"
JANUARY 24, 1987
Debbie Harry
"French Kissin' in the USA"
"In Love With Love"
JANUARY 31, 1987
Bruce Hornsby and the Range
"The Way It Is"
"Mandolin Rain"
FEBRUARY 14, 1987
Paul Young
"WarGames"
"The Long Run"
Buster Poindexter
"Heart of Gold"
FEBRUARY 21, 1987
Willie Nelson
"Partners After All"
"Blue Eyes"
FEBRUARY 28, 1987
Robert Cray Band
"Right Next Door"
"Smoking Gun"
Eddie Van Halen
"Stompin' 8H"
MARCH 21, 1987
Percy Sledge
"When a Man Loves a Woman"
MARCH 28, 1987
Wynton Marsalis
"J Mood"
"One Mustaad"
APRIL 11, 1987
Anita Baker
"Sweet Love"
"Same Ole Love"
APRIL 18, 1987
Timbuk 3
"Just Another Movie"
"Hairstyles and Attitudes"
MAY 9, 1987
Suzanne Vega
"Marlene on the Water"
"Luka"
MAY 16, 1987
Los Lobos
"Is That All There Is"
"One Time, One Night"
MAY 23, 1987
Roy Orbison
"Crying" / *"Pretty Woman"*
"In Dreams"

1987–1988

OCTOBER 17, 1987
Sting
"We'll Be Together"
"Little Wing"
OCTOBER 24, 1987
L.L. Cool J
"Go Cut Creator Go"

The Pull
"The and That"
OCTOBER 31, 1987
The Cars
"Strap Me In"
"Double Trouble"
NOVEMBER 14, 1987
Simply Red
"Suffer"
"The Right Thing"
NOVEMBER 21, 1987
Cher
"I Found Someone"
"We All Sleep Alone"
DECEMBER 5, 1987
Bryan Ferry
"The Right Stuff"
"Kiss and Tell"
DECEMBER 12, 1987
David Gilmour
"Ah, Robertson, It's You"
Buster Poindexter
"Hot Hot Hot"
DECEMBER 19, 1987
Paul Simon and Linda Ronstadt
"Under African Skies"
Linda Ronstadt
"Los Laureles, La Cigarra"
JANUARY 23, 1988
James Taylor
"Lonesome Road"
"Sweet Potato Pie"
"Never Die Young"
JANUARY 30, 1988
Robbie Robertson
"Somewhere Down the Crazy River"
"Testimony"
FEBRUARY 13, 1988
Terence Trent D'Arby
"Wishing Well"
"Under My Thumb"
FEBRUARY 20, 1988
Randy Travis
"What'll You Do"
"Forever and Ever, Amen"
FEBRUARY 27, 1988
10,000 Maniacs
"What's the Matter Here"
"Like the Weather"

1988–1989

OCTOBER 8, 1988
Keith Richards
"Take It So Hard"
"Struggle"
OCTOBER 15, 1988
The Sugarcubes
"Birthday"
"Motorcrash"
OCTOBER 22, 1988
Randy Newman
"It's Money That Matters"
"Dixie Flyer"
NOVEMBER 5, 1988
Edie Brickell and New Bohemians
"What I Am"
"Little Miss S"
NOVEMBER 12, 1988
Johnny Clegg and Savuka
"I Call Your Name"
"Take My Heart Away"
NOVEMBER 19, 1988
Tracy Chapman
"Baby, Can I Hold You" / *"Freedom Now"*
"Mountains O' Things"
DECEMBER 3, 1988
The Bangles
"In Your Room"
"Hazy Shade of Winter"
DECEMBER 10, 1988
Bobby McFerrin
"Drive"
"The Star-Spangled Banner"

DECEMBER 17, 1988
Little Feat
"Let It Roll"
"Hate to Lose Your Lovin'"
JANUARY 21, 1989
Anita Baker
"Giving You the Best That I Got"
"Just Because"
JANUARY 28, 1989
John Hiatt
"Paper Thin"
"Slow Turning"
FEBRUARY 11, 1989
Luther Vandross
"She Won't Talk to Me"
"For You to Love"
FEBRUARY 18, 1989
Cowboy Junkies
"Sweet Jane"
"Misguided Angel"
FEBRUARY 25, 1989
Gipsy Kings
"Bamboleo"
"Djobi Djoba"
MARCH 25, 1989
Elvis Costello
"Veronica"
"Let Him Dangle"
APRIL 1, 1989
Living Colour
"Cult of Personality"
"Open Letter to a Landlord"
APRIL 15, 1989
Dolly Parton
"Why'd You Come in Here Lookin' Like That"
"White Limozeen"
APRIL 22, 1989
John Mellencamp
"Pop Singer"
"Jackie Brown"
MAY 13, 1989
Fine Young Cannibals
"She Drives Me Crazy"
"Good Thing"
MAY 20, 1989
Tom Petty and the Heartbreakers
"Free Fallin'"
"Runnin' Down a Dream"

1989–1990

SEPTEMBER 30, 1989
Neil Young
"Rockin' in the Free World"
"Needle and the Damage Done" / *"No More"*
OCTOBER 7, 1989
Rickie Lee Jones
"Satellites"
"Ghetto of My Mind"
OCTOBER 21, 1989
Billy Joel
"We Didn't Start the Fire"
"Downeaster Alexa"
OCTOBER 28, 1989
Don Henley
"The Last Worthless Evening"
"The Boys of Summer"
NOVEMBER 11, 1989
Eurythmics
"Angel"
"(My, My) Baby's Gonna Cry"
NOVEMBER 18, 1989
David Byrne
"Dirty Old Town"
"Loco de Amor"
DECEMBER 2, 1989
k.d. lang
"Pullin' Back the Reins"
"Johnny Get Angry"
DECEMBER 9, 1989
Linda Ronstadt and Aaron Neville
"Don't Know Much"
"When Something Is Wrong"

DECEMBER 16, 1989
Tracy Chapman
"Gimme One Reason"
"All That You Have"
JANUARY 13, 1990
Harry Connick, Jr.
"It Had to Be You"
"It's Alright with Me"
JANUARY 20, 1990
Bonnie Raitt
"Thing Called Love"
"Have a Heart"
FEBRUARY 10, 1990
Quincy Jones
"Back on the Block"
"We Be Doinit"
FEBRUARY 17, 1990
Aerosmith
"Janie's Got a Gun"
"Monkey on My Back"
FEBRUARY 24, 1990
Technotronic
"Pump Up the Jam"
"Get Up! (Before the Night Is Over)"
MARCH 17, 1990
The Pogues
"White City"
"Body"
MARCH 24, 1990
Eric Clapton
"No Alibis"
"Pretending"
"Wonderful Tonight"
APRIL 14, 1990
The Smithereens
"A Girl Like You"
"Blue Before and After"
APRIL 21, 1990
The B-52's
"Cosmic Thing"
"Channel Z"
MAY 12, 1990
Spanic Boys
"Keep On Walking"
Julee Cruise
"Falling"
MAY 19, 1990
The Notting Hillbillies
"Railroad Worksong"
"Love You Too Much"

1990–1991
SEPTEMBER 29, 1990
Sinéad O'Connor
"Three Babies"
"The Last Day of Our Acquaintance"
OCTOBER 6, 1990
Hothouse Flowers
"Give It Up"
"I Can See Clearly Now"
OCTOBER 20, 1990
The Time
"Jerk Out"
"Chocolate"
OCTOBER 27, 1990
Mariah Carey
"Vision of Love"
"Vanishing"
NOVEMBER 10, 1990
World Party
"Way Down Now"
"Ship of Fools"
NOVEMBER 17, 1990
Paul Simon
"The Obvious Child"
"Proof"
"Late in the Evening"
DECEMBER 1, 1990
Faith No More
"Epic"
"From Out of Nowhere"

DECEMBER 8, 1990
Edie Brickell and New Bohemians
"Woyaho"
"He Said"
DECEMBER 15, 1990
The Neville Brothers
"Brother Jake"
"River of Life"
JANUARY 12, 1991
Vanilla Ice
"Ice Ice Baby"
"Play That Funky Music"
JANUARY 19, 1991
Sting
"All This Time"
"Mad About You"
"Purple Haze"
FEBRUARY 9, 1991
INXS
"Bitter Tears"
"Suicide Blonde"
FEBRUARY 16, 1991
Deee-Lite
"World Clique"
"The Power of Love"
FEBRUARY 23, 1991
Whitney Houston
"I'm Your Baby Tonight"
"All the Man I Need"
"My Name Is Not Susan"
MARCH 16, 1991
Black Crowes
"Thick and Thin"
"She Talks to Angels"
MARCH 23, 1991
Fishbone
"Sunless Saturday"
"Everyday Sunshine"
APRIL 13, 1991
R.E.M.
"Losing My Religion"
"Shiny Happy People"
APRIL 20, 1991
Michael Bolton
"Love Is a Wonderful Thing"
"Time, Love and Tenderness"
MAY 11, 1991
Chris Isaak
"Wicked Game"
"Diddley Daddy"
MAY 18, 1991
Elvis Costello
"The Other Side of Summer"
"So Like Candy"

1991–1992
SEPTEMBER 28, 1991
Public Enemy
"Can't Truss It"
"Bring Tha Noize"
OCTOBER 5, 1991
Color Me Badd
"I Wanna Sex You Up"
"I Adore Mi Amor"
OCTOBER 12, 1991
Tom Petty
"Into the Great Wide Open"
"Kings Highway"
OCTOBER 26, 1991
Bonnie Raitt
"Something to Talk About"
"I Can't Make You Love Me"
NOVEMBER 2, 1991
Skid Row
"Piece of Me"
"Monkey Business"
NOVEMBER 16, 1991
Mariah Carey
"Can't Let Go"
"If It's Over"
NOVEMBER 23, 1991
Tin Machine
"Baby Universal"
"If There Is Something"

DECEMBER 7, 1991
Hammer
"Too Legit to Quit"
"Addams Groove"
"This Is the Way We Roll"
DECEMBER 14, 1991
James Taylor
"(I've Got to) Stop Thinkin' About That"
"Shed a Little Light"
JANUARY 11, 1992
Nirvana
"Smells Like Teen Spirit"
"Territorial Pissing"
JANUARY 18, 1992
Robbie Robertson
"Go Back to Your Woods"
"The Weight"
FEBRUARY 8, 1992
C+C Music Factory
"Here We Go Let's Rock and Roll" / "Gonna Make You Sweat"
"A Deeper Love"
FEBRUARY 15, 1992
Teenage Fanclub
"The Concept"
"What You Do to Me" / "Pet Rock"
FEBRUARY 22, 1992
Red Hot Chili Peppers
"Stone Cold Bush"
"Under the Bridge"
MARCH 14, 1992
Garth Brooks
"Rodeo"
"The River"
MARCH 21, 1992
En Vogue
"Never Gonna Get It" / "Hold On"
"Free Your Mind"
APRIL 11, 1992
Pearl Jam
"Alive"
"Porch"
APRIL 18, 1992
Annie Lennox
"Why"
"Legend in My Living Room"
MAY 9, 1992
Bruce Springsteen
"Lucky Town"
"57 Channels"
"Living Proof"
MAY 16, 1992
Vanessa Williams
"Save the Best for Last"
"The Comfort Zone"

1992–1993
SEPTEMBER 26, 1992
Bobby Brown
"Humpin' Around"
"Good Enough"
OCTOBER 3, 1992
Sinéad O'Connor
"Success Has Made a Failure of Our Home"
"War"
OCTOBER 10, 1992
Spin Doctors
"Little Miss Can't Be Wrong"
"Jimmy Olson's Blues"
OCTOBER 24, 1992
Arrested Development
"Tennessee"
"People Everyday"
OCTOBER 31, 1992
10,000 Maniacs
"These Are Our Days"
"Candy Everybody Wants"
NOVEMBER 14, 1992
Morrissey
"Glamorous Glue"
"Suedehead"

NOVEMBER 21, 1992
Sade
"No Ordinary Love"
"Cherish the Day"
DECEMBER 5, 1992
Neil Young
"From Hank to Hendrix"
"Harvest Moon"
DECEMBER 12, 1992
Black Crowes
"Sometimes Salvation"
"Non-Fiction"
JANUARY 9, 1993
Bon Jovi
"Bed of Roses"
"Wanted Dead or Alive"
JANUARY 16, 1993
Madonna
"Fever"
"Bad Girl"
FEBRUARY 6, 1993
Mick Jagger
"Sweet Thing"
"Don't Tear Me Up"
FEBRUARY 13, 1993
Paul McCartney
"Get Out of My Way"
"Biker Like an Icon"
"Hey Jude"
FEBRUARY 20, 1993
Sting
"If I Ever Lose My Faith in You"
"Love Is Stronger Than Justice"
"Every Breath You Take"
MARCH 13, 1993
Mary J. Blige
"Reminisce"
"Sweet Thing"
MARCH 20, 1993
Soul Asylum
"Somebody to Shove"
"Black Gold"
APRIL 10, 1993
Peter Gabriel
"Steam"
"In Your Eyes"
APRIL 17, 1993
Lenny Kravitz
"Are You Gonna Go My Way"
"Always on the Run"
MAY 8, 1993
Midnight Oil
"Truganini"
"My Country"
MAY 15, 1993
Willie Nelson and Paul Simon
"Graceland"
"Still Is Still Moving to Me"

1993–1994
SEPTEMBER 25, 1993
Nirvana
"Heart-Shaped Box"
"Rape Me"
OCTOBER 2, 1993
Cypress Hill
"Insane in the Brain"
"We Ain't Goin' Out Like That"
OCTOBER 9, 1993
Aerosmith
"Cryin'"
"Sweet Emotion"
OCTOBER 23, 1993
Billy Joel
"The River of Dreams"
"All About Soul"
OCTOBER 30, 1993
Smashing Pumpkins
"Cherub Rock"
"Today"
NOVEMBER 13, 1993
James Taylor
"Memphis" / "Slap Leather"
"Secret of Life"

NOVEMBER 20, 1993
Stone Temple Pilots
"Creep"
"Naked Sunday"
DECEMBER 4, 1993
Paul Westerberg
"Knockin' on Mine"
"Can't Hardly Wait"
DECEMBER 11, 1993
Tony Toni Toné
"If I Had No Loot"
"Tell Me Mama"
JANUARY 8, 1994
Blind Melon
"No Rain"
"Paper Scratcher"
JANUARY 15, 1994
Counting Crows
"'Round Here"
"Mr. Jones"
FEBRUARY 5, 1994
Salt-N-Pepa
"Shoop"
"Whatta Man"
FEBRUARY 12, 1994
UB40
"C'est la Vie"
"Can't Help Falling in Love"
FEBRUARY 19, 1994
Crash Test Dummies
"Mmm Mmm Mmm Mmm"
"Afternoons and Coffeespoons"
MARCH 12, 1994
Aretha Franklin
"A Deeper Love"
"Willing to Forgive"
"Chain of Fools"
MARCH 19, 1994
Snoop Doggy Dogg
"Gin and Juice"
"Lodi Dodi"
APRIL 9, 1994
Dwight Yoakam
"Pocket of a Clown"
"Fast as You"
APRIL 16, 1994
Pearl Jam
"Not for You"
"Rearview Mirror"
"Daughter"
MAY 7, 1994
The Pretenders
"Night in My Veins"
"I'll Stand By You"
MAY 14, 1994
Janet Jackson
"Throb"
"Any Time, Any Place"

Shows without a Musical Guest
DECEMBER 2, 1978
Host Walter Matthau
APRIL 5, 1982
Best of New SNL
JANUARY 22, 1983
Host Lily Tomlin; she performed as singer Purvis Hawkins
MARCH 24, 1984
Best of SNL
MARCH 2, 1985
SNL Film Festival
MAY 4, 1985
Best of SNL '85

Dick Ebersol was the NBC executive in charge of the development of the original *Saturday Night*, and he also took over as producer of the show from April 11, 1981 to April 13, 1985. Ebersol commented that if he were writing his *Saturday Night Live* epitaph, it would note three things. First and foremost, that the show brought him "the best thing I ever had in my life—my wife," Susan Saint James, whom he met when she hosted the show on October 10, 1981, and married six weeks later. Secondly, that he "had the good fortune to hire Lorne Michaels to produce this original vision." And finally, that the four years in which he served as producer "saved the show from extinction." The following are further reflections on his SNL experiences:

ON "DISCOVERING" EDDIE MURPHY:
It was clear the minute I walked into the room, the first time I walked into *Saturday Night Live*, that there was a megastar there and I still to this day cannot believe that anybody could miss that. None of us have ever taken any credit for finding him out somewhere else. Eddie was clearly right there, but he was an exalted extra—they had him warming up the audience. It's just mind blowing to me, even now, to think of the fact....Even if the material sucked, Eddie had something to bring to it, to bring a smile to your face.

ON HIS FINAL SEASON AS PRODUCER, 1984-85
I said to myself, "If George Steinbrenner can buy free agents, why can't I?"...I certainly think there was a murderer's row of young male talent on that show. And you can see Julia Louis-Dreyfus getting her legs as a real comedian. And Jim Belushi was getting a clear persona; his brother John was a gigantic presence, but I still believe Jimmy is the better actor.

ON LARRY THE LOBSTER:
I'm still stunned to this day that they voted to save him and as everybody in the studio knows, he died anyway—but the people at home wanted to save him.

Great Sketches (1980-85)

Frank Sinatra

1 *"Start shooting the press./They're just in the way./Don't let them be a part of it/My USA."* Frank (Joe Piscopo) is getting ready for the presidential inauguration: "You sent for me, Mr. Sinatra?" asks Reagan (Charles Rocket). Sinatra offers a few observations: "During rehearsal I noticed you were always in the front. Who do you think people are tuning in to see?"

"Number two—your acceptance speech. I'm not in it." Reagan swears he's rewriting it. "Good boy, Ronnie. I've been thinking in my skull about this Bush cat. He obviously does not *capisce* my role in the new administration."

"Oh, no, Mr. Sinatra. Georgie loves you!" "Not enough. He's out." More advice: "I think Nancy would make a groovier vice president." Nancy Kissinger? asks Reagan. "Your broad, your old lady, your chick!" "Oh, you mean Mommy!"

2 President Reagan addresses the nation "to talk to you about one of the most important questions that confronts the nation today: "Is Frank Sinatra a hoodlum?" And the Chairman is there to answer for himself. Frank, are you a hoodlum? "No, Ron, I am not." Do you associate with hoodlums? "No, Ron, I do not." Do you know Carlos Granatelli? "You mean Fingers?" Yes. "No."

3 Francis Albert is saddened to see "thousands and thousands of beautiful American guys and chicks out of work" in the auto industry. Worker Jerry Hemphill (Tony Rosato) shows that Japanese cars are made out of thin aluminum, like beer cans, while American cars "are built solid, like this American-made J.C. Higgins bowling ball." And bowling balls easily crush beer cans. But that can't help sweet little Melissa (Gail Matthius), who is in a wheelchair because her father's import ran into a cow.

Frank also shares the pain of vet Harold Duffy (Tim Kazurinsky), who lost an arm in WWII. "When we were shooting *From Here to Eternity*, I'd have to leave the set *every* day, because of the tears in my eyes."

Joe Piscopo

4 Mary Gross of Weekend Update reports on a recent Reagan legislative victory. In an interview the presidential consultant Frank Sinatra is asked how they persuaded the swing voters: "I can tell you in one word: 'Muscle.' We *leaned* on them, Mary. We let them know that if they did not cooperate, things would not go so good for them, if you catch my drift."

5 It's "Mick!," the Rolling Stone's first variety special, and the guests include "Mister Francis Albert Sinatra." Sinatra testifies: "I've always had this theory: Rock singers make me puke. Except for this, man. Mick, you're hip. You and your partner, what's-his-name, the guy who looks like walking death. You guys have penned some bouncy tunes that I've always wanted to sing."

6 The honorary entertainment director of the White House, Francis Albert Sinatra, celebrates the president's birthday. He alters "My Kind of Town": "*My kind of chief executive,/We're talkin' chief executive./Shoots down Qaddafi, Ron Reagan does,/Takes naps when he wants to, Ron Reagan does.*"

Then he does a little something for "our First Chick": "*When she gets hungry, the Third World can wait./She buys her china, at one grand a plate./Threads by Adolfo, that chick, she looks great./The First Lady [is a] champ.*"

And how about the secretary of state? "*He's bad, bad, bad Al Haig./Tougher than the Red Brigade./Badder than ol' King Kong./Meaner than a neutron bomb.*"

A few lines about the dancing Ron junior: " '*Fairy tales can come true, Ron it happened to you...*' Mr. President, I'm sure you feel the same way about Ron junior that I do about Frank junior."

7 Frank introduces *Frank Sings Tunes the Young People Will Enjoy*. To that end, Frank brings in Stevie Wonder (Eddie Murphy). He's very much into that tune Stevie does with the Beatle kid—"you know, the one who looks like a broad?"

The song is "Ebony and Ivory," which, Stevie explains, is about racial equality; but Frank doesn't get it: "When I think of *Ebony*, I think of a magazine that most people do not buy. When I think of Ivory, I think of a soap that floats." The keyboard metaphor is "too artsy for the public, *capisce*?" This is 1982, let's get to the point.

FRANK: *You are black and I am white*
Life's an Eskimo Pie,
Let's...take a bite!
That was groovy thinkin',
Lincoln, when you set them freeeeee...
We all know
Cats are the same,
Maine to Mexico—
Good...Bad...
Guys and chicks...
STEVIE: *I am dark and you are light.*
FRANK: *You are blind as a bat and I have sight.*
Side by side, you are my amigo,
Negro, let's not fiiiiight...
STEVIE: *Ebony, ivory,*
Living in perfect harmony.
FRANK: *Salt and pepper,*
Sammy and Dean,
Stevie and me are peachy keen.
STEVIE: *You are white.*
FRANK: *You are black—and who cares?*

8 Sinatra is a guest on Gumby's Christmas special. "I know you have many marvelous friends in the world of animation. I bring you greetings in song." He sings his version of the theme from *The Flintstones* (a yabba-dooby-doo time) and closes with a special "Silent Night":
Silent night, holy night,
It's okay, everything's all right
'Round that virgin chick, she had a kid,
Who grew up to be famous, you all know what he did.
Sleep! It's quiet in Heaven!
Sleep! Heavenly peace.

9 Bob Hope (Dave Thomas) has invited Woody Allen (Rick Moranis) over, as well as Frank. Woody asks the camera: "What can I possibly have in common with Frank Sinatra?"

"How about Mia Farrow," reminds Bob; and Frank wonders, "How's it feel to have seconds?" Hope and Sinatra want to enlist Allen's help in reelecting Reagan: "Me and Hope, we cover one segment of voters, and you cover the other. You know, like the faggots, the commies, the liberals, and that sort of thing." Under duress (he prefers "not to become part of a highway"), Woody agrees to direct Reagan's commercials: "But make 'em funny. Not like your last couple of movies."

Joe Piscopo and Eddie Murphy

10 Live from Las Vegas, it's the game show "What Would Frank Do?" with host Dom LaMagna (Danny DeVito). "Okay, Frank drops in unexpectedly to his favorite restaurant, Patsy DiAmore's Villa Capri. He notices his favorite table is occupied. The maître d' comes over. What would Frank do?"

Contestant number one (Robin Duke) thinks Mr. Sinatra would leave quietly after asking the maître d' about his family, fly back to Palm Springs, and have a lovely dinner on his jet. "What are you, from Mars?" The next contestant, the hairdresser Dion (Eddie Murphy), in town for a convention, answers: "Frank would buy the entire restaurant, then he could have his favorite table every time he wants." Contestant number three (Rhea Perlman) thinks "Frank would call Jilly and his goons and have them rearrange the customers' faces and then make the owner sleep with the fishes and break his sons' legs."

Dion had it right and he goes on to be the big winner. His prize: a trip to New York, New York. *"You're gonna wake up in a Dunfey classic hotel…"*

11 Frank has arranged for his friend Sammy Davis, Jr. (Billy Crystal) to host *Saturday Night Live*. Sammy calls Frank out as his first guest. *"Once there was a cat with one eye,/Wanted to host on* Saturday Night./*They wouldn't let this black, Jack—/So I gave 'em a smack!"* After an interruption they do a duet: *"So anytime I'm feeling blue/Because you're a black Jew/It can be outtasight./Live from New York, it's a groovy thing,/The Candyman can on Shabbas Day,/Live from New York, it's Saturday Night!"*

FIRST AIRED: JANUARY 17, 1981

The Honeyrooneys

Ralph: Me and my pal Norton are going bowling. Hey, Norton! Come down here! [*To audience, referring to city backdrop*] Did you ever notice how fake these buildings are? [*A knock at the front door*] And how quickly Norton comes downstairs?

Norton: Hey there, Ralphie boy, what do you say there, pal o'mine? How you doing, Alice. Ralph, I'm a bit on the hungry side, mind if I take a bite out of your refrigerator?

RALPH KRAMDEN PLAYED BY "ANDY ROONEY" (JOE PISCOPO)
ED NORTON PLAYED BY EDDIE MURPHY
AIRED: APRIL 17, 1982

Eddie Murphy and Joe Piscopo

Joe Piscopo

Andy Rooney

Ever notice how annoying my voice is? Of course, you can turn it off. I can't! Ever notice it gets dark at night? Where does the sun go? Nobody knows. Ever notice how much rouge I have on my cheeks? Of course, some people think it makes me look like a clown...

PLAYED BY JOE PISCOPO
AIRED: OCTOBER 3, 1981

ma's room and say 'bitch.' Did she slap you? Then you did it right!"

Mr. Robinson's friend Mr. Speedy (Gilbert Gottfried) comes to the door with a $125 "chemistry kit": "You should never play with chemicals unless you know what you're doing, boys and girls. Can you say 'Richard Pryor'?"

2

It's one hell of a day in my neighborhood,
A hell of a day for a neighbor.
Would you be mine?
Could you be mine?
I hope I get to move to your neighborhood someday.
The problem is that when I move in, y'all move away.
So come on up for some coke or some smoke.
You bring the stash, 'cause Robinson's broke.
Would you be mine?
Could you be mine?
Won't you be my neighbor?

"We're all alone today. You know why? My wife walked out on me. I'm so glad the bitch is gone." Mr. Landlord (Tim Kazurinsky) brings Mr. Robinson a present. "Oooo, look,

Eddie Murphy

Mr. Robinson's

The amiable Mr. Robinson is a lot like the personable children's television host Mr. Rogers—the main difference is that Mr. Robinson's "wonderful, magical city of fantasy" is the ghetto. "Oh, look, a bombed-out building! Could you live in it? Could you corner somebody in it and take his wallet? Our neighbors are having so much fun, our friends can hardly wait to go out and play. Ooh, look! Mr. Taxicab Driver is driving through our neighborhood. Think he'll pick up one of the people from our neighborhood? No way. Can you say 'throw a coke bottle'? Well, since I have to walk to work—I can't catch a cab—I gotta walk sixty-three blocks, so I'll see you tomorrow."

1 "My wife will be home soon—Can you say 'bitch'?" In fact, "that's our special word today." "Walk into Mom-

boys and girls, an eviction notice. Can you say 'scumbucket'? That's our special word for the day." Robinson says he *did* have the rent money, but it "mysteriously disappeared": "Then suddenly my wife showed up in a new dress. You want to see that dress, boys and girls?" He holds up a torn dress, which has a large bootprint on it.

Then it's off to the magical land of make-believe to visit a scumbag—a puppet of President Reagan. The president has no answers for Robinson's questions, so the middle finger stands alone: "I think I speak for all black people!"

3

It's one chilly day in my neighborhood,
A chilly day for a neighbor.
Would you be mine?
Could you be mine?

I used to have a winter coat, but it got stole.
I ain't been outside in a week 'cause it's too damn cold.
I hope you're warm in Beverly Hills.
When the earthquake comes, I hope you get killed.
Would you be my—
Wish you was my—
You wish you was my neighbor.

Mr. Landlord has turned off the heat because Mr. Robinson didn't pay his rent. "Mr. Landlord sure is mean. Can you say 'mutha'? When you say it one way it means mom. Try saying it this way: MUTHA!"

We meet Robinson's friend Nelson: "He's a mean mutha. He's what we call a py-ro-man-knee-ack." Nelson takes care of the heating problem by torching the landlord's apartment—and Robinson heats himself by the flames. "Oh, that's a nice warm fire, boys and girls."
This evenin', this evenin'
I burned up my landlord,
And I don't feel blue
'Cause when they put him in the soil,
I'll go down and turn on my oil.
A very happy tomorrow to you.

Neighborhood

4 Today's word, "scumi," is in *Soul Train* scrambleboard style, and Mr. Robinson rearranges it to form "music." Robinson is going to play his new drums. "Drums come from Africa, but these drums come from the Apollo Theater, where Smokey Robinson's band is performing and they left his van open in the back of the place. I ripped him off."

But Robinson's drumming disturbs his neighbor (Mr. T), who breaks through the door and prepares to do the same to Mr. Robinson. "Hello, boys and girls. The new word for the day is 'pain.'"

5

It's a beautiful day in the neighborhood,
A beautiful day for a neighbor.
Would you be mine?
Could you be mine?

Eddie Murphy and Mr. T

I married a woman who said she was rich.
I spent all her money, walked out on the bitch.
Would you be mine?
Could you be mine?
Won't you be my neighbor?

Today's word is "ontapanure." Learning to make money is easy. Mr. Robinson is selling things "lying around the house," like a car stereo. "How long do *you* think it would take Mr. Robinson to get one of these out of that BMW? Would you believe twenty-seven seconds?" He also has gold chains and lots of wallets, including one with a pants leg hanging on it: "That's what happens when you get in a rush, boys and girls." And there are some earrings too: "Uh-oh. Looks like there's a little piece of ear left on this one."

6 Mr. Robinson has just been given a basket left by an old friend named Juanita. ("You know, friends like to give things to each other. I gave something to Juanita one night. Eight times one night.") What could it be? "Here's a riddle, boys and girls: What's black and Puerto Rican and has my eyes?" It's today's new word: "bastard." "Can you use this word in a sentence? Cabdrivers can."

Mr. Robinson explains where babies come from: "When two people love each other very much, they lay down and the man gives the woman twenty dollars." Robinson learns that this little bundle can bring a thousand dollars on the black market. "Babies really *are* a bundle of joy!"

7

I've always wanted to live in a house like yours, my friend.
Maybe when there's nobody home—I'll break in!
It feels real good to walk streets again
After being in jail doing seven to ten.
Would you be mine?
Won't you be mine?
I wish you was my neighbor.

Mr. Robinson gives a lesson in careful shopping. The receipt in his grocery bag reads $46.79: "That's a lot of money for a lady who could only afford to give me a quarter to carry it to her car. I felt so bad for her that I carried it all the way to my apartment for free. I guess she learned a lesson in careful shopping, didn't she? She learned that forty-six dollars worth of groceries is worth more than twenty-five stinkin' cents."

A good comparison shopper doesn't have to spend a lot either. "This turkey has the same nutrition as a T-bone steak. But if you compare the two packages like I did, you'll see the steak fits under your clothes a whole lot easier."

8 Mr. Robinson has been talking to children in the park about what they want to be when they grow up: "A fireman? Really? You want to have a burning wall fall on your head while you're trying to save some bitch's cat? Naw, you don't want that."

He has a small dog with him, who is two years old: "Why, in human years, that means he'd have dropped out of school by now." Robinson shows how to pursue a career in telephone soliciting: "Hello? Is this Mrs. Herbert Green?...This is?...Good! Is your dog missing?...Why don't you go check?" In the meantime the boys and girls learn a new word, "ransom." Let's use it in a sentence: "I *ransom* dog out the yard and now I got it. Mrs. Green, do you know today's new word?"

9 Christmas is a time for giving, and Mr. Landlord has given Mr. Robinson an eviction notice. That's why Mr. Robinson wears a Santa suit to sneak into his building. "But this suit isn't just a disguise. No! When I add this Salvation Army kettle and this bell, it becomes a small business."

Mr. Robinson actually has a lot in common with Santa. "We both like to climb into people's houses late at night. Only, Mr. Santa Claus likes to leave things. Mr. Robinson prefers to take a few things away every now and then."

Mr. Robinson tears the heads off ordinary dolls and sticks on a head of cabbage to create Cabbage Patch dolls: "I can sell these to little stupid kids for about fifty dollars each." Today's word is "X-mas." Another word that begins with "x"? X-con. And when Mr. Landlord bangs on the door, Mr. Robinson remembers another "x" word: x-scape!

First aired: February 21, 1981

Buckwheat

Buh-Weet Sings

Eddie Murphy and Tim Curry

Boy, id been a nong tibe since dem days," the No-Longer-Little Rascal observes. "Hi, I'm Buh-Weet, amembuh me?" The lovable star of the Little Rascals has a new adult career as a pop singer. In fact, Buckwheat (Eddie Murphy) has sold more albums than Elvis, or The Beatles—in Kenya! And here in America his debut album is "numbah eighting wid a bullet, and we hopin' id donna doe dold." Follow the tragic story of Buckwheat and his valiant comeback effort.

1 Buckwheat introduces his album *Buh-Weet Sings*: "dum ub my bavorite tongs. Ids all ite here in dis uhn petacular opper," Take a wisten: "*Munce, tice, fee tines a mady.*" Also on the album are the songs "Wookin' Pa Nub" ("*Wookin' pah nub in all da wong paces, wookin' pa nub*") and "Una Pa Noonah Banka." Send $49.95 to Buh-Weet, Bah Firty-Free, New Nork, New Nork. "Take it fum Ow Gang, yo gang will nub it. Buy my wecord! O-tay!"

2 Mick Jagger (Tim Curry) hosts a television special. Guests include the Mandrell Sisters (Christine Ebersole, Robin Duke, and Mary Gross), Shari Lewis (Robin Duke) and Lamb Chop, and—"I can't believe it! Buckwheat! What are you doing on my first network special?" "Hi, Mit Dagger! I wad dus atoss da hall, tabing a new peshal paced on my album *Buh-Weet Sings*."

3 Tom Snyder (Joe Piscopo) hosts a kids program, "The Uncle Tom Show." Buckwheat is a guest, pushing his new album, *Buh-weet Sings por de Tids*. Selections include "*No, no, no de moat, dently down de deam./Meneny, meneny, meneny, meneny, nipe id bud a deam,*" and the song from *Mary Poppins*, "Tuperpalitaginistusexpianadoshus."

"Thanks Buckwheat, I got to be honest, I don't know what the hell you just said but I enjoyed it anyway!"

4 A musical performance by Buh-Weet and de Dup-weems. They perform "Top! in du Name of Nub" and their pirst dold wecord, "Aby Nub." The set ends with Buckwheat mixing with the audience and singing "Meech Out an Dutch."

5 Robert Blake returns to his roots with a reunion of his colleagues from the Little Rascals. Alfalfa (Mary Gross) has been singing in Vegas with Falana, Spanky is still a pig, Darla (Julia Louis-Dreyfus) has been "turning tricks in Washington" and wears a stole made out of Petey, while Froggy has been serving time after taking revenge on the doctor who removed his tonsils and ruined his voice. Buckwheat has just played Carnegie Hall, and has a warm greeting for Bawetta.

6 The camera slowly crawls up a pair of designer jeans. Calvin Klein? Nmm-mmm. Jordache? Nmm-mmm. Sassoon? Nmm-mmm. Now the model's face can be seen, and he asks, "Buh-weet? *Yes!*" Buckwheat Jeans: with "Otay" on the back pocket.

7 "The Shooting of Buckwheat: America Stunned," Ted Koppel (Joe Piscopo) reports the shocking news and we go to the videotape: "No oddagaffs, peas," Buckwheat requests as he waves to his fans. A voice calls, "Hey, Mr. Wheat!" and shots ring out.

The live coverage switches to St. Vincent's Hospital. Koppel delivers the tragic news: "Buckwheat is dead." A new program identification runs: "Buckwheat Dead: America Mourns. Brought to you by Texxon. Life goes on, and Texxon is there. Because Buckwheat would have wanted it that way."

Coming Thursday night at 9: *The Buckwheat Story* on NBC. O-tay!

Mary Gross

8 "He's hot, he's sexy, and he's dead." David Susskind interviews Buckwheat's bodyguard Burger Johnson (Eddie Murphy), who declares that "Buckwheat was the greatest performer that ever lived." But Burger goes on to say: "Buckwheat was a sleazeball. It's all in my new book, *Buckwheat Was a Sleazeball*. It's all there—the nastiness, the brutality, the kinkiness, the drugs, the fact that that little nigger slapped me in front of the queen of England."

Burger claims: "Many times he would say to me, 'Burger, go round up twelve strangers off the street. I'm gonna sex 'em down.' " To prove his point, Burger airs a home video: Buckwheat shoots out his TV set, burns his caterer with a cigarette, and uses two women to "make a Buh-Weet sandwich."

9 Buckwheat answers the door—after putting on a fake beard. He says in a clear voice, "I'm sorry, I'm not allowed any visitors. I've been quite ill." As the man leaves, we hear, "Whew! Dat mud a tose nun! I better bactice my peach nesson."

The bell rings again and it's Alfalfa (Mary Gross): "Open your shirt please. My friend Buckwheat had a big tattoo on his chest. It said 'Mother.' " The tattoo now says "Tom Smothers," and Buckwheat slips: "I'm his miggest pan."

Apparently, Buckwheat staged his own "tilling," as he was receiving death "trets." "I never dun nubbin do no-body," he claims. But Alfalfa reminds him of the time Buckwheat put a frog down his pants, just as he was about to sing in front of class. Alfalfa pulls out a gun—"I've been waiting all my life for this moment"—and shoots Buckwheat for real.

O-Tay!

FIRST AIRED: OCTOBER 10, 1981

Eddie Murphy

§ ome would call Velvet Jones (Eddie Murphy) a mere pitchman, but the leader of the Velvet Jones School of Technology describes himself as an educator. His school helps many, many people make lots and lots of money: "We can even help you to get your high school dequibalency degree!" Here is what Velvet has to offer you:

1 "Are you a female high school dropout, between the ages of sixteen and twenty-five? Are you tired of doors being slammed in your face when you apply for a job? Are you tired of laying around in bed all day with nothing to do? Well, you never need get up again, because in six short weeks I can train you to be a high-paying ho. That's right. It's a known fact that a good ho can make up to fifteen hundred dollars a week. Just think—fifteen hundred dollars a week, without even leaving the comforts of your own bedroom.

"Sound too good to be true? Just send for my new book, *I Wanna Be a Ho*, and if in six short weeks you're not confident that you can make big money as a ho working for me, just send the book back for a full refund! It's as simple as that!"

A student (Robin Duke) confirms Velvet's claims: "You get to meet new people, travel, wear nice clothes, make

Velvet Jones

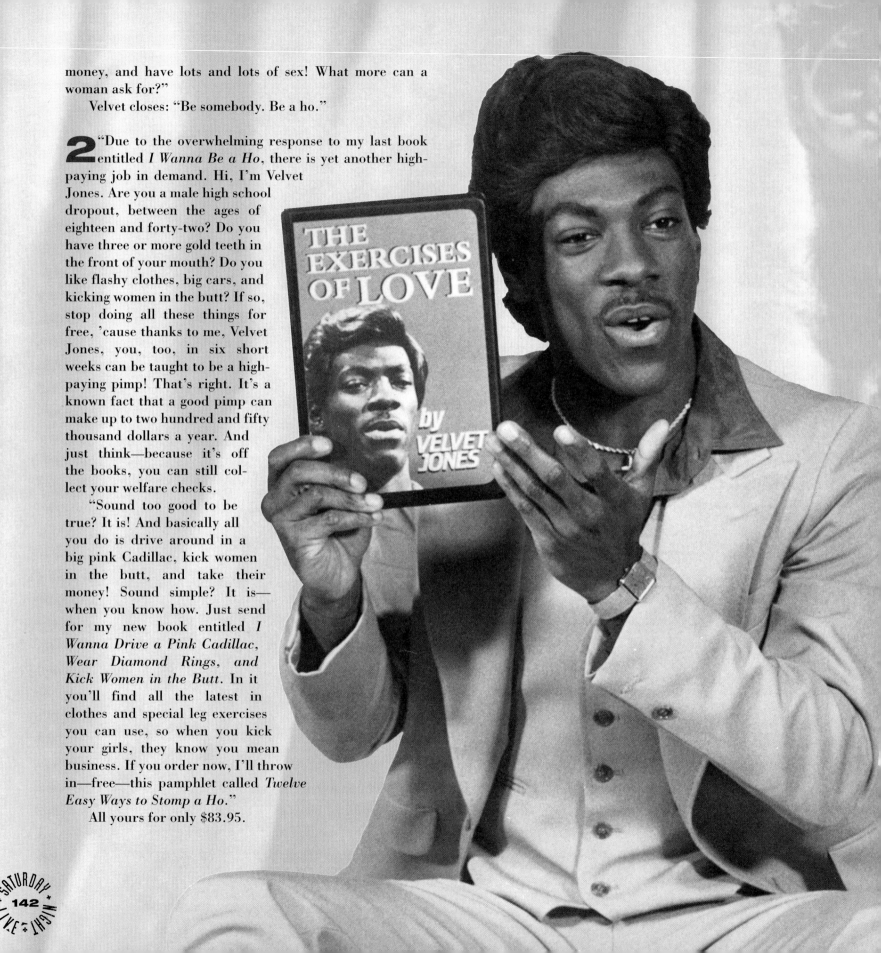

money, and have lots and lots of sex! What more can a woman ask for?"

Velvet closes: "Be somebody. Be a ho."

2 "Due to the overwhelming response to my last book entitled *I Wanna Be a Ho*, there is yet another high-paying job in demand. Hi, I'm Velvet Jones. Are you a male high school dropout, between the ages of eighteen and forty-two? Do you have three or more gold teeth in the front of your mouth? Do you like flashy clothes, big cars, and kicking women in the butt? If so, stop doing all these things for free, 'cause thanks to me, Velvet Jones, you, too, in six short weeks can be taught to be a high-paying pimp! That's right. It's a known fact that a good pimp can make up to two hundred and fifty thousand dollars a year. And just think—because it's off the books, you can still collect your welfare checks.

"Sound too good to be true? It is! And basically all you do is drive around in a big pink Cadillac, kick women in the butt, and take their money! Sound simple? It is— when you know how. Just send for my new book entitled *I Wanna Drive a Pink Cadillac, Wear Diamond Rings, and Kick Women in the Butt*. In it you'll find all the latest in clothes and special leg exercises you can use, so when you kick your girls, they know you mean business. If you order now, I'll throw in—free—this pamphlet called *Twelve Easy Ways to Stomp a Ho*."

All yours for only $83.95.

3 Paulette Clooney (Robin Duke) is suing Velvet Jones for false advertising. Her attempts to use his methods have failed miserably. "This weirdo comes over and says he'll give me three bucks to put my fist in my mouth—like this!" she says, describing the best she did.

Velvet accuses Paulette of skipping chapter 3, "Would I Make a Good Ho?" "Not everyone can be a ho," Velvet states. "I think we can clear this up in three words: 'The bitch ugly.' " The judge concurs.

4 Secret Serviceman James West (Robert Conrad) searches for General Ulysses S. Grant (Tim Kazurinsky) at the best brothel in Washington—run by Velvet Jones: "One of you hos better bring me a mint julep before I kick your butt! And one of you hos better get that door before I kick your other butt!"

West knows Jones as a "disgruntled runaway slave turned mad scientist, inventor, and trafficker in white slavery." Velvet, however, prefers to think of it as affirmative action: "My hos are happy hos. Listen to they sing!" West demands custody of the drunken Grant, but Velvet wants ten thousand dollars. "That's not ransom, that's his bar bill—and I'm not even mentioning the three dollars he owes for the two minutes with Curlene!" Jones escapes in a time machine, to one hundred years in the future.

5 Velvet tells the audience he has died from overexposure: "You will never see me again on this show, because tonight I died from overexposure." He introduces friend Paulie Herman, the Jersey Guy (Joe Piscopo), who says "I, too, know all too well the difficulties of overexposure, having appeared on this show one too many times. So I am pleased to announce that Velvet and I are moving to the Garden State of New Jersey." Velvet tries Paulie's "I'm from Jersey! Are you from Jersey?" while Paulie does his "Be a ho. Are you a ho?"

6 "Who among us has not dreamed of faraway places and intertwined lovers? Hi. I'm Velvet Jones. If you love love as I do, I know you will want to buy my latest Velvet Jones Harlequin Romances. There are many exquisite titles to choose from."

He reads from *Velvet Love*: " 'When she touched her lips to the glass, LaWanda felt her heart move inside her. The fire in her eyes beckoned me. I knew in that instant that the three dollars I had spent on wine would not go to waste.'

"Wasn't that romantic? But wait. There's more. Allow me to read from my personal favorite: 'Suddenly I saw her, standing at the gates of the Lincoln Tunnel. Dare I approach her? My heart pounded in my chest. I felt a burning in my loins I had never felt before. Thus I realized that I had been...*Kicked in the Butt by Love*.' Yes, endless evenings of romance can all be yours if you order now. Who wrote the book of love? Velvet! It's as simple as that."

7 "Hello, I'm Velvet Jones. Are you out of shape but would like to get in shape in order to have more sex? I can show you how to do it. The easy way. It's all here in my exciting new videocassette...*The Exercises of Love*, by Velvet Jones." Comes complete with demonstrations by the lovely Velvettes. "Yes, it's all here: the squatting, the thrusting, the grunting, and the groaning. Take it from Velvet, these are exercises you will want to watch again and again."

Be somebody. Be a ho.

FIRST AIRED: OCTOBER 17, 1981

Gumby

"I'm Gumby. I am Gumby, dammit. G–U–M–B–Y. Never have five words weighed so much." Gumby (Eddie Murphy) is "an entertainer, an actor, and an eraser." Is he over the hill? His agent does note that he's been having trouble getting Play-Doh commercials, but the man himself maintains that he is "a very rich piece of gum, baby."

He has not had an easy time of it, being a "green Jew," but he is "the one who broke the color barriers for all the other cartoons of today—for your Pink Panthers and your Heckle and Jeckle." Gumby speaks coarsely and likes to smoke a big cigar. He has little affection for his former partner Pokey (Joe Piscopo): "A lame, plug nag," "Mr. No Work, Mr. Washed-Up, Mr. Nobody." But some say that it's Gumby who suffers—from a big head ("a big crooked head, I might add").

Gumby's Career:

1 Tom Snyder (Joe Piscopo) is hosting his children's show, "The Uncle Tom Show," with guest Gumby, who has written an exposé on the industry: *I'm Gumby, Dammit.*

"Don't let anyone tell you that the casting couch does not exist in the cartoon industry. I want you to know, and I'm not afraid to sit on your show, Tom, and tell you who they were. For instance, Betty Boop. She was on the casting couch. Also, Josie *and* the Pussycats. Them too. And believe it or not, Wilma Flintstone. The woman is a slut, Tom. She made it to Bedrock on her back, and I'm not ashamed to tell you this."

What about rumors of Gumby's own loose ways? "Not me, Tom, but you know who got a way with the girls? Magilla Gorilla. He'll get in bed with anyone. I've caught him in bed with Mr. Peebles before."

2 It's "Merry Christmas, Dammit!": "I am Gumby, and I want to say before I get started it's about time the swines at the network gave me my own special. I've been sitting in my living room watching specials with nobodies, like Frosty the Snowman and Rudolph the Red-Nosed Reindeer for years. Hey, Rudy! Drop dead, baby, this is my special! We know why the nose is red, Rudy! *Glug glug gla-glug.*" He has a treat for the kids: "Wanna hear Gumby tell a Christmas story? Then gather around and keep your damn mouths shut!"

3 Bruce Dern is suited as Gumby and offers to tell a St. Patrick's Day story. The real Gumby interrupts: "Drop dead, you bastard, there's only one Gumby, all right, and that's me, okay? I'm Gumby, dammit, me!"

Gumby agrees to hear his story, which features Saint Patrick bashing leprechauns over the head. "I

like that," Gumby admits. "I didn't know you felt that way about leprechauns."

4 It's *Late Night with David Letterman*, and Dave (Joe Piscopo) introduces guest Gumby. "Cut the crap, Letterman, you know why I'm here, I'm here to push my special—let's push it, baby." It's a bloopers compilation called "Pardon Me, Dammit, I Blew It." It features Pokey sneezing during Marvin Hamlisch's arpeggio, set-

ting the pianist off on a rampage of whining. Letterman's teasing doesn't go over with Gumby: "Don't be sassy with me, I'll smack you in the mouth!"

5 Gumby is reuniting with Pokey for a television special, but the horse is late for rehearsal: "Why am I working with this no-talent, drunken, hypochondriac horse? That nag could not get a job on a merry-go-round!"

Pokey finally shows: "I got chest pains. I was at the doctor. I feel terrible." Gumby is not sympathetic and is particularly offended by Pokey's flatulence: "The last thing I need is a big fat orange horse breaking wind, stinking up the place!" Gumby also outlines an important distinction: "You are not working with me. You are working *for* me, all right? Now, before this you were nowhere. I

Eddie Murphy and Joe Piscopo

got into a hansom cab last week, who's pulling the cab? You."

6 Young Gumby (Gary Kroeger) is turned down by the casting agent (Joe Piscopo) for *The Victor Mature Story*. "But I'm flexible," Young Gumby protests.

"Cut!" Gumby cries—he is directing *The Gumby Story*. Later in the film, the agent gets a call for a green, rubbery, slope-headed guy who can twist himself into a pretzel—and a star is born.

But the executive in charge of production (Jim Belushi) shuts down this "turkey." It can't be the writing or the directing that's the problem, since Gumby did both—so he attacks the actor playing Young Gumby.

7 In "Broadway Gumby Rose," some show-biz old-timers (Martin Short, Billy Crystal, and Christopher Guest) are hanging around the delicatessen, trading stories, and Gumby joins them. He's been in Nashville recording commercials for fish. "I am a star, okay? I'm not a fish salesman!" The waiter (Rich Hall) demands seventeen dollars and change from Gumby; on November 6, 1958, at five-thirty P.M., he allegedly ran out on his bill for a Morey Amsterdam sandwich.

I'm Gumby, dammit.

FIRST AIRED: MARCH 27, 1982

Eddie Murphy

GREAT MOMENTS

Larry the Lobster

Eddie Murphy: Would you throw your pet dog or cat or hamster into boiling water? No! No you wouldn't. You know why? Because those pets have a name. And so does this thing here. His name is Larry. Larry the Lobster. And you know what we're going to do? Larry's life is in your hands. I'm dead serious, this is what we're going to do, listen to me. We've asked NBC—this is not a joke—to get up two special phone numbers so you people at home can call in and vote. Now this show is live and we're really doing this; this is not a joke. You want to save Larry the Lobster, dial 1-900-720-1808. That number again [*Speaks quickly*] 1-900-720-1808. If you want to kill him...

Tony Rosato: Let's boil that sucker!

Eddie: If you want to kill him, dial 1-900-720-1809. That's [*Speaks slowly*] 1-900-720-1809. Now unless you call in to save him, we're going to boil Larry's little butt right here on national television. Now you call in. The phone company is going to charge you fifty cents, but isn't it worth fifty cents to save Larry's life? Or look at it this way: Isn't it worth half a buck to see us boil Larry on TV? So call now—

you've only got an hour—operators are standing by.

Eddie [*Later in the show*]: In just a little while, we're going to find out if Larry lives or Larry dies. But first I want to say that I think Larry here has been a good sport about all of this. For that reason, if Larry lives, Larry's really gonna live. Mel, tell 'em about it.

Announcer: If Larry lives, we'll give him a night on the town he'll always remember, beginning with a luxurious ride in a limo provided by Eastwind Limousine. First stop, Broadway, and the Mark Hellinger Theater, where Larry will enjoy the hit musical *Sugar Babies*. After the show, Larry will go backstage, where he'll meet stars Ann Miller and Mickey Rooney. Then, it's back to the limo to the fabulous Rainbow Room, where Larry will dance to the music of Cy Oliver and his orchestra. Larry, it's all yours if our viewers decide to save you. Otherwise, it's a one-way ticket to a burning, boiling hell.

Final Tally:
KILL LARRY: 227,452
SAVE LARRY: 239,096

AIRED: APRIL 10, 1982

Robin Duke and Joe Piscopo

can't eat any of this. We have diverticulitis"). The waiter (Tony Rosato) tries to get them out as quickly as possible—eventually offering them the meal on the house ("I didn't know it was going to cost this much") and driving them home.

2 Doug and Wendy travel by plane. They are to be seated next to Danny DeVito ("But we wanted to sit in the nonsmoking section"). After they wrestle with their luggage ("But it'll stick out and I won't have any room for my feet") and headsets ("Mine isn't working"), the stewardess announces that the flight is overbooked, and everyone runs for the door.

3 The Whiners are having trouble conceiving; their doctor (Ron Howard) suggests that stress may be a problem ("Well, Wendy's mom is staying with us"; "Doug lost his job"; "Our apartment was robbed"; "And I don't feel attractive!"). They rule out adoption, since "it wouldn't be a real Whiner," and Doug insists: "My genes must live on." So the doctor shuttles them off to an artificial insemination specialist.

Doug Whiner's (Joe Piscopo) and Wendy Whiner's (Robin Duke) most noticeable attribute is their incredibly loud, nasal, and whiny voices, which they use to complain about nearly anything, and everything. Add to this their pathetically slouched posture—possibly caused by exhaustion from their diverticulitis—and it is safe to say that nobody can clear a room like the Whiners. They live in New Jersey, in a lovely home with a badminton court. Childless when we first meet them, they eventually adopt a little girl (Drew Barrymore), as hopelessly annoying as they are.

The Whiner Chronicles:

1 The Whiners return to the restaurant where they had their first date. They have to wait ("But I wanted to sit down right away"), then switch tables ("But we wanted to sit over there"), and even have trouble ordering ("But we

4 The Whiners adopt a nasty little girl, Wanda, who has been rejected by three thousand couples and forty-two single parents: "I don't want to live in New Jersey! It smells like cheese!" She is as annoying as they are—and she even has diverticulitis. "We love her!" Wanda says: "I'm gonna be a Whiner!" The process usually costs five hundred dollars and takes six months, but for this case the adoption agency makes an exception: "I'll give you ten dollars and you can take her today."

5 Doug and Wendy stumble onto a bank robbery. The bandits (Brad Hall and Gary Kroeger) take them

hostage and are so annoyed by their whining ("You'll get the chair for this") that they shoot them. Doug is wounded—but he thinks his diverticulitis is cured.

6 Doug is in the hospital with a gunshot wound. He shares a room with a gravely ill patient (Sid Caesar) on life-support machines. Wendy visits, and the couple's whining brings the other patient to his feet: "You're up and around—that's nice. What are you doing?" Announcing, "I'm going to shut you up!" he then tries to kill them.

7 The Whiners arrive late for a taping of *SNL* ("We had to take a nap") and a page (Julia Louis-Dreyfus) gives them standing room ("But I can't see!"). They're not too happy about the host, Joan Rivers ("She's so loud"), or the musical guests, Musical Youth ("They shouldn't be up so late"), and they wind up opening the show with their whining.

8 Wendy finds Doug's war medals. Flashbacks of Vietnam show that he drove his captors crazy and they actually let him go—he did not "escape."

9 The Whiners are the one millionth visitors to the Big Apple ("I hate New York"; "We wanted to go to Toledo!") and the guests of "Two on the Town." Hosts Rob Weller (Gary Kroeger) and Melanie Anderson (Julia Louis-Dreyfus) show them the sights, from the view from atop the Empire State Building ("It's so crowded down there"), to hot dogs *al fresco* ("Don't you have anything easier to digest?"), to *Cats* ("They smell") on Broadway. Finally they introduce the Whiners to a real taste of New York—a mugging. But the muggers give them back their money and run away.

FIRST AIRED: APRIL 10, 1982

The Whiners

Billy Crystal

Sammy

Christopher Guest, Billy Crystal, Martin Short, Jim Belushi, and Mary Gross

1 The metal detector at the White House has rejected Sammy Davis, Jr.'s (Billy Crystal) jewelry, but once inside he tells Reagan (Joe Piscopo), "What a gas it is to be here with you, the ultimate cat," and cracks a joke about not being crazy over the house's color. Sammy is grooving on the whole experience: "I've got the *shpilkes* and the *nachas*—it's like a surf and turf, you know what I'm saying?"

Reagan wants Sammy's help: "A campaign song?" asks Sammy, and sings one used by his friend in India: "*Who can take the British,/Bring them to their knees/With passive resistance and some curry if you please?/The Gandhi-man,/The Gandhi-man can.*" Sir Ron asks, "Would you do a hug for me?" "Any place, anytime," says Sammy, jumping into Reagan's arms. "Not *me*—Hart and Mondale, hug *them!*" Sammy's happy to do his part: "I will hug these guys right out of their political careers."

2 Sammy is telling Frank Sinatra (Joe Piscopo) that he feels bad about not being asked to host *Saturday Night Live.* "Sammy, the show *sucks.*" "But Frank, it's a hip thing to do, and I'm into hipness," Sammy argues.

Host you will, Frank declares. Together they go to NBC and Frank interrupts Don Pardo's audience warm-up— "Don, it's good to see you. Listen, do me a favor, get me some towels for my room"—and announces that Sammy will be tonight's host. They sing a duet: "*So anytime I'm feeling blue/Because you're a black Jew/It can be outtasight./Live from New York, it's a groovy thing,/The Candyman can on Shabbas Day,/Live from New York it's Saturday Night!*"

3 Host Jesse Jackson confesses to Sammy, "doing this show scares me to death...You're black, you were Christian, you're Jewish, you were poor, you're rich, you've got that eye thing. I mean, you're the whole Rainbow Coalition!" Jackson does his George Bush impression. "Do you have another one?" Sammy asks. "Because you're cooking, man." They close with Sammy teaching Jackson how to open the show in Yiddish.

4 Host Ringo Starr brings out "old friend" Sammy Davis, Jr., and reveals that Sammy frequently collaborated with the Beatles, especially on *Abbey Road*. "It was a labor of love, so much fun, the Mops, the Mop Tops," recalls Sammy. Apparently Sammy even told Paul to take off his shoes at the cover shoot. The two sing each other's hits, and Ringo further discloses, "You *are* the walrus!"

5 Sammy is a guest on Jackie Rogers, Jr.'s (Martin Short) "$100,000 Jackpot Wad": "I'll tell you, Jaxola, I'm just standing here *kvelling*," Sammy insists. "To win money for these cats that you don't know, well, that's *exciting.*" Sammy must describe foods to his partner, Rajiv (Christopher Guest). "This is a little hot spicy number..." "Rita Moreno!" "No, babe, it comes from a cucumber, they let it sit in a barrel with its brothers so it becomes something else." "A caterpillar!" They move on to bagels. "Now, this is one of my people's favorite kind of things..."

FIRST AIRED:
MARCH 17, 1984

Joe Piscopo and Billy Crystal

Davis, Jr.

GREAT CHARACTERS

Donny and Marie

Marie: For the Osmonds, Christmas is a joyous time for the whole family to get together.

Donny: Yeah, Marie. But things sure have changed since you got married!

Marie: Well, what about you, Donny? You've got a wife at home!

Donny: You're right. I guess Christmas just won't be the same this year. [*Sings*] *I'll have a blue Christmas without you...*

Marie: I'll be so blue thinking about you...

Donny and Marie: Decorations of red/On a green Christmas tree/Won't mean a thing/If you're not here with me./I'll have a blue Christmas, that's certain./And when the blue heartache...

[*They have gradually gotten very close; now they stop singing and kiss passionately.*]

Gumby: Donny and Marie! Hey, hey, hey, cut it out! Is this how you kids go Hawaiian? Give me a break here!

DONNY OSMOND PLAYED BY GARY KROEGER
MARIE OSMOND PLAYED BY JULIA LOUIS-DREYFUS
GUMBY PLAYED BY EDDIE MURPHY
AIRED: DECEMBER 11, 1982

Baseball Players

"Not only were they great ballplayers, they gave us Smelt Night too."—Yogi Berra

Pictured is Leonard "The Rooster" Willoughby (Billy Crystal), who was "so fast, he hit a line drive up the middle and he got hit in the head sliding into second base." His colleague was "King Carl" Johnson (Christopher Guest): "In the old time, of course, I'd play a whole doubleheader with a broken leg."

AIRED: OCTOBER 13, 1984

Mary Gross and Julia Louis-Dreyfus

Chi Chi Consuela

Chad Web: Who's your favorite ghostbuster?

Consuela: I like the black one.

Chi Chi: The black one? He didn't do nothing.

Consuela: But he was a ghostbuster. They didn't give him enough to do, but he would have been a great ghostbuster if they would have given him a great ghostbuster job and said, "Go do that and be successful with it."

CHI CHI PLAYED BY MARY GROSS
CONSUELA PLAYED BY JULIA LOUIS-DREYFUS
CHAD WEB PLAYED BY JIM BELUSHI
AIRED: NOVEMBER 10, 1984

Gary Kroeger and Julia Louis-Dreyfus

Martin Short and Billy Crystal

The Guru

Many great questions press upon my soul and I feel compelled to share them with you. For instance, why is the tidy bowl man so happy about living in a toilet? Why do Latin American dictators insist on wearing sunglasses and skinny little moustaches when they *know* it only makes them look sleazy? Exactly what are we saving daylight time for? Did you ever get a letter from a girl who draws pretty little hearts and flowers on the envelope? Why is it that this girl will undoubtedly be fat? Why, if I kill a baby seal, am I a terrible man, but if I squash a baby cockroach I am a *good* man? But, you say, the seal is a helpless animal in the wild, while the cockroach is a pest...then I would say, "How would you like to have a few hundred baby seals living under your sink?"

PLAYED BY TIM KAZURINSKY
AIRED: FEBRUARY 19, 1983

Tim Kazurinsky

Kate & Ali

Kate: Ali, you eat these biscuits before they get cold. I've slaved over them all day, and you haven't eaten a one.
Ali: Kate, Kate, don't tell me what to do. If you put another biscuit in my face, I'm gonna knock you upside your head. I am still the greatest of all time.
Kate: Well, that kind of talk will get you nowhere. It's pure sham, and you know it. Like my father, I abhor sham. Always have. Never did like it at all.
Ali: Kate, you are driving me crazy.
Kate: Oh, you!
Announcer: Yes, it's Kate and Ali. Watch the sparks fly when a four-time Oscar winner and a three-time world heavyweight champion move in together with no questions asked.

KATHARINE HEPBURN PLAYED BY MARTIN SHORT
MUHAMMED ALI PLAYED BY BILLY CRYSTAL
AIRED: DECEMBER 1, 1984

Fernando

Billy Crystal and Howard Cosell

In one of his deeper moments Fernando (Billy Crystal) declares: "People want to know so much about the stars. We have no royalty in this country. We're it. You know what I'm saying, darlings." Accordingly, he gives the darlings what they want.

After two stints at *Saturday Night Live*'s news desk, Fernando hosts his own starry-eyed talk show. "Fernando's Hideaway" offers celebrity chitchat, marvelous stories of Old Hollywood, and bits of plain homespun philosophy—the most unforgettable being, "It is better to look good than to feel good."

His romantic accent comes from having "American teeth and a Spanish mouth." His definition of love: never having to say "I'm sorry, this never happened to me before." But of course, he adds, "I'm kidding you. I am a kidder."

1 The big news story: the upcoming television season. Fernando mourns the loss of the marvelous, Corinthian-leather-skinned Ricardo Montalban's *Fantasy Island*. He does, however, look forward to *60 Menudos*, featuring "sixty fourteen-year-old investigative reporter-Ricans."

Nancy Reagan (Mary Gross) shares pictures from China. A snapshot from the beach prompts Fernando to reflect, "Only in America can the president have bigger breasts than the First Lady." He recalls their Hollywood past: "We never slept together, did we? You would remember *that*!"

2 Fernando reports on where the stars vacation. This year "*the* place to be seen" is a brand-new resort, the Betty Ford Rehabilitation Center: "I tell you, talk about

SATURDAY NIGHT LIVE 154

Ringo Starr, Billy Crystal, and Barbara Bach

Night of a 1,000 Stars! They said they didn't look good when they went in, but after thirty days there, they looked marvelous. Absolutely marvelous."

3 The booth is empty, and Fernando does not feel marvelous. He looks marvelous, but he does not feel marvelous. Barry Manilow had promised an interview, but he is "one busy *caballero*" and has backed out. One of Fernando's crew pretends he is Manilow instead. "What is your definition of love?" Fernando asks "Manilow," and offers his own answer: "I'm done, let's get some Chinese food."

4 Fernando welcomes Ringo Starr and Barbara Bach, who looks marvelous. He asks whether Starr can be addressed as Ring and moves quickly from chitchat about the Fab Four—"that Beatles thing really took off, didn't it?"—to a topic that interests him more: Bach's exercise regimen and her grunts in the film *Caveman*. Fernando's new definition of love: "never saying 'I'm sorry, this never happened to me before.' "

5 Fernando visits Phil Donahue's green room ("another talk-show host with gray hair, but he doesn't look as marvelous as me"). The upcoming show has promising guests: a Nazi, two midget transvestites, and the marvelous-looking subway vigilante Bernhard Goetz (Rich Hall). Goetz agrees to appear on Fernando's show, and a thrilled Fernando wants to call his producer immediately—but he makes the mistake of asking Bernhard for a quarter.

6 *Saludos*, Darlings, from Radio City Music Hall, home of tomorrow's Night of 100 Stars. Fernando is "standing here in a gray cashmere coat and a towel Red Buttons gave to me. Let's go in, because I'm freezing my castanets off, I'll say that to you now!" He visits Teri Garr, who looks marvelous, even if she has some hair on her outfit and "it looks like Lorne Greene has been rolling around on your

body there for a while." Fernando speaks with Susan Lucci, Morgan Fairchild, Ann-Margret, and Lynn Swann ("I have been a fan of yours for many years and I have seen most of the movies that you have been in"). After all the glitter, Fernando concludes: At the Night of 100 Stars, *he* looked the most marvelous.

7 Siskel and Ebert visit the Hideaway. Fernando is "steamed" that David Hasselhoff's not up for an Oscar: "He talks to the car, the car talks back, he has great hair." Gene laments that Mariel Hemingway's breast enlargement stole attention from her performance in *Star 80*. "How big did she get her breasts?" Fernando wants to know, and the critics argue over her cup size.

8 Fernando's guests are "the greatest stars in the history of the world right now," Mr. T and Hulk Hogan, and they look humongous. They glare as Fernando asks: "Hulk, what is your definition of love?" "What are your Passover plans?" "Do you yearn to return to your theater roots?" Fernando compares Hogan's flexing pecs to "Dorothy Lamour from behind, on her way to the commissary!" and asks whether the muscles have pet names.

9 Fernando introduces "a legend in his own mind," Howard Cosell. "I got to ask you, from the bottom of my heart, did you really puke on Don Mattingly's shoes? That must have looked marvelous!"

Fernando declares: "*The Battle of the Network Stars* is, to me, the epitome of sports. Carl Lewis is great, but to see Adrienne Barbeau running in slow motion, bompedy-bompedy-bompedy, with her ABC team, you know, with those nipples bursting through the thing—*they look marvelous*, I've got to tell you."

You look marvelous.

FIRST AIRED: MAY 5, 1984

Ed (Martin Short) is a kind and decent man—as decent as decent can be—with certain clear passions in life. One is his undying respect for *Wheel of Fortune* host Pat Sajak, to whom he has written over forty letters of encouragement. Another is his love of music—and in particular, the triangle. But Ed is an excitable fellow, and often his passions lead to a variety of problems—"Why do I always forget to wear the oven mitts?"—but everything always seems to be decent in the end, we must say.

1 A suicidal Mr. Quigley (Christopher Guest) has one more *Wheel of Fortune* contestant to interview—Ed: "This is a very decent office. So often high ceilings can be effective!" Ed fantasizes about becoming Sajak's best friend, but then he stops himself: "Oh, like that really

Jesse Jackson and Martin Short

Ed Grimley, Jr.

makes sense, like I suppose Pat Sajak doesn't have like over a million friends probably." Quigley tells Ed he has been accepted, and Ed thanks him—"for being so decent, I must say." Ed is hailing a taxi when Quigley's falling body lands on him. But they're both okay—and Ed's cheerful attitude inspires Quigley to go on living.

2 Jesse Jackson, traveling by air, wants to get some sleep, but at the last minute Ed takes the window seat. He's returning from a very decent trip, a prize courtesy of *Wheel of Fortune*: "It was the best! Give me a break. I went mental!" A demon appears at Ed's window, and the stewardess (Julia Louis-Dreyfus) settles his nerves: "It must be in my head. Probably just an undigested piece of bologna, I suppose." The demon reappears, and Ed opens the door of the plane. He's sucked out. "This is just dumb. This is stupid," Jackson complains, and ends the sketch.

3 Thanksgiving is imminent and the anticipation is making Ed mental. He pulls his pumpkin pie out of the oven: "Oh, perfect! Gee, I wish I'd put on some sort of an oven mitt at this point." While looking through his telescope he sees his seemingly decent neighbor, Mr. Wilson (Ed Asner) kill his wife (Pamela Stephenson). Wilson pushes his way into Ed's apartment, and as they talk he eyes Ed's telescope. Ed, ever generous, tells him, "If you or your late wife would like to borrow it perhaps…" Wilson proceeds to strangle Ed—until Ed's dad (Christopher Guest) arrives: "What are you doing to my son, I must say?"

4 Ed, already late for his triangle lesson, goes mental over his late bus. He joins a man from Europe (Ringo Starr)—"that can be quite decent, I must say"— who is hit by lightning, repeatedly. Ed gives him his lucky coin and

SATURDAY NIGHT LIVE

156

Martin Short

Tina Turner and Martin Short

6 Ed shares a hospital room with Mr. Faraccio (Jim Belushi), a mafioso. Ed is excited, as tomorrow is his birthday: "Every year, it's like one of the most decent, happiest days of my life. I don't know how it works out that way." A happy Ed plays air triangle to a recording of *Peer Gynt*.

A "doctor" (Christopher Guest) produces a syringe for Ed. "Prepare to breathe your last, Mr. Faraccio," he warns. Ed helplessly tries to explain that he has the wrong man: "I'm as doomed as doomed can be, you know." Just then Uncle Basil (Howard Cosell) enters: "Unhand my nephew, I must say! 'Cause what you're doing is far from decent, you know!"

7 It's Christmastime, Ed's cookies burn, and he is going completely mental. "Perhaps if I play my triangle, that could lift my spirits back to a more festive frame of mind." The Devil (Jon Lovitz) materializes and offers Ed a fifty-dollar gift certificate at the department store of his choice—in return for a small consideration payable at a later date. Ed refuses: "I feel your intentions are less than honorable, and I don't think I'd fare well in Hell, what with the heat and all." Incensed, the Devil chases Ed—but Ed drives him back with his picture of Pat Sajak. "So honest, so sincere...so filled with decency!" says the Devil. "In defeat I take my leave."

I'm going mental.

First aired: October 6, 1984

leads him away from the bench. As Ed returns to retrieve his triangle tires squeal and the man's body flies by; the coin didn't work, so he returns it.

5 It's the gustiest of gusty days—so gusty that when Ed opens his window, he can barely stand upright. Miss Malone (Tina Turner)—"the woman of my dreams"—calls to borrow some oranges. Ed goes so mental that he doesn't check his fridge until after she hangs up—and it is overflowing with onions. When Miss Malone arrives, he tries to pass off his onions. She does accept his offer of "a spare pot pie made of turkey materials mostly that would be so easy to heat up," and they dance together.

Martin Short and Ringo Starr

Synchronized Swimming

Featuring Gerald (Harry Shearer), Lawrence (Martin Short), and their director (Christopher Guest).

Gerald: Oh, it's not going to be easy. My brother and I know. Men have never done synchronized swimming in a sanctioned competition in this country. Officially, it's got like a zero acceptance rate.

Lawrence: I don't swim.

Gerald: Lawrence doesn't swim. So, I mean, no, of course not, no one's going to just walk up and hand us a gold medal. Men's synchro isn't even in the '88 Olympics yet.

Lawrence: That's okay, 'cause we could use the time. 'Cause I'm, I'm not that strong a swimmer.

Gerald: But, I mean, that just means, you know, for '92, we're a lock for the gold.

Gerald: I remember, it was a Friday. I was coming home. My wife, Abby, asked me, "Honey, is there something wrong?" And I said, "No, there's nothing wrong. I've made a decision. I'm leaving the accounting firm, and Lawrence and I are going to pursue a dream that we have, and that basically synchronized swimming is going to be our lives for the rest of this century.

Director: One, two, three, four, here it goes. This is like a mirror between you, and then he goes this way, and then let's say you were to point at each other. You're doing the same thing, aren't you? No, you're not angry at him—

Gerald: No, I'm not.

Director: No, you're just pointing at him. Hey, you! I know you. I know you. Let's hear the waggle. The waggle. Yes, just let me see this…Yeah, you remember that…Maybe not.

Director: Working with them has also given me a goose, if I may use that

Harry Shearer and Martin Short

expression. I've been directing regional theater, "Shakespeare in the Park," and if I ever do that again, I'm going to, you know, kill myself with a Veg-O-Matic.

Director: We dig a hole, we dig a hole, we dig a hole…

Director: And the great thing about these boys is they are thinking gold. I mean, who would want to wear bronze anyway?

Director: Be aware of the waterlines. So start holding your noses now! And hold

your breath! Count: one, two, you're underwater—I am too, but I'm talking, just pretend—two, three, four, look at the fish going by, you see people's feet. Can you hold it any longer? No, so burst out of the water, and aren't you glad to be out of the water? Lawrence, aren't you glad?

Lawrence: Yes.

Director: Yes!

Director: Although the judges don't count it, deck work is a very important part of Lawrence's preparation for the gold and that's allowed to come from within him. He can be surprisingly creative.

Gerald: The underwater part is really challenging. In a way, it's what makes this sport a sport. The male rules are a lot tougher. We can only touch the bottom with the balls of our feet, or else it's five-eighths of a point off.

Lawrence: The music is chosen to express different moods: happy, underwater…We'll argue about it sometimes, but I think Gerald trusts my tastes.

Gerald: There just comes a time in your life where you have to take yourself to the limit. We have the opportunity to do something that no one has ever done before. And we're going for it.

AIRED: OCTOBER 6, 1984

Frankie (Christopher Guest) and Willie (Billy Crystal) are messengers—though they try other skilled occupations as well. They have two main topics of discussion: the secretary on the thirty-fourth floor at Shedelman's Suits who has a thing for Frankie ("She was all over me, drove me nuts") and how they experience pain. The question of the secretary is easily resolved—after all, "a stallion's got to run"; but there are always new sources of pain to be shared.

1 In an elevator, Frankie and Willie wonder who will take part in the next presidential debate: "The same guys as last time, I guess." Willie doesn't understand debates: "I don't know who wins." Frankie agrees: "They never flash the scores or nothin'."

Willie said it happened to him last week; matter of fact, he pounded his hand in frustration on the, uh..."Metal thing?" Yeah, says Willie, and it really hurt. Frankie knows what Willie means, having recently put his head in a vise in the basement; he hated that. Willie hates it too: It's like when he sticks his feet into a movie seat and cuts off his circulation. And that's like Frankie stapling his lower lip to his desk blotter—which reminds Willie of pushing a spindle up his nose through his tear duct, sort of like Frankie taking a cheese grater to the back of his legs...

2 Willie and Frankie are night watchmen. Frankie's shoulder hurts; every time he walks by exposed bolts, they dig into his arm. Frankie knows pain. The other day, he bought one of those linoleum knives—the kind with the double edge—and he just spread his toes apart and kind of sawed back and forth and poured on Tabasco sauce.

Willie knows what he means. The other day he took one of those, uh..."Meat thermometers?" Yeah, and he shoved it in his ear as far as it could go, and took one of those, uh..."Ball peen hammers?" Yeah. "That must have smarted! What I hate is when you go into the kitchen, open the drawer, pull out a..." Carrot scraper, Willie correctly guesses. "Carrot scraper, and you stick it up your nose, work it around real good, till your mucous membrane is all worn away." The pain peaks with Frankie's rolling back and forth, nude, on a gross of thumbtacks.

3 The two are construction workers this time, and as before, Willie misses their previous job. Willie's finger is killing him. Frankie knows what he means, having nicked

Billy Crystal and Christopher Guest

his "hiney" shaving and then squatted in a bowl of gin. It's like pushing golf tees into your navel with a snow dome, or feeding your tongue into a movie projector, or sticking knitting needles into your nipples and twisting them like propellers on a B-29 bomber: "Sounds great, but it hurts like hell. I hate it."

4 Willie points out to Frankie that their new job—as part of a waterskiing human pyramid—doesn't make meeting people very easy. But it's not as bad as when you stand on a hot plate for an hour or so, or seal your eyes shut with Krazy Glue, or whack your Adam's apple with a Wiffle bat, or puncture your Adam's apple with tweezers, or get your tongue stuck in the garbage disposal. ("So it flaps around like the plastic flags at the opening of a supermarket?" "Yeah!")

5 Frankie and Willie are messengers again, and Willie loves it. The Shedelman's secretary was just all over him in the copier room. Frankie's not surprised: "Women are slaves to our guided missiles of love." Leaving the secretary pains Willie. Like power drilling under your toenails. Like stapling bologna to your face. Like shoving your face in a piranha's fishbowl, or slamming the trunk of your car on your tongue, or sticking one of those six-inch replicas of the Empire State Building up your nose just to see how far it'll go. "I must have been up to the..." "Ninety-fifth floor?" "Yeah, had to be, because the..." "Transmitter was sticking out of your forehead?" "Yeah!"

FIRST AIRED: OCTOBER 20, 1984

Do You Know What I Hate?

A week in the life of *Saturday Night Live* is unlike any other kind of week. Populated by night owls, driving at a furious pace, culminating in what is still the only live network variety or comedy show, every week is a new adventure.

Far from the glitz of Hollywood, the offices of *Saturday Night Live*, on the seventeenth floor of 30 Rockefeller Center, look more like the home of a shoestring start-up company. Most of the furniture resembles the kind that many New Yorkers claim from the streets in the middle of the night; the main refreshment is coffee; and the dress code is distinctly casual. To be sure, there are no longer bunk beds in anyone's office, but many a writer spends many a night crashed on couches that would not meet with their mother's approval.

The week begins on Monday night, when story ideas are pitched for the first time in very rough form and the writers begin their work. But for most people, the real operation doesn't start until Tuesday. From then through the rest of the week, a crew of approximately 250 people assembles sets in Brooklyn, designs and creates costumes, composes and records music, and much more, as the race to Saturday night is on.

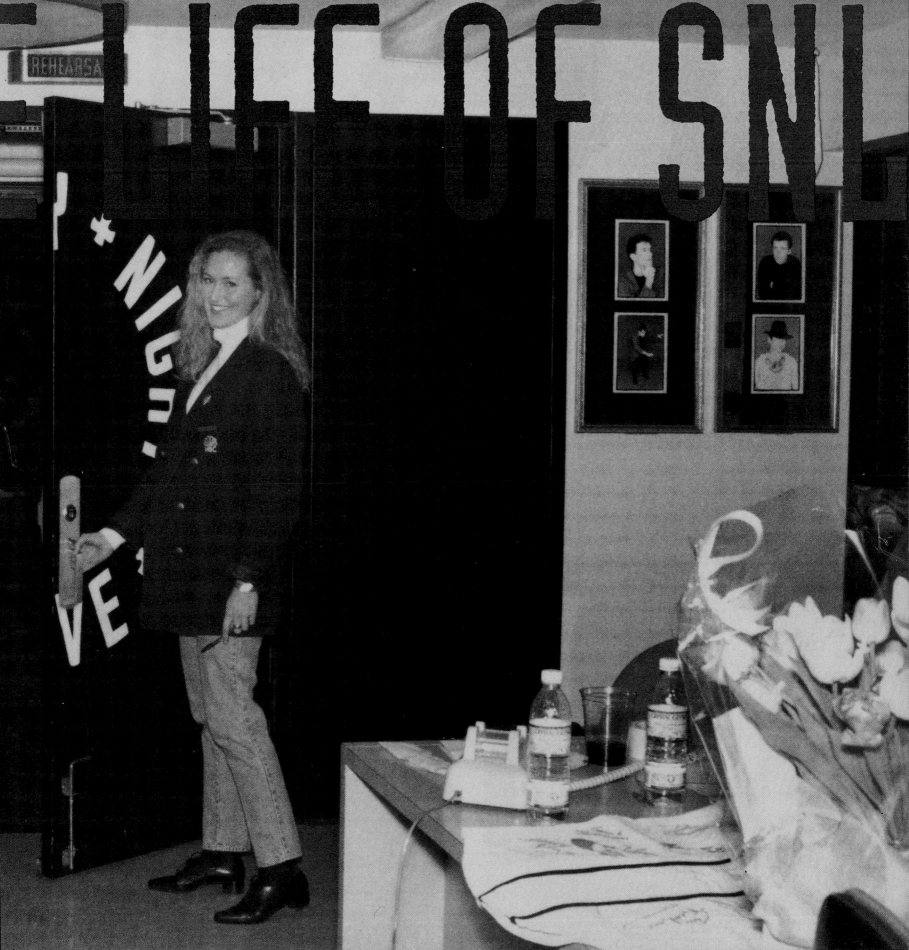

Ryan Shiraki from the Talent Department and associate producer Liz Welch, who spends the day making sure the host meets with all of the writers.

Tuesday

Melanie Hutsell and Ellen Cleghorne work on an idea.

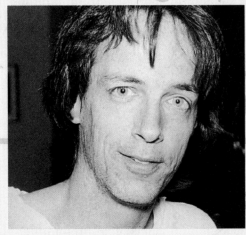

Writer Fred Wolf.

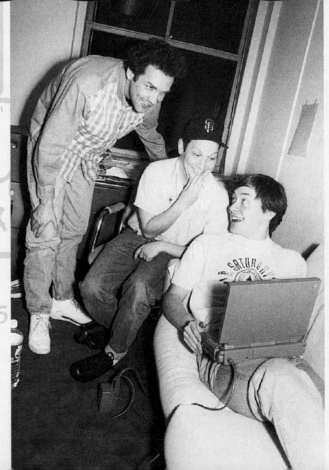

Norm MacDonald, Rob Schneider, and Lew Morton are on to something amusing.

Producer Jim Downey (*right*) enjoys a light moment with David Spade and Chris Farley on Tuesday night.

Edie Baskin photographs the hosts every Tuesday, taking the pictures that viewers see every time the show comes back from commercial (called "bumpers").

Inspiration typically doesn't strike while sitting at a desk—Sarah Silverman captures the moment.

The end product.

Filmmaker Tom Schiller, who has been with the show on and off since the very beginning.

After an all-nighter and a nap on the couch, writer Ian Maxtone-Graham does some quick grooming before the next day's work.

Wednesday

SATURDAY · LIVE · NIGHT

SNL SHOW #827

HOST: BALDWIN/BASINGER

Wednesday afternoon is when the show first starts to take shape. The entire cast and crew piles into a conference room, as writers and performers read different sketch ideas. In a typical week thirty-five sketches will be proposed; this week eleven pieces then get the go ahead. Of those, another three are cut after dress rehearsal.

This meeting is truly the first audience for most pieces, and the atmosphere is friendly but competitive. Everybody wants to get their work on the air, and while Lorne makes the final decisions, the reaction of the read-through crowd can be very important.

After the read-through the hosts sit down with Lorne Michaels and key personnel to discuss the possibilities. While most hosts are happy to go with the instincts of the people who make the show work, sometimes they have strong feelings about particular sketches.

A WEEK IN THE LIFE OF SATURDAY NIGHT LIVE

DEPARTMENT   _Writing / Performing_

DEPARTMENT HEADS   _Jim Downey_

DEPARTMENT MEMBERS   _David Spade's Week_

PLEASE DESCRIBE YOUR WEEK AS IT UNFOLDS:

MONDAY
Call in sick

TUESDAY
Come in late. Tell people
I was sick yesterday. Write sketches

WEDNESDAY
read sketches Realize I have nothing
in the show. Tell people my
sketches weren't written funny cuz I
was sick monday.

THURSDAY
Rehearse
sketches I was put into after they
took a feature player out.

FRIDAY
Call mom in
arizona + tell her not to stay up Sat

SATURDAY
Tell other performers its a bad audience
+ play other miscellaneous mind games. Pat myself
on back.

PLEASE SAVE ALL DRAWINGS, NOTES, SKETCHES, MEMORABILIA
FROM THIS WEEK FOR THE 20TH ANNIVERSARY BOOK.

It looks like just another meeting, but producer Jim Downey calls the Thursday rewrite session the most important one of the show. The writers hone one another's pieces, and rough sketches start turning into finished drafts. Once again they'll be working through the night.

Thursday

A week in the life of David Spade.

Taped on Thursday evenings, the promos for the show have to be quick, clever, and memorable—which is a lot to ask of ten seconds. Here Lorne consults with Alec and Kim as David Spade looks on.

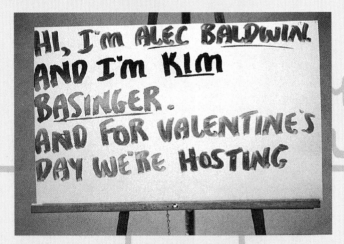

HI, I'M ALEC BALDWIN. AND I'M KIM BASINGER. AND FOR VALENTINE'S DAY WE'RE HOSTING

Even the smallest detail lands on cue cards. Here are the cards for Kim and Alec's promos.

A gallery of long-time and key show personnel:

Top, *left to right*: director Dave Wilson and associate director Bobby Caminiti; lighting designer Phil Hymes; stage managers Joe Dicso and Bob Van Ry; technical director Stacey Foster.

Middle, *left to right*: supervising producer Ken Aymong; production designers Eugene Lee, Keith Raywood, and Akira Yoshimura; graphic designer Bob Pook.

Bottom, *left to right*: coordinating producer Audrey Peart Dickman; Jim Signorelli, director-producer of commercial parodies; production designer Edie Baskin; and sketch music adapter Hal Wilner.

The Anatomy of a Costume

Making Kim's Dress

The Costume Department has to assemble or create dozens of costumes for each show, depending upon the complexity of the show itself. Here we follow one original creation, Kim Basinger's dress for her role with Phillip the Hyper-Hypo (played by Mike Myers).

Costume designer Melina Root's original sketch and fabric swatch.

Doug James sews Kim's dress for dress rehearsal.

Ready to roll.

The dress in action, at dress rehearsal. Basinger liked the dress so much that she kept it after the show was over.

Lorne Michaels, in his office on the seventeenth floor.

Lorne Michael's ninth floor office, which overlooks the studio where the show is shot. Choice viewer mail is posted on the left side of the bulletin board; cast and host photos are on the right.

SEPTEMBER 25	OCTOBER 2	OCTOBER 9	OCTOBER 23	OCTOBER 30	NOVEMBER 13	NOVEMBER 20	DECEMBER 4	DECEMBER 11
CHARLES BARKLEY	SHANNEN DOHERTY	JEFF GOLDBLUM	JOHN MALKOVICH	CHRISTIAN SLATER	ROSIE O'DONNELL	NICOLE KIDMAN	CHARLTON HESTON	SALLY FIELD
NIRVANA	CYPRESS HILL	AEROSMITH	BILLY JOEL	SMASHING PUMPKINS	JAMES TAYLOR	STONE TEMPLE PILOTS	PAUL WESTERBERG	TONY TONI TONE

JANUARY 8	JANUARY 15		FEBRUARY 5	FEBRUARY 12	FEBRUARY 19		MARCH 12	MARCH 19
JASON PATRIC	SARA GILBERT		PATRICK STEWART	ALEC BALDWIN KIM BASINGER	MARTIN LAWRENCE		NANCY KERRIGAN	
BLIND MELON	COUNTING CROWS		SALT N PEPA	UB40			ARETHA FRANKLIN	SNOOP DOGGY DOG

MARISA TOMEI

APRIL 9	APRIL 16		MAY 7	MAY 14
KELSEY GRAMMER	DREW BARRYMORE	DANA CARVEY		
	PEARL JAM			

MICHAEL RICHARDS

The rise and fall of prospective hosts and musical guests is charted on this bulletin board in Lorne Michaels's ninth-floor office.

Friday

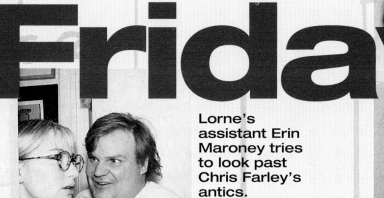

Lorne's assistant Erin Maroney tries to look past Chris Farley's antics.

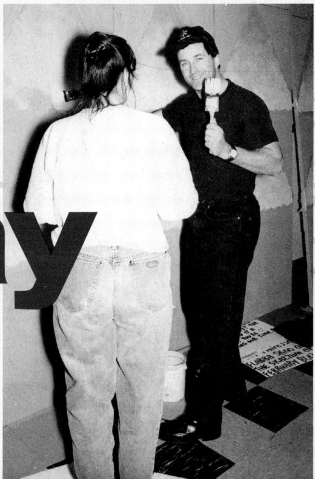

The glamour of hosting. Alec lends a hand painting the scenery for his House of Pain sketch, in which he plays a sadistic trainer who scares (or beats) fat people into eating less.

Saturday

Tickets are drawn by lottery at the beginning of every season, and the demand for the remaining house seats is always intense. The star power of the Baldwin-Basinger show makes it a particularly hot ticket. Here Danny Goldstein spends the morning sorting out the ticket madness.

The SNL band rehearses on Saturday morning.

Before dress rehearsal, everyone meets to see the monologue for the first time on it's feet, as Lorne Michaels addresses the group.

Setting Up

The Weekend Update Set

It's hard to imagine how cramped the space is at studio 8-H where the show is shot. Up to twelve complete sets are crammed into every available space at any one time. For the sake of convenience, the Weekend Update set comprises a few pieces, easy to set up and easy to break down.

In about five minutes, while the musical guests play and commercials are run, the Weekend Update set is put together in front of "home base," which is where the host delivers the monologue.

To keep Update as fresh as possible, writing begins in earnest on Saturday morning. Here Al Franken and Kevin Nealon go through a week's supply of newspapers in search of material.

Norm MacDonald and writer Steve Koren.

Update material can continue to change throughout the day. Kevin Nealon and Herb Sargent make some last-minute changes, while relaxing on an empty set.

Saturday

In the hour between dress rehearsal and the broadcast of the show itself, Lorne Michaels meets with Kim and Alec and key personnel. The cast and crew are brought in for technical and performance notes and the show is pared down by as much as thirty minutes. The master board reveals the changes: a new cold opening is put in place, the Bike Messenger, Company Mixer, and Visualization (Kim with a lecherous psychiatrist) sketches are all cut, and the MacIntosh Post-Its commercial parody will wait until next week.

SHOW #827

HOST: BALDWIN/BASINGER

Jay Mohr and David Spade wait backstage for the Canteen Boy and Hollywood Minute pieces, respectively (as Spade attempts to rattle Mohr's concentration).

Mike Myers prepares for his role as Phillip the Hyper-Hypo. Melina Root lends a hand.

Phil Hartman reviews his script as his dresser Dan Adkins stands by.

Ellen Cleghorne practicing for her role as Denise "Who Let Her Kind in Here?" Washington in the "Goodfellas" opening sketch (called the "cold opening"). Writer Dave Mandel looks on.

The Anatomy of a Sketch

Making Romantic Man

Longtime director Dave Wilson blocking the sketch on Friday, with the actors in the background.

It looks big on your television screen, but each set is shoehorned into a different corner of the studio. A long view puts it in perspective.

Blocking a tricky move in which Mike Myers, Alec Baldwin, and Phil Hartman simultaneously light one another's cigarettes with suave ease.

Making a sketch come to life can be a tedious process. Here Julia Sweeney and Chris Farley search for motivation, or patience.

A lot of viewers don't notice how much original music is featured in the show. A typical week includes a couple of jingles as well as one or two original songs. Romantic Man features the song shown on the left, written and composed by Marilyn Suzanne Miller (who also wrote the sketch) and Cheryl Hardwick.

How many people does it take to set a table? Saturday afternoon the sets are "dressed," as all the important props and details are put in place.

Left: Jim Downey, Marilyn Suzanne Miller, and Lorne Michaels, watch the sketch at dress rehearsal, and discuss some last-minute modifications. Julia Sweeney's hair will change, and Alec Baldwin adopts a French accent.

At blocking on Saturday—almost there.

Dress rehearsal: Julia's hair will change again, and it's on to air.

Even people in the studio, and the studio audience, wind up watching a lot of the show on monitors. Here UB40 enjoy a piece while waiting to go on.

The amount of time it takes to apply makeup can determine the running order of the show, with the most complicated pieces often coming at the opening. Here Rob Schneider is transformed into Microscopic Elvis.

Adam Sandler gets miked by Jan Switkas for Canteen Boy.

Kevin Nealon warms up the audience just before the show starts. "You had a great time; I was very funny," he assures them.

Saturda

Wigs, wigs, wigs—enough to get through a week.

Talent coordinator Marci Klein sifts through CDs looking for potential musical guests.

The man behind the voice: Don Pardo in his announcer's booth.

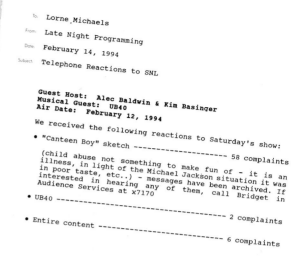

NBC   MEMO

To: Lorne Michaels
From: Late Night Programming
Date: February 14, 1994
Subject: Telephone Reactions to SNL

Guest Host: Alec Baldwin & Kim Basinger
Musical Guest: UB40
Air Date: February 12, 1994

We received the following reactions to Saturday's show:

• "Canteen Boy" sketch -------------------- 58 complaints

(child abuse not something to make fun of - it is an illness, in light of the Michael Jackson situation it was in poor taste, etc..) - messages have been archived. If interested in hearing any of them, call Bridget in Audience Services at x7170

• UB40 ------------------------------------- 2 complaints

• Entire content --------------------------- 6 complaints

cc: Andrew Brewer
     Jim Downey
     Herb Sargent
     Mike Shoemaker
     Caroline Stevens

Every week NBC telephone operators field calls from viewers, and submit a log. In his Week in the Life questionnaire, Andrew Brewer from NBC Standards and Practices noted, "Canteen Boy needs to be toned down a little. Not as worried this week as others...." But as the call memo reveals, viewers felt differently.

In dress rehearsal (*left*), Adam Sandler and David Spade play two of the Baldwin brothers in this "Family Feud" sketch (with Tim Meadows playing famous author James Baldwin, graciously substituting for Daniel Baldwin). But in the show itself (*right*), Stephen and Billy Baldwin play themselves.

Quick Change

There are no plush dressing rooms for cast members. When there's time—which means more than two minutes—they change in simple stalls with a curtain hanging in front. When there isn't time, everything comes off and on again wherever there's enough space to rip your shirt off.

And sometimes there's no time at all. In this week's show Alec Baldwin raced out to introduce UB40 with his shirt unbuttoned and his belt halfway on. With seconds to spare, he lost the belt and followed the shouted direction to "stand behind Kim."

Here Kevin Nealon goes for the quick-change option.

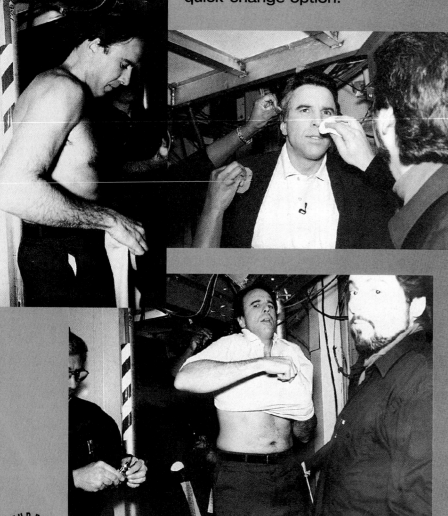

Finally, it's 11:30 and the show opens without a hitch. After the Goodfellas cold opening and the opening montage, Kim and Alec do their monologue together, in which Kim confesses: "I wanted to host the show alone—because you're not funny, and it makes me nervous to be around you."

Everyone gathers onstage for the traditional good nights (if you really stayed up until 1:00, you'd know what we were talking about).

aturday

Every week cast, crew, and friends head to another New York hot spot for the cast party, which can run until 6:00 A.M. This week's party is at Main Street, on Manhattan's Upper West Side.

Alec Baldwin and Kim Basinger relax with friends and relatives.

Ellen Cleghorne, associate producer Mike Shoemaker, guest writer Jim Emerson, and Julia Sweeney.

Adam Sandler.

Stephen Baldwin with friends Michael J. Fox and Tracy Pollan.

SATURDAY
182
LIVE NIGHT

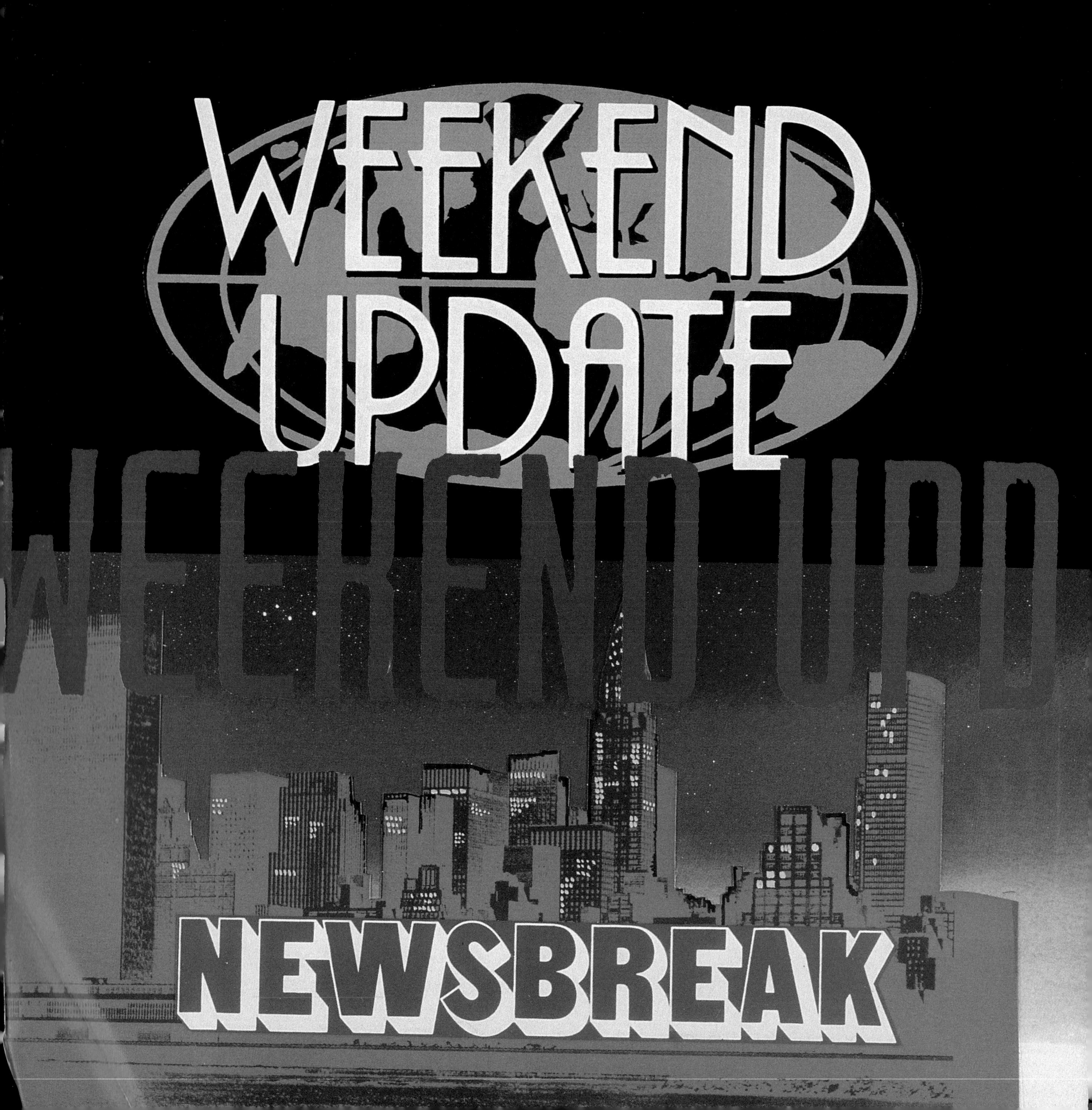
WEEKEND UPDATE
WEEKEND UPD
NEWSBREAK

WEEKEND UPDATE

DENNIS MILLER

ATE / POLITICS

WEEKEND UPDATE

KEVIN NEALON

It was announced today that the small African nation of Chad has changed its name to Brian. In the spirit of Third World solidarity, the nation of Tanzania has changed its name to Debby.

This just in: Generalissimo Francisco Franco is still dead.

Secretary of State Kissinger stated today that he is tired of using his silly accent in public and will begin to speak in plain English. This will in no way affect the content of what he is saying.

In a speech to the Athens, Georgia, Chamber of Commerce, presidential contender George Wallace said, "I don't judge a man by the color of his skin. I judge him according to how well you can see him in the dark when he smiles."

UNICEF fell under attack this week when Syria formally protested the charity's new Christmas card, which says, in ten different languages, "Let's kill the Arabs and take their oil!"

This bulletin just in: From Madrid, Spain, comes the word that Generalissimo Francisco Franco is still dead. Doctors say his condition is unchanged.

Confusion continues over the Angolan situation throughout the world. The Japanese prime minister is said to have commented, "I always thought Angola was a sweater."

CHEVY CHASE

Good evening, I'm Chevy Chase, and you're not.

Good night and have a pleasant tomorrow.

DAN AYKROYD

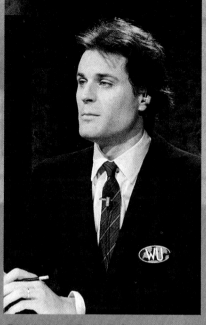

CHARLES ROCKET

Good evening, I'm Charles Rocket. Here now the news.

I'm Charles Rocket. Good night and watch out.

JANE CURTIN

Good evening, I'm Jane Curtin. Here now the news. Our top story tonight:

That's the news. Good night and have a pleasant tomorrow.

BILL MURRAY

GAIL MATTHIUS

BRIAN DOYLE-MURRAY

Good night and good news.

BRAD HALL

That's all for tonight. For SNL News, I'm Brad Hall. Good night.

DENNIS MILLER

Good evening. What can I tell you?

That's the news and I am outta here.

MARY GROSS

CHRISTOPHER GUEST

That's the news. Good night.

KEVIN NEALON

I'm Kevin Nealon, and that's news to me.

Generalissimo Francisco Franco has been critically dead now for eleven weeks, and his doctors refuse to speculate on how long he can last in his present condition.

This week the FDA banned red dye no. 2, saying the red coloring agent is suspected of having cancer-causing qualities. Coincidentally, it was reported this week that Ronald Reagan revealed he was undergoing treatment for cancer of the hair.

In reviewing Update for the past twelve editions, we find we have been unreasonably unfair to Gerald R. Ford. Beginning tonight, Weekend Update declares a moratorium on stories that might be interpreted as accusing the president of stupidity and clumsiness. In the future we shall treat the office of the president with the respect it deserves, and eliminate all questionable references to our chief executive.

Dateline Washington: This morning an unidentified man fell out of a second-story window of the White House and landed headfirst in the Rose Garden. Whoever it was somersaulted to a waiting helicopter, bumped his head on the rotor blade, and was carried in the craft by Secret Service agents, then took off for Andrews Air Force Base for the first leg of a trip to Vail, Colorado.

Emily Litella

Violins on television, saving Soviet jewelry, conserving our natural racehorses—these are the issues that work Emily Litella (Gilda Radner) into a frenzy. Her editorial responses also address such burning controversies as busting schoolchildren, an airplane hijacking masterminded by crustaceans, the Eagle Rights Amendment, and reinstating the deaf penalty ("I myself occasionally have difficulty with my hearing, but I know I wouldn't want to be punished for it").

Eventually Emily becomes an official Weekend Update correspondent, joining her colleagues Cheddar Cheese, Mr. Adenoid, and Miss Clayton (whom she also calls Bitch). Her career even includes a turn as a political reporter assigned to cover Congresswoman Stella Abzug live from City Hall as she prepares to "throw her cat in the ring." And we meet Emily's sister, Essie (Ruth Gordon), with whom she discusses such issues as that new fad, transcendental medication, those ships disappearing in the Magruder Triangle, flea erections in China, and Ralph Nader's proposal that cars be equipped with air fags.

Gilda Radner

Some of the Issues of Emily's Time:

•What's all this fuss I hear about endangered feces? That's outrageous. Why is feces endangered? How can you possibly run out of such a thing? Just look around you—you can see it all over the place. And besides, who wants to save that anyway?

•What's all this fuss I hear about making Puerto Rico a steak? Let me warn all of you: If you make Puerto Rico a steak, the next thing they'll want is a baked potato—with sour cream and chives and little bacon bits. And then they'll probably want a salad bar! Why, they'll be lined up for miles!

•What's all this fuss I hear about the 1976 presidential erections? I know that they erected a monument for Mr. Lincoln and President Washington, but that's because they're dead! Hopefully, the 1976 president won't be dead, so he won't need an erection!

•What's all this fuss I hear about pouring money into canker research? How much can you learn about a tiny sore inside your face! Why waste your money, America? Cankers *can* be beaten. Don't eat grapefruit. And if you do have cankers, don't fiddle with them. Keep your fingers out of your mouth!

*Oh. That's different.
Never mind.*

EMILY'S ANSWERING MACHINE

"Hello. This is Emily Litella. I'm not home right now, but I will call you back as soon as possible. Just leave your name, number, and what time you called after you hear the sound of the Jeep."

Roseanne Roseannadanna

Ostensibly Weekend Update's consumer affairs reporter, Roseanne Roseannadanna inevitably winds up covering some issue of personal hygiene instead—things that get stuck in your teeth, polyester clothes that retain odors, belly-button lint, warts, the inside of her mouth, people who eat fish ("Sure, it comes from the sea, but what's so great about that? It swims around, plays with other fish, swims some more, eats, sleeps, goes to the bathroom, all in the same place"), and much more.

Roseanne loves spotting celebrities, particularly when they are doing something embarrassing or disgusting. She's the kind of person who likes going to Elaine's " 'cause you get to see a lot of real famous celebrities with a little bit of spaghetti sauce right here. And if they don't wipe it off right away, it gets all hard and dry and crusty, like a blotch, and when they open their mouths, the blotch separates, and when they close their mouths, the blotch comes back together again."

Each report concludes with some old-fashioned wisdom from Roseanne's relatives, from her father to her optimistic aunt Pollyanna Roseannadanna and her musical cousin Lola Falana Roseannadanna. Roseanne's outlook is probably best summed up in Grandmother Nana Roseannadanna's words: "Life is just like fruitcake. When you look at it, it's rich and sweet with honey and sugar and spice, and it tastes delicious and good and makes your mouth water. But if you look at it real close, there's little chunks of green things that taste real weird and you don't know what it is."

Gilda Radner

Things on Roseanne's Mind:

• Did you ever stub your big toe on the car or drop something heavy on your foot and the toenail on the big toe turns different colors like purple and brown and green and then it hangs there and falls off in your sock? And you're left with a toe with no nail and a sock that has a nail in it.

• Did you ever find a thing between your teeth and you don't know what it is? You look at it and you play with it on your fingers. And you say, "What is this thing? I don't remember eating that." And then you flick it away or wipe it under the chair.

• You know what roughage is? That's the food that goes right through you like a fast train and drags other stuff along with it so they don't hang around too long to rot and stink up your insides. Imagine, if you could, the inside of your body as a big, long curving pipe like under a sink, with all these ugly germs and pieces of red meat and diet soda and Twinkies and monosodium glutamate and stuff sittin' there clogging up everything. But then this roughage stuff, like a piece of carrot, comes along just like a can of Liquid-Plumr and it cleans out everything.

• Let me ask you this: Did you ever eat a hamburger and there's a hard thing in it? It's a toenail. You know it's not part of the hamburger, but you separate the meat and the lettuce and the pickle to one side of your mouth—and you come around with your tongue and you take out this thing and it's like a bone. But it's not a bone. I keep asking myself, Roseanne Roseannadanna, if they can make a coffee I like with no caffeine, how come they can't make a hamburger I like with no toenails?

It just goes to show you, it's always something.

1978

Belushi Rant

Well, the latest reports from NASA say that the Skylab space station will fall to earth around the end of June. Many people are concerned that the debris might pose a safety hazard. But this is really a paranoiac notion for people who are uninformed. I've been reading up on this, and according to the experts who built this thing, the odds are one in one hundred and fifty that some person may be torn to shreds by a hunk of blazing metal. I read another article that said that there is an organization, who call themselves the Chicken Little Society, that said if Skylab hits the World Trade Center, it would knock it over. Ha-ha-ha. That's a spectacular fantasy, but not something that a knowledgeable man would worry about. After all, it's only a hundred and eighteen feet long and weighs seventy-seven-and-a-half tons. But don't worry, it's not as if you'd be standing there and get hit by this thing the size of a house.

John Belushi

Oh, no. Don't worry about that. You see, when this thing starts burning up, it's supposed to break into five hundred pieces. Now get this: The biggest pieces to reach the ground will be a fifty-one-hundred-pound air-lock shroud and a thirty-nine-hundred-pound lead-lined film vault. They will be traveling four hundred feet per second on impact. Hey, no problem. No danger there. No. Of course someone might get hurt. Someone could be huddling in his basement with a helmet on, and three tons of sizzling steel could crush him like an ant. So maybe you're thinking, "I know it's silly, but I don't want to be there when this stuff hits, okay? So where can I go? South America? Alaska? Malibu? Mill Valley?" But you know what? They have no idea. [*John picks up globe and heavy metal representation of Skylab.*] When this thing hits the dense part of our atmosphere, it's going to skip around—like this. And you know what? They don't know where it's going to fall, but they do know the five hundred pieces will be spread out in a path four thousand miles long and a hundred miles wide. [*John begins gouging the globe with the Skylab object.*] Oh-oh, here comes Skylab. Hey, there's a fisherman in his boat—*whup*! Oh, it's smashed to pieces. Hey, there's a mom and dad at the zoo, aren't those bears funny—whoa! Now they're like gum on the bottom of a shoe. Hey, there's John Belushi in New York. He's not worried about Skylab. No. That's silly. What do you know? He's sizzling like a pizza underneath a two-ton lead-lined film vault! But did he have any reason to worry or be afraid? The government takes fifty percent of the money he earns every year. They could be spending it on mass transit and solar energy and cleaning the environment—but NOOOOO! They have to spend millions sending up huge chunks of steel so they can scream back to earth to maim and kill innocent people—AAGH! Skylab! AAGH! It's coming! AAGH!

Point-Counterpoint

Jane Curtin and Dan Aykroyd

Jane Curtin: Dan, only a reactionary ass such as yourself could oppose full diplomatic relations with China. As President Carter said, it is a simple recognition of reality. How can we ignore eight hundred million people? But then again, I guess it's your habit to ignore reality. You're a paranoid schizophrenic, Dan, whose politics are obviously born out of some buried infantile trauma. You hide from reality, constructing a world to justify your own hostile incapacity for love and compassion. Go ahead, Dan, live in your dark lonely world; the rest of us will extend our hands in friendship to eight hundred million human beings, saying, "Hi, you do exist, let's be friends."

Dan Aykroyd: Jane, you ignorant slut. My personality profile is not at issue here any more than is your inability to achieve orgasm. The issue is Tai-

wan. How can we expect to have the confidence of any free nation when we stab one of our most faithful allies in the back? I suppose you'd like to conduct our foreign policy the way you conduct your private life! Hopping from bed to bed with anyone that can do you some good. Then what do you have? An old dried-out scuz that no decent man would be seen with. Is that what you want for America? It's too late for you, Jane, but our country still has some dignity left.

Jane: Good night and have a pleasant tomorrow.

Bill Murray, Stargazer

Thank you, Jane, Dan. Hello, everybody, and I *mean* that. Now get out of here. I mean it. Hello. I hope everyone had a *primo* summer. Yours truly, the party animal, went insane for three months. Speaking of fun, tonight I'm reviewing *The Deep*, Columbia Pictures' box office smash of this summer. The same guy who wrote *Jaws*, Benchley, wrote it, and they gave him *multo dinero* to do it.

Anyway, I haven't seen the film yet. I haven't seen the film yet, but people I know say, "Well, Jacqueline Bisset *looks* great, but the film is despicable." When I think of myself, I think of a guy with no preconceptions, and I love that about myself. When movie taste is involved, you can't trust anybody, so I'm going to screen a clip of the movie right now and tell you what I think.

Nick Nolte, lose the mustache. Lose it. Who are you kidding? You look like a Denver cop. Give me a break, *please*. That's not the Nick Nolte I know and loved in *Rich Man, Poor Man*. Now don't call me a bitch either, Nick. I'm sorry, that's the way I feel. Now get out of here.

Robert Shaw...you disturb me, Robert. I used to love you. And I don't think there's anyone who's more respected in the industry. But your accent, what are you? Scotch, English, Irish, Welsh? You sound like you're always selling macaroons or Lucky Stars or something. Now fix that, will you? And regain my respect, *please?*

Jackie Bisset. Your time has come. Your charm and body fill the screen. But you've got to do this stuff that doesn't stretch you as an actress. You can be a success, honey, *if* you look out for Jackie Bisset. Don't let any of the little-minded people try to make you what you're not. You're you. Be it. Just be Jackie.

That's my first review of the season. If you didn't like it, I'm sorry, but that's the way I feel. Now get out of here. I mean it.

Mother Teresa, the nun whose work in the slums of Calcutta won her the Nobel Peace Prize, has already decided how she'll spend her prize money. This week she goes shopping for a Mercedes 450 and then plans to, "get the hell out of this jerk-water town."

Gerald R. Ford said yesterday that he will not run for president in 1980. Ford said he thinks President Carter will be reelected because, "An incumbent president would have to be an idiot to lose. The incumbency is a great advantage. I wish I had it when I was president."

The National Safety Council has announced that about four hundred people will be killed on the highways during this four-day Christmas holiday period. That amounts to four deaths every ten minutes. So, during the course of our Weekend Update newscast, we would like to say good-bye to Roy Klein, Laurie Zaks, and the Schindler twins.

It's official. Gerald Ford will not be a candidate for president this year. Announcing his decision at a press conference today, Mr. Ford said, "I believe that this country is in very grave danger, both at home and abroad, and I have decided that I am simply too stupid and inept to deal with the problems we face."

Don Novello

Father Guido Sarducci

Gossip columnist for _L'Osservatore Romano_, the Vatican newspaper

Well, we got a new pope. He's a wonderful pope, even though he's not Italian. I really thought that Cardinal Felonio would get it. He had a good campaign, he had a nice button, a good slogan. _Felonio est unum_—"Felonio is the one." It's hard to come up with good slogans in Latin—there aren't many slang words. They say he had some big bucks behind him; some said it was Episcopalian money—I think that might have hurt his chances. These cardinals had an interesting idea. Their slogan was _Tota via cum Spanzollo et Russo_—"All the way with Spanzollo and Russo." Their idea was that being pope in modern times is too much for any one man, and if they got elected, they were going to split up the job. They were also going to call themselves Pope John Paul Two—and one of them would have been known as John Paul Two One, and the other would be John Paul Two Two. One would have been pope on Monday, Wednesday, and Friday, and the other on Tuesday, Thursday, and Saturday, and they would switch off every other Sunday. Cardinal Barcelli—what a wonderful, wonderful pope he would have made! Everybody likes him—he's holy and he's smart too. Only trouble with him was that he looks just like Joe Garagiola.

FATHER GUIDO SARDUCCI PLAYED BY DON NOVELLO

Chico Escuela

Jane Curtin: Now we'd like to welcome a new member to our Update team. The former all-star second baseman for the New York Mets, Chico Escuela. Welcome, Chico. Chico will be covering the sports scene for Weekend Update.
Chico Escuela: Thank you. Thank you bera, bera much. Besaball been bera, bera good to me. Thank you, Hane....Pete Rose. Besaball been bera, bera good to Pete Rose. Three-point-two million dollars _para_ Pete Rose. Charlie Hustle—you bet. Thank you bera, bera much. _En fútbol. En_ Dominican Republic, _fútbol_ is—how you say it?—soccer. Your _fútbol?_ I don't know. _En_ National Hockey League: I don't know hockey. _En_ besaball—besaball been bera, bera good to me. Thank you—thank you bera, bera much, Hane.
Jane: Great job, Chico. I'm glad that we haven't hired just another stupid ex-jock sportscaster.

CHICO ESCUELA PLAYED BY GARRETT MORRIS

Garrett Morris

Joe Piscopo

Dr. Jack Badofsky

Five-hundred thousand Americans now have a new enemy hitting them below the belt: *genital herpes.* This is not to be confused with *facial herpes.* If you get it here, it's *herpes simplex.* Down there, it's *herpes complex.* If you get it in both places, it's *herpes duplex.* There are many, many new virulent strains of herpes I'd like to tell you about. The first is *whorepes.* This is transmitted solely by prostitutes who do not bathe regularly. *Whorepes* should not be confused with *Hopis,* which you get from certain tribes of Indians. Any contact at all with filthy midgets can lead to a nasty case of *twerpes.* If you should make love to a person who works at a Sno-Kone stand, you could get *slurpes.* And sleeping with a green giant could give you *Le-Sueur-peas,* and kissing your canary can cause a bad spell of *chirpes.*

DR. JACK BADOFSKY PLAYED BY
TIM KAZURINSKY

Tim Kazurinsky

Joe Piscopo, SNL Sports

Hello again, everybody. Joe. Piscopo. Live. Saturday Night Sports. The big story. Today. This afternoon. This network. NBC broadcasts a football game with no announcers. They just put statistics on the screen with *no announcers!* You like that, Don Ohlmeyer, executive producer, NBC Sports? No announcers? Just statistics? "Joe Piscopo. Sports announcer. Six-one. Melodious voice. Curt Gowdy: A lot of money. Howard Cosell: Even more money. Joe Piscopo: Minimum wage." Exciting? Revolutionary? Innovative? Boring! This is Joe Piscopo. Saturday Night Sports. Just like to say: Christmas. Merry. New Year. Happy. Goodwill. Men. Peace. Earth. Charlie.

Rich Hall

Paul Harvey

Hello, Americans, I'm Paul Harvey. Y'know, recently we've heard so much about President Reagan's Star Wars technology; and though I'll admit it sounds like fun, before we commit to such an exorbitantly expensive undertaking, shouldn't we consider other fun forms of domestic protection? Such as Wham-O technology. Yes, Wham-O. Who remembers Hula Hoops? The Wham-O Corporation recently submitted to the Pentagon details for the Wiffle rocket. It's true. Think of the savings to our military. Incidentally, did you know all the components are available at your True Value Hardware Store?

Page two: Reagan speaks of exchanging trade secrets with the Russians. Why not exchange Nerf technology? Cover the earth with Nerf, and missiles would be absorbed just like a giant sponge. Fun for the whole family. Yes, the list goes on. Slinky-powered transport vehicles; Pez rocket launchers. Come on, America. Let's put our toy companies to work, then ask ourselves: [*Sings*] "*War. Un-hunh, uh-hunh. What is it good for? It's been good for Hasbro. Two hundred million GI Joes. War. Uh-huh. Good God, y'all. What is it good for?*" I'm Paul Harvey. Good day!

PAUL HARVEY PLAYED BY RICH HALL

Dr. Herman Tarnower, creator of the famous Scarsdale Diet, was buried yesterday after being shot to death by his lover, Mrs. Jean Harris of Virginia. The funeral was a testimonial to the success of Dr. Tarnower's weight-loss plan, the casket being carried by one pallbearer and five helium balloons.

Yes, it's that time of year again. The annual Newfoundland harp seal slaughter is under way, but this year no one should feel bad about it. A Canadian naturalist and seal expert reports that the baby harp seal is a vicious little animal that despises human beings, lies, cheats, carries a gun, and has bad breath. It is also masochistic and loves to be clubbed on the head by Norwegians. One hundred and eighty thousand of the beasts should get it this season, and we say, good riddance.

At The Hague today, the World Court condemned Iran for violations of international law. Since the World Court has no actual punitive powers, the best it could do was require the Ayatollah Khomeini to serve on jury duty at the Court next week. However, the Court said Khomeini could get out of it if he proves he runs his own business and can't afford to get away.

Late tonight President-elect Reagan announced that he intends to keep at least one of his campaign promises, and will appoint a black to his cabinet. The new administration's secretary of defense is to be Shirley Temple Black.

Mr. Subliminal

An article in a London tabloid has linked the British intelligence service with bugging the Royal Family. I'd like to comment for a minute on this royal scandal....There's nothing I'm more sick of hearing about [*BUTTAFUOCO*]. It's not like the Royals are doing anything indecent [*INBREEDING*]. Now, supposedly, there's a tape of Charles and Di arguing, and in one of the conversations Di suggests she's been putting on such a charade, she should be an actress [*PORNO*]. I agree [*NICE BOD*]. Putting up with Charles—I mean, who does he think he is [*TAMPON*]? They say there are even tapes of Queen Elizabeth. What can she possibly have to hide [*PREGNANT*]? I just don't think anyone should dump on the Royals [*BAD TEETH*]. But soon they're actually going to be giving tours through Buckingham Palace [*PEEP SHOW*]. This whole episode, could anything be more embarrassing to a family [*ROGER CLINTON*]? I don't think so.

MR. SUBLIMINAL PLAYED BY KEVIN NEALON

Kevin Nealon

A. Whitney Brown

The Big Picture

Well, my friends, a hundred and forty Soviet dissidents saw the clear blue sky of freedom this week as part of a new Soviet policy known as *glasnost*, which is the Russian way of saying, "Welcome back, sorry about the frostbite. See you soon." Of course, the Russians have had periods of openness before, only this time they say it's for real, no fooling. The genuine article. You know, the last time I heard that, I was buying a Rolex in Times Square. I even remember the time. It was 4:03. It seems like it's always 4:03. Same thing is happening in China, but individual rights are an even lower priority in the Chinese culture. Because the issue just doesn't come up that often—you're born, you're short, you have straight black hair, why rock the boat? It's not easy to stand out in a crowd of a billion people. A billion people. That means that even if you're a one-in-a-million kind of guy, there's still a thousand just like you. When I put China and the Soviet Union into the Big Picture, I see two great nations, painfully emerging from a period when each was ruled by a paranoid old man clinging to a fossilized worldview and occasionally lapsing into senility, fantasy, and isolation. You have to feel sorry for a country in that situation. That, my friends, is the Big Picture.

PRESENTED BY A. WHITNEY BROWN

VICTORIA JACKSON'S MOVIE REVIEW

Four stars is a pretty good movie. It's not the best, but it is well worth watching, in my opinion. Three stars is the best. Rush out and see this movie, they don't make them any better. Two stars is the worst—don't waste your time or money, it's the bottom of the barrel. And one star is pretty good too.

Queen Shenequa

Queen: Thank you, Kevin, or should I say, *Asante sana abaragani.*

Kevin Nealon: What? *Abassi...*

Queen: It's Swahili. You know, Swahili, the language we speak in the Bronx. It's a greeting. Hi, y'all, this is Queen Shenequa back from Harlem, where I learned all about Kwanzaa today. "Kwanzaa" is a Swahili word, and it means "Santa don't come to *my* house!" I'm so glad we've got our own holiday. When I was a kid, I was tired of people asking me, "What did Santa bring you, what did Santa bring you?" Santa comes down the chimney. I live in the projects. Where's he going to come in from, the incinerator? You know what I mean, Kevin?

Kevin: *Aburugani...*

Queen: Kwanzaa is a seven-day holiday and you pray a lot. On the first day we pray for our lost brothers and sisters. On the first day I'm going to pray for Michael Jackson. I'm gonna pray he gets his mind back. Now what's wrong with that child? Has anyone seen his mind, 'cause he clearly lost it sometime after *Thriller.* Singing about it doesn't matter if you're black or white. If it doesn't matter, then why are you so white? Of course it matters, because if it didn't matter, you would just leave it the way it is. Why bother changing something if it doesn't matter? If you change something, then it matters; if it doesn't matter, you just leave it alone, right, Kevin?

Kevin: Abaragani!

Queen: Yes! Another Swahili name: Milli Vanilli. "Milli Vanilli" translates to "I'm not singing, you? Nuh-uh!" Milli tried to commit suicide by jumping out of a window—well, he didn't really jump, he got somebody else to jump for him. On a serious note, I'm going to pray for Nelson Mandela, who was in town this week addressing the United Nations. His first visit was heralded with ticker tape parades, and that's all right because some of my sisters and brothers didn't get it. You know, when he came before? 'Cause I was hanging out with my stupid girlfriend Christine. She said, "Well, why are they giving him a ticker tape parade?" I said, " 'Cause he was in prison for twenty-seven years." She said, "So? My father was in prison for twenty-seven years, they didn't give him no ticker tape parade." I said, "Christine, it's different. See, Nelson Mandela was in prison for liberating his people, and your father was in prison for liberating those TVs from their department store." She's stupid. I'm praying for her too. Her mind is out there frolicking into madness with Michael. So much to pray for, Kevin, I better get me some knee pads, what do you think?

QUEEN SHENEQUA PLAYED BY ELLEN CLEGHORNE

Ellen Cleghorne

196

The Hollywood Minute

Let's get started. Mariah Carey had a big hit this year with a remake of the Jackson 5's "I'll Be There." Mariah, you know why he sang that song? So you don't have to. It's called originality. Look into it.

Tom Selleck is *Mr. Baseball*. Come on, I've seen better stories on the place mats at Burger King. It's called TV. Stay on it.

L.A. Law season premiere aired this week. Guess what? Didn't watch it, didn't tape it.

The *Encyclopædia Britannica* guy. This kid needs a serious beating. "Remember me?" Yes, and you're an idiot.

Ross Perot. Good person, smart businessman; thinks he's going to be president. Guess what? It's not gonna happen; it's called the Bronze. Get used to it.

Kris Kross. Guess what? It's a short ride. Save some money.

[*Pictured: LaToya Jackson.*] Hi. I'm a mess. [*Pictured: Keith Richards.*] Hi, I'm Skeletor. Have we met? [*Pictured: Vanilla Ice.*] Hi, I'll rap for food. [*Pictured: Slash.*] Mmmbbbuhmmmbuh-mmbuh.

Hey, Michael. Do me a favor: Put a fork in yourself, 'cause you're done. It's called peaked with *Thriller*. Deal with it.

[*Pictured: Madonna.*] "Hey, Dad, look, I wrote a book." It's called *Chlamydia*. Get used to it. [*Pictured: George Bush.*] Ten days and counting. It's called Public Speaking Tour. Get ready for it. That's The Hollywood Minute. Kevin, back to you.

PRESENTED BY DAVID SPADE

David Spade

Cajunman

Adam Sandler

Here to talk about his recent trip to Daytona Beach is our party correspondent, the Cajunman.
Kevon!
What's that smell, Cajunman?
Onion.
All right, Cajunman, I understand that you go down to Daytona Beach just about every year.
Tradition.
You look like you got some color

there too.
Suntan lotion.
All right, Cajunman. You're down on Daytona Beach a lot. How's your body looking?
Definition.
Then how do you stay thin?
Metabolison.
And?
Liposuction.
All right—anyway, Cajunman, I've heard you do a lot of drinking down there occasionally.
Inebriation.
What kind of beer were you drinking?
Pabst Blue Ribbon.
Now somebody told me that you guzzled, like, thirty-two beers in some beer-guzzling contest. What happened after that?
Hallucination.
What'd you see?
Satan.
Anybody with him?
Jim Morrison.
Whoa! That would have freaked me out, how'd you handle that?

Defecation.
I can imagine. So you also judged a wet T-shirt contest, is that right? How were the contestants?
Oh, Kevon—
What made you decide on the winner?
Melons.
Did you have any luck with her?
Rejection.
That's too bad.
Lesbion.
Cajunman, Cajunman, how did you know that?
Intuition.
Cajunman, what's the matter?
Depression.
Oh, Cajunman, there's plenty of other women out there. You'll find someone.
"Love Connection."
Okay, well, thanks for coming, Cajunman. You want me to say hello to somebody?
John Goodmon.
Okay, I will.

CAJUNMAN PLAYED BY ADAM SANDLER

Operaman

1 *Billionerro, Ross Perot*
Mi confuso
Es Frank Perdue? Oh?

[Pictured: George Bush.]
Ssh, ssh, el doze-oh.
Shhhhhhh, el doze-oh
[Pictured: Los Angeles.]
El inferno violencia
Armageddon
[Pictured: George Bush.]
Shhhhhhh, el doze-oh
No disturba Presidente

[Pictured: Daryl Gates.]
La chiefa policia
No dispatcha gendarme
Morono, no respondo,
No excusa bagga doucha

Messier
El choke-oh
Il Cupo de Stanley
Arrivederci

Carnac finale
Termino bella notte
Carnac adio
El beginno
El chin-o
Jay Leno
no oh oh oh oh oh oh

Saturdia Noche Viva
Endo seasone
Operaman
Bye-Bye

2 *Perot es candidato*
No, No candidato
Si, Candidato
No, No candidato
Do ah poopa
Or get off da potta!

Oh solo mia
Mia solo
Soon-Yi incesta
Woody addio

Es Madonna?
No, es Bambina
Es Madonna?
No, es Virgin-ah
Ah! El cracko!
Es Madonna!

[Pictured: Dan Quayle
and Murphy Brown.]
Enuffo! Enuffo!
"Topico over exposo!"

Leno chin-o. El produché.
Mucho close-oh Mucho
boffo
El peacockoh ultimatum
Leno chin-oh blow her
off-oh.

Fergia, Fergia
Nippola, Nippola
Nippola, Nippola
Nippola, Nippola
Cantalopas
El protrudo
Operaman
Grande stiffo
Bye-Bye!

3 *Base-ballah*
Es upsetta
Negro-phoba
Anti-Semitah
Biggest problema
Marge-Bella
Is that she fire-ah
Lou Piniella!

Home Alone-oh
Mucho dinero
Little bambino million-
air-oh
Mucha lira
Money to lend-oh
Operaman
Make-ah new friend-oh

Amy Fisher
Buttafuoco

El-knock-oh
El-shoot-oh
In jail-oh
No bail-oh
Senora
You're a whore-ah

So-oh-oh-oh-oh-oh
Malia
Bon appetito

Tatum cinema! Actressah
No! Es mama! Tu es
mama!
Paper Moon-oh, mi
Oscar-oh!
You forget-oh
Bad News Bear-oh!
Ah ah ah ah ah ah ah ah
ah

[Pictured: George Bush.]
Adieu
Arrivederci
Hasta la vista
White-a House-a too
de-loo

Au Revoir
Shalom
Sayonara
Ciao
Chucko and Diana

Feliz Navidad
Bella Hanukkah
Operaman
Bye-Bye

OPERAMAN PLAYED BY
ADAM SANDLER

Adam Sandler

Pat: Dear Diary, It's twelve o'clock and once again I find myself alone. Dick's leg swelled up today and he was in intense pain. Good! The ocean is calm here at San Clemente—quite a contrast to the stormy final days in the White House. I'll never forget the night of August seventh. I had just gone down to the pantry to get some refreshment, when I heard Dick's voice. As usual, he wasn't speaking to me; he was talking to Abe Lincoln...

Nixon: Well, Abe, you were lucky. They *shot* you. Come on clot! Move up to my heart! Kill me! KILL ME!

[*Julie and David Eisenhower enter.*]

David: Ah, Mr. President, Julie and

Dan Aykroyd and John Belushi

The Final Days

Featuring Pat Nixon (Madeline Kahn) at her desk in San Clemente, Richard Nixon (Dan Aykroyd), Julie Eisenhower (Gilda Radner), David Eisenhower (Chevy Chase), and Henry Kissinger (John Belushi).

I were thinking maybe you should go upstairs and get some rest. Maybe things will look brighter in the morning.

Nixon: Shuddup! Ugh, he looks like Howdy Doody!

Julie: Daddy, you're not going to resign, are you?

Nixon: No, no, a pessimist would resign. I'm an optimist.

Julie: It's the pessimists who want you to resign, isn't it, Daddy?

Nixon: That's right, Princess. Remember that army hospital I visited in Vietnam? There was a young enlisted man from Des Moines, Iowa. He had been hit in the eye with a surface-to-air missile. And he had only four pints of blood left in his body, and as you know, a man usually has eight pints of blood in his body. Now the pessimists in this country would say that boy was half empty, while I like to think that he was half full.

David: That's right, Mr. President. You know, I was talking to two reporters from *The Washington Post* this morning, and they said they thought you were half crazy, but I told them I like to think of you as half sane.

Nixon: Thank you. Now, if you'll leave me alone, I'm in the middle of a meeting.

David: Meeting?

Julie: Okay, Daddy, if it'll make you feel better.

[*Nixon walks over to JFK portrait.*]

Nixon: You! Kennedy. You looked so good all the time. They're gonna find out about you too. The president having sex with women within these very walls. That never happened when Dick Nixon was in the White House. Never. NEVER! NEVER! NEVER! NEVER!

Pat: Never...never...never...never... never...never. I think Henry Kissinger was the first one to suggest that resignation was inevitable. He told Dick not to think of it as a resignation, but as "humiliation with honor." I think the last time they spoke to each other was on the same night...

Nixon: Never! Never! Never!

Kissinger: Mr. President, Mr. President. I just spoke mit your lovely daughter und charming son-in-law, und zey expressed a deep concern for your well-being, which I, of course, share, und zey suggested zat I come down und cheer you up.

Nixon: Henry, you know, I'm not a crook. I'm innocent! [*Long pause*] I am! I'm telling you, Henry: I had nothing to do with the bugging of Watergate; I had nothing to do with the cover-up, with the breaking into Daniel Ellsberg's psychiatrist's office, or with the man who was killed in Florida.

Kissinger: Vhat man vas killed in Florida, Mr. President?

Nixon: You don't know about the little Cuban who...ah...never mind. Henry, get down on your knees and pray with me.

Kissinger: Mr. President, you've got a big day tomorrow, vhy don't ve get in our pajamas und go sleepy.

Nixon: Don't you want to pray, you JEW BOY!

Kissinger: I don't vant to get into zat again, Mr. President. Excuse me, I've got to go varn the Strategic Air Command to ignore all presidential orders.

Nixon: All right, thanks, Henry. Jewboy! Jewboy! Jewboy!

Pat: Dick wasn't anti-Semitic...he hated all minorities. I remember once an aide referred to the Vietnamese as gooks and Chinks. Dick said that was all wrong. He said a Chink is someone from China and a Gook is anyone of Oriental persuasion. A Chink is always a gook, but a gook isn't always a Chink. But Dick's prejudice didn't prevent minority admirers from supporting him....

AIRED: MAY 8, 1976

Ford-Carter Debate

Featuring moderator Ruth Clusen (Lily Tomlin), Gerald Ford (Chevy Chase), Liz Montgomery (Jane Curtin), Tom Burke (John Belushi), Earl Roland (Garrett Morris), and Jimmy Carter (Dan Aykroyd).

Clusen: Good evening, this is Ruth Clusen of the League of Women Voters. Welcome to the first of three televised presidential debates between Republican candidate Gerald R. Ford and his challenger, Governor Jimmy Carter of Georgia, the Democratic nominee for president. This first debate will be limited to a discussion of domestic issues, so let me introduce the three journalists who will be asking the questions: Liz Montgomery of *The Washington Post*, who was selected by the League of Women Voters because of her expertise in economic matters; Tom Burke, *Rolling Stone* magazine, for his incisive reporting of the Washington bureaucracy; and...Earl Roland of the *Chicago Tribune* because he is a Negro. Now, at the request of President Ford, Mr. Tommie Bell, the senior linesman of the National Football League, will toss the coin to determine who will be asked the first question.

Ford: I'll take the side with the head on it.

Bell: Heads it is. The president will receive.

Clusen: All right. Thank you, Mr. Bell. Ms. Montgomery?

Montgomery: Mr. President, Governor Carter has accused you of hiding in the White House instead of meeting the people. How do you answer that charge?

Ford: I was not hiding, I was simply lost for a little while. The Secret Service found me and now everything is just fine.

Clusen: Mr. Burke, a question for Mr. Carter.

Burke: Governor Carter, your son Chip has admitted to smoking marijuana. As president, you would be the chief law enforcement officer of the country. What is your attitude on the decriminalization of marijuana?

Carter: Mr. Burke, as much as I love my son Chip, if I were to come upon him smoking marijuana, I would have him arrested. I would, however, grant him an executive pardon, but not until he had gone through the due process of the legal system, so that all questions could be answered before the American people. This would be a pardon, not amnesty. Amnesty would be condoning the smoking of marijuana, while a pardon would be merely forgiving him for its use.

Clusen: Mr. President, rebuttal?

Ford: No, thank you, I've just had dinner.

Clusen: No, sir. It is your turn to rebut on the answer that Mr. Carter gave concerning his son's smoking dope.

Ford: I see no reason for name-calling here. Mr. Carter's son is no dumber than my son and I see no reason for calling him a dope. I wouldn't call my son Susan a dope.

Clusen: Mr. Roland, any questions?

Roland: Which one is Ford?

Clusen: Ms. Montgomery, go ahead.

Montgomery: Governor Carter, you turned that question about mari-

Chevy Chase and Dan Aykroyd

leader Benigno Aquino. The ruling was made after a federal witness testified that Aquino, in fact, died of asphyxiation, after some bullets he'd been chewing "went down the wrong pipe."

Paul Castellano was let go by the parent company earlier this week. Anonymous sources cite creative differences as the reason for the abrupt dismissal, which took place at curb level outside the Sparks Steak House on Manhattan's East Side. That's the Sparks Steak House, where beef is the specialty of the house, but occasionally you'll hear the word "duck" bandied about.

The National Board of Education's Write-the-Script-to-*Rocky-IV*-Before-You-See-the-Movie Contest had to be canceled this week when 1,752 entries tied for first place, correctly duplicating the written screenplay right down to the last comma.

This just in: Godot finally showed up. He was rude, and we asked him to leave.

1986

Lee Iacocca's autobiography entered its fifty-first printing, with 2,610,000 copies in print. However, the Chrysler Corporation announced it is recalling 800,000 copies because of a cracked flyleaf and several jammed metaphors, which could be fatal if read too fast.

juana around so that you could talk about pardons: Is this an oblique reference to Watergate? Are you perhaps hoping to make some political gains by recalling the dirty laundry of Watergate?

Carter: No. Certainly, I could not benefit by reminding the American people that they were forever denied the truth and due process of law from the ugliest scandal in our nation's history, when President Gerald R. Ford pardoned his predecessor, the first president ever to resign in disgrace, Richard M. Nixon. No, no, my friends, I will not belabor the fact that Mr. Ford was appointed by the most corrupt president in the history of this great—

Clusen: Governor, you have ten seconds to wrap this up.

Carter: So, I would say no, Watergate, *W-a-t-e-r-g-a-t-e*, Watergate has no place in these debates.

Clusen: President Ford. You have two minutes to rebut.

Ford: I'd have to go along with Governor Carter on that. I would keep Watergate out of this. I wouldn't remind the people of it.

Clusen: Next question. Mr. Roland.

Roland: Mr. Ford. How do you and Mr. Carter differ on abortion?

Ford: Of course, Mr. Roland, this is a very delicate and controversial issue for the American people and I have given a great deal of long, hard thought to both sides of what might be thought of as the most sensitive issue of the campaign. What was the question?

Roland: Abortion!

Ford: Mr. Roland, I support a constitutional amendment allowing the states to decide their own abortion laws. This would allow a woman who wants an abortion to travel to another state—

Clusen: Mr. Carter. Rebuttal?

Carter: I think my stance on the abortion issue is perfectly ambiguous and ill-defined, and I see no reason to elaborate any further.

Clusen: Ms. Montgomery, a question on economics?

Montgomery: Yes. Mr. President, you have called the Humphrey-Hawkins bill "fiscally irresponsible," and you say it will have a price tag of possibly sixty billion dollars. But isn't it true that the jobs provided by the bill will create up to a hundred and fifty billion dollars in increased production, using Walter Heller's figure that for every one percent unemployed, there is a resulting thirty-seven-billion-dollar loss in GNP? Now, at the present rate of taxation on GNP of thirty-nine percent, doesn't this come to about the same sixty billion dollars in increased revenues?

Ford: It was my understanding that there would be no math questions. I'm prepared to answer any questions about domestic issues. Perhaps you would like to know something about me and Betty?

AIRED: SEPTEMBER 18, 1976

Danny DeVito and Phil Hartman

Gorbachev-Reagan

Featuring Mikhail Gorbachev (Danny DeVito), Ronald Reagan (Phil Hartman), and their limousine driver (Kevin Nealon).

Gorbachev: It is important dat we not expect too much from dis Summit. But it is a first step. And from such a step many—Please, Ron, would you stop staring at my forehead!

Reagan: Oh, I'm sorry, I did it again, didn't I. I'm trying so hard not to. I've got kind of a mental thing about it. Please continue.

Gorbachev: Never mind, it wasn't important. Anyway, here we are in Washington, D.C. Please, give me the grand tour.

Reagan: Well, to begin with, as you can imagine, Mikhail, our nation's capital is rich with history. See that building over there with the big pillars—

Gorbachev: Lincoln Memorial.

Reagan: Whatever. Anyway, that's where Jean Arthur talked Jimmy Stewart out of giving up in *Mr. Smith Goes to Washington.*

Gorbachev: "With malice toward none. With charity to all."

Reagan: No, I believe she said, "You can't quit now. Not you, Jeff." Oh, look over there. The Iwo Jima Memorial...have you ever heard the story behind that?

Gorbachev: I'm not sure.

Reagan: Well, evidently, John Wayne didn't want to play that part.

Gorbachev: I see.

Reagan: Duke had his heart set on doing *Slattery's Hurricane.* But he was under contract to Warner Brothers at the time, and, well, Jack Warner phoned Duke's agent, Lew Wasserman, and said, "Lew, if the Duke doesn't do *Sands of Iwo Jima,* he'll be shagging tennis balls for Tyrone Power."

Gorbachev: I'm sorry. Who?

Reagan: Tyrone Power. Anyway, Duke did the movie, and was nominated for an Academy Award. Now, you know who would have played Duke's part if he'd gotten his way?

Gorbachev: To play John Wayne's part. I—I don't know.

Reagan: Forrest Tucker.

Gorbachev: It is strange how these things happen.

Reagan: Oh, look! The Pentagon. You, of course, would know this from *Seven Days in May, Fail Safe,* and so on. Remember the really big war room in *Fail Safe?*

Gorbachev [*Lying*]: Yes.

Reagan: Well, it's in there. I've never seen it, but in the event a war breaks out, they'll take me there, evidently.

Gorbachev: Would it be possible for me to see this war room? It would be fascinating to compare it to the film.

Reagan: Well, I don't see why not. You're on the VIP tour.

Driver: Ah, Mr. President. I'm afraid we can't visit the war room.

Reagan: Why not?

Driver: Well, sir, I'm quite certain that the war room would be off-limits to Premier Gorbachev...be-ing that he's such a high-ranking Soviet official.

Reagan: Oh, right. You know, sometimes I forget that we're mortal enemies.

Gorbachev: Well, Ron, often I think that if the circumstances had been otherwise [*Reagan begins staring at the birthmark again.*], you and I could have been great...Well, we could have been good...if...[*Irritated, Gorbachev covers up the birthmark with one hand and points out the window at the Jefferson Monument.*] What monument is that?

Reagan: Hmm. It might be the Tomb of the Unknown Soldier.

Driver: It's the Jefferson Memorial, sir.

Reagan: Ah.

Gorbachev: Is very beautiful.

Reagan: Yes, it is. Must be quite a story behind that. Oh! Oh! There's the Washington Monument. And here on this very field is where the saucer from *The Day the Earth Stood Still* landed. And I figure that the robot Gort stood...right... *there!* Right there!

Gorbachev [*recalling fondly*]: *Klaatu barada nikto.*

Reagan: Yep. *Klaatu barada nikto.* I always wondered what those words meant.

Gorbachev: It means Live from New York, it's Saturday Night!

AIRED: DECEMBER 5, 1987

Bush-Dukakis Debate

Featuring Peter Jennings (Tom Hanks), Diane Sawyer (Jan Hooks), Sam Donaldson (Kevin Nealon), Michael Dukakis (Jon Lovitz), and George Bush (Dana Carvey).

Jennings: Good evening. I'm Peter Jennings here in Los Angeles awaiting the start of the second and final presidential debate between Michael Dukakis and George Bush. As you may know, the League of Women Voters withdrew their sponsorship of this debate, citing unreasonable demands by both campaigns. In fact, one of the conditions made by the Bush camp requires us to tell you what's on other channels. On HBO is *The Sensuous Nurse,* starring Ursula Andress and Udo Kier; on Showtime, *The Making of "Who Framed Roger Rabbit,"* an entertaining look at this summer's blockbuster hit; and on ESPN, a repeat of the LSU–Georgia Tech Southeast Conference showdown. And the Democrats have asked us to announce that C-SPAN will be rerunning the Bentsen-Quayle debate at four A.M. Eastern time. Well, this debate is about to start, so let's go to the moderator, Diane Sawyer.

Sawyer: Good evening, I'm Diane Sawyer of *60 Minutes.* Welcome to the second presidential debate between Vice President George Bush and Massachusetts governor Michael Dukakis. Gentlemen.

Our panel of questioners are Elizabeth Dowd of the Cleveland *Plain Dealer,* Sam Donaldson of ABC News, and syndicated columnist Carl Rowan. The first question goes to Governor Dukakis and will be asked by Elizabeth Dowd.

Donaldson: Governor Dukakis!!! Governor Dukakis!!!

Dukakis: Sam.

Donaldson: Your leadership style has been described as technocratic, cool, emotionally dead. Even your closest advisers admit that sometimes you are distant and aloof, a bit of a cold fish. Pundits are saying that one of the reasons you trail in the polls is that you are uninspiring, and seem totally devoid of passion.

Dukakis: What's the question?

Donaldson: Well, I suppose the question, Governor, is do you have the passion necessary to lead this country?

Dukakis: Sam, that kind of aspersion to my character quite frankly makes me—well, there's no other word for it—enraged. Maybe I shouldn't say that in the heat of the moment, but I can't control myself. I apologize for flying off the handle. And I'm just sorry my kids had to see me like this.

Sawyer: Mr. Bush. Rebuttal.

Donaldson: Mr. Vice President!!! Mr. Vice President!!!

Bush: Sam.

Donaldson: Do you really think SDI or Star Wars will work? Do you really think it's possible to create a shield that would prevent any or all nuclear missiles from striking the United States?

Bush: I'm glad you asked me that, Sam. Because tonight I can reveal something that's just been declassified. The key to SDI, to the whole concept, is a Time Machine. It's a beautiful idea. Let's say the Soviets launch a surprise attack, and a few of their missiles do get through our floating network of particle beam lasers. Then we use the Time Machine. We go back in time, before the surprise attack. It's defensive, it's clean, and it'll save our kids in the event of a Russian first strike. Now, who could be against that?

Dana Carvey and Jon Lovitz

Sawyer: Governor Dukakis?

Dukakis: Well, if such a Time Machine were possible, I'd like the vice president to explain why we haven't been visited already by time travelers from the future. You can't tell me that responsible members of a future government of the United States wouldn't, with access to a Time Machine, come back to reverse some of the mistakes, cockamamie mistakes, made by this administration. Of course they would. This idea is ridiculous. Spending billions and billions on a Time Machine whose very existence defies logic is, in my mind, lunacy.

Bush: Well, Mr. Massachusetts, Harvard Yard Brainiac. You may prove to yourself that it's impossible, but I think I'm like most Americans who'd rather see a Time Machine with an American flag on the side and not a hammer and sickle.

[Applause.]

Sawyer: Please, as I warned you before, hold down your reaction. It will only come out of your candidate's— *[She is hit by popcorn.]* That was uncalled for. Next, Sam Donaldson, with a question for Governor Dukakis.

Donaldson: Vice President Bush. There are millions of homeless in this country—children who go hungry and lacking in other basic necessities. How would the Bush administration achieve your stated goal of making this a kinder, gentler nation?

Bush: Well, that is a big problem, Sam, and unfortunately the format of these debates makes it hard to give you a complete answer. If I had more time I could spell out the program in greater detail, but I'm afraid, unfortunately, in a short answer like this all I can say is we're on track—we can do more—but we're getting the job done, so let's stay on course, the thousand points of light. Well, unfortunately, I guess my time is up.

Sawyer: Mr. Vice President, you still have a minute-twenty.

Bush: What? That can't be right. I must have spoken for two minutes.

Sawyer: No, just forty seconds, Mr. Vice President.

Bush: Really? Well, if I didn't use the time then, I must have just used the time now, talking about it.

Sawyer: No, no, Mr. Vice President, it's not being counted against you.

Bush: Well, I just don't want it to count against Governor Dukakis's time.

Sawyer: It won't. It will come out of the postdebate commentary.

Bush: Do you think that's a good idea?

Sawyer: You still have a minute-twenty, Mr. Vice President.

Bush: Well, more has to be done, sure. But the programs we have in place are doing the job, so let's keep on track and stay the course.

Sawyer: You have fifty seconds left, Mr. Vice President.

Bush: Let me sum up. On track, stay the course. Thousand points of light.

Sawyer: Governor Dukakis. Rebuttal.

Dukakis: I can't believe I'm losing to this guy.

Sawyer: And now Carl Rowan with a question for Vice President Bush.

Donaldson: Mr. Vice President!! Mr. Vice President!!

Bush: Sam.

Donaldson: Mr. Vice President, wouldn't you agree that a lot of people after watching Dan Quayle's performance last Wednesday are, quite frankly, worried about his ability to step into the job of president should something, God forbid, happen to you?

Bush: Sam, let me answer that question this way. I'm in perfect health. I jog every day. Pulse rate forty-three. Ticker's fine. I pledge that I will spend more than any president ever has on Secret Service protection. And I will go down in history as the president in the bulletproof bubble. Guys…

[A glass "bubble" is lowered.]

Bush: Carl Rowan. Would you do the honors? Go ahead, aim at my heart, Carl. *[Carl Rowan fires gunshots at Bush, which ricochet, and the bubble is lifted back up.]* So you see. There's nothing to worry about.

Sawyer: Gentlemen, let's go to your closing statements. Governor Dukakis, you're first.

Dukakis: I am the son of Greek immigrants. My parents were little people. Little swarthy people. So I understand the American dream. *Yo comprende el dremo des Estados Unidos. [He does the same again in Greek, then French, then Hebrew.]* The question you have to ask yourself on November eighth is whose judgment you trust. Do you trust the judgment of a man who traded arms to the Ayatollah and used that money to fund an illegal war in Central America? Or do you trust a son of a Greek immigrant who can think and talk in complete sentences. I think the choice is obvious.

Sawyer: Vice President Bush.

Bush: Well, let me answer some of that. First of all, I didn't know that the money from the Iran arms sales was going to the contras. I was told the money was going for the bombing of abortion clinics. Now this election is about the future. Yes, we want change. But we are the change. Do we wanna go back to the malaise days of Jimmy Carter? I don't think so. So once again, stay the course; we're on track. The thousand points of light. Thank you very much.

Sawyer: And thank you, gentlemen, for sharing this debate with the American public. I'm Diane Sawyer, saying good night.

Aired: October 8, 1988

Not Another Vietnam

George Bush (Dana Carvey) is seated in the Oval Office.

Good evening—happy holidays. Once again it's that festive season. Tonight our Jewish friends observe the fifth night of Chanukkah—the celebration of a military victory won centuries ago in a part of the world where today four hundred thousand brave Americans await my order to annihilate Iraq. None of us want war—but as commander in chief I am ever cognizant of my authority to launch a full-scale orgy of death there on the desert sand. Probably won't—but then again I might. And if we do go to war, I can assure you—*it will not be another Vietnam*. Because we learned well the simple lesson of Vietnam: "Stay out of Vietnam." They'll beat you bad, *b-a-a-d*. But this time is different, because the world is behind us. Critics say, why is the U.S. doing all the work? Not true. *Seventy-eight* countries are contributing to Operation Desert Shield. Not all are sending troops—sure. But giving what they are able. From Belgium, nylon helmut covers. From New Zealand, socks, ranging from sizes six through twelve. Six is small. Twelve, that's big. Me, I'm a ten and a half. Could wear a ten. Wouldn't be prudent. From the Congo, Ray•Ban sunglasses—two pair. From Yugoslavia, men's swimming trunks. From Mexico, salsa. And the list goes on. You see, world behind us, not like Vietnam. And this time, our strike will be swift and deadly. I know you're watching, Saddam. And time is running out. The deadline—the morning of January fifteenth. One month from today. And when that morning dawns, you won't be hearing the chirping birds. You'll be hearing something very different—something like this…

[*Bomb whistle*]

Then nuthin'. You wait—*kaboom*. Then—

[*Bomb whistle*]

—nuthin', you're lucky, it's a dud. Then—

[*Bomb whistle*]

—*kaboom*. Short fuse, heh, heh, heh. And finally the last thing you'll hear as you pass into oblivion: Live from New York, it's Saturday Night!

AIRED: DECEMBER 15, 1990

Dana Carvey

Gulf War Briefing

Featuring Secretary of Defense Richard Cheney (Phil Hartman), Lt. Col. William Pierson (Kevin Nealon), and nine reporters (Mike Myers, Dana Carvey, Julia Sweeney, Tom Davis, Jan Hooks, Conan O'Brien, Tim Meadows, Adam Sandler and Chris Farley).

Secretary of Defense Richard Cheney: And so, to sum up, while this war is by no means over, it is certainly fair to say that we have inflicted heavy damage on the Iraqi war machine, and every day brings victory for the coalition that much closer. Now I'm going to hand the floor over to Lieutenant Colonel Pierson, who will field your questions.

Lieutenant Colonel William Pierson: Thank you Senator Cheney. I'm happy to take any questions you might have with the understanding that there are certain sensitive areas that I'm just not going to get into. Particularly, information that might be useful to the enemy. Yes?

Reporter #1: What date are we going to start the ground attack?

Pierson: Well, as I mentioned a moment ago, there are certain sensitive areas which we are just not going to go into, and that is certainly one of them. Yes?

Reporter #2: Sir, knowing what you know, where would you say our forces are most vulnerable to attack, and how could the Iraqis best exploit those weaknesses?

Pierson: Well, again, this falls into the area of information that might be useful to the enemy, and I just can't divulge it right now.

Reporter #3: Sir! Which method of hiding scud missiles is working best for the Iraqis?

Pierson: Now, this again is a good example of information that could help the enemy, and I just can't answer that.

Reporter #4: I have a two-part question. Are we planning an amphibious invasion of Kuwait, and if so, where exactly will that be?

Cheney: Excuse me. If I could interrupt here, I just want to underscore what Colonel Pierson said at the start of Q&A. There are two general categories of questions that we are simply not going to be able to address. One, those that would give our enemy advance warning of our actions, and two, those that would identify any points of weakness or vulnerabilities to the Iraqi forces. So let's reopen the floor to questions.

Reporter #5: I understand that there are passwords that our troops use on the front lines. Could you give us some examples of those?

Pierson: No, that is something I really cannot comment on.

Reporter #6: Yeah! Are we planning an amphibious invasion of Kuwait? And, if so, where?

Pierson: I believe that question was asked and if you recall, I already answered it, or said I could not answer.

Reporter #7: Sir, what would be the one piece of information that would be most dangerous for the Iraqis to know?

Pierson: No can answer! I have time for two more questions. Yeah?

Reporter #8: Yes, Farud Hashami, *Baghdad Times.* Where are your troops, and can I go there and count them.

Pierson: Nope! Last question.

Reporter #9: Is there anything that you can tell us that would lower the morale of our fighting men?

Pierson: No. Really, the only thing we're at liberty to say at this time is LIVE FROM NEW YORK, IT'S SATURDAY NIGHT!

AIRED: FEBRUARY 9, 1991

Kevin Nealon

The most restrictive antiabortion legislation in any state has been passed in Idaho this week. The bill would allow doctors to end a pregnancy only in cases of rape, in cases of incest, and in case the woman goes to another state to get the abortion.

It was revealed this week that the contras are breaking up because one of them is dating Yoko.

Congress has been spending long hours this week trying to find a way out of the budget crisis. Among the dozens of interim proposals was one by New York senator Alfonse D'Amato to burn down the Capitol for the insurance.

United Nations inspectors flew helicopter missions to search for Scud missile sites in Iraq for the first time this week. Although the inspectors found no Scuds, they did find Waldo three times.

The man who invented the "severe tire damage" parking-lot spikes died recently. A hospital spokesman said he would have lived had the ambulance not had to go all the way around to the south entrance of the hospital's parking lot.

Abu Dhabi, the country that harbors the scandal-ridden financial institution BCCI headquarters, announced today that it will be changing its name to Abu Dhabi Du and its capital to Bedrock.

205

*A*nnouncer: NBC's *Saturday Night Live* will not be seen tonight so that we may bring you this NBC News Special, "Debate '92: The Challenge to Avoid Saying Something Stupid." And now, here is your moderator, Jane Pauley.

Pauley: Good evening. I'm Jane Pauley, and welcome to St. Louis for the first in our series of three presidential debates. Tonight's debate among President George Bush, Arkansas governor Bill Clinton, and diminutive Texas businessman Ross Perot will begin in just a moment. But first let me introduce my fellow panelists, CNN anchor Bernard Shaw and ABC News political correspondent Sam Donaldson. Now let's meet the candidates. Gentlemen. The first

of primitive Third World country. The fact is, Arkansas did have a long way to go, but we've made progress. When I started as governor, we were fiftieth in adult literacy, and last year, I'm proud to say, we shot ahead of Mississippi. We're number forty-nine and we're closin' fast on Alabama. Watch out, Alabama, we got your number!

Bush: Can I say something here? Two years ago I went on a fishing trip in Arkansas with Baker, Fitzwater, Quayle, and myself. We were chased and assaulted by a couple of inbred mountain people. I was sworn to secrecy as to those events, but suffice it to say, they felt that Dan Quayle—and I quote—"sure had a purty mouth." Now if that's the kind of progress Bill Clinton brought to

you see, this election is about who can take the heat, who you want there when that secured phone in the White House rings at three A.M. Do you want someone who will answer the phone politely, "Hello, this is the president. Speak slowly and clearly and tell me what the problem is." Or do you want someone who's cranky, who says, "This better be important," or "Do you realize what time it is," or simply says, "Shut up!" hangs up the phone, and *sleeps like a baby while the world burns!*

Pauley: Thank you, gentlemen. Now Bernard Shaw has a question for Governor Clinton.

Shaw: Yes, Governor Clinton. If Kitty Dukakis were raped and murdered, would you favor the death penalty for her assailant?

Debate '92

question will be asked by Sam Donaldson.

Donaldson: Governor Clinton. Let's be frank. You're running for president. Yet your only experience has been as the governor of a small, backward state with a population of drunken hillbillies riding around in pickup trucks. The main streets of your capital city, Little Rock, are something out of Li'l Abner with buxom underage girls in their cutoff denims prancing around in front of Jethro and Billy Bob, while corncob-pipe-smoking, shotgun-toting grannies fire indiscriminately at runaway hogs.

Clinton: I'm sorry, Sam, do you have a question?

Donaldson: My question is, How can you stand it? Don't you lose your mind living down there?

Clinton: Sam, you must have watched too many of my opponent's TV spots. I'm tired of the Bush campaign trying to portray my home state as some sort

Arkansas, *I don't think we need it in the White House!*

Clinton: That's not fair. Just this year we passed Mississippi to become forty-first in the prevention of rickets.

Perot: Can I jump in here? Why are we talking about Arkansas? Hell, everybody knows that all they got down there is a bunch a ignorant inbred crackers. Peckerwoods, catch me? Now can we talk about the deficit? While we've been jabbering, our deficit has increased by half a million dollars. That's enough to buy a still and a new outhouse for every family in Little Rock.

Clinton: Will you shut up!

Perot: Hold it there, cracker boy, I'm not finished.

Bush: See that right there. Kind of makes you wonder whether these men have the temperament to be president. Would you tell Prime Minister Major to shut up? Would you call Boris Yeltsin a 'Crackerhead'? Who wouldn't you tell to shut up? 'Cause

Pauley: Mr. Shaw, really. You don't have to answer that, Governor Clinton.

Clinton: No, no, I'm happy to answer that. Obviously none of us want to see Kitty Dukakis raped and murdered, but if she had to be murdered I would hope it would be in Arkansas—because no state is tougher on crime. Last year we passed Florida to become number two in executions by lethal injection and first in crushed by heavy stones.

Pauley: Mr. Perot? Rebuttal.

Perot: I was hopin' we'd get into the issues, but if this is the way the game is played, fine. So, if somebody were to lay a finger on Kitty Dukakis, I wouldn't kill him right away. That'd be too easy. I'd wait for a hot Texas day, see. Tie him to a stake. Get an ant trail goin'. You know, Texas red ants. Inch long. Just love to bite into human flesh. Catch what I'm saying here? See, they're eatin' him alive. Nice and slow like. And I'd sit with him in the shade under an umbrella, maybe with a lemonade, sit back, say to the fella, "How do you like them apples?" And he'll be screamin', "When am I gonna die?" and I'd say, "I don't know exactly, and frankly, I resent your question." Catch me?

Pauley: Thank you. Now let's turn to the deficit. President Bush. During your term, the deficit has grown by over a trillion dollars.

Bush: I know.

Pauley: Honestly now, don't you feel some kind of tax hike will be needed to reduce the deficit?

Bush: Jane, the answer is no. I WILL NEVER RAISE TAXES AGAIN! NEVER, EVER, EVER,

Dana Carvey, Phil Hartman, and David Spade

EVER…NEVER, EVER AGAIN, AND I MEAN NEVER, EVER, EVER, EVER, NEVER, EVER!! NEVER!!! NEVER!!!!!!

Pauley: Thank you, Mr. Pres—

Bush: NEVER, EVER, EVER—

Pauley: Mr. President, please.

Bush: — EVER, EVER AGAIN!

Pauley: Sam Donaldson, with a question for Governor Clinton.

Donaldson: Governor Clinton. This week the big story has been your 1969 trip to Moscow and your involvement in antiwar activities. Some have even suggested that while in Moscow, you had meetings with KGB agents. Isn't it fair to say that you haven't really told the American people the full story?

Clinton: Sam, this kind of attack shows how desperate the Bush campaign has become. Yes, I did go to Moscow by train in 1969. And while

on the train I struck up a conversation with a man in the seat next to me. He gave me a package to take to Moscow and instructed me to leave it folded in a newspaper in a kiosk across from Lenin's tomb. I've explained this many times. Yes, the KGB did subsequently pay my way through law school, but that was the last contact I had with the KGB until years later when Hillary and I were having problems, and it was a KGB agent, Nikolai Kuznetsov, who let me stay at his place for a while until we patched things up.

Donaldson: But isn't it true that during one of the peace demonstrations you burned an American flag in Red Square?

Clinton: I tried to burn an American flag once. I didn't like it, it gave off

---

Featuring Jane Pauley (Julia Sweeney), Bernard Shaw (Tim Meadows), Sam Donaldson (Kevin Nealon), Bill Clinton (Phil Hartman), George Bush (Dana Carvey), and Ross Perot (Dana Carvey and David Spade).

---

toxic fumes, so I didn't inhale.

Perot: Can I say somethin' here?

Pauley: Mr. Perot.

Perot: I think that's just sad.

Pauley: President Bush?

Bush: Once again. All comes down to trust. Who's been there? I've been with Mitterand, I've met with Major. I know the White House. I know the door out to the Rose Garden doesn't lock unless you *pull it.* I know the toilet in the Lincoln Bedroom will run all night unless you jiggle that handle. *It's not enough to flush it. You've got to jiggle it!* I know Air Force One. I know that seat 8G does not fully recline. If we are flying the prime minister of Canada to a trade conference, I alone can say, *"Mr. Mulroney, seat 8G does not fully recline. I suggest you use another!"*

Pauley: All right, Mr. Bush. Our time is up. Each candidate will be allowed a brief closing statement. Governor Clinton.

Clinton: Thank you, Jane. We've

talked about many issues tonight. But this election is really about one thing: change. Over the last twelve years more and more Americans have found themselves working longer and harder for less and less. We need to invest in our people again. Because together, all of us, pulling as a team, we can do it! Thank you.

Pauley: President Bush.

Bush: My fellow Americans. This election is about leadership and trust. Now our opponents have tried to portray us as the party of the rich and privileged, ignoring the fact that our economic program has created more opportunity for more Americans than in any twelve-year period in history. Well, let me tell you something: I'm not worth three-point-three billion dollars, and I wasn't educated at Ox-

ford. *But I knew how to lead this country to victory in the Persian Gulf and I can do it again here at home!*

Pauley: Mr. Perot.

Perot: This whole thing fascinates me, really. See, you don't have to be a Ph.D. at Harvard to know that our kids are going to inherit a four-trillion-dollar deficit. And that's just a crime. Now, if I'm president, we start cleaning up this mess on day one. It's gonna take some sacrifice. No doubt about it. But I know the American people are ready to sacrifice as long as it's fair. This is your country. Let's take it back.

Pauley: Thank you, Mr. Perot. Don't you have one last thing to say?

Perot: No, I can't. I'm on tape. Why don't you do it, live-boy.

Bush: Live from New York, it's Saturday Night!

Aired: October 10. 1992

Phil Hartman and Dana Carvey

Perot-Stockdale

Featuring Ross Perot (Dana Carvey) and Admiral James Stockdale (Phil Hartman).

Perot: There you go—that was vintage. That was the finest moment in any debate. Talk about pinnin' the tail on the donkey, that's just what you did. You were just A-1 in that debate. You had an H-bomb, them other fellas had slingshots.

Stockdale: Ping-Pong match. It was like a—

Perot: Yes, sir. You won hands down—them press people are loony. People saying you're a drag on the ticket, they musta been watchin' a different show. When you were quiet there for an hour, that was world-class. Showed you ain't just talk. Quiet man, lot goin' on upstairs. Them others just went shootin' their mouths off.

Stockdale: Who am I? Why am I here?

Perot: You're the admiral and you're takin' a joyride. Oh, I get it. You're quotin' yourself. "Who am I?" That line was precious. And you know, when you were wanderin' around there, remember that? When it looked like you were gonna walk on over to Gore's podium? That was— Margot and I just loved that. Showed you were restless, had places to go, people to see.

Stockdale: I'm all out of ammo.

Perot: Heh, heh, heh. Perfect, and the part when you were stoppin' and stutterin'—grand slam. Showed you weren't rehearsed. President needs to be spontaneous, not like those other two. And the American people know it.

Stockdale: Gridlock.

Perot: That's right. And the way your mind drifted, showed you're open to new ideas. And when you took your glasses off and on, nervously, and when you forgot your hearing aid was off, like you didn't know where you were, well, that was just stunning. And I adored it, and so did Margot, and all my kids.

Stockdale: I'm hungry.

Perot: Admiral, we ate at Denny's a half an hour ago. You had a double cheeseburger. Your belly's full. I rest my case.

Stockdale: Where are we?

Perot: Ain't this pretty country, Admiral? And aren't you havin' fun? We're miles from anywhere. Take a look, Admiral. There's a ten-point buck deer. That's beautiful. Symbol of American strength.

Stockdale: Where?

Perot: Right over there. There, I'll pull up, you get a better look. See, there? [*Perot "helps" Stockdale out of the car and speeds off.*]

Aired: October 24, 1992

pen on typical McDonald's restaurant.

Cashier: All right, that's a Quarter Pounder with cheese, small fries, and a Coke.

Clinton: All right, boys, let's stop here for a second. I'm a little parched from the fog.

Aide: Sir, we've only been jogging for three blocks. Besides, Mrs. Clinton asked us not to let you in any more fast-food places.

Clinton: I just want to mingle with the American people, talk with some real folks, and maybe get a Diet Coke...or somethin'.

Aide: Fine. But please don't tell Mrs. Clinton.

Clinton: Jim, let me tell you something. There's gonna be a bunch a things we don't tell Mrs. Clinton about. Fast food is the least of our worries.

Second Cashier: Oh, my God! It's Bill Clinton!

Clinton: Hey, nice to meetcha. How are you? That's an adorable baby. What's your name, sweetheart?

Customer: [*Holding baby*]: Her name is Shakira.

Clinton: Now that means "African princess," doesn't it?

Customer: Why, yes!

Clinton: Well, she certainly is beautiful enough to be a princess. Are you gonna finish those fries?

Customer: Ah, no. Would you like some?

Clinton: Well, if you're not gonna eat 'em...Mmm, these are good. Shakira, you take good care of your mom now. [*Moves on.*] Hi, how are you? Good to meetcha. How we doin' over here?

Les: Les Holmgren. Holmgren Hardware. Voted for you, sir.

Clinton: Thank you, Les. So you own your own hardware store?

Les: Yes, indeed, sir. Since 1972.

Clinton: Well, good for you. You know, we want to create a network of community development banks that lend to small businesses like yourself. I see your boy doesn't like pickles.

Les: Nah, he hates 'em.

Clinton: You mind? Attaboy. So, good luck to ya. We're gonna wake up every day thinkin' about you. Oop, missed one.

O'Brian: Governor, I'm Kevin O'Brian, the manager. And I just want to thank you for dropping by, again.

Clinton: Well, thank you, Kevin.

wash it down? Ahhh! That hits the spot.

O'Brian: Your Egg McMuffin, Mr. President.

Clinton: Thank you, Kevin. You have any of that sweet and sour sauce? You know, the kind that you dip McNuggets in.

O'Brian: For your McMuffin?

Clinton: Or the barbecue sauce.

malia…but it's not getting to the people who need it…because [*Brings McMuffin back to himself*]…it's being intercepted by the warlords. [*Finishes McMuffin*] And it's not just us. It's other countries too. [*Grabs a McNugget from yet another customer*] Your McNugget is aid from Great Britain. [*Starts to take it to previous customer, but*

Clinton-McDonald's

Featuring a cashier (Chris Rock), Bill Clinton (Phil Hartman), a presidential aide (Kevin Nealon), second cashier (Melanie Hutsell), a customer (Ellen Cleghorne), Les Holmgren (Chris Farley), Kevin O'Brian (Tom Arnold), a college-aged customer (Julia Sweeney), and the other customer (Rob Schneider).

You got a real American family place here. Is it too late for an Egg McMuffin?

O'Brian: Well, we stop serving breakfast at eleven. But for you…

Clinton: Thanks so much.

O'Brian: And should I check to see if I can scare up some of those sausage patties?

Clinton: You read my mind.

Aide [*Whispers*]: Ah, sir, maybe you'd prefer a McLean burger, or the garden salad is very nice.

College-Aged Customer: Governor Clinton. Ah, I'm a sophomore in college, and I may have to drop out because my parents can't afford tuition.

Clinton: Speak of the devil, that's one of those McLean sandwiches. Are those any good?

College-Aged Customer: Would you like to try it?

Clinton: Well, just a bite. Mmm. That's not bad. You know, my National Service Trust Fund would allow every student to— Mind if I

Tom Arnold, Rob Schneider, Kevin Nealon, Phil Hartman, Tim Meadows, and Jim Pitt

Whichever.

Other Customer: You can use mine.

Clinton: Great. Just pour it right on.

Other Customer: I have a question.

Clinton: That's it. Pour it all on.

Other Customer: Do you support the decision to send troops to Somalia?

Clinton [*Taking a bite*]: Mmm, that's a good question. Yes, I do, and let me tell you why. See, right now, we're sending in [*Holds up his McMuffin*]…food [*Puts McMuffin in front of other customer*]…to So-

then gobbles it down] Inter-cepted by warlords. [*Looks around; finds…*] This man's Filet-O-Fish over here is relief from Italy. [*Pops it in his mouth; a muffled…*] Warlords. And you can send all the food you want. [*Grabbing…*] A McDLT, hot apple pie, it's just gonna end up with [*Eating*]…the warlords. Now, with a broad-based international military force, we can make sure that the…McRib Sandwich…[*Grabs a McRib and sets it on other customer's tray*]…gets to the people who need it. [*Then he just picks it up and gulps it down.*] Can I get a Coke?

Aide: Ah, sir, I think we should probably continue your jog. We've only gone about an eighth of a mile.

Clinton: All right. You guys up for a real run?

Aide: Yes, sir.

Clinton: Race you to Pizza Hut!

AIRED: DECEMBER 5, 1992

THE CURRE

Great Sketches (1985-94)

He's the producer of *Saturday Night Live*, friend of Ferdinand Marcos, husband of Morgan Fairchild (whom he's seen naked), and much, much more. Yeah, that's the ticket. Who is this dashing man of many talents? Allow him to introduce himself:

"Hello, my name is Tommy Flanagan (Jon Lovitz), and I'm a member of Pathological Liars Anonymous. In fact, I'm the president of the organization. I didn't always lie. No, when I was a kid, I told the truth. But then one day I got caught stealing money out of my mother's purse. I lied. I told her it was homework—that my teacher told me to do it. And she got fired. Yeah, that's what happened. After that, lying was easy for me.

"I lied about my age and joined the army. I was thirteen at the time. Yeah, I went to Vietnam and I was injured catching a mortar shell in my teeth. And they made me a three-star general. And then I got a job in journalism, writing for the *National Enquire*— Er, *Geographic*; yeah, I was making twenty thousand a y— Month. In fact, I won the Pulitzer Prize that year. Yeah, that's the ticket.

"And then my cousin died, Joe Louis, and I took it hard. Maybe too hard—I tried to kill myself. Yeah, I *did* kill myself. Sure, I was medically dead for a week and a half. It was a woman that brought me out of it—Indira Gandhi. Yeah, right, and she told me about Pathological Liars Anonymous. Oh, you'd be surprised how many famous people belong. In fact, at one of the meetings I met my wife, Morgan Fairchild. Yes, I'm a changed man now, and all because of Pathological Liars Anonymous. Why, I—I even have my picture on the cover of *Newsweek* magazine. Yeah, every day. Yeah, that's the ticket."

Some Other Whoppers:

•Tommy visits his mother (Nora Dunn): "You look two—ah, five years younger than you did last year." As Mom recalls, Tommy never lied when he was a child—unlike the "escaped convicts who used to leave the girlie magazines un-der your mattress." Apparently he was a smart student—so smart, she says, "they made you stay back a year and help the other kids."

•Tommy is chatting with Jerry Hall. He's into rock and roll too; he's played with everyone. Not the Stones, though: "I *manage* them. I wrote all their songs too. Remember the song 'Satisfaction'? I wrote it." Well, actually, he just changed the original title, "I Can't Get No Service in This Place." He and Mick were in Vietnam together, and Tommy

Jon Lovitz.

The Liar

saved his life. Jerry says Mick was never in Nam. Well, that's how Tommy saved his life—he stopped him from going.

Jerry knows Tommy's a fraud, because she's Jagger's wife—although, she says, "we're not exactly married" and she has no ring. Jagger appears and agrees that he knows Tommy: "Remember last weekend when I didn't come home? I was with Tommy. We went fishing together—yeah, fishing. That's the ticket!"

• Tommy presents Oprah Winfrey with an Oscar "on behalf of Pathological Liars Anonymous." Oprah remarks, "But I thought that only the Academy could give these out?" "We're the parent company," he replies. "We did a recount. You won by five hund— Ah, a thous— Ah, one vote! Yeah, yeah, that's it—Best Actress in *The Purple Rose of Cairo*." She corrects him: "No, no, *The Color Purple*." "Well, now you're being silly—that didn't win anything."

• Tommy, it appears, has been two-timing Park Avenue matron Margaret (Sigourney Weaver). He told Margaret he was at the Masters when he was actually in Atlantic City with Laura (Nora Dunn): "He even bought me these earrings." Margaret notes she used to have a pair exactly like them, but they were stolen by the burglars Tommy chased away.

Tommy arrives from his lunch with the president ("I'm the new spokesman for the State Department. Sure I am. Turned out the old guy was *a liar*") and faces the music. It turns out Tommy has a double. He's a spy—a double agent!

• Rosanna Arquette, in satin lingerie, is practicing for the new "Neck with the Producer" sketch: "Kiss me, you fancy dresser, it makes me dizzy." "Lorne Michaels" appears—or is it Tommy?—and Rosanna asks: "I say one line and then we make out for five minutes? I just don't get the joke." Tommy brushes aside her concerns: "It's conceptual,"

Jon Lovitz, Mick Jagger, and Jerry Hall.

he explains, "a political statement, yeah, a plea for the homeless. It's, ah, subtext. A hidden message. You have to read between the lines." The real Lorne Michaels arrives, and as Tommy slips out, Lorne looks at the "Neck" script: "This isn't bad. It's funny and it makes a nice point about the homeless."

• A bartender can't believe Tommy makes two million dollars a year gelding sheep. "No, I said *welding* sheep." Why would anybody want to weld sheep? "I just told you—for two million dollars a year!"

• Tommy Flanagan appears on Weekend Update as Oliver North's attorney, protesting his client's complete innocence. How does Tommy know? "'Cause it was me, yeah, that's the ticket—isn't that special!" He and his wife, Morgan Fairchild, were CIA spies; Tommy, disguised as a fish, was caught and taken to the Russian Tea Room, where he was "filleted and eaten." And so on.

Anchor Dennis Miller breaks in to ask, "What does this have to do with Colonel North?" "Nothing," allows the Liar. "That's my point. He had *nothing* to do with it."

• Away for over a year, Tommy explains his absence: "Just this morning I was doing my wash— I was in Washington, D.C. Yeah, that's the ticket! And I was sitting in the White House—which I painted—with my dog—uh, secretary, Barbara Bush—who I've seen naked." The president walks in on this "dangerous liaison" and appoints Tommy as a liaison for Yasir Arafat, as both are members of the PLO—Pathological Liars O-nonymous.

Yeah, that's the ticket.

First aired: November 16, 1985

Dana Carvey.

Church Lady

"Church Chat" is a religious talk show hosted by Enid Strict (Dana Carvey), whose primary mission is revealing Satan in his many earthly disguises: "You remember him, don't choo? The Prince of Darkness, the Antichrist, the Beastmaster. His Satanic Majesty, Beelzebub, the Wicked One, the Foul Fiend? His Lustiness, the Father of Lies, Old Horny, the Sin Stud, the Great Confuser? And in case you've just joined in, we're talking about the red-hot, tight-buttocked Hairy Host of Hell. Probably rings a little bell in your head now, doesn't it? Well, isn't that special."

Some call her "smug and self-satisfied, on [her] high throne, judging everyone," the kind of person who "twists everything people say into some kind of a sordid perverted thing!" But as far as Enid is concerned, she is simply superior—as she often demonstrates in the Superior Dance at the finale.

Along with her celebrity guests, Church Lady is often joined by National Bible Student of the Year Ginny Barton (Victoria Jackson). Despite Ginny's angelic credentials, Church Lady always suspects the worst of poor Ginny ("Not much blood makes it up to our little brain when our tingly naughty parts are engorged").

But can Church Lady really be so good? Hasn't she ever strayed? "Well, one time I peeked through a hedge and saw Mr. Bob mowing his lawn in his Bermuda shorts. And to fight my demonic urges, I popped a butter-rum Life Saver and sucked away like there was no tomorrow."

Church Lady's Crusades:

1 Today's first guest is Christopher Durang: "Tell me—when you wrote your dirty little sex play *Sister Mary Ignatius*, who was your collaborator? Was it by any chance…SATAN!" Next is Sally Kellerman, who finds "this whole Satan thing kinda silly": "Oh. Well. Perhaps you'd find burning in eternal hellfire silly as well." Finally, Church Lady gives a "big 'Church Chat' hello" to Zuul (Sigourney Weaver, in a reprise of her role in *Ghostbusters*) who truly is possessed by the "hot, tight-buttocked Beastmaster." Church Lady calls for Billy (Phil Hartman) to bring holy water, just as Zuul ravages him.

2 "Halloween. Innocent little holiday for the kiddies or a night on the town for Satan?" The answer is apparent as Church Lady looks inside her jack-o'-lantern: "Oh, what do we have here? A raging inferno of satanic hellfire….Isn't that special." Ginny Barton makes her first appearance. She missed church for the first time in 758 weeks, because she was helping her boyfriend's grandmother: "Apparently some of us come to church when it's conveeenient."

Also joining Church Lady are an outspoken Rosanna Arquette and Ric Ocasek, dressed in black leather: "We like ourselves, don't we, Ricky—with our black leather pants stretched tight across our bulbous crotch region?" She says a prayer against him: "Starting to feel a little prickly heat in your groin area, Ricky?" After Rosanna calls her "a sexually repressed, closed-minded little bitch," Church Lady suggests they get someone less "judgmental" to host the show, like...SATAN!

Dana Carvey and Rob Lowe.

3 Enid announces that she will not be seen on *Saturday Night Live* tonight. She wishes to protest the selection of the guest host, Mr. Samuel Kinison, who made some references to Christ and crack as a guest comedian two weeks ago. "Viewers, I implore you, do not watch this show! Do not watch this show!" But a boycott is not enough: She marches backstage to confront the "Sin Sergeant," the "diabolical disciple of depravity," the "paunchy prince of perdition."

4 Rain has kept many away from the church potluck luncheon and, as Church Lady warns, "those absentees afraid of a little moisture will be praying for rain when they're burning in eternal hellfire." Ginny arrives late, explaining that she got "tied up." Church Lady comments, "Well, isn't that special. Apparently some of us need little accoutrements to help us perform our dirty little sex acts." Competitive as ever, Church Lady belittles Ginny's "little luncheon dish," a cherry Jell-O jubilee, and declares her own ninety-five-quart turkey casserole "just a little bit superior": "Therefore I do my little Superior Dance for you."

5 Guest Shirley MacLaine (Jan Hooks) is asked about a phrase in her book *Out on a Limb*: "I am God." Church Lady sniffs, "I don't think the Father is a sassy little redhead."

The Satan Bowl takes place the following day, an event

where "large, sweaty men collide at a high rate of speed to the apparent delight of onlookers...and the fans scream like little Beastmasters, drink beer, and spit up." Appropriately, Church Lady's guests are Joe Montana and Walter Payton. Montana talks about snapping the ball: "Is that when a heavyset gentleman squats down and passes the pigskin between his thighs, where your hands are nestled near his bulbous naughty place?"

6 Church Lady's first guest is Danny DeVito, and they discuss his movie *Tin Men*, which is rated R: "Apparently some of us have to use the 'F' word to be funny." Ann Landers (Nora Dunn) is on next to discuss safe sex: "In these times of strange germs and viruses, isn't it silly to have plastic covers for your furniture and not for your children?" But Church Lady favors "celibacy or *s-e-x* in a monogamous Christian marriage—doors locked, lights out, in the missionary position." Willie Nelson joins them, and Church Lady wants details about all the girls he's loved before.

7 Church Lady explores television ministries: "Responsible Christian broadcasters or greedy media sluts? You be the judge." She welcomes Jim (Phil Hartman) and Tammy Bakker (Jan Hooks). Church Lady breaks down the fifteen minutes it took for Jimmy to have his "tryst" at the Lucky Stiff Motel: "So there we are, our naughty parts all engorged and tingling, leaving us, let's see, two minutes to fornicate." Tammy becomes hysterical and mascara streams down her face. "Well apparently, Tammy, Mister Mouth is moving, but we have no idea what we're saying, do we?" Satan is behind it all, and Church Lady proclaims our times "a big fat romp in the park for the Beastmaster."

8 Church Lady questions Ginny Barton about her behavior around Minister Bob: "Your schoolgirl crush flaming out of control, your naughty parts engorged and tingling, your bulbous buttock region thrusting and releasing."

The next guest is Dennis Hopper: "Brilliant, misunderstood genius or Satan worshiper? You be the judge." Dennis is not the wild man he once was; at one time he attended orgies: "Apparently that is where strangers gather in their birthday suits and frolic on a moist, three-tone shag carpet area to the jungle rhythms of Nat King Cole."

9 In a display of open-mindedness, Church Lady presents a guest who worships a different Lord: Iranian diplomat Rashashimi Khadudi Hasumi-imi-humi (Jon Lovitz). She's sure that Mohammed is a lovely little prophet, but the United States has Jesus on its side: "You remember, Christ our Savior, the Son of Man, the King of Kings, the baby prince, the heavenly host, the cloud stud, Jay Ceeeeee!"

Next Enid welcomes Sean Penn. "Now, Sin...excuse me, *Sean*...you're married to Madonna. So she's named after the mother of our Lord. But she doesn't quite live up to the same standards, does she?" A clip from Madonna's "Open Your Heart" video is shown, and Rashashimi is thrilled: "I will give you two million drachma for the dancing woman!" Sean takes a swing at Church Lady, but she knocks him out.

10 A viewer writes: "I am shocked at the number of people who bring their children to total strangers in Santa suits and allow them to hold their young ones firmly on their pelvic region, offer them candy, and whisper, 'Don't be afraid to tell me what you *really* want.'" As Church Lady reveals, the same letters that spell Santa can also spell SATAN.

Enid's first guest is Jessica Hahn (Jan Hooks), who denies that she was a teenage prostitute: "I am not a whore," she protests. "And I am not the Church Lady," says Enid. Danny DeVito is back, promoting his new movie, *Throw Momma from the Train*. "What a charming title, Daniel. So it's a *family* picture, just in time for Christmas." He recommends that she get her package wrapped every once in a while.

11 The first guest is the Reverend Pat Robertson (Al Franken): Presidential candidate? Or newfound Sa-

tan worshiper? You be the judge. "So we put the electoral college ahead of the Bible college," says Enid. Next up is Jimmy Swaggart (Phil Hartman): "I'm a sinner! I have sinned against you!" "Well, what a news flash," jabs Enid. "I'm not going to whitewash it," Swaggart vows. "I let my church down and I let my family down." Enid: "And didn't we let something else down...like our trousers?"

12 Guest Geraldo Rivera has failed to show, apparently due to a broken nose. "I guess some of us can only keep our obligations when it's conveeenient." Enid has found "the next best thing": a monkey, Bobo, along with Steve Barnes (Matthew Modine) from Christian Farm Safari. "Steve, Bobo is naked, and his little naughty parts are touching me right now. I thought you said these were Christian animals."

Jan Hooks, Dana Carvey, and Fred Savage.

The next guest is Morton Downey, Jr. He is smoking ("sucking on a Satan stick"), which prompts Enid to note that the Bible says the body is a temple: "I guess our temple apparently is a dumpster." He says what she really needs is "a little Morton Downey, Junior Junior": "Listen, piano mouth! You are on *my* show, and I am the [*bleeped*] Church Lady, and no one [*bleeped*] with me!"

13 Church Lady is practicing her nightly ritual—praying for strength in resisting the Devil. It's time to exercise and she touches her toes: "Up to heaven and down to hell. Up to heaven and down to hell." Next comes running in place; she imagines Satan is after her: "Run from Satan! Keep those knees up! Satan is on your buttocks, Satan is on your buttocks!"

But she has a visitor: Satan (Jon Lovitz). He has come to make peace for this one night, and he hands her a Christmas gift. She feels awful, she didn't get him anything. Satan's gift: a little devil doll for her dashboard.

14 The 1980s are drawing to a close, and it's been a ten-year party for the Beastmaster. It's time to battle Satan in the nineties, beginning with tonight's first guest, Olympic gold medalist Nadia Comaneci (Jan Hooks), who swears that her new husband in Florida "loves and respects my mind." "I'm sure he also respects your ability to twist your body into a hot, sweaty little pretzel, ready to be smeared with man mustard," Church Lady comments, and denies she means anything by her remarks—then "sneezes": "*AH-slut. AH-slut.*"

The second guest is Leona Helmsley (Nora Dunn), whom Enid taunts about her impending incarceration. The next arrival is Andie MacDowell, star of *sex, lies and videotape* ("What a *charming* title"), a film about a husband who fornicates with his in-laws.

15 Enid's first guest—"and she's hardly a guest, because she's family"—is her niece Enid (Fred Savage), a Church Lady in miniature. They introduce the first Official Tabloid Slut of the Nineties, Marla Maples (Jan Hooks). Marla claims that she and Donald Trump "are just close friends." "And Enid is just a little boy in a dress," retorts Church Lady.

The Donald himself arrives, and he warns Enid that he could buy and sell both her and her "little freak show." The Enids blame his "special" tantrum on worship of the wrong "G"—Greed.

16 It's St. Patrick's Day—a harmless Irish tradition, or a chance for people to fornicate like drunken little Beastmasters? Enid welcomes Rob Lowe; they have agreed to avoid certain sensitive topics. Once they finish off the list of approved topics ("Acrylic blends versus cotton, which do you prefer, Rob?"), it's time for Rob to keep his half of the bargain. Enid pulls out a paddle and gives him a good spanking. "Thank you, Church Lady, may I have another?" She loses control—"Don't you ever, ever, ever do that again!"—and shouts at her guest's behind: "Get out of his buttocks, Satan! Leave his buttocks! Leave his buttocks, Satan!"

17 Enid's first guest is Saddam Hussein (Phil Hartman): "Welcome to our show, Sodomy." Later she is joined by her mentor, her inspiration, the wind beneath her wings—her sainted mother (John Goodman). Mother thinks Saddam looks like someone. Could it be Uncle Walter? Julie Peters, the town slut? SATAN?

The United States is the great Satan, snaps Saddam,

Roseanne Arnold and Dana Carvey.

and your entrails will be food for the grinning hyena that gorges on your rotting flesh. Well, isn't that special? A quarrel breaks out, and Mother and Enid take Saddam down, forcing him to say the opening words of the show.

18 Dana is finishing a Colorado stand-up performance, announcing his final appearance as Church Lady: "After tonight, she's dead." He and Jon Lovitz drive along the ice-covered roads and tumble down a hill. A title appears: *Misery II.*

In a remote cabin, Dana wakes to the face of his Number-One Fan (Roseanne Arnold), who declares: "I just don't know what I would do if anything ever happened to the Church Lady, you know? I swear to God, I think I would just go completely *insane!*" Later, the Fan dresses Dana as Church Lady and makes him perform.

Dana strikes back: "Die, witch, die! Isn't this special! Isn't this convenient!" But she keeps getting up. Shots ring out, and the Fan dies. Lovitz is the rescuer. "I thought you were dead," Dana cries. "*Acting!*" replies the master thespian. He then kills Dana and slips on Enid's wig and glasses: "Well...isn't that special."

Well, isn't that special.

FIRST AIRED: OCTOBER 11, 1986

Sweeney Sis

You must have pressed 'L' for lobby. Join us!" Such is the welcoming spirit of Liz (Nora Dunn) and Candy (Jan Hooks), two sisters who live to entertain. They play the motel circuit, hitting such hot spots as the Holiday Inn, the Ramada, and their traditional haunt, the Blarney Stone ("We're having too much fun. Call the fun police"). Their act almost always begins with "Everything's Coming Up Roses" and usually features some signature scat and their trademark tune, "The Trolley Song." It's hard to tell the sisters apart, though as Liz confides: "She's the brains, I'm the nut." "Guilty!" They are often joined by their accompanist, Skip St. Thomas (Marc Shaiman). Let's bring the room down for a minute.

The Sweeneys On Tour:

1 The Sweeney Sisters appear with host Bill Smith (Kevin Nealon) on "Instant Coffee." First, though, they perform a medley, including "Everything's Coming Up Roses," "Yesterday" (which they believe in), leading into "Tomorrow" and more. They correct the plug Bill made: "By the by, we're not playing the Blarney Stone Inn, we're playing at the Blarney Stone Inn *Lounge*."

2 A wisecracking emcee (Robin Williams) is entertaining at the Baycrest Jewish Retirement Home: "Sit down, Saul, before the nurse gives you a piña colonic." Then, from around the corner at the Blarney Stone...it's the Sweeney Sisters! They've prepared a special medley, featuring "*L'Chaim*," "It Was a Very Good Year," and several tunes from *Fiddler on the Roof*. "*Hava Nagila / Have two Nagilas / Have three Nagilas / They're veee-ry small!*" they belt. The emcee and Morty Meshugener (Paul Simon) treat the girls to what they remember of "Alone Again, Naturally," punctuated by the odd "oy!"

3 Liz brings Roger (William Shatner) to Candy's Christmas wingding ("I don't know about the ding, but how about a wing?"): They're engaged! What better way to cele-

brate than with a medley? A medley it is, themed around bells and heartfelt repartee: "It's not gonna be easy to be the Lone Ranger out there by myself!" Their customized version of "Silver Bells" goes down particularly well: "Who are you calling a ding-a-ling?" "You!" "Okay!"

4 It's Chinese New Year at Wo Sun Ting's (Paul Shaffer) restaurant, where they give away free rabbits every half hour. The latest winner is Ching Change (Dana Carvey), owner of the Pet Chicken Shop ("Business no good, chicken make lousy house pet"). Wo hurries on the hot act he discovered on American New Year's at the Blarney Stone. The sisters' selections include "Here Comes Peter Cottontail" (it's the Year of the Rabbit) and a simultaneous duet of "Everything Is Beautiful" and "I'd Like to Teach the World to Sing." "You are on a roll tonight," Candy teases, "—an egg roll!"

5 The Sweeneys play a party at the Ramada, celebrating a new primate house at the zoo. Charlton Heston, the unwilling guest of honor, has been brought there by a limo driver (Phil Hartman) who thought he would enjoy the party, which features *Planet of the Apes*. Liz and Candy offer more themed selections, including "The Lion Sleeps Tonight," a touch of "Shock the Monkey," and "Yes, We Have No Bananas" ("I lied," says Candy, pulling one from the fruit bowl).

6 In a farewell performance before they set out on an eighteen-city summer tour, the Sweeneys sing a medley of good-bye songs: "Hello! Goodbye!" "Bye Bye Birdie," "See You in September," "Sealed with a Kiss," "What I Did for Love," "So Long, Farewell," and the Beatles' "The End."

7 Candy has found her Prince Charming in Dutch (Robert Mitchum), but he's slow in dumping his current wife. He does want to set Candy up in a condo, so she never has to work a smoky dive again. Liz arrives to rehearse the new medley; Candy hasn't learned it, and the Blarney Stone wants them to headline Wild Turkey Night:

ers

"Shooters are only fifty cents. Should bring in a big crowd." Candy says the act is over, but she'll sing the new medley one last time. Their conflict is spelled out in song, and through the power of music, these "Such Devoted Sisters" are "Reunited," and it feels so good.

8 The Sweeneys acknowledge a shy Paul Simon in the audience. They have one thing to say to Paul: "Slow down! You move too fast!" Hey, where will they see Paul next? "Are you going to Scarborough fair?" Liz reminisces about her stacks of Simon and Garfunkel records: "And she didn't even have a record player," Candy jibes. "But I was hearing something," Liz insists. "The sounds of silence!"

One sister is a rock, the other an island; they coax Simon into joining them in a rendition of "Fifty Ways to Leave Your Lover." Then Candy brings the room down for a minute: "Paul Simon. What do those words mean to me? A lot. *'Like a bridge over truh-uh-buhled waters—you've laid yourself down!'*"

9 The Sweeneys are in jail. Their cellmates are other female "entertainers." The street-smart Doreen (Melanie Griffith) notes: "You two look like a couple of high-priced girls. You ought to be workin' Vegas." "Well, thank you.

Nora Dunn and Jan Hooks.

That's something we are sort of striving for," Candy bubbles. Skip bails the sisters out, but they can't leave yet. "It's great to be here at Precinct Forty-Three. And you guys have been so nice to us during our stay we'd like to leave you with a little gift. *'Please release me, let me gooooo.'*" "A medley of "favorite prison songs" follows; "Tie a Yellow Ribbon 'Round the Old Oak Tree," "Chain of Fools," "Chain Gang."

10 Big sister Audrey (Mary Tyler Moore) pays a surprise visit to the Sweeneys' Holiday Inn gig. The three need to powwow, "and how!" Audrey has just left her cheatin' husband, Frank. The first number is "We Are Family." The man-trouble medley is dedicated to Audrey: "The Man That Got Away," the theme from *Mahogany*, "Do You Know the Way to San Jose," "D.I.V.O.R.C.E.," "The Way We Were," and a rousing "One Less Bell to Answer." Overcome by emotion, Audrey pulls a microphone from her purse and joins in, and the medley becomes more optimistic: "I Will Survive," "Hit the Road, Jack," "These Boots Were Made for Walking," and more.

FIRST AIRED: OCTOBER 18, 1986

"I am Hans and I am Franz and we just want to pump…you up."

Hans (Dana Carvey) and Franz (Kevin Nealon) introduce themselves as two pumped-up guys from a small village of "veight" lifters in Austria, who came to the United States, following in the footsteps of their cousin, the greatest bodybuilder in the history of the world. Maybe you heard of him—Arnold Schwarzenegger. Like Arnold, they wear athletic sweats and lifting belts and have bulging muscles. But they will not tolerate undisciplined Americans:"We can't make you pump up, and if you're not going to do it, don't be jerking us around, we don't have the time….If you don't think this matters, maybe we should take a belt to your buttocks until it is all black and blue and swollen."

Hans and Franz

Pumping Up:

1 Hans and Franz declare, "We're not here to cut you down, we're here to pump you up." For those who are very serious about the pump, the "veight" lifters have a video, "Pumping You Up." On it you see that when a pathetic loser walks into a room, everyone knows it because they can smell him. "If you don't work out, someone should grab you by your jockstrap and give you the wedgie of your life."

2 Hans and Franz introduce Helmut (Phil Hartman): "Everywhere you look Helmut is covered with baby

fat, but he is a grown man." Hans says: "His buttock is soft like jam. I wish I had a biscuit to put that buttock on." If his pectorals drooped "any lower, he'd step on them." They will follow Helmut's progress over the coming weeks, but nothing comes easy. If you have a problem with that, maybe you should be disciplined. "*Ja*. Maybe I should take off my sweatshirt after a long hard workout and wring it out into a glass and make you drink it."

3 Hans and Franz present the "typical injured person," the victim of a car accident (Scott Rozbicki, played by Paul Simon). They advise Scott to get rid of the crutches, which look like the side of a crib. They lift him up and dangle him; his back is arched, and he's in obvious pain. Which is good: No pain, no gain. "Here's my prescription for you: Take two of these [*Shows fists*] and call me in the morning."

Helmut returns after three weeks. Hans and Franz note that there's progress on the pectorals: "Three weeks ago we could have sat down on a stool and milked you like a cow. Helmut is now like half man, half cow, because he didn't work the muscle evenly." Now, do they milk him or pummel him?

4 Hans and Franz reply to Jimmy the Greek Snyder's observation that "white people have smaller thighs than black people." This inane remark made Franz's blood boil so much, he didn't even have to pump his muscles the day he heard it: "I only wish I could have spent [the day] pummeling a certain fat-butted oddsmaker." Hans brags, "That little Webster guy on television, he could live inside one of my thighs"—and there would still be room for that Sammy Davis, Jr., guy. And Michael Jackson. And Gary Coleman.

5 Why did the Americans fare so poorly in the Olympics? Franz knows: "I can answer that in one word, my friend—puny. The puny man just stands there panting, with his tongue hanging out like a dog." Hans chimes in, "*Ja*, and if you're going to be a dog, why don't you lick yourself in public and scrape your butt on the driveway." Of course, the *real* Olympics are in the summer, for sports like weight lifting. As for winter events: "Look, Mr. Olympic Man, watch me slide around in the snow like a baby."

Hans and Franz bring on a Baby Olympian, the American skier Billy Cooper (Judge Reinhold), who placed forty-seventh in the preliminaries. Hans and Franz are surprised he did that well: "Your body looks like a little pretzel stick." "*Ja*, instead of Mr. Cooper, your name should be Mr. *Salty*."

6 Hans and Franz address their alleged use of steroids: "We're just like yogurt—all natural, no chemicals." "But there is no fruit at the bottom of us, only muscle, and not just at the bottom but throughout, as if we were pre-stirred muscle yogurt." Enough talk—but they must clear the air about Greg "Stuganis," who won two gold medals "just for making a puny splash": "If Franz and I ever hit our head on the board, the people would look up and say, 'Where is the board?'"

7 Hans and Franz are camping out, under the open sky. Hans is in a reflective mood. No, he would never go to Mars: "I would become weightless, and that is my worst nightmare." On Mars, even a puny man could lift

Dana Carvey and Kevin Nealon.

Dana Carvey and Kevin Nealon.

shown (FBI warning: Rebroadcast will result in serious pummeling). Glasses of red wine await; they just want to take—*clink!*—you out.

10 Critics have said that Hans and Franz's methods wouldn't work for the average, garden-variety girly-man. To answer their critics, Hans and Franz show a picture of the pathetic Joseph William Zieglefreud (Steve Martin), whom they have since turned into the embodiment of perfect pumpitude. Joseph is then wheeled out on a dolly; every muscle of his body, save his head, is gigantic—in fact, Joseph can't move at all below the neck. But a slight lack of flexibility is a small price to pay for such pumpitude. Should any girly-man kick sand in his face and Joseph were a little more flexible, he'd kill the girly-man.

11 In "Honey, I Shrunk Hans and Franz" the two have been accidentally shrunken by the ultimate girly-man, Rick Moranis. Franz assures us that he is still twice the size of a Flintstones vitamin, and "not a Barney—a *Fred*." Hear Hans now and believe him later—no shrunken girly-man could ever lift a whole lemon as Franz does, or curl pistachio nuts like Hans ("I can also bench-press a cashew!"). Spotting a mouse, they ridicule its flabby belly and skinny little arms.

12 Thanksgiving greetings from Hans and Franz, who caution: "It's not an excuse to stuff your face like the fat pig losers you are." Tonight they demonstrate the most powerful flabosuction machine in the free world: "From thirty-five meters it can convert an elephant into a dachshund." But they're not here to paint obscure imagery, they're here to suck...you out. More specifically, they'll suck out guest Roseanne Barr (Victoria Jackson). Something goes wrong during their demonstration: The "flab receptacle" overflows, spraying yellow goo everywhere.

13 It's Valentine's Day and the men are alone—but don't be thinking they are losers: "We could very easily come out here with a lovely *Liebchen* on each arm," but it would only provoke a " 'flabalanche' of jealousy and envy." They sing valentines to their true love—their muscles: "*I just called to say I pumped you!*"; "*You're once, twice, three times the size of a normal muscle*"; and "*Losers in the night, / Exchanging flab, / Muscles are not tight, / Their tone is bad.*"

a man-size weight. They hear animals howling: "Listen to me now and hear me later, Mr. Bear. If you think we are easy prey, then maybe you should take a look at *this*!" They flex, but something advances; they shout, before realizing it's only the park ranger (Al Franken): "You did not frighten us. You are sadly mistaken."

8 Hans and Franz announce the opening of their new gym in Wayne, New Jersey, The Pumpatorium, managed by Victor (Danny DeVito). Victor's opinion of flabby losers: "These losers need discipline! They are fat, lazy pigs who should only be dead! You hear me? Dead! Dead! Dead! Dead!" Enough talk. Arnold Schwarzenegger comes by and his cousins fawn over him: "You are the embodiment of perfect pumpitude!" They flex for him, but he's sickened: "You pathetic losers, I hate the way you guys talk! Look at your buttocks—soft like marshmallow! You guys are lucky we don't have a campfire here, believe me." But Arnold softens on them: "It doesn't matter how pumped you are, as long as you reach your full pump-tential."

9 "A lot of you ladies wrote in saying 'Dear Hans and Franz, I'm tired of my girly-man. I want a real man. Please date me.'" They introduce their new video, "A Fantasy Dinner Date with Hans and Franz." A preview is

14 Guest Patrick Swayze is complimented on *Ghost*: "In the movie, you play a properly pumped-up man who rises to heaven." Swayze has written a book on flexibility. Hans and Franz demonstrate "flex ability" but cannot imitate Swayze's split: "*Ja*, well, either way. It's all flexibility." After Swayze leaves, Franz cannot concentrate: "What are these feelings I'm experiencing? Why do I keep thinking about Patrick Swayze? Wanting to get to know him better, to possibly bunk and train with him."

15 Atop a camel, Hans and Franz report from Kuwait. Tired of waiting for the ground war to start, they launch Operation Muscle Storm: "Come out, you Iraqi girly-man! You know, Hans, they should change the name of Iraq to '*I am a loser*'!" "*Ja*, and Baghdad to 'Flabdad.'" They deride their skinny-legged camel as well: "Spend a few months on the StairMaster, then we'll talk."

16 Hans and Franz readdress the issue of steroids: The only "stare-oid" problem they have is people staring at their pumpitude. They discuss Cousin Arnold's new movie and boast that he could rip Steven Seagal's skinny little arms off and use them as dental floss. Seagal himself appears, but he's not angry: "You see, I follow Zen." "We know Zen," says Franz. "First we lift the barbell, *zen* we lift another, *zen* another, *zen* another." Seagal offers a convincing demonstration, but they conclude: " 'Mind over matter' is fine, but let's not forget muscle over matter!"

Dana Carvey, Arnold Schwarzenegger, Danny DeVito, and Kevin Nealon.

17 Cousin Arnold has made a motivational tape with Hans and Franz teaching schoolchildren the importance of exercise. Hans notes "it's very important to properly oil your body" and also recommends shaving all body hair. But Arnold is disgusted: If they don't stop teaching competition over exercise, he will twist their flab into a pacifier and have them suck on it until they poop in their diapers.

18 Hans and Franz celebrate Halloween by passing out goodies: brewer's yeast, bee pollen, metabolic bulk enhancers, eggs, and a vision of perfect pumpitude. A mother (Catherine O'Hara) complains that her unpumped son, who wears a Superman costume, was taunted. Hans notes, "I strapped a baby to a leg press once, and he thanked me when he was two." Franz is thanked with a punch in the gut. He could very easily not have vomited, but he did not tense his abdomen.

We just want to pump…you up.

FIRST AIRED: OCTOBER 17, 1987

Dana Carvey, Steve Martin, and Kevin Nealon.

Master Thespian

Acting!

PLAYED BY JON LOVITZ
AIRED: DECEMBER 7, 1985

Jon Lovitz.

Pat Stevens

Pat Stevens: I'd like to congratulate George on his startling victory in New Hampshire. He's doing well in the South, he's had a wonderful reign as vice president—tell me, are you proud of your son?

Barbara Bush: Pat, George is not my son. He's my husband.

Pat: Oh, heavens, I guess I dropped a fly in your soup! Well, she looks so much older, I hardly think it's my *faux pas!*

[*Later in the same episode*]

Liz Dole: I am a career woman. I graduated from Duke University, studied at Oxford, got a law degree at Harvard University. I served in the Nixon and Ford administrations, I was Officer of Human Affairs, I was head of the Federal Trade Commission, and I was of course public liaison to President Reagan before I became Transportation Secretary. And now I just help my husband campaign.

Pat: Do they ever call you Wonder Woman? That's terrific. Now, Barbara, I understand you've written a book about the family cocker spaniel and you've been working on a rug.

Barbara: Yes, I have been needlepointing a 14-foot rug for some time on and off. The book is just something I work on occasionally, for fun. But I'm most interested in my work to combat illiteracy and my involvement in support of the arts. I've raised five children—

Pat: Well, that's enough to turn anybody's hair gray!

PAT STEVENS PLAYED BY NORA DUNN
BARBARA BUSH PLAYED BY PHIL HARTMAN
LIZ DOLE PLAYED BY JAN HOOKS
AIRED: FEBRUARY 20, 1988

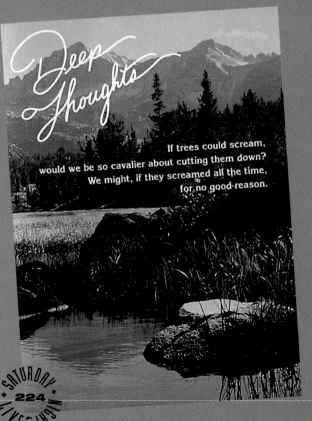

Deep Thoughts

If trees could scream, would we be so cavalier about cutting them down? We might, if they screamed all the time, for no good reason.

Phil Hartman, Nora Dunn, and Jan Hooks.

John Malkovich, Jan Hooks, and Nora Dunn.

Attitudes

Len Tukwilla: Well, I make driftwood hats…
Linda Dano: Uh-huh.
Len: Earmuffs…
Linda: Wow.
Len: Shoes…
Linda: Super.
Len: Wine racks…
Linda: No!
Len: Mobiles…
Linda: Great!
Len: Backscratchers…
Linda: Super!
Nancy Glass: Len Tukwilla. Driftwood artist. Dreamer. Finder. Seeker. Maker of driftwood things.

LEN TUKWILLA PLAYED BY JOHN MALKOVICH
LINDA DANO PLAYED BY NORA DUNN
NANCY GLASS PLAYED BY JAN HOOKS
AIRED: JANUARY 21, 1989

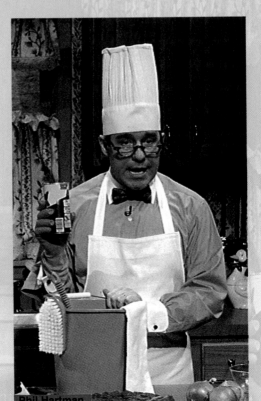

Phil Hartman.

Anal Retentive Chef

People try to tell you that the secret to peppersteak is the seasoning—but we know different, don't we. Uh-huh. It's getting all the pieces the same size. And that's what I've done here. Beaut— Uh-oh. This one's a little bigger than the rest, so we'll just discard that one…and I don't think this little wrinkly one belongs in here…and this, well, I just don't like the look of that one at all. In fact, why don't we just start over and throw this out.

PLAYED BY PHIL HARTMAN
AIRED: APRIL 1, 1989

Deep Thoughts

The face of a child can say it all, especially the mouth part of the face.

Wayne's World

Mike Myers and Dana Carvey.

Party! Party hearty! It's Friday, ten-thirty, it's time to party. I'm your excellent host, Wayne Campbell. With me as always is Garth." "Party on, Wayne." "Party on, Garth." So begins the hottest show on Cable 10, Aurora's community-access channel. Wayne Campbell (Mike Myers) and Garth (Dana Carvey) are in front of the camera, with the unseen Terry and Mark on the cameras and their new switcher, Neil.

Regular guests include Nancy (Jan Hooks) from school ("She's an excellent babe. Let's get right to the point. Do you stuff?") and Garth's dad, Beev (Phil Hartman), who owns the Wishing Well Convenience Store.

The Complete Party:

1 Beev is the first guest, and Wayne asks Garth: "At home is he a goof, or what? Does he tell you not to do stuff like read the magazines?" We learn that, "He's just a normal dad. I wish he'd get his teeth fixed so people wouldn't call him Beev." Wayne offers a list of the Top Ten Things Beev Says, including, twice, "Are you gonna buy that magazine? This isn't a library." Number one is, "Hi, my name is Beev—I'm a big fag." An angry Beev bans Wayne from the store.

Next up is Nancy, who reveals what chicks think of them: "A lot of girls like Garth because he's real quiet. But most girls think you're conceited, Wayne." A shock to Wayne: "No way." "Way," she insists. "No way," he protests, and she reinforces the point with another "Way." Wayne also takes a call from a viewer whose girlfriend has thrown up on him.

2 Wayne, Garth, and Nancy are back. Wayne has made amends with Beev by agreeing to let him do a commercial. While Beev reads his pitch, Wayne holds up a sign that identifies Beev as a "big fag." Wayne sees Nancy "hanging off" Garth and assumes she's his chick now, which provokes a volley of insults: "You're being majorly gimpish."

"You're a gimpoid." "You're in-the-style-of-the-gimp." "You have simulated gimp-look."

Math teacher Miss Simpson (Mary Tyler Moore), clad in a studded leather jacket and tight black leggings, joins them. "It's really weird to see you out of class," confesses Garth, "it's like seeing a movie star on the street."

3 Tonight's unbelievable guest is Wayne Gretzky. It has always been Gretzky's fantasy to have a cable show called "Wayne's World"; Campbell's own fantasy is to play hockey with Gretzky. With that, Wayne and Garth fade into a dream. To the sounds of "Dream Weaver," Wayne goes one-on-one with Gretzky and wins the heart of his wife, Janet Jones ("She's more than a babe; she's a babe-aholic, and she needs help!") "I guess it was all a dream. *Or was it?*" A hockey stick has somehow appeared on his lap.

Mike Myers and Dana Carvey.

WAYNE'S TOP TEN
1. MADONNA
2. KIM BASINGER
3. GARTH'S MOM
4. HEATHER LOCKLEAR
5. IRENE RYAN
6. FARRAH FAWCETT
7. BETTY RUBBLE
8. JOSEPHINE BAKER
9. ELLE MACPHERSON
10. JULIA ROBERTS

4 Wayne introduces the coolest senior in school, Rick (Bruce Willis): "You can't even get near him in the smoking area because of the sea of babe-itude that surrounds him." Rick announces this year's cool word: "sphincter" (last year's were "pail" and "bucket"). Nancy arrives as Rick leaves: "You see Rick on the show and you bolt over here like a mental case. What a nympho. But I tell you he's got the hots for you." "Really?" "Fished in!" She accuses them of being pail and really bucket, which Wayne dismisses: "Nobody says that anymore."

5 Wayne and Garth review movies: *Steel Magnolias* is a "chick flick." *The Bear* sucked donkeys. They split on *Crimes and Misdemeanors*. To Wayne, "it wasn't so much a movie as it was an essay of man in society. Although the topic of free will versus determinism is fascinating, I would hardly call it entertainment." Garth just thought it sucked. Finally, *Batman* was megaexcellent: "He shoots, he scores!"

Their guest is Aurora's police chief, Mark Wilson (John Goodman). "Umm, Police Chief Wilson?" "Yes?" "A homosayswhat." "What?" "A homosayswhat." "What?" "A homosayswhat." "What?" "Exactly."

Mike Myers, Brad Whitford, Joe Perry, Steven Tyler, Dana Carvey, Joey Kramer, and Tom Hamilton.

6 Wayne and Garth welcome Mr. Hemphill (Ed O'Neill), their driver's ed teacher: "You know, Mr. Hemphill, having you on is kind of like having a king on the show. So, welcome, you're heinous!" Wayne and Garth perform an anti-drinking-and-driving public service announcement. As the drunk driver, Wayne pantomimes "driving" his couch while Garth whisks cutout "trees" back and forth to simulate motion. *Ka-boom!*

7 Garth's cousin Barry (Tom Hanks) is a roadie for Aerosmith and has convinced them to appear on the show. They're in the Campbell breakfast nook, as the "Nook Cam" shows. Garth flips: "Oh man, they're *actually here*! I'm not worthy, I'M NOT WORTHY!!!" Barry and Wayne argue over whether roadies are the bottom feeders in the great babe food chain: "There's a ton of chicks who would rather go out with the roadies than with the band." "Shyeah right. And later on monkeys might fly out of my butt!"

Aerosmith joins them and Garth is so excited, "I think I'm gonna hurl!" Wayne asks the band about their drug and alcohol use, Steven's lips, and the decline of communism. Steven Tyler notes that "until you remove the Stalinist era party apparatchiks, there will be no real change in the Soviet Union," but Tom Hamilton disagrees: "If you study history, you'll see that since the rise of the nation-state, socialism has been an historical inevitability, dude." The show closes with the band and the hosts jamming on the "Wayne's World" theme.

8 Wayne and Garth offer their Oscar picks. *Batman* claims Best Movie and Best Babe, as well as Best Movie Junk You Can Buy. Guest Lisa Harwin (Debra Winger) is here to defend her reputation: The rumors are "that you're a...well, a slut. That you're a ho. That at the

drop of a hat you lift tail." Time for "Chick Court!" Swearing on Wayne's guitar, Lisa denies that she's been out with four guys in a week, and ridicules Wayne's informant as a gimp extraordinaire. Wayne asks, "Lisa, now that your name is cleared, do you want to go out with me?"

9 It's "Movie World" again. They liked *Pretty Woman*. "They should introduce stern legislation to curb such dangerous levels of babe-ocity." Wayne found *Opportunity Knocks*, starring Dana Carvey, funny. Garth? "Sucked!" The first guest is Mrs. Hilary Algar, Garth's mom (Candice Bergen). Wayne says, "For a mom, you're a fox. I'm serious. You're such a fox you should be on the Fox Network." Wayne falls into a fantasy inspired by the *Summer of '42*— whichs ends with Wayne in her bed. But the dream sequence goes awry: "That's my mom, you pig! *Ka-boom! Ka-boom!*" Garth guns Wayne down, before he wakes up.

10 It's "Wayne's World After Hours," from Garth's living room. "This week we'll be looking at three adult selections: *Bright Lights, Big Titties*; *Field of Reams*; and the new Madonna 'Justify My Love' video." Wayne warns those "easily horned out" to leave the room: "She'd give a dog a bone." Garth feels funny, like when you climb a rope in gym class. *Schwing!* But Police Chief Mark Wilson stops the video transmission.

11 Wayne and Garth have spent three days watching the Gulf War without leaving the basement ("we just whizzed in the laundry room sink"). It's a media circus: They've got three TV sets—one tuned to CNN, one to ABC, and one to NBC. Why no CBS? "I'm sorry, their coverage sucks! Dan Rather—*not!*" Their Best/Worst list of media coverage includes: Worst Name: Wolf Blitzer. "It's so obvious the guy made it up for the war." "Yeah, it's like, 'We now take you to our war correspondent, Howitzer Explosion Guy.'" ABC wins Worst Map for some sandbox thing: "I built a volcano in the third grade that looked better."

12 Joe Pesci is Wayne and Garth's pick for Best Supporting Actor: "We didn't see *GoodFellas*, but Pesci is such an excellent name. Like I'm feeling a bit Pesci, you know, I could or could not eat fish. I'm just Pesci." Julia Roberts wins Best Actress: "There's no contest. She's such a babe. *Schwing!* Tent pole action."

13 Madonna is named the Number One Babe of All Time—and Wayne notes, "the beauty of it is...I've had her!" In a dream sequence Wayne and Garth find themselves in Madonna's room. She and Wayne play truth or dare. "Have you ever made love to two women at the same time?" "Um…yes?" "I believe you—not!" "Well, I might…" "Yeah, you might—and monkeys might fly out of my butt!"

Wayne dares Madonna to make out with him. She does, and other performers from her video appear: "Isn't that Prince?" Madonna sees the snakelike dancer: "Wow, look at the unit on that guy"—who turns out to be Garth.

14 It's the Best and Worst of the Summer of 1991 awards. Best International News Event: "The ill-fated coup d'état in the Soviet Union," mostly because "it's such a cool word." Worst Magazine Cover goes to *People*'s choice of Patrick Swayze as the Sexiest Man Alive: "He's got that humungoid melon! His head has its own weather system!" *Vanity Fair*'s nude and pregnant Demi Moore wins Best Magazine Cover. "We thought it was very appropriate…*not!* Hey, Demi Moore, how about a little Demi less."

15 Wayne and Garth look back at 1991. There was the William Kennedy Smith trial and Garth "got pubes." They present the Top Ten Reasons Why We're Bummed Communism Fell: Number nine is the "inevitable collapse" of Yakov Smirnoff's career; number seven is Katarina Witt's losing the sweet taste of forbidden fruit ("now she's just another cute chick in an ice show with a tight skater's butt"); number two is that there are no more bogus Soviet rock bands to make fun of.

16 It's another Oscar rundown: Worst Hair? Juliette Lewis: "She looked like a Jim Henson creation gone horribly wrong." Recalling a gross scene in *The Silence of the Lambs*, Wayne thinks he's got a hurl on deck and Garth's going to chunder—but they hold that honk. "Chunkage contained." Best Babe goes to Rebecca De Mornay: "Rebecca De *Hornay*, more like." Finally, Best Cleavage goes to Demi Moore: "Hello, I'd like two pickets to Tittsburgh, please!"

17 Wayne and Garth present Top Ten Things We Love About Bill Clinton. Universal health care and his huge head start the countdown. His short running shorts, nicknamed "banana hammocks," come in at number seven: "Were they designed by Heinrich Nutslinger?" They love the Fleetwood Mac theme—*not.*

"Here's a quarter, *buy* a clue." Other choices are the Gore daughters ("*Schwing!* Finally there's some talent in the White House!") and Claudia Schiffer: "Okay, she has nothing to do with Bill Clinton, but we just thought she was majorly spankable."

18 Wayne's girlfriend, Cassandra, trick-or-treated as a brick, and he went out as a bricklayer. Garth, dressed as Barney, got his ass kicked. They review *The Remains of the Day*: Wayne calls it "a tour de force portrayal of the repressed emotions of the English psyche set against the backdrop of fascistic prewar Britain." Garth? "Sucked!" *Jurassic Park* was really cool, and Laura Dern was a babe-a-saurus. Tyrannosaurus Sex. A major chickadactyl.

19 Wayne's watching Heather Locklear, on *Melrose Place*: "She's the leader of the Bod Squad." In a dream sequence he lands in bed with Heather's character, Amanda. Is he worthy? "Last night was okay, but don't let it get to your head." Wayne encounters the entire *Melrose Place* gang, including Billy (Adam Sandler)—"Sorry, man, I seem to be allergic to emasculation. By the way, Billy, close your mouth. You've been catching flies there, chief"—and Sydney (Sarah Silverman), "the psycho hose-beast." Amanda keeps popping in, always in a new business outfit, to remind Wayne that she is a very busy advertising executive. She won't tolerate bastards who try to control her, and Wayne is diddle-liddle-la-ed back to the basement.

Party time! Excellent!

First aired: February 18, 1989

Sprockets

"Sprockets" is a talk show for mod West Germans who are interested in the collision of the German avant-garde and American culture. The black-clad, bespectacled host, Dieter (Mike Myers), is the typical angst-ridden German. He bombards his guests with bizarre and often disarming questions—and is especially fascinated by the textural, macabre elements of "pure *amerikanische Kultur*." When a guest's answer becomes too "tiresome," Dieter quickly changes the topic, often asking the guest to touch his beloved but temperamental monkey, Klaus—who is often asked to give him *fünf*.

Welcome to "Sprockets":

1 Dieter's guest is Butch Patrick (Ben Stiller), the actor who played Eddie on *The Munsters*—a "brilliant satire of a postnuclear American society." To Dieter, Eddie was an "Every-Vampire."

He asks his guest, "Can I touch your widow's peak? It is *most* bizarre." Dieter's monkey bites Butch and draws blood. Dieter savors the moment: "I would have liked you to play Eddie completely covered in sores, abrasions, lesions."

2 Dieter introduces this week's guest, the art critic Heike Mueller (Nora Dunn): "Not only is she a genius, she is also my *lover*"; her reviews "are harsh and without mercy." Heike thanks Dieter for the compliment.

She recounts a performance piece by Chuckles—an artist whom they both agree would be completely misunderstood. Why, they wonder, is it that the truly brilliant are doomed to a life of obscurity, surrounded by a sea of mediocrity, only to end up covered in sores in a pool of their own filth?

3 Jimmy Stewart (Dana Carvey), "obsessed outcast whose dark visions drive us to the edge," discusses his new book, *Jimmy Stewart and His Poems*. Jimmy agrees that "good poetry is about destruction." Apparently his poem "Funny Little Pooch" was composed after he had hitchhiked through Paraguay and settled in with a fifteen-year-old whore who then left him, taking all his possessions.

Dieter lavishes praise: "Jimmy Stewart, you are a running sore, running from yourself, yet your scab heals us all." Jimmy recites a passage from "My Kitten, My Pal." Dieter's evaluation: "That poem pulls down my pants and taunts me."

öst deutsche televonken ② east german television

4 A busy week in Berlin: The Scabs on Canvas exhibit opens and the Berlin Wall comes down. Dieter is joined by the brilliant countercultural filmmaker from the East, Gregor Voss (Woody Harrelson), the man behind *The Dead Coat* and *Irritant #4*.

"Gregor Voss, your presence intimidates me to the point of humiliation. Would you care to strike me?" A clip is screened, and Dieter rhapsodizes: "That film looks at me when I am naked and calls its friends!" But he's soon disillusioned by Voss's newfound love for Western kitsch: "You were the greatest auteur of emptiness, my personal *Gesellschiest*, and now I watch you drink beer from a hat. I would never drink from headgear. You may not touch my monkey."

5 Dieter faces the press. Why, they ask, is he preparing to shoot his monkey, Klaus, into space? "Because art is dead." And why now? "Christmas is traditionally the time when most suicides occur." The questions become tiresome, and everyone is invited to touch the monkey for the last time. Suddenly Klaus throws a lever and the rocket takes off, with Dieter's entourage on board: "Yes, we are doomed, and I am filled with remorse, and it is most delicious."

6 "Dieter's Dance Party" features Schreibmaschine's "Weird Nun." Gerhard (Dana Carvey) and Elsa (Jan Hooks) are picked from the crowd: "Your hair is grotesque. What did you think of the song on a scale of one to fourteen?" Gerhard finds it hellish yet exquisite—a nine; Elsa finds it bourgeois and banal—a negative three. Dieter derides her adolescent attempt to be clever and gives the song a fourteen: "It had a good beat and it was easy to dance to."

After a message from Clearasil (*Macht das pimplen kaput!*), Dieter greets trendsetter Etienne (Rob Lowe), the genius behind such brilliant dances as the ermine, the Belorussian stomp, and the parsnip. But Etienne is passionate about the lambada, a dance both masturbatory and obscene that draws Dieter like a moth to flame.

7 Guest Karl-Heinz Schelker (Kyle MacLachlan) previews the finalists in Germany's Most Disturbing Home Videos competition—works submitted by ordinary Germans "who just happen to record the everyday occurrences of the grotesque and profane." Dieter is so excited that his genitals are sucked up into his body cavity. The four finalists are:
• A fat Bavarian man in a diaper cavorts under a garden sprinkler. ("Brilliant, truly disturbing.")
• A man kicks another man in the testicles. The pain is so great, he has to vomit. ("His agony was gorgeous; I need to be slapped.")
• The body of a dead man is discovered in a park ("which, in itself, is not that disturbing") and is turned over to reveal "Ants! Ants! Ants!"
• In a Hanover gallery a couple is looking at a painting when the man's lederhosen fall to the floor.

8 A very special Weihnachten (Christmas) show. Saint Nicholas is played by Henri Kon-

ninjkirke (Dennis Quaid), the star of the hit sitcom *Don't Put That Sausage in Your Mouth, Mrs. Nederlander*. Henri "plugs his show with the subtlety of a flying mallet." To Dieter, the traditional German Christmas is "tedious and bourgeois." When Henri reminds him of the delight of a freshly made Christmas meat helmet, Dieter admits, "You're right. I have become so jaded that someone should strike at my genitals with a toffee hammer. That would fix my wagon."

9 It is springtime, and Dieter is as happy as a little girl. His guest is Veronika Goethe (Catherine O'Hara), known for her blockbuster movie *This Squid Has One Too Many Arms*. Veronika's latest role is in the new comedy *The Head in a Rusty Metal Box*. The clip, compelling yet tedious, leaves Dieter "spent, like a man who is forced to wear his genitals like a pendant."

10 Dieter introduces a German *Dating Game* called "Love Werks." Bachelor Wolfie Schreiber (Jason Priestley) enjoys "appraising antiques and then smashing them, and he hates his father."

Bachelorette number one (Victoria Jackson) is a nurse who wants to be an actress; number two (Julia Sweeney) is "by night a dominatrix," who by day works at the Lego factory outside of Baden-Baden; number three, the deep-voiced Susan (Phil Hartman), has just got out of prison; and number four is Wolfie's mother (Siobhan Fallon).

Number two's perfect date "would be impossible under existing German laws, but would involve a lot of humiliation, a sound spanking, and of course, coffee and chocolate fingers." Number three promises to "push you to the ground, pee on you, chanting '*Haus* on fire. *Haus* on fire. Put it out.' " After being forced to drink antifreeze, "you would wake up in excruciating pain with a size seven poop chute."

And the winner is Susan, the she-male: Wolfie declares, "I abhor chocolate fingers, and she/he reminds me of my father."

Mike Myers.

11 Euro Disney has just opened, and Dieter is as happy as a little girl. The filmmaker Graus Grek (Woody Harrelson) is, however, thoroughly disgusted: "I threatened to gnaw at my own genitals like a small woodland creature in protest." He plans a counterculture theme park, EuroTrash—"a celebration of the repellent and painful in everyday European life." Attractions will include the Boring Teacups ride in Ennui Village; Insane Frontier Land, home of the Diseased Bear Jamboree; and the Poke at the Turk ride.

12 Dieter is dreaming: He is greeted by a young woman, then by his mother, then by Marv Albert, then by a talking caribou. The young woman reappears and invites Dieter to fondle her conical breasts; she drops a six-pack on Dieter's crotch. Suddenly Susan, the she-male, is with them: "I want to poke out your eyes and make love to your skull." A diapered man spits food out of his mouth, and a caribou chauffeurs them away. Dieter opens his robe to a *Frau*, who screams when she sees the monkey's head

and shoulders that cover his pubic area. "Touch my monkey! Touch him! Love him!"

13 It's "*Das Ist* Jeopardy," with contestants Gunther Strauss (Chris Farley), who collects rare smoked sausages and likes to make cheese whistles; Veronika Koenig (Nicole Kidman), who is interested in brine and grows her hair as a hobby; and the returning champion, Susan, the she-male.

Wrong answers cost contestants money and cause painful electric shocks to be administered to pensioner Frau Schreiber (Julia Sweeney). Categories are Pain, Fear, Art, Inert Gases, Countries That Are Weak, and Things That Begin with "P." The winner receives a tongue bath from the House of Velvet.

Now is the time on Sprockets when we dance.

FIRST AIRED: APRIL 15, 1989

Jason Priestly, Mike Myers, Victoria Jackson, Julia Sweeney, Phil Hartman, and Siobhan Fallon.

GREAT CHARACTERS

Nora Dunn and Victoria Jackson.

The Big Bitch Bull Dyke Bust Out of '89

[*Inside a tunnel, Zsa Zsa Gabor is digging with a spoon, holding a poodle in her other arm. Leona Helmsley is behind, holding a gun on her.*]

Zsa Zsa Gabor: I can't go on any longer, dahlink.

Leona Helmsley: You wanna rot in that stinkin' joint!? Keep digging!

Zsa Zsa: I'm not made for this type of thing. New York is where I'd rather stay.

Leona: Shut up!

Zsa Zsa: I get allergic smelling hay.

Leona: Shut up! And you better keep that dog quiet!

Zsa Zsa: He can't help it. He's very nervous.

Leona: I'm giving you five seconds to shut that mutt up.

Zsa Zsa: Please, Froo Froo. Mommy needs you to be quiet.

[*The dog barks. Leona pumps two bullets into the dog.*]

Zsa Zsa: Froo Froo! Ohh! My little Froo Froo!

Leona: Stop that whimpering. I said, stop that whimpering!

Zsa Zsa: Dahlink, I am stopping the whimpering already.

Leona: Then what the hell is that?

[*At this moment, Jim Bakker breaks through into the tunnel, whimpering.*]

Jim Bakker: Oh, praise the Lord, thank God. I thought you were the cops. Unh, unh, unh…

Leona: Jim Bakker.

Zsa Zsa: Thank God, dahlink. Someone from show business.

Leona: How the hell did you get here?

Jim: I was tunneling out of the men's prison, and I, I got lost, uh…

[*He goes into a fetal position and whimpers.*]

Leona: You little wimp. Get out of that fetal position. I've got an eighty-five-year-old husband who's senile and incontinent and he's still twice the man you are.

LEONA HELMSLEY PLAYED BY NORA DUNN
ZSA ZSA GABOR PLAYED BY VICTORIA JACKSON
JIM BAKKER PLAYED BY RICK MORANIS
AIRED: OCTOBER 7, 1989

Chippendales

Barney, we all agreed that your dancing was great, your presentation was very sexy. I guess in the end, we just thought Adrian's body was much, much better than yours. You see, it's just that, at Chippendales, our dancers have traditionally had that lean, muscular, healthy physique, whereas yours is, well, fat and flabby. [*Barney starts to vamp*] No, Barney. No. No. No. Barney, we've made our decision.

JUDGE PLAYED BY KEVIN NEALON
BARNEY PLAYED BY CHRIS FARLEY
ADRIAN PLAYED BY PATRICK SWAYZE
AIRED: OCTOBER 27, 1990

Patrick Swayze and Chris Farley.

Toonces, *the Driving Cat,*
The cat who could drive a car.
He drives around
All over the town,
Toonces, the Driving Cat!

Even though Toonces, a gray tabby, repeatedly drives their car over cliffs (often with them inside), his owners, Lyle (Dana Carvey) and Brenda Clarke (Victoria Jackson), still encourage his efforts—recording the crashes on home movies and sending him to driving school.

On the Road with Toonces:

1 Steve Martin (in a onetime appearance as Toonces's co-owner) and Brenda discover that their cat can drive—sort of: "I saw him up there fooling around at the steering wheel. I guess I just assumed he could drive." Toonces drives away: "I guess he CAN drive!" "Yeah! Just not very well!" Next they worry about Toonces's driving test: "That written part is pretty hard." Kevin Nealon administers the test, and over a cliff they go.

2 Brenda and Lyle are out with Toonces when they are approached by Martians. Toonces escapes and drives wildly in search of help—crashing right through the wall of the office of forest rangers John Goodman and Kevin Nealon. He types a message: "My owners Lyle and Brenda Clarke of 3130 Meadow Lane are being held captive by Marshens." ("He mispelled Martians," notes one ranger.) "Get in the car with me and I will drive you to them."

They go along ("This cat's all over the road!") and over a cliff. Everyone joins the Martians and go for a ride in the spaceship, with Toonces taking the helm—and they crash into the Washington Monument.

3 Toonces, in a cowboy hat, appears at the bar of Sis (Debra Winger) and Bud (Dana Carvey) in "Urban Toonces." The cat gestures for a drink. Asked for ID, he produces his suspended driver's license. They see he's only four years old: "Well yeah, in cat years that's like twenty-eight years old—he's okay. You're okay." "You know you better check and see if he's got real money—he might try to pay us in dead birds or sumpin'."

Toonces rides the mechanical bull to much acclaim. Later that night he is out driving, and Sis wonders, "Do you think we should let him drive after drinking that shooter and everything?" But Bud is calm: "That was hours ago. Besides, he had a big plate of tacos or sumpin'." Toonces, look out!

4 Miss Daisy (Jan Hooks) complains to her chauffeur, Hoke (Quincy Jones), about his driving. He quits, jumping out of the moving car, and it crashes. As Miss Daisy recuperates, her son (Phil Hartman) tells her that he has hired a new chauffeur, "one who wouldn't talk back." It's Toonces, who takes over with the inevitable results.

5 Candice Bergen and her cat, Spunky, have come over to watch home movies of Toonces crashing in various holiday spots—over the falls at Niagara ("What a view we had that day") and into the Grand Canyon (it's "really deep, isn't it?"). They even see a clip of Toonces as a kitten, driving a toy car over a small wall of rock.

Candice suggests that Spunky take them for a drive, since he has just finished driving school. As Spunky gets dressed, Toonces chloroforms him and leaves him in the closet. Disguised as Spunky, Toonces takes the wheel, and over the cliff they go.

6 Toonces is dreaming that he's in charge of the Baby Chick Division: "These chicks are helpless and you'll be totally unsupervised. Think you can handle it?" Toonces nods. He goes for a drive, and his owners praise him. "He's the best driver of anybody." In the dream Toonces talks, too, in both English and French. The dream ends with the car flying over a cliff, suspended in midair.

7 Sarah Connor (Linda Hamilton) and her son John (Edward Furlong) are trying to escape from the Terminator (Phil Hartman),

A-1 DRIVING SCHOOL
REPORT CARD

Name	SPUNKY	
		A+
Driving		
Conduct		
Attendence		
Punctuality		
Extra Credit for Helping Grade Papers		

Toonces

but he has come to warn them about the Tooncinator. "So let me get this straight. They sent a cat who can drive a car back through time so he could kill us?" Yes. "A robot cat. And he can drive—just not very well."

The Tooncinator, wearing leather and shades, is impervious to gunshots and car crashes. "He'll be back." Trying a new tack, they allow him into their car. Sarah says, "He wasn't trying to kill us, after all. He was just trying to catch up to us, to be our kitty!" Should they let him drive? "Well, of course, he's a very advanced cyborg, with all sorts of sophisticated…Tooncinator, *watch out!*"

8 It's Flippy, the Flipping Chihuahua, the Flippingest Dog You'll Meet. Unfortunately, he goes flipping into the street and, *splat*, is run over. Brenda and Lyle are in the car with Toonces: "Did we just hit something?"

9 Stone Phillips (Mike Myers) and Jane Pauley (Julia Sweeney) apologize for recent NBC mishaps: the car report for which "NBC used incendiary devices to be sure the trucks caught fire" and the segment on faulty building construction for which they placed "several explosive devices at key structural points throughout the building."

They also apologize for the Olympic Triple-Cast ("We now admit it was an ill-conceived, idiotic idea from start to

Victoria Jackson, Steve Martin, and Toonces.

finish—although we wish to point out that no incendiary devices were used"); for letting David Letterman go ("We now admit that Jay Leno is not as good"); and for the *SNL* sketch in which actors Mike Myers and Dana Carvey made fun of Chelsea Clinton ("It was a cheap and unnecessary shot made by a desperate and overrated performer.")

Stripped of their limo privileges, they leave the studio together in a car-service sedan. Toonces is at the wheel.

10 Isabelle (Kirstie Alley) and Penelope (Julia Sweeney) are riding in a horse-drawn carriage, discussing their futures. Isabelle is to marry John Wilkes Booth; Penelope is to marry Rasputin and is on her way to her doctor, Typhoid Mary. Isabelle and her husband will live in Krakatoa; Penelope is headed for Hiroshima. Isabelle's brother is on the *Titanic* looking for a whale, Moby Dick. Penelope carries a tsetse fly, a present for her

nephew. Isabelle is getting married on April 18, 1906, in San Francisco and hopes that something awful doesn't happen, like an earthquake. Penelope plans to drop her friend off at Dead Man's Curve. But they are going too fast. It's not the regular driver! "It's Toonces! The Cat Who Could Drive a Horse-Drawn Carriage!" The whole group goes over a beautiful cliff.

Toonces, look out!

First aired: May 20, 1989

Nude Beach

Featuring Bob (Dana Carvey), Doug (Matthew Broderick), Jack (Kevin Nealon), Ted (Dennis Miller), Bill (Jon Lovitz), Victoria Jackson, and Nora Dunn

Bob: Is this great or what?
Doug: I feel a little self-conscious, Bob. I mean, I've never been to a nude beach before.
Bob: Aw, listen, Doug, you don't have to worry about that here. The people at this club, they're not hung up about that kind of thing. That's what's great about it, everyone's just here to relax.
Doug: Really?
Bob: Yeah, yeah. Believe me, in a few minutes, you'll forget all about it. C'mon, I'll introduce you to some of the guys.
Doug: Okay…thanks, Bob.
Bob: Hey, guys!
Jack: Hey, Bob. Hey, your penis looks great today.
Bob: Thanks, Jack. Yours too.
Ted: Hey, Bob.
Bob: Hey, Ted. How's your penis?
Ted: Not bad.
Bob: Good. Hey, I'd like you guys to meet Doug.
Jack: Hey, Doug.
Doug: Hey, guys.
Jack: Hey, pretty small penis there, Doug.
Doug: Huh?
Ted: Yeah. You could pick a lock with that penis.
Jack: Hey, that's okay. There're plenty of guys around here with small penises. Bill's got one. Hey, Bill—come on over here and show him your penis! Bill, this is Doug.
Bill: Hey, Doug.

Doug: Hey, Bill.
Bill: So I guess you have a pretty small penis.
Doug: Yeah, I guess so.
Bill: Well, that's okay. I hear it really doesn't matter to women.
Doug: Yeah, I read that.
Jack: Okay, you two, enough small penis talk.
Ted: Hey, guys, wanna see my pictures from Barbados?
All: Yeah, sure.
Ted: Okay. That's me with some friends on a catamaran.
Jack: Penis looks great.
Ted: Thanks. Here's me, playing tennis with my father.

Kevin Nealon, Dennis Miller, Matthew Broderick, and Dana Carvey.

Bob: Hey, you've really got your dad's penis.
Ted: Yeah. By the way, Jack, *what* have you done with your penis? Looks *super!*
Jack: Oh, I go to this place on Long Island. They do great work.
Ted: Wow. You got the address?
Jack: Sure.
Ted: Great. I'll write it on my penis so I won't forget.
Bill: So, Doug, where you from?
Doug: Montpelier, Vermont.
Jack: Oooh…cold up there. Must be tough on the penis.
Bob: Bill, you're from Denver, right?
Bill: Yeah…
Ted: Good penis town.

Victoria: Hey, everybody!
Jack: Hey, girls.
Nora: Hey, who's the new guy with the penis?
Bob: Oh, that's Doug.
Victoria: Hey, Doug.
Doug: Hi.
Nora: Hey, pretty small penis.
Doug: Yeah.
Victoria: That's okay.
Doug: Hey, thanks.
Nora: Hey, Dave just made a great sand penis sculpture. You should come see it before the tide comes in.
Victoria: Yeah, it's got testicles and everything.
Ted: Great. We'll check it out.
Bill: See, Doug, you had nothing to worry about.
Doug: Yeah, I guess not.
Jack: Hey, who wants to sing the club anthem?
All: Yeah!
Bob: Okay, I'll start. "*I once had a penis sing to me / His penis penis song / And when that penis penis sang, / Here was the penis's song / He'd sing me.*"
All: "*Penis, penis, penis, penis, / Penis, penis song. / Penis, penis, penis, penis, / Penis all day long. / Penis, penis, penis, penis…*"
[*Jack steps forward.*]
Jack: Hi. I'm Kevin Nealon. What you just saw was an attempt to make an important point—that wherever you go, no matter how you look on the outside, we're all pretty much the same. You know, when the Standards Department was dissolved here at NBC, we welcomed it as an opportunity to deal with issues like these in a frank way. And to be honest, we're a little disheartened by the snickering we heard during this presentation. It kind of makes us wonder if there's room for serious discussion of these subjects on television. So to those of you who missed the point—grow up. Really.
All: "*Penis, penis, penis, penis, / Penis all day long—*"

AIRED: OCTOBER 15, 1988

Frank Sinatra

Frank describes "that nickel rocket they call stardom": "You're ridin' the express elevator to the penthouse overlooking Success Street, the main drag through Dreamtown. When I first took a bite out of that brass ring, it left such a bad taste, I wanted to spit that thing out that horses have in their mouth when they're gettin' led around. But I'm just a saloon singer from Hoboken, not a thesaurus. Know this, sweetheart: One day you wake up, and you're top dog, on the top rung of that top...*thing* up there. And you're eating breakfast off some five-hundred-dollar broad's chest. That's when you get on your knees and thank the Big Man that he told the lady Fame to tap you on the shoulder."

1 Sinatra is talking to "Georgie Michael" (Dana Carvey) about fame: "The point is, you've got talent. Not like that guy who plays Mork." Michael wants Frank to look at his butt: "I don't swing that way, baby!" "My butt's very important. I feature it in every single video. You've seen the biggest butts in the business, and I want you to be honest: Is my butt as good as Bing Crosby's?" Then Michael has the nerve to criticize Frank's butt: "It must be all wrinkled and sagging." "You're damn right my ass is shot, baby. I *worked* it off!"

2 *Announcer:* The Sinatra Group. An unrehearsed discussion of current issues in the recording industry. With panelists Sinéad O'Connor [Jan Hooks], Billy Idol [Sting], 2 Live Crew star Luther Campbell [Chris Rock], and Steve Lawrence [Mike Myers] and Eydie Gorme [Victoria Jackson]. And now here's the moderator, Frank Sinatra.
Frank: Issue number one: censorship. They got the records with the labels now, people gettin' arrested. What the hell's going on? Sine-aid O'Connor!
Sinéad: Well, I think it's a bloody shame that freedom of expression is suppressed in this country—
Frank: Yap, yap, yap. Billy Idol!
Billy: I think they're all a bunch of tight-assed old farts—

Frank: Get a haircut. Luther Campbell!
Luther: Well, man, I had my run-ins with censorship all year—
Frank: Can't understand a word.
Luther: Said, I was censored all year—
Frank: You don't know what censored is, junior. Censored is being dumped by Columbia because Mitch Miller doesn't like the way your career is going. It's having million-dollar pipes and nowhere to play 'em. Am I right, Steve and Eydie?
Steve: Yes you are, Frank.
Eydie: Absolutely, Frank.
Frank: You bet I am. Next issue: this crap with MTV. With the nudity and all. What is this crap? Sinbad O'Connor.
Sinéad: Well, I think it's bloody awful. But it's typical of entertainment in a male-dominated society.
Frank: Boo-hoo. You had me and then you lost me. Billy Idol.
Billy: I think it's great—
Frank: Shaddap. Luther Campbell.
Luther: Well, that's my bread and butter, man—
Frank: Once more around, pal. Sounds like pops and buzzes from here.
Luther: I said, that's my bread and butter, man.
Frank: No, you're wrong, schoolboy. You don't *need* to work blue. You'll never play the big rooms with that crap. Ask Redd Foxx. You don't need the blue stuff, kid, you got talent.
Luther: But I don't have talent.
Frank: You've got it, kid. You listen to me. You got a Ben Vereen quality, I can't put my finger on it. Take the high road, baby.
Luther: I swear, man, I don't have any talent. None. This is all I got. Tell him, man.
Billy: Yeah, he sucks.
Sinéad: He's not talented.
Frank: No. Bob Goulet—*that's* not talented. You got talent, you got a Dionne Warwick/Falana kind of thing goin', Steve and Eydie.
Eydie: Oh, you're right, Frank.
Steve: Absolutely. He's great.
Frank: Of course he is, you brownnoses. Look at you,

you're just swimmin' in my wake. Issue number three: This bald chick, what's with her head? Let's start with the chick. What gives, cue ball? I'm lookin' at you, I'm thinkin' fourteen in the side pocket.

Sinéad: I can't believe you're talking about my hair with all the bloody starvation and suffering in the world right now.

Frank: Come on, swing, baby. You're platinum. Billy Idol.

Billy: I think she's really quite attractive.

Frank: Check out his papers. Luther Campbell!

Billy: You watch it, mate!

Frank: Easy, baby. And what's with the sneering crap? Don't do that to the people. They *wanna* like you. That's what killed Dennis Day. Contempt for the audience. Luther Campbell! What about the chick's head?

Luther: Be honest, I don't care about the head. I like the butt.

Phil Hartman and Sting.

Frank: I hear you, baby. Forget the head. Put a bag over it and do your business. Am I right, Steve and Eydie?

Steve: You bet, Frank.

Eydie: You know it, Chairman.

Frank: You were a little slow that time.

Steve and Eydie: Sorry, Frank.

Frank: Forget it. You're all right. You could pick up a check once in a while...

Eydie: Frank, that's not fair—

Frank: Shut up. Okay, issue number four: Milli Vanilli. What is this faggot crap? Uncle Fester!

Sinéad: I don't understand the question.

Frank: I'll tell you what you better understand. Next time you see Old Glory ridin' up that pole, you better sing that anthem, darling. You're lucky you're a chick, or you'd be nothin' but a stain on the road and a crew cut! Our founding fathers went to the mat for you, baby!

Sinéad: It's not my flag. I'm Irish.

Frank: Oh. Well then, stay off of this stuff [*Mimes drinking*]! That's the curse of you people. Billy Idol!

Billy: I forgot the bloody question.

Frank: I'll give you the question. What the hell's with this devil stuff? This whole black mass, and the whole six-six-six, coffins thing. Don't think the Big Man ain't keepin' score, baby. He put you in the penthouse, and He can kick you down to the gutter with these two.

Steve and Eydie: Hey! Geez!

Frank: Shut up, you wastes of space. Just be glad you get to hang with me.

Steve: You're right, Frank.

Eydie: Sorry.

Frank: It's your choice. You can open for me at the Meadowlands, or headline at the Tick Tock Inn. Okay, Luther!

Luther: I think Milli Vanilli got what they deserved.

Frank: Can't understand a word. Next issue: Rita Hayworth or Ava Gardner. Who would you rather nail? I disqualify myself, since I've done them both.

Billy: I think you're a bloody stupid old fart.

Frank: You're all talk, blondie! You want a piece of me? I'm right here!

Billy: Don't provoke me, old man.

Frank: You don't scare me. I got chunks of guys like you in my stool!

Billy: All right. I'll rip your bloody head off.

Frank: Steve—go kick his ass!

Steve: What?

Frank: You heard me!

Eydie: Do it, Steve.

Steve: Huh? Well, okay.

Billy: You got it! [*He punches Steve in the gut.*]

Frank: Next week, the Grammy Awards. Where the hell is Vikki Carr's album? Bye-bye. Keep the hand up, Steve!

3 It's the First Annual Sinéad O'Connor Awards ceremony, and the most important award—"The Person Who Best Represents Everything I Despise About the Music Industry"—goes to Frank Sinatra! "Maybe I'm from the old school, but when the people take the trouble to give you an award, you damn well better show up. You don't throw that boycott crap in their face. I'm talkin' to you, Zippy! You're not in the side show anymore, you're in the center ring!" He also has a few words for cohost Paul McCartney (Dana Carvey): "Stay off the funny stuff, Ringo!"

4 Nancy Reagan (Jan Hooks) receives a "derivery" of Chinese food. The deliveryman whips off his disguise: It's Frank! "After we *shtup*," he explains, "we could have some Chink food." He's made it with every First Lady since Eleanor Roosevelt, and Nancy's got the best "rack"—"but you could eat off Bess Truman's ass." Nancy calls her love to bed: "Just come here, greaseball, and make me pay!" Frank and Nancy couple energetically. Plaster falls onto Ron's (Phil Hartman) head as he's addressing the nation: "That's just Frank and Nancy going at it," Ron explains.

5 Following the rerelease of *Spartacus* with a previously excised bathing scene with homoerotic overtones, moviegoers can soon see another restored classic, *Ocean's Eleven*. It contains a bubble bath scene between the young Sinatra and Sammy Davis, Jr. (Tim Meadows): "I don't know. Sittin' here with you now, I got some kooky thoughts knockin' around in my brain! Your skin. Your skin is like— What I'm tryin' to say is, if you got out of this tub

and put on a dress, I'd take you out for the biggest steak you've ever seen!" Sammy explains that if a cat digs cats, and if it's all right with you, then it's all right with the man upstairs.

6 Woody Allen (Dana Carvey) has just sat through a public screening of *Husbands and Wives*. Mia Farrow (Jan Hooks) turns up, as does Frank Sinatra. "I let you fly the coop once, Mia, now I'm clippin' your wings. I can't bear to watch you play musical Jews!"

He counsels Woody: "Look, we're all weak, baby. Sometimes a guy's gotta trade up for a new set of wheels. But you made one mistake: You gotta keep your mitts off the *kinder*. Believe me, I thought about it myself a few times, but I took my business to the *john*. When you're a one-man band, nobody gets hurt!"

7 Casey Kasem presents a videotape of Frank recording *Duets*. He's finishing with Barbra Streisand (Mike Myers): "Cut it, that's a keeper. Hit the road, Babs. The meter's running. See the door? Use it." Next up is Bono (Adam Sandler). Frank charges into "I've Got You Under My Skin," and charges out just as fast: "I'm ninety-three, baby. When you're pushing a century, there is no 'take two'!"

Liza Minnelli (Rosie O'Donnell) blows in for a verse of "The Lady Is a Tramp": "Your money's on the dresser, baby, I'm done with you." Anita Baker (Ellen Cleghorne) arrives next with Kenny G (Jay Mohr). She leaves, and G leaves soon after: "Enough with the horn, already! I haven't heard screeching like that since Ava Gardner!" Wynonna (Melanie Hutsell) and k. d. lang (Rob Schneider) appear. "Never heard of them. Next?"

And Nancy Sinatra (Julia Sweeney) and Frank Sinatra, Jr. (Dave Attell) are turned away: "This ain't no charity. I gave you the name, now get out!"

Bono returns, demanding a second take. "You're getting on my nerves, potatohead!" Frank slugs him and declares the record complete.

8 Kevin Nealon presents Frank on Weekend Update to conclude his curtailed Grammy speech. "Thanks, Chevy. Okay. Here's the rest of my speech. 'Thanks for the award. Drive home safely. Good night.'"

FIRST AIRED: SEPTEMBER 29, 1990

Chris Rock, Victoria Jackson, Mike Myers, Frank Sinatra, Jan Hooks, and Sting.

Nat X

THE DARK SIDE With NAT X

ive, from Compton, California, a city so bad it has a drive-by shooting lane, it's "The Dark Side" with Nat X (Chris Rock). The only show on TV written by a brother, produced by a brother, that's strictly for the brothers. "The Dark Side" is also the only fifteen-minute show on television. Why only fifteen? "Because The Man would never give a brother like me a whole half hour. The Man will give Pat Sajak, Joan Rivers, and Rick Dees an hour, but a brother like me, no way." We all know who The Man is: "I'm talking about the same man who made the black jellybean the worst-tasting candy on earth." The same man "who tells you the black cat's bad luck and the white cat is pussy." Not to mention the same man who invented pool, "a game that isn't won until the white ball knocks all the colored balls off the table."

The show often features Nat's Top Five list ("Why five? Because The Man would never give me ten of anything. I'm lucky to get five!") and the menacing "White-Man Cam," which makes it look as if Nat is behind steel prison bars. "I haven't had that much fun since I saw Weezy Jefferson naked!" The Sandman (Chris Farley) is often called upon to sweep Nat's guests away when they become irritating.

Chris Rock.

1 Nat counts down the top five reasons why white people can't dance:

5. Too busy counting their money.
4. Too busy counting my money.
   3. Small thighs make it hard to dip.
   2. They're inferior.
   1. They can—they're just waiting for the waltz to come back.

His first guest is Jimmy Smits from *L.A. Law*. Nat suspects Smits's Colleagues don't treat him like an equal: "I mean, when something's missing on the set, I bet they come to you first." Smits answers no: "Do they know you're not white?" They do. "Then they blame the black guy, then!" Next up is pro boxer Gerry Cooney (Kevin Nealon). Visiting "The Dark Side," Nat notes, is "the only time you can get this close to a black man without getting your ass kicked."

2 Nat recognizes Black History Month: "Isn't that nice. The Man gives us February because it's the shortest month of the year! It's also the coldest month of the year, just in case we wanted to have a parade." His first guest is General Colin Powell (Tim Meadows): "Now when you report to the president in his *White* House,

Chris Farley and Chris Rock.

5 Nat has a video hookup with Michael Jackson (Chris Rock). Nat blasts Jackson for singing that it doesn't matter if you're black or white: "Why don't you try to get a taxicab? Try to marry a Kennedy girl!" Nat issues a shocking revelation: "I'm your father!"

6 It's Nat's first show after the L.A. riots: "I want to say hello to all our fans watching on brand-new TVs. Thanks for leaving the studio alone." Nat introduces the Rodney King jury, all of whom wear disguises, including one (Phil Hartman) sporting a paper-bag mask inscribed Please Don't Kill Me: "Sit your twelve white asses down." A Batman-masked juror (Julia Sweeney) says they saw the entire incident on tape. "The *whole* tape? What part did I miss—the part where Rodney picks up his eye?"

7 Nat complains about the movie in which "Whitney Houston's hugging up on that white boy Kevin Costner! What's up, Whitney, couldn't you get a black bodyguard? Why don't you borrow one from Eddie Murphy?" Nat admires guest Joe Jackson's (Sinbad) talents: "I'm not talking about your guitar playing, I'm talking about your left hook. I saw you hit Jackie so hard his Afro came off!" Naturally, he's curious about Michael: "Was it all surgery, or did you smack the black off him?"

FIRST AIRED: NOVEMBER 10, 1990

does he make you shine his shoes?" Nat surmises that Bush gave Powell power so that "just in case he ever blew up the world, he could blame it on a black man." Vanilla Ice (Kevin Bacon), the so-called Elvis of Rap, joins them: "I call Vanilla Ice Elvis because I wish he was dead!"

3 We learn that Nat relaxes by going bowling, "taking that big black ball and throwing it into those ten white pins with red necks." Andrew Dice Clay (Steven Seagal) is the guest. Nat invents a nursery rhyme: "There once was a whitey named Dice, / Who looked like Fonzie on steroids./ Blah blah blah blah,/Blah blah blah blah, / My big black foot in your ass!"

4 A viewer asks what would have happened to Pee-wee Herman had he been black: "Not only would he have been arrested, but they'd have given him another ten years for blocking the screen with his big African-American penis."

Nat welcomes LaToya Jackson (Victoria Jackson): "Sit your no-talent ass down!" He wants to know, "What's up with Michael? What the hell, the boy got a brain in a jar?" LaToya plugs her *Playboy* pictorial: "We saw what you had last time! What you got now, a third boob or something?" Spike Lee pays a surprise visit, and Nat says to LaToya, "Scoot your I-wish-I-was-Janet-ass over." Nat notes Spike's X baseball cap: "I seen these hats all over town, but I ain't seen a dime yet!"

Victoria Jackson, Spike Lee, and Chris Rock.

Zoraida

Zoraida: I could hook you up right here to be a Security Agent!

Kirstie Alley: Okay, look. I am an actress and I don't really have time for this and I don't want a job as a security agent.

Zoraida: Who you gettin' loud with?

Alley: I am gettin' loud with you. I am an actress, get it?

Zoraida: Oh, no no no no— Excuse me— I'm an actress too because right now I'm acting like I didn't hear what you just said to me. Because if I did, I think I would be kicking your unemployed ass right now! What'd you say? No no no no. What'd you say? Come back and say it to my face! Hey, Kirstie Alley—what makes you think I won't cut you?

ZORAIDA PLAYED BY ELLEN CLEGHORNE
AIRED: APRIL 17, 1993

Ellen Cleghorne.

George Wendt and Dana Carvey.

Carsenio

Carsenio: You are my main man. Are you my main man?

George Wendt: Well, I guess so…

Ed McMahon: Main man, yes!

Carsenio: "Cheers." That is a fresh, fly show. Now tell me, George, I wanna ask you this, how often do you do the wild thing?

George: Johnny, Johnny, what are you doing here? Why don't you stick to what you do best?

Carsenio: Well, I like to think what I do best *is* the wild thing! Is this dope? Is this dope stuff? Look at this!

George: Johnny, c'mon now. I'm concerned about you. A drastic personality change like this can really be very dangerous.

Carsenio: Dangerous? I did not know that. Did you know that, Ed?

Ed: Yes.

George: You shouldn't feel embarrassed, this is rather common among people your age.

Ed: Secondary Latent Personality Displacement, O Great One.

Carsenio: Well that is some wild, wacky stuff. But what about these people, *whoop whoop whoop*…?

George: Johnny, the truth is, they're morons.

Carsenio: Morons? Morons? I did not know that.

CARSENIO PLAYED BY DANA CARVEY
ED MCMAHON PLAYED BY PHIL HARTMAN
AIRED: MAY 18, 1991

Pat

A lot of people say, "What's that?"
It's Pat.
A lot of people ask, "Who's he? Or she?"
A ma'am or a sir, accept him or her
For whatever it might be.
It's time for androgyny—
Here comes Pat!

Pat O'Neal Reilly (Julia Sweeney) is a very sexual being—the only problem is, no one knows what sex Pat is. Of course, on one level Pat is just like the coach of the New York Knicks, with one big difference: This Pat's never coached a professional basketball team. Age thirty, height five eight, sex—yes, please—Pat works as an accountant. It's an attractive career path, being such a male-dominated field. But let's be clear. Pat only dates people of the opposite sex. Chris (Dana Carvey) is Pat's on-again, off-again special someone. But that sweet face and long-flowing hair can be deceptive. Chris is not what he/she appears to be—a decent human being.

 Some of the confusion is surely because Pat is the product of a broken home. Ever since Jean ran off with "that thing," poor Frances has had to be both mother and father to Pat.

 What else do we know about this complicated person?
•Pat played Peter Pan in high school.
•Pat enjoys watching *Tootsie*.
•Pat never carries a wallet or purse, just a Le Sportsac.

 And so each episode brings a new series of attempts to figure out what he/she is.

The Many Lives of Pat:

1 Pat talks—or flirts—with Bill (Kevin Nealon), an underling at work. Pat's a little cranky, having been jilted by Chris for Terry, and it is that time of the month—bills.

2 Coworker Sue (Roseanne Arnold) chats with Pat. Sue asks Pat for a key to the ladies' room, but Pat can't give her one—since Pat isn't a supervisor. Pat's sweetheart, Chris, appears at the end. Poor Chris has cramps—from the StairMaster.

3 Pat goes to the drugstore and the clerk (Catherine O'Hara) can't wait until Pat leaves. Pat needs razors (Pink Daisy or blue Gillette?—the Gillettes are cheaper), aftershave lotion (Vaseline Intensive Care), antiperspirant (Secret—strong enough for a man, but made for a woman), and something a little embarrassing—prophylactics. "I think contraception is the responsibility of both partners."

4 Pat gets a haircut for tonight's formal affair: "I look like a million bucks—I feel so sexy!" The perplexed barber, Dominick (George Wendt), brushes Pat extra clean around the chest and below the waist—to no avail.

5 It's Pat's birthday and Pat's parent Frances (Kirstie Alley) comes by for lunch. "You look so young you could be siblings," a coworker comments. Frances passed out when Pat was born, and awakened only when the doctor cried, "Congratulations, it's a baby!" Everyone sings, "*For Pat's a jolly good person!*"

6 Pat joins a health club. Having just seen *Return to the Blue Lagoon*, Pat would like to have a body like that—which is to say, Pat wants to be bigger in all the right places. But the trainer can't figure where those places are hiding, until Pat goes to the locker room. Unfortunately, the program is interrupted by a news update on the Louisiana governor's race, so the mystery continues.

7 Pat reluctantly agrees to play strip poker with the coworkers: "I feel so naughty!" The women have spritzers and the guys drink beer, but Pat passes on both, having taken an antihistamine for allergies. Aerosmith's "Dude (Looks Like a Lady)" plays as the game starts—and by morning, only Pat is still dressed, the night's big winner.

MENS
LOCKER ROOM
←——

WOMENS
LOCKER ROOM
←——

Julia Sweeney.

8 In a scene reminiscent of *Basic Instinct*, Pat is being interrogated: "Which one of you put on the condom?" "We put it on together, like the sex manual suggests." Pat's legs open slowly—but the crotch of the tan polyester pants allows no clues. Who would Pat prefer as a partner on a desert island, Armand Assante or Nicollette Sheridan? Assante: "His skills in hunting and fishing would be superior to Nicollette's."

9 Pat is looking for a roommate in "Single White Person." Hedra (Melanie Hutsell) finds Pat "so wonderfully complicated!" and soon becomes obsessed with Pat. "Maybe she's in love with you," says friend Graham (Joe Pesci). "Maybe she's gay. Or straight. Or bi. I don't know—all three." Hedra masquerades as Pat and puts the moves on Chris. Pat breaks it

Kirstie Alley, Julia Sweeney, and Kevin Nealon.

Dana Carvey.

up and Hedra attacks: "You bitch! Uh, you son of a bitch! I mean, you creep!"

10 The account manager, Carl (Christopher Walken), is mystified by this "accountant person": "The question of his/her gender has thrown me for a loop. It's rattling, it's unsettling, and not at all the norm....I see others attempt questions. Pat answers with ambiguities that only amplify my curiosity. The light forms an image that hits my eyes, but my brain cannot unscramble the code." Poor Carl is driven to suicide. Pat's assessment: "What a weirdo!"

11 Miranda Richardson and Stephen Rea are seated at a bar, and they are fascinated, even aroused, by the pub's entertainment: It's Pat, performing a hands-flowing rendition of "The Crying Game." Who knows the mysteries of the human heart?

12 A castaway (Harvey Keitel) longs for the intimacy of a woman, or even the companionship of a good male friend. Like an answered prayer, Pat washes ashore: "Oh, my God, it's a...person." Nineteen days later the castaway tells his diary all he can about Pat: "We have had sex eight times, and I still don't know whether Pat's a man or a woman." The castaway finally asks point-blank, but as Pat answers, an audience member (Adam Sandler) cries: "No! No! Don't tell us, Pat! We don't want to know if you are a man or a woman! The fact that we don't know is all the fun!"

FIRST AIRED: DECEMBER 1, 1990

The Receptionist

Featuring Michael Tassoni (Kevin Nealon), the Receptionist (David Spade), Roseanne Arnold, Dick Clark's mother (Julia Sweeney), and Jesus (Phil Hartman).

Tassoni: Hi, I'm here to see Mr. Clark.
Receptionist: Okay, and you are...?
Tassoni: Michael Tassoni.
Receptionist: And this is regarding?
Tassoni: Mr. Clark is buying a few custom-made suits from our company and he asked me if I would stop by today and take his measurements.
Receptionist: Right, so you don't have an appointment.
Tassoni: Well no, not really, I mean he...
Receptionist: Okay, if you could just have a seat.
Tassoni: But...
Receptionist [Whispers]: Thanks.
[Roseanne Arnold enters and tries to walk into office.]
Receptionist: Uh, uh, hi! Hello!
Roseanne: Oh, hi. I'm here to see Dick.
Receptionist: And you are...?
Roseanne: Are you kidding?
Receptionist: No, ma'am.
Roseanne: Roseanne...Arnold. Ring a bell?
Receptionist: And he would know you from?
Roseanne: Maybe from my own show that happens to be number one in the Nielsens.
Receptionist: Right, and is that some sort of contest or something? I don't...
Roseanne: Are you seriously this stupid? I have my *own* TV show, like Bill Cosby.
Receptionist: Right, and he is...?
Roseanne: A TV star, like me!
Receptionist: TV?
Roseanne: Yeah, you know, *TV*, where an electron gun sends electron particles out of a cathode-ray tube and they travel over the airwaves to a satellite, then back down to earth in a rectangular box that unscrambles them so people can stare at them?
Receptionist: I'm no stranger to sarcasm.
Roseanne: Listen, peewee, forty million people see me every Tuesday night.
Receptionist: I only watch PBS. Please forgive me. I'm sure you're very famous, and if you could just have a seat, it won't

Phil Hartman and David Spade.

be long.
Roseanne: Don't talk down to me, you little tick, or I'll throw you back on the mangy dog's ass you jumped off of.
Receptionist: Using that tone won't get you in any faster. I suggest you wait your turn. Now, do you need a parking validation, or...
Roseanne: No! [*She sits and lights a cigarette.*]
Receptionist: Would you be a lamb and not smoke? Thanks.
Roseanne: This guy gets under my skin like a chigger.
Receptionist: Uh, I heard that.
Roseanne: Good.
[An elderly woman enters. She is very emotional.]
Dick's Mother: Excuse me...this is very hard for me. I'm Dick Clark's biological mother. I gave Richard up for adoption when he was three weeks old, and not a day goes by when it doesn't tear me apart inside, not knowing if I made the right decision. I know he's spent years looking for me, and I'm finally ready to see him. I have an aching void inside me, and seeing his face is the only thing that could—
Receptionist: I'm sorry, I was on the phone, did you have a question?
Dick's Mother: No, I'm sorry, this was a bad idea.
Receptionist: No, no. You can stay. But can I ask you a favor? Would you be a dove and wait over there for him. We like to keep this area clear. Thanks.
Roseanne: By the way, I just made your whole year's salary while I was sitting here. Just thought I'd let you know that.
Jesus: Hello, my son.
Receptionist: Hi. And you are...?
Jesus: I am the Lord. I'm here to get on the airwaves that Richard Clark controls to tell the world I have come back as I promised.
Receptionist: Now, did you have an appointment, or...?
Jesus: My son, don't you recognize Me from the Bible?
Receptionist: I'm not a big reader. If you could just have a seat.
Jesus: Listen. *Friend* —
Receptionist: I know, if you could just have a seat. Thanks.
Roseanne: Isn't he the worst?
Jesus: He really is.
Tassoni [To Jesus]: Can't you do something?
Jesus: I will in a minute.
Receptionist: Threatening me with eternal damnation won't get you in any faster. [*Phone rings.*] Dick Clark Productions! And you are...?

AIRED: FEBRUARY 22, 1992

Bill Swerski (Joe Mantegna) and his fellow Super Fans, Pat Arnold (Mike Myers), Todd O'Connor (Chris Farley), Carl Wollarski (Robert Smigel), and Bob Swerski (George Wendt), gather regularly to air their views on WCBM–767, though usually without Bill, the victim of a series of heart attacks. The show is broadcast live from Ditka's in the heart of Chicago, the City of Big Shoulders and home, of course, to a certain football team which has carved out a special place in the pantheon of professional football greats—that team which is known the world over as…Da Bearssss! And occasionally they also recognize a certain team from a certain town known for its Polish sausage and soon to be known as the home of…Da Bullssss.

The broadcasters are fueled by a steady diet of bratwurst, Polish sausage, knockwurst, pork chops, and, of course, cheese fries. They love their teams, but most of all they venerate the man who made the Bears giants, Coach Ditka—"a man whose courage and good grooming set a standard for an entire city. His hairstyle was like the man himself: sharp, unmovable, water-resistant."

The Season of the Super Fans:

1 The local sons are seven-point underdogs against the Giants—but not to the Super Fans. Their predictions: "62–3, Bears." "79–zip." Carl calls the Bears, 52–14, much to his fellow Super Fans' disbelief. Bill's pick? "At the end of the game there will be two teams of contrasting moods heading off the field, one glum, one gleeful—the gleeful of which being Da Bearssss. Seventy-four to two."

Their civic pride is on the line: "I mean, which building would you rather have, the Empire State Building or the Sears Tower?" It's unanimous: Da Searssss.

2 Bob Swerski sits in for his brother Bill, who is recovering from a heart attack. They forecast the day's matchup with the Detroit Pistons. Pat sees a Bulls victory,

149–23; Carl expects the Bulls to win 149–52. Todd predicts a 402–0 shutout—but Michael Jordan *will* be held to under 200 points.

Back to "a more serious topic, Da Bears": Somehow, the home team recently lost to the Giants 31–3. Ditka had his mind on more important things: "There was a war on, my friend." The waitress asks whether they ordered the nachos or the beers. Da Beerssss!

3 Da Bears have just come off of back-to-back defeats, and Carl thinks Ditka has shown a lot of compassion. As for the day's game with the Bills, Carl foresees a low-scoring affair: Bears 31, Bills -7. Negative seven? "Watch Ditka find a way." Todd was

Chris Farley, Robert Smigel, Mike Myers, and George Wendt.

kind enough to show up, even though earlier this week he had suffered another heart attack; nothing major, but he must limit his pork intake to 400 grams a day: "The doc says a small piece of Polish sausage is lodged inside the lining of my 'eart."

Now on to basketball: How many times will the Bulls repeat their championship? "Minimum eight-peat." Michael Jordan stops by the table, and the Fans have a few questions about his participation in the upcoming Olympics: The teams look to be lopsided—"why don't you just play these countries by yourself?"

4 Da Bears are going to demolish the Detroit Lions in the day's game; but first we reflect on our Thanksgiving heritage. In a school play Pat's nephew Tommy Arnold (Macaulay Culkin) plays a pilgrim: "Look at this bountiful meal the Indians have prepared for us! Pork chops, strip steak, kielbasa, baby back ribs, and a side of home fries." An Indian sage smokes a peace pipe and tells the future: "Bears ninety-six, Lions fourteen"—and "that's the half-time score, my friend!"

Super Fans

Back at Ditka's the Fans are joined by Bob's daughter Denise Swerski, Miss South Side of Chicago (Beth Cahill). Carl, Todd, and Pat are charmed; she's got a real Mrs. Ditka quality. They try to impress her: "Look how many chops I polished off."

5 Due to a lack of interest, the Super Bowl broadcast is pre-empted in Chicago in favor of far more entertaining fare: "Bob Swerski's Quiz Masters." The categories: Bears, Ditka, Bulls, Famous Ditkas Through History, Ditkationary, and Grab Bag. The questions are flying.

Greatest movie of all time? *The Bear*. Greatest nineteenth-century novelist? Flaubert. Tastiest cheese available to man? Camembert. The decisive final question: Bears versus Bulls? Todd has the right answer: "The senseless waste of pitting these two mighty forces of nature against each other like matter versus antimatter would be a tragedy, not only for the teams involved but for our planet. All nations must band together to ensure that such a conflagration never takes place."

6 Todd, Carl, and Pat appear on Weekend Update to comment on game seven of the Bulls-Knicks playoffs. They discuss Knick coach Pat Riley as Todd holds up a photo of Mike Ditka. "Where have we seen that sharp hairstyle before?" And what about the names of the teams? "What the hell's a Knick?" Carl has an idea: "It's what a New York man gets when he shaves his legs before going into a Greenwich Village bar."

7 This week's broadcast is from the Richard M. Butkus Trauma Center at Halas Memorial Hospital ("the place for hospital ribs"). Each patient has his own barbecue sauce IV ("a sweet road to recovery, my friend") and call buttons for a nurse and/or a rib-eye steak sandwich. Bob and Todd will bounce back from their heart attacks— as will "a certain assemblage of burly gladiators known to all as Da Bears. Although technically mathematically eliminated from the playoffs, do not count them out, my friend."

8 Bob Swerski issues an open letter to the Chicago Bears: "Today, history witnessed one of the most monstrous acts of betrayal ever committed in the annals of man." Yes, Ditka has been fired, and this despicable act of savagery shall forever bring disgrace on…Da Bearssss. Todd cannot join his fellow Fans in writing, for upon hearing the news, "he suffered his most massive heart attack to date." The Super Fans return their season tickets (prebought through 2032), as well as all their fan paraphernalia.

Da Bearssss!

FIRST AIRED: JANUARY 12, 1991

Sting and Rob Schneider.

Richard Laymer (Rob Schneider) of the Accounting Department, commonly known as the Richmeister, presides over the room in which the photocopier is located. Rich has a strange way of addressing people, but as coworker Sandy ("Sandita, the Sandstress," played by Julia Sweeney) explains, "It's just his way of trying to be nice."

Makin' Copies:

1 We meet Rich's coworkers Tom ("Tom-may! The Tom-ster! Tom-Tom! Mr. Tom! Tom-may! Toooom," played by Mike Myers), Randy (mistakenly called "Billay! The Billster! Billy-Bill-Bill!" and played by Kevin Nealon), Sandy, and Steve (Phil Hartman). "Stevearama" finds Rich "kind of annoying" but tries the argot himself, and Rich is soon "makin' friends with the Stevenator."

A celebrity appears: "Sting! Der Stinglehoffer. Makin' copies. Stingatollah. Stiiiiing. Sting-a-ling-a-ding-ding-dong."

2 "Baron von Steve" discovers a glitch in the Xerox-olla. In comes "Xerox Repair Man, the Guy Who Checks the Toner, Toner-Checker Man, The Guy Who Took a Swing at Me" (Kevin Bacon). "Admiral Checkley von Toner, Tony Tone Tone" must remove the machine for repairs. The Sandita notes that the copier is Richard's whole life: "If they take it away, it'll kill him." Richard, devastated, has no recourse but to wheel in the coffee machine.

3 It's a farewell party for Drew (Jeremy Irons) and the Richmeister comments on everyone's drinks: "Captain Steve of the SS *Vodka*. Stevie Stolichnaya!" A tipsy "Dan-o" (Chris Farley) lifts "Tina-Nina" (Victoria Jackson) onto the photocopier, and Rich instantly dials "Security, Secure-a-rama". He gives Drew a surprise going-away present, the Xerox Telecopier 7009 man-

Rob Schneider.

Mak'Ln'

The

ual. "Oh, no," Drew protests, "I couldn't possibly accept this. You need this." But Rich has it memorized.

4 Nico Tenelli (Steven Seagal), a rebellious cop, has been demoted to a desk job, and his first duty is—photocopying. "Detective Tenelli, makin' copies. The Guy Who Breaks the Rules! The Rulebreakster! The Lone Wolf, *El Lobo Solo.*"

Nico turns violent on Rich, who narrates his own abuse: "Oh, no, the Richmeister, thrown through the coffee machine. Potential concussion for the Richman. Nico, losing control. Got me by the ankles. The Anklemeister."

5 A new worker, Larry Hansen (Jeff Daniels), habitually works people's names into well-known melodies, like the opening theme of Beethoven's Fifth Symphony: "*Ste–ven–Le–viiiiine; Ste–ven–Le–viiiiine.*") Sandy ("Sanditized for Your Protection") notices that the Richmeister feels threatened: "Rich just feels this whole name thing is his area." Steve and Richard fight to attract the Randibulator's attention: "*Oh, Randy / Well you came, and you gave without taking.*" Randy judges them "equally irritating."

6 "The Rand Old Opry, the Randster, Randomly Selected for Your Listening Pleasure, Randy" notes Rich is reusing old nicknames. "The Randipulator doesn't know how hard it is to keep coming up with new names." Has the Richmeister always been this way? Steve wonders, and Rich plunges into "a flashback—*el backo de flasho.*"

Young Rich (Macaulay Culkin) is in school: "Cindy, the Cindstress. The class babe, makin' her pencils sharp. Froggy, The Frogginator. The Guy with the Warts. Frogman. The Guy Who Likes to Eat the Paste."

7 An *L.A. Law* parody. Grace Van Owen (Susan Dey) sulks at the copier. "Grace! The Grace Lady, makin' copies. Princess Grace, back from Graceland!" She announces that she's leaving the firm: "No more copies for the Partridge Girl! Laurie Partridge, not really playing the keyboards, not even plugged in! No electricity for the Partridge-inator."

8 It's the office Halloween party: "Captain Hook! Larry from Accounting! The Walk-the-Plankster! Baron von Plankenstein." Randy comes as "Madonna, the Dirty-Bookinator, fifty bucks, too expensive for the Richmeister." And Laura (Catherine O'Hara) is "the Let-Them-Eat-Cakestress, the Signorina Guillotina, Mademoiselle No Head, the Bloody Spurtstress Marie Antoinette—The Mayor of Choppoquiddick!"

Then the Grim Reaper appears. Richard is to die from the copy machine's radiation, but his endless nicknaming drives the Reaper away.

9 David Koresh (Mike Myers) is demanding that his religious statement be aired on the radio: "Copies will be released to the press as soon as they're ready." "Jesus! Makin' copies! The Christmeister!" Yes, Rich is at the copier. "Five hundred copies for the Lamb of God!" A woman enters (Melanie Hutsell): "Becky! Wife number five of the Son of God! Mrs. Jesus can't make her copies. Christ, hogging the machine! More work for the Man from Galilee!" Another wife enters: "Number twelve! Also her age! No age limit for the King of Kings!"

FIRST AIRED: JANUARY 19, 1991

Macaulay Culkin (*center*).

Richmeister

COFFEE TALK
with Linda Richman

Talk Amongst Yourselves

I'll give you yet another topic:

1. The Progressive Era was neither progressive nor an era. Discuss.

2. The Holy Roman Empire was neither holy nor Roman nor an empire. Discuss.

3. Did Truman drop the atomic bomb to defeat the Japanese or to scare the Russians? Discuss.

4. Franklin Delano Roosevelt's New Deal was neither new nor a deal. Discuss.

5. The peanut is neither a pea nor a nut. Discuss.

6. The Italian neorealist movement in film was neither Italian nor neo nor particularly real. Discuss.

7. The Partridge family were neither partridges nor a family. Discuss.

8. A ThighMaster is neither a thigh nor a master. Discuss.

9. The chickpea is neither a chick nor a pea. Discuss.

10. Duran Duran is neither a Duran nor a Duran. Discuss.

Mike Myers.

"Coffee Talk" begins as a call-in show for true Noo Yawkers. Paul Baldwin (Mike Myers), the original host, likes to "talk about coffee, New York, daughters, dogs—you know, no big whoop, just coffee talk." Long story short, Paul gets *shpilkes* in his *genecktagesoink* after two episodes and moves to Boca Raton to recuperate.

When Linda Richman (Mike Myers) first substitutes for Paul, she makes it clear that she doesn't know from coffee, but she does know about Barbra Joan Streisand. Under Linda's direction the show becomes more coffee klatch than coffee talk, with a healthy dose of Yiddish and a close look at Barbra's latest activities.

A single woman living in a New York apartment building, Linda was once married to an adagio dancer with turquoise hair and carpal tunnel syndrome—may he rest in peace. Everything was fine until she started harboring secret thoughts of opening her own needlepoint boutique. They divorced after thirty years of marriage. She has a daughter, Robin, who is engaged to Michael—a goy. And did we mention that she has a hiatus hernia?

4 It's Robin's birthday. Linda and her other best friend, Liz Rosenberg (Madonna)—"Don't talk to me, I'm having a bad hair day"—discuss the Oscar nominations for *Prince of Tides* and complain that Barbra has not been nominated for Best Director. They also discuss Madonna, who Liz says is a call girl: "Madonna is a tramp—feh!" But Linda retorts, "Madonna's legs are like two sticks of butter lashed together in a rough-hewn manner." Liz and her mother (Roseanne Arnold), who is gassy and has female troubles, are always fighting, but they reconcile on the air, and *everyone* is *farklempt*.

As they sign off, Barbra herself appears: "All this talk about food—I'm getting hungry, girls." Linda says, "I have to go and die now."

5 Linda is joined by her sister Judy (Glenn Close): "She's got Land O Lakes written all over her." Linda's daughter is engaged. Unfortunately, her fiancé Michael is a goy: "He might as well have the word 'gentile' tattooed on his forehead." He has "one of those button noses like a Muppet—I swear, he could be made out of felt and I wouldn't know the difference."

Coffee Talk

Let's Schmooze:

1 Paul takes "cawls" in his loft, no big whoop—although one caller talks of parking his car in Harvard Yard. He should have called "Boston Talk."

2 Paul is joined by Audrey (Delta Burke), his former "thing" from the building. We learn that dogs cannot drink coffee in New York—it's against the law. Who knew?

3 Linda substitutes for Paul. She and her best friend, Sheila Arnstein (Kirstie Alley), discuss Barbra—her great body, her great hands, her forthcoming movie, *The Prince of Tides*, and the mere fact that she got out, a poor *mieskeit* from Brooklyn with a hook nose. They reminisce about *The Way We Were* and Redford's beautiful *goyisher punim*. They are joined by Sheila's husband, Saul (Phil Hartman), a *zhlub* who would rather park far away than circle the block for a good parking spot.

Judy asks Robin about the ring and warns her to be on the lookout for a "canardly"—meaning you can hardly see it: "They don't know from diamonds, these people."

6 Linda flirts with her handsome neighbor Claude (Bill Murray) from 4C, whom she met in the laundry room. "A tall drink of water," he works as a casting agent, specializing in grotesques. He used to weigh seven hundred pounds but slimmed down with Deal-a-Meal, and when he had finished the diet, Richard Simmons drove by his house and honked.

Claude and Linda bemoan Barbra's absence from the list of Oscar nominees, even though she didn't do anything. "They should give her one just for keeping her nose."

7 Not an episode of "Coffee Talk," but Linda on a cruise ship. She chats with a fellow passenger (John Goodman), an attractive, single, and—thanks God—Jewish gentleman. They discuss other cruises they've taken, the

highlight of each being the copious amount of food served. Linda's first cruise was to the Yucatán: "You can have triple entrées." She once went to Russia on a barge—actually they parked the barge alongside Russia—and discovered that they have great pizzas at the Hermitage. But she didn't like Japan: "Japan has no pastry."

8 It's Mother's Day and *alayne vay yeshtayne* Linda is "alone like a dog," since Robin is with her mother-in-law. Robin's best friend, Stacy, calls in—she's half Episcopalian, half Jewish, so Linda calls her "a Pissy Jew." She also has great legs: "The left one is salted; the right one, Land O Lakes." They commiserate on what a hard day it must be for Soon-Yi.

Linda's *mamale* calls in from Coral Gables to ask why Linda didn't visit: "If I wanted to travel, believe me, I wouldn't take a guilt trip."

9 It's Halloween, and Linda is dressed as Barbra Streisand circa 1968, during her *Up-the-Sandbox-What's-Up-Doc?*-white-lipstick-knee-length-patent-leather-boots-and-colors-that-don't-exist-in-nature phase.

Unfortunately, Linda is home alone—her friend who was going to have a party has come down with *shpilkes*. So Linda is giving goodie bags to the *kinder* and discussing Barbra, notably her relationship with André Agassi. "Barbra—the kid's twelve years old!"

10 Linda is joined by her new boyfriend Patrick O'Callahan, (Charlton Heston): "Can you believe it? An Irish cop and me? It's like a sitcom. I feel like *Bridget Loves Bernie: The Golden Years.*"

Indeed, Patrick loves Linda, and he's even tried to pick up her way with words: "I love all your *stick*." "That's *shtick*." "I feel like such a *smuck*." They talk about living together: "If you should move in, I never want to hear the sentence 'Where should we put the tree?' " But Patrick has bigger things in mind—he proposes marriage.

11 Linda has just seen Barbra's New Year's Eve concert—"I looked at her and thought, I just can't believe it's not butter"—and now it's time to shed those extra pounds from last year.

Richard Simmons surprises Linda with a customized Deal-a-Streisand: "It makes me so *farklempt*, those extra pounds." Highlights include:

- *"People, people who eat pizza, Have the highest cholesterol in the world."*
- *"I can't bring you blintzes anymore."*
- *"Memories, wipe the cream off apple pie. You don't need those extra calories. Kiss the fat good-bye."*

12 Linda greets family friend Helen Hunt, who is three-quarters Methodist and one-quarter Jewish: "A Moo-shoo." Again Linda laments Barbra's failure to earn an Oscar nomination, while Helen points out that she didn't do any film work that would qualify. "I do not care. That is not the point." Linda's pulling for Spielberg: "He could marry ten *shiksas*, each with pug noses, for all I care. What that man has done as a filmmaker and a Jew!" Helen likes Holly Hunter, but Linda demurs: "Mute, shmute. She didn't have to memorize a single word."

13 The owner of Linda's building, Leila (Heather Locklear), is dying of jealousy over Linda's Streisand tickets. "My sister Judy's husband, Sid, went to the same bungalow colony in the Catskills with the nephew of a guy whose neighbor is Barbra's booking agent's father. It was a piece of cake." A caller has the nerve to suggest that $350 a ticket is too steep: "Would you pay one dollar each day to hear Barbra sing?" Linda asks. "Well, that works out to three hundred and sixty-five dollars a year, which leaves you fifteen dollars for the baby-sitter—it's a *bargoon*. So take your negativity elsewhere, you pig."

It's like buttah!

FIRST AIRED: JANUARY 19, 1991

Mike Myers, Barbra Streisand, Madonna, and Roseanne Arnold.

Stuart Smalley (Al Franken) is a caring nurturer, a member of several twelve-step programs, but not a licensed therapist. He is also codependent, an adult child of an alcoholic, a recovering overeater, and a perfectionist. And he has had to overcome many family problems as well: Dad is "a big stinking drunk" who calls him "Waste of Space"—"Thank you, Dad, for the self-esteem"; Mom is "perverse...a total loon and in complete denial about Dad's drinking." When Stuart tells her he's in ACOA, she keeps thinking he's a member of the ACLU. In fact, "everyone in the Smalley family is either an alcoholic or a codependent."

But Stuart maintains a good attitude, and through affirmations and positive visualizations he helps himself and others through life's little problems. His visualization of a perfect day is Al-Anon in the morning, a terrific Gamblers Anonymous picnic at lunch, and an Adult Children of Alcoholics dance.

1 Having blown a previous program, Stuart decides to do today's show "in the now"—only he blanks: "That's okay, because that's what going on now. Nothing. Except I'm beginning to panic. Which is okay, because it's my panic, and I own it. And I'm thinking, I don't know what I'm doing, they're going to cancel the show. I'm going to die homeless and penniless and no one will ever love me."

2 A hair replacement infomercial displaces Stuart to a late-night time slot. Stuart used to be afraid of his anger: "So I stuffed my anger. And I stuffed my face. And that's why I weighed three hundred pounds." He starts to feel guilty and wonders, "Maybe the show is garbage and they should cancel it." But he fends off his Stinking Thinking with an affirmation.

Al Franken.

Stuart Smalley

3 Today Stuart wants to share his "experience, strength, and hope with any Kurds who might be watching." Stuart likens the Kurds' situation to his three-year relationship with a rage-aholic named Dale. It's "okay" to be angry with Bush and Hussein, "a very sick person who obviously hates himself and is taking it out on you." Finally, he modifies his affirmations for the Kurds: "I'm glad I'm a Kurd. I am fun to be with. Because I'm good enough, I'm smart enough, and people like me. Well, not everybody. But that's their problem. And your problem. Okay, I'm sorry, this is not my best show."

4 "Hello. I'm Stuart. And I'm an overeater." Stuart visits Weight Watchers, where that's not said: "But I just like it when people say, 'Hi, Stuart.' " Something awful happens—the scale was miscalibrated, so everyone's three quarters of a pound heavier than previously told. As the meeting ends, Stuart concedes it was "very good, you know, for a Weight Watchers meeting."

5 Stuart welcomes guest Michael J. (Michael Jordan). Ever empathetic, Stuart imagines Michael lying awake at night, thinking, "I'm not good enough, everybody's better than me, I'm not going to score any points, I have no business playing this game."

Michael disagrees gently, and Stuart responds, "Denial ain't just a river in Egypt." He does feel pressure occasionally, Michael concedes, and gamely recites an affirmation: "Hello, Michael. I don't have to be a great basketball player. I don't have to dribble fast or throw the ball in the basket. All I have to do is be the best Michael I can be."

Al Franken and Michael Jordan.

6 Stuart is joined by his cousin Leon (Kiefer Sutherland), who has his own show in Canada, "Today's Meditation with Leon Smalley": "I'm going to do a great show today, and I'm going to give of myself because I'm joyful, I'm happy, and goshdarnit, I'm free!"

Stuart wonders aloud: "The three things in the mirror—why not, 'I'm creative, I'm original, I made this up myself'?" He then realizes that "carrying around resentment is like carrying around baggage you really ought to check." But when Leon announces that his show is moving to Lifetime, Stuart confesses his sick and destructive envy. Recommending "a checkup from the neck up," Leon forgives Stuart, and Stuart forgives himself.

7 Stuart's guest is his nephew Kyle S. (Macaulay Culkin), son of an absentee alcoholic father and an overeating mother in rehab. They've just returned from a delightful Alatot meeting.

8 Stuart greets his sister Jodie S. (Roseanne Arnold), a gratefully recovering overeater: "You look terrific, Sis. Look at you—all in one chair!" Also appearing is one of Jodie's former husbands, Bobby Hensal (Tom Arnold), a cross-addicted chemical dependent fresh from a rehab stint.

Suspecting codependency, Stuart asks Jodie to swing a soft bat at a pillow representing "Bobby's disease," which tried to run her down in his car, hit a parking meter, and took a shot at her. Bobby takes the bat and pounds Stuart: "It's my fault. I'm not a licensed therapist. This was not my best show."

9 Stuart discusses something he knows nothing about: politics. "The only politicians I really admired were Martin Luther King, although a woman in Al-Anon said he was a compulsive sex addict; and Mahatma Gandhi, although a woman in OA said he had an eating disorder." Stuart is voting for Bill Clinton: "The Democrats keep nominating these codependents." Michael Dukakis, he notes, "was in severe denial and very shut down emotionally."

10 As a treat to his inner child, Stuart wears a Halloween costume between his customary sweater and yellow shirt: "It's a skeleton, because it's scary and because it reminds me that I am a human being. And that's okay. That's what I am. And besides, I think it makes me look thinner." He had considered dressing up as a feeling: "But what does dread look like? Other than my mother." Stuart refuses to "enable any little sugar addicts" and gives trick-or-treaters rice cakes.

11 Stuart dreads spending the holidays with his parents. "You know, sometimes I get this fantasy of seeing Norman Rockwell in a meeting, and he stands up and says, 'Hi, my name is Norman, and I paint lies.'"

Stuart can't decide whether or not to go: "I'm just *should*-ing all over myself. Oh, God, I can't believe I bought a nonrefundable ticket. I should have sent the money to Somalia or something. They're going to cancel the show, I'm going to die homeless and penniless, I'm twenty pounds overweight, and no one will ever love me—except my parents, so I should go home."

12 Depressed by Valentine's Day, Stuart considers his intimacy issues: "I learned what love is from my parents. Which is that you find that one special person who was placed on the planet just for you, and then put them through forty years of living hell."

Then he critiques Valentine's cards with messages like "Your Love Is All I'll Ever Need" and "You're Everything to Me": "I'm sorry, I thought I was in the Valentines section, not the codependency section."

13 Stuart greets guest Charles B. (Charles Barkley). Stuart, as Charles sees him, is "really messed up." Charles talks about how happy he is: "I'm the best basketball player in the world. There is nobody better."

"Then I guess you've won a lot of championships," muses Stuart. Well, no. Sensing that "Cleopatra isn't the only queen of denial," Stuart brings on someone who knows Charles's suffering: Muggsy B. (Muggsy Bogues). Charles derides the "ugly midget," but Muggsy's sensitivity ("I know how badly you wanted to beat the Bulls….And I love you!") melts Charles's heart.

14 Stuart helps a divorcing couple, Lorena and John B. (Rosie O'Donnell and Mike Myers). Forced sex with John has made Lorena angry. "What did you do with that anger?" asks Stuart, and learns she cut off his penis.

He then asks John, "When Lorena cut off your penis, how did that make you feel?" John answers, "It hurt a lot." Stuart has Lorena apologize to John's penis: "Hello. I was very angry at you. But that doesn't make you a bad penis! I'm sorry I cut you off and threw you in a field. I'm glad they found you and reattached you."

15 Stuart's guest is Martin L. (Martin Lawrence), who is clearly an angry man. Martin complains, "I'm *still* waiting on *my* forty acres and a mule!" "Okay, is this something our producer promised you?" asks Stuart. "Sometimes he overcommits, which is one of his problems. He's a people pleaser."

Eventually Martin lets down his facade. His father wasn't there for him as a boy—"He had to *work*!" Stuart says, "My father, too, was a slave, and his master was the bottle." "Word?" "Word!"

I'm good enough, I'm smart enough, and doggone it, people like me.

First aired: February 9, 1991

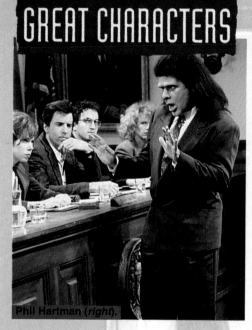

Phil Hartman (*right*).

Unfrozen Caveman Lawyer

100,000 years ago, a caveman was out hunting on the frozen wastes when he slipped and fell into a crevasse. In 1988, he was discovered by some scientists and thawed out. He then went to law school and became Unfrozen Caveman Lawyer.

Ladies and gentlemen of the jury, I'm just a caveman. I fell on some ice and later got thawed out by some of your scientists. Your world frightens and confuses me! Sometimes the honking horns of your traffic make me want to get out of my BMW and run off to the hills or whatever. Sometimes when I get a message on my fax machine I wonder, "Did little demons get inside and type it? I don't know!" My primitive mind can't grasp these concepts. But there is one thing I do know. When a man like my client slips and falls on a sidewalk in front of a public library, then he is entitled to no less than two million in compensatory damages and two million in punitive damages. Thank you.

PLAYED BY PHIL HARTMAN
AIRED: MARCH 14, 1992

Beth Cahill, Siobhan Fallon, Melanie Hutsell, and Mary Stuart Masterson.

Sorority Girls

Di: Oh my God, could you die? I felt like he loved you.
Pam: He was loving you.
Di: He was loving you.
Meg: He hated me. Oh my God, I can't believe he so completely hated me.

DI PLAYED BY MELANIE HUTSELL
PAM PLAYED BY BETH CAHILL
MEG PLAYED BY SIOBHAN FALLON
AIRED: JANUARY 11, 1992

Chris Farley and Paul McCartney.

The Chris Farley Show

Chris Farley: Do you remember when you were in The Beatles, and you were supposed to be dead, and there were all these clues, and everyone thought you were dead. That was a hoax, right?
Paul McCartney: Yeah, I wasn't really dead.

AIRED: FEBRUARY 13, 1993

Ike Turner

Ike Turner: Yeah! Thank you, Kevin Nealon. Well it's Valentine's Day, you dig? Yet all anybody can talk about is Nancy Kerrigan, and who did or didn't hit her. Well, I got one thing to say, baby, I didn't touch her! I wasn't even there! Everybody's always trying to blame Ike—Ike never did nothing!
Kevin: Okay, Ike, how about back to Valentine's Day, remember?
Ike: Damn, Kevin Nealon, you riding me tonight, you know that? You want Valentine's Day, I'll give you Valentine's Day, there you go!

IKE TURNER PLAYED BY TIM MEADOWS.
AIRED: FEBRUARY 12, 1994

Kevin Nealon and Tim Meadows.

Buh-Bye

Thank you for flying Total Bastard Airlines. As we indicated at the start of the flight, we at Total Bastard Airlines are bitter about the career paths we have taken, and we do tend to take that out on our passengers. We at Total Bastard Airlines realize that in your travel plans we know you have a choice of many airlines, but we'd like to thank you for flying the blue skies of Total Bastard.
Passenger: Hi, uh, could you arrange for me—
Steward: Buh-bye.

Stewardess: Yeah, buh-bye.
Passenger: I have this carry-on—
Steward: Here's me: Buh-bye. Here's you: I wanna say something important! Me: Buh-bye. You: I'm Joe Carry-on, let me through, I'm a big man. I don't check nothing. Me: Buh-bye. You: I'm cool, I wear a suit, no *way* am I a loser. Well, you're wrong, now buh-bye.

PASSENGER PLAYED BY TIM MEADOWS
STEWARD PLAYED BY DAVID SPADE
STEWARDESS PLAYED BY HELEN HUNT
AIRED: MARCH 19, 1994

David Spade, Tim Meadows, Helen Hunt, and Tom Davis.

Mike Myers, Adam Sandler, and David Spade.

Gap Girls

Customer: What about these pants, aren't they, I don't know, aren't they too big?
Christy: Not at all, just belt 'em!
Lucy: Yeah, just get a belt, and you cinch 'em!

CUSTOMER PLAYED BY MIKE MYERS
CHRISTY PLAYED BY DAVID SPADE
LUCY PLAYED BY ADAM SANDLER
AIRED: JANUARY 9, 1993

Index

Saturday Night Live By The Numbers

1. Number of live shows: 367
2. Highest rating/share ever: 16.0 / 47 (October 13, 1979)
3. Lowest rating/share ever: 4.2 / 16 (November 8, 1975)
4. Total number of cast members (not including featured players): 56
5. Number of shows on which Chevy Chase was a cast member: 30
6. Number of shows on which Chevy Chase was host: 6
7. Number of Beatles that have appeared on the show: 3
8. Number of Rutles that have appeared on the show: 4
9. Number of times the show was broadcast on a seven-second delay: 2
10. Number of English lines spoken by John Belushi's Samurai: 1
11. Number of 60s pop songs performed by Reverend Jesse Jackson: 2
12. Number of Dr. Seuss stories read by Reverend Jesse Jackson: 1
13. Number of *Star Trek* parodies: 3
14. Number of times set designer Akira Yoshimura has portrayed Mr. Sulu in a *Star Trek* parody: 3
15. Number of seats in Studio 8H: 292
16. Number of Presidents to say "Live from New York…": 1
17. Number of show announcers: 2
18. Number of show directors: 2
19. Number of times the word "cheeseburger" was spoken in the first Olympia Restaurant sketch: 80
20. Number of times the word "douchebag" was spoken in the Lord and Lady Douchebag sketch: 12
21. Number of times the word "penis" was used in the Nude Beach sketch: 43 (17 spoken/26 sung)
22. Number of times a cast member said the word "fuck" on the air: 2
23. Number of movies featuring characters that previously appeared on *Saturday Night Live*: 10
24. Number of show's writers who went on to host a talk show: 2
25. Number of show's performers who later joined the cast of *In Living Color*: 2
26. Number of sports figures who have hosted or co-hosted: 17
27. Number of political figures who have hosted: 5
28. Number of musicians or bands that have hosted: 19
29. Number of hosts who are now dead: 12
30. Number of cast members who are now dead: 3
31. Number of cast members whose brothers later joined the show: 3
32. Number of people who have portrayed Richard Nixon: 2
33. Number of people who have portrayed Gerald Ford: 1
34. Number of people who have portrayed Jimmy Carter: 3
35. Number of people who have portrayed Ronald Reagan: 7
36. Number of people who have portrayed George Bush: 2
37. Number of people who have portrayed Bill Clinton: 1
38. Number of adults who have portrayed Dan Quayle: 2
39. Number of children who have portrayed Dan Quayle: 1
40. Number of complaints NBC received after Sinéad O'Connor tore up a photo of the Pope: 4,484
41. Number of calls supporting O'Connor: 725
42. Number of complaints NBC received about Martin Lawrence's monologue: 627
43. Number of calls supporting Lawrence: 3
44. Number of shows produced by Jean Doumanian: 12
45. Number of shows the program was not named *Saturday Night Live*: 41
46. Number of times the show has been performed outside of New York: 1
47. Number of times the show has been performed in Brooklyn: 3
48. Number of openly gay cast members: 1
49. Number of openly Canadian cast members: 5
50. Number of cast members who married another cast member: 2

Key

2. Host and Musical Guest: Steve Martin and Blondie.
3. Host and Musical Guest: Candice Bergen and Esther Phillips.
5. October 11, 1975 to October 30, 1976.
7. George, Ringo, and Paul.
8. Dirk, Barry, Stig, and Nasty.
9. December 13, 1975 (Host: Richard Pryor); May 12, 1990 (Host: Andrew Dice Clay).
10. "I can dig where you're coming from," to Richard Pryor in Samurai Hotel on December 13, 1975.
11. "Red Rubber Ball" and "Jean" on October 20, 1984.
12. *Green Eggs & Ham* on September 28, 1991.
13. May 29, 1975 (Host: Elliott Gould); December 20, 1986 (Host: William Shatner); February 5, 1994 (Host: Patrick Stewart).
16. Gerald Ford on April 17, 1976.
17. Don Pardo and Mel Brand.
18. Dave Wilson (1975-1986, 1989-1994) and Paul Miller (1986-1989).
19. January 28, 1978 (Host: Robert Klein).
20. May 24, 1980 (Host: Buck Henry).
21. October 15, 1988 (Host: Matthew Broderick).
22. Paul Shaffer on March 15, 1980 (100th Anniversary Show); Charles Rocket on February 21, 1981 (Host: Charlene Tilton).
23. *The Blues Brothers, Gilda Live, Wayne's World, Mo' Money, Bob Roberts, Mr. Saturday Night, Coneheads, Wayne's World 2, It's Pat,* and *Stuart Smalley.*
24. Chevy Chase and Conan O'Brien.
25. Damon Wayans and Chris Rock.
26. Fran Tarkenton, O.J. Simpson, Bill Russell, John Madden, Bob Uecker, Alex Karras, Billy Martin, Howard Cosell, Hulk Hogan, Joe Montana, Walter Payton, Wayne Gretzky, Chris Evert, George Steinbrenner, Michael Jordan, Charles Barkley, and Nancy Kerrigan.
27. Senator Julian Bond, Mayor Ed Koch, Senator George McGovern, Rev. Jesse Jackson, and Presidential Press Secretary Ron Nessen.
28. Paul Simon, Kris Kristofferson, Ray Charles, Art Garfunkel, the Rolling Stones, Frank Zappa, Rick Nelson, Deborah Harry, Johnny Cash, Olivia Newton-John, Stevie Wonder, Ringo Starr, Madonna, Paul Shaffer, Willie Nelson, Dolly Parton, Quincy Jones, Sting, and Hammer.
29. Desi Arnaz, Anthony Perkins, Ruth Gordon, Broderick Crawford, Frank Zappa, Rick Nelson, Ted Knight, Strother Martin, Ray Sharkey, John Candy, Billy Martin, and Sam Kinison.
30. John Belushi, Gilda Radner, and Danitra Vance.
31. Dan Aykroyd (Peter, 1979-80); Bill Murray (Brian Doyle, 1980-1982), John Belushi (Jim, 1983-1985).
32. Dan Aykroyd and Tony Rosato.
33. Chevy Chase.
34. Dan Aykroyd, Joe Piscopo, and Dana Carvey.
35. Chevy Chase, Harry Shearer, Charles Rocket, Joe Piscopo, Randy Quaid, Phil Hartman, and Robin Williams.
36. Jim Downey and Dana Carvey.
37. Phil Hartman.
38. Dana Carvey and Michael J. Fox.
39. Jeff Renaudo.
45. The program was known as *NBC's Saturday Night*, then just as *Saturday Night*, before the March 26, 1977 show.
46. February 20, 1977, in New Orleans.
47. October 16, October 23, and October 30, 1976, when the NBC election unit took over Studio 8H.
48. Terry Sweeney.
49. Dan Aykroyd, Robin Duke, Martin Short, Phil Hartman, and Mike Myers.
50. Julia Louis-Dreyfus, Brad Hall.

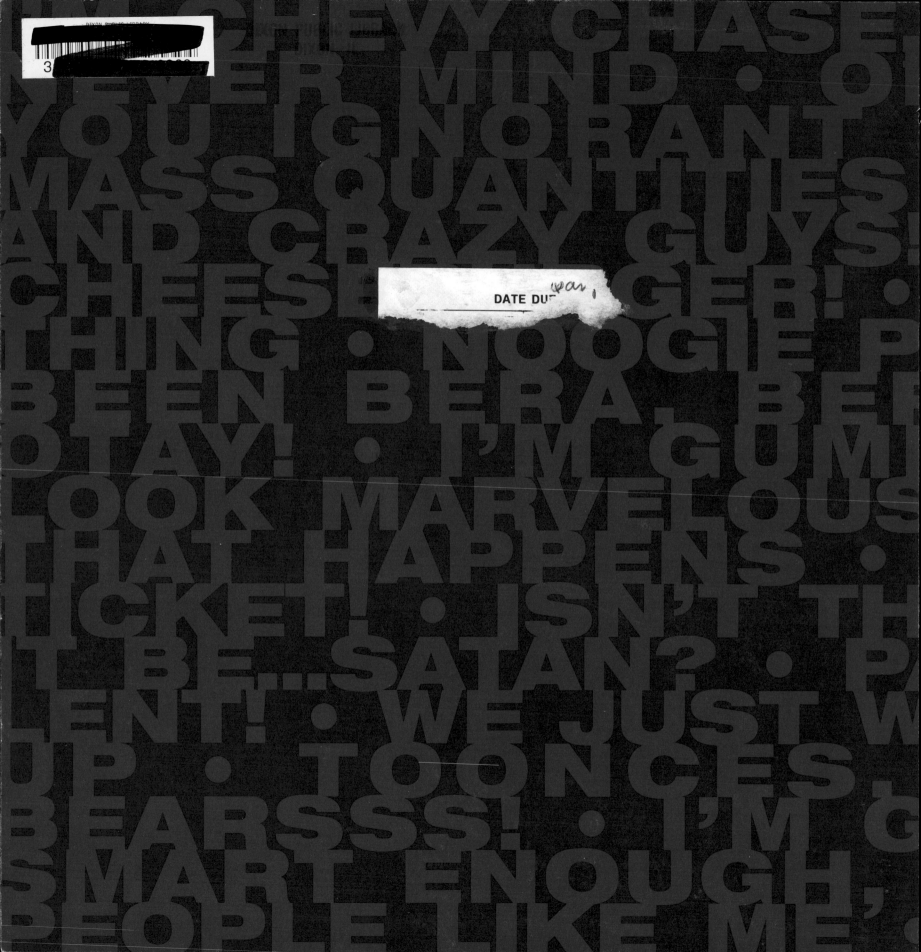